UTOPIA IN ZION

SUNY Series in Israeli Studies
Russell Stone, Editor

UTOPIA IN ZION

The Israeli Experience
with Worker Cooperatives

RAYMOND RUSSELL

STATE UNIVERSITY OF NEW YORK PRESS

Published by
State University of New York Press, Albany

© 1995 State University of New York

For information, address State University of New York
Press, State University Plaza, Albany, N.Y., 12246

Production by E. Moore
Marketing by Fran Keneston

Library of Congress Cataloging-in-Publication Data

Russell, Raymond, 1946–
    Utopia in Zion: Israeli experience with worker cooperatives \
Raymond Russell.
        p.   cm. — (SUNY series in Israel studies)
    Includes bibliographical references and index.
    ISBN 0-7914-2443-X (HC : acid-free paper). — ISBN 0-7914-2444-8
(pb. : acid-free paper)
    1. Cooperation—Israel.   I. Title.   II. Series.
HD3532.2.A4R87   1995
334'.095694—dc20   94-19576
                                                                            CIP

10 9 8 7 6 5 4 3 2 1

CONTENTS

vi   Contents

TABLES

FIGURES

INTRODUCTION

There is a great deal of experimentation with various forms of worker ownership of businesses going on in the world today. In the United States, for example, the federal government has been providing encouragement for the formation of employee stock ownership plans, or ESOPs, since 1974. As these ESOPs have grown in size, they have acquired controlling interests in some of America's largest and best-known firms, such as Avis Rent-a-Car and the Polaroid corporation; as this work goes to press, United Airlines seems to be in the process of joining this group. Similar government-sponsored programs to encourage employees' participation in the ownership of their workplaces are currently in operation in many other parts of the world (Russell, 1992). Governments that have recently been especially active in promoting employee ownership include those of Russia, Poland, and other formerly socialist states of Eastern Europe. These governments often include ownership by employees or by citizens as part of their privatization plans, because these programs offer a politically attractive compromise between these countries' socialist past and their current hopes for a capitalist future (e.g., Logue and Bell, 1992; Blasi, 1992; Weisskopf, 1992; Krajewska, 1993).

Both in the United States and elsewhere, these innovations in ownership are often embarked upon as if they were entirely new and unprecedented reforms. The truth, however, is that the world has already accumulated a tremendous amount of experience with the ownership of businesses by their workers. The research project whose results are reported here was undertaken in the hope that much information that is relevant to our current political and

economic choices can be gained from the study of these past experiments in worker ownership.

The idea of worker ownership of businesses is almost as old
as capitalism itself. Capitalism creates many forms of separation
between workers and their work, and worker ownership has been
seen by many visionaries as a way to bring the two back together.
Since early in the nineteenth century, virtually every Western
economy has witnessed repeated if sporadic experimentation with
workers' cooperatives, employee shareholding, and other means of
promoting worker ownership.

Already by the second half of the nineteenth century, many of
these efforts had begun to be dismissed as impractical dreams.
Worker cooperatives, in particular, were increasingly disappointing
their well-wishers. They were not spreading through capitalist
economies and outcompeting their conventionally owned rivals, as
John Stuart Mill and many others had hoped. The few that had succeeded economically were increasingly perceived as failures in
other respects. Many worker cooperatives showed signs of "degen-
erating" back into conventional capitalist businesses. They made
increasing use of hired, nonmember labor and also appeared to be
imitating the autocratic decision-making practices of their capitalist competition. After studying their history, the Fabian socialists Sidney and Beatrice Webb concluded in 1920 that "All such associations of producers that start as alternatives to the capitalist
system either fail or cease to be democracies of producers" (Webb
and Webb, 1920, p. 29).

For Frederick Engels and other Marxists, such failures illustrated the difference between a socialism that was "utopian" and
one that was "scientific." Reforms like workers' cooperation and
employee shareholding were dismissed by them as voluntaristic efforts to wish one's way to socialism. Such ameliorative innovations begin by ignoring the coercive power of markets and the
state, but in the end are forced to conform to their dictates. For
Marxists, these failures demonstrate that the only way to create an
alternative to capitalism is to seize the state and to use this
weapon to abolish capitalism by force.

In the twentieth century, most socialists heeded the Marxists' advice and concentrated their efforts on the state. But within
the Jewish community in Palestine and later Israel, a utopian variety of socialism continued to flourish (Buber, 1958).

A number of factors worked together to lead Israel to take

this exceptional course. One is that the Zionist project that lies at the heart of modern Israel is itself an exercise in utopianism. It is an effort to find a new and unknown land—a "utopia," or "nowhere" in the literal sense of the term—and to create a new and better society within it.

There were also some very practical considerations that encouraged the socialism of Israel's Zionist pioneers to develop in this utopian direction. They were socialists who had no state and would-be workers who had no work. By the early decades of this century, the Zionist immigrants to Israel began to realize that if they were going to have any kind of economy in Israel at all, they would have to create it themselves, from scratch. And since the challenge of establishing new businesses in Israel required more resources than most individual immigrants possessed, they saw practical reasons as well as ideological ones to pool their resources and create institutions that would be collectively rather than individually owned.

It is for such reasons that a country as small as Israel contains one of the largest and most unusual assortments of worker-owned institutions in the world. The most famous of these are the collective agricultural settlements known as kibbutzim. More numerous and more populous than the kibbutzim are the more individualistic agricultural cooperatives known as moshavim. Another large number of enterprises is owned collectively by Israel's General Trade Union Federation, or Histadrut, through its economic subsidiary, the Chevrat Ovdim. These Histadrut-owned ventures include a number of industrial enterprises, known collectively as Koor; a construction firm, the Solel Boneh; and Israel's largest financial institution, the Bank Hapoalim, or Workers' Bank.

In addition to all of these unique institutions, Israel also has a sizable population of worker cooperatives of a more classic type. The best known of these are two large bus cooperatives, Egged and Dan. Egged, which in 1988 had 4,692 members and another 3,400 hired employees, takes care of bus transportation everywhere in Israel except in Tel Aviv; Dan, with 1,811 members and 1,508 non-members, serves Tel Aviv itself. As of December 1988, when this study began, the entire population of producer, transportation, and service cooperatives in Israel was officially recognized as consisting of a total of seventy-five organizations, which together employed 16,562 workers. Although smaller than the kibbutzim, moshavim, and enterprises owned by the Chevrat Ovdim, this population of worker cooperatives has historically accounted for between 1 and 2 percent of Israel's nonagricultural labor force. This places the relative size of this worker cooperative sector second only to Italy's within the Western world (Ben-Ner, 1988a, p. 8).

I had been aware of many of these unique features of the Israeli economy for years, having read about them in the works of Preuss (1960, 1965), Viteles (1966, 1967, 1968), Daniel (1976), and others. I did not have a chance to study these institutions firsthand, however, until I spent a semester at Tel Aviv University on a Fulbright fellowship in 1989–90.

As the focus of my own research, I chose the worker cooperatives rather than the kibbutz, moshav, or Chevrat Ovdim. This was first of all because these organizations had been the subject of less previous research and were less widely known outside of Israel. More importantly, however, I felt that since these cooperatives were more similar in structure to the forms of worker ownership that we most frequently encounter outside Israel, they might also be more likely to yield lessons that would be relevant to the work of researchers and practitioners in other countries.

I must acknowledge at the beginning that the story I have to tell here is not a very encouraging one. Despite some favorable circumstances and early successes, the population of worker cooperatives in Israel has on the whole not done very well. These cooperatives now seem to be disappearing from virtually every field in which they once flourished, with the exception of bus transportation, over which they enjoy a monopoly. And in most fields in which worker cooperatives can still be found, most of them are in quite advanced states of degeneration, with hired nonmembers performing the bulk of the labor in the vast majority of them.

Rather than ignoring these problems, this book seeks to confront them head on. It examines both the rise and fall of this population in some detail. It makes efforts to give credit for achievements wherever such credit is due. Where the news is mostly bad, this account does not shirk from telling it, but it also attempts to salvage constructive lessons wherever possible from these defeats.

This book views both the growth and decline of this unique organizational population as consequences of the changing institutional environment in which it was situated. Such influences are especially relevant to this story, because the formation of worker cooperatives is always to some extent a "utopian" act. Worker cooperatives are often created with an explicit intention to provide a better alternative to capitalism. Where this is not the case, one can usually identify some additional element that subordinates the self-interest of the individual organizational founders to the pursuit of some broader social values or the good of a larger group. In Israel, this utopian element was supplied by a labor Zionist ideology and political economy that gave more legitimacy and resources to cooperative and collectively owned organizations than to more individualistic alternatives. It was this normative and political climate that for many decades encouraged new immigrants to Israel to create organizations that would be cooperatively rather than individually owned. And it was the gradual transformation of these institutional circumstances that did more than anything else to cause the decline of this population of firms.

Scholarship on the history of Israeli society and its labor economy can be divided into an older generation of scholars, typified by Eisenstadt (1967), who attribute Israel's unique labor-owned organizations largely to the Zionist and socialist values of the immigrants, and a younger generation, typified by Shafir (1989) and Shalev (1992), who emphasize the role of economic factors. The "institutional" perspective adopted here (Stinchcombe, 1965; Meyer and Rowan, 1977; DiMaggio and Powell, 1983, 1991) attempts to avoid both of these two poles. It acknowledges that most organizational founders are simultaneously subject to both economic and normative influences. They are virtually always trying to establish entities that can withstand competitive pressures and meet their economic needs, but they do not initiate their entrepreneurial activities in a social or political vacuum. The organizational models they choose are always selected from among those that are made available to them by their society and their era, and that are identified by their industry, society, and state as being both viable and appropriate, which is to say "legitimate."

These points apply with special force to the Jewish community of Palestine and later Israel in the early and middle decades of the twentieth century, when a new economy and society were being self-consciously created by a Zionist leadership and an immigrant labor force. Any attempt to attribute the history of the Israeli worker cooperatives over this time period either solely to normative considerations or solely to economics would be equally one-sided and would fail to appreciate the powerful combination of both ideological and economic motivations that made the Jewish economy of Palestine and later Israel so unusually productive of labor-owned institutions. The kibbutz, the Histadrut, and Israel's worker cooperative movement grew as rapidly as they did not by forcing Jewish immigrants to choose between their values and their interests, but by appealing simultaneously to both. And while this was true of the Jewish workers, it applied with even greater force to their leaders and to the unique political economy that they created in Jewish Palestine with the help of Zionist philanthropists abroad. By the time Israel achieved its independence in 1948, these forces had created a uniquely pro-cooperative public opinion that was now combined with the coercive power of the state.

But independence also brought new immigrants and new problems. As both Israeli society and the Israeli economy became increasingly diverse, the earlier pro-cooperative consensus gradually unraveled, both in the opinion of the public and in the policies of the state. These social changes were epitomized by the electoral victory of the Likud in 1977, in which Israel's traditionally pro-cooperative Labor government was for the first time replaced by a government that was openly hostile to the Histadrut and to the kibbutzim.

The first steps in this evolution are described in chapter 1, which focuses on the relationship between Israel's worker cooperatives and the Histadrut. Incorporation into the Histadrut brought both important legitimation and powerful patronage to the Israeli worker cooperatives in their early years. But it was never an unmixed blessing, and in the end it probably did the Israeli worker cooperatives more harm than good. In its relationship to the worker cooperatives, the Histadrut saw itself as a watchdog as well as a sponsor. In its roles as a trade union and as guardian of Zionist and socialist values, the Histadrut was scandalized by the tendency of the worker cooperatives to make increasing use of hired labor. The Histadrut's frequent complaints and campaigns to root out this practice probably did more than any other single factor to discredit the idea of forming worker cooperatives in Israel.

Chapter 2 offers a quantitative analysis of factors that affected the formation and dissolution of Israeli worker cooperatives from the 1920s through the 1990s. Theories derived from the population ecology of organizations are used to show that in the early years, the growth of the Israeli worker cooperative population had a tendency to feed on itself, as the formation of worker cooperatives in one year helped to popularize the very idea of forming worker cooperatives and thereby stimulated the formation of still more worker cooperatives in subsequent years. But in later years, the same process began to work in reverse. Deaths of existing worker cooperatives tended to outnumber the births of new ones, and these deaths had a significantly measurable effect in discouraging future births. Later analyses in chapter 2 indicate that the formation of worker cooperatives in Israel was also adversely affected by a number of changes that took place in Israeli society as a whole, including the reduction in the rate of immigration that began in the 1950s and the loss of political power by the Labor Party and its allies in the election of 1977.

Chapter 3 and 4 examine two internal transformations in the Israeli worker cooperatives that have done more than any other factors to damage their reputations in the eyes of the Israeli public: their increasing reliance on hired labor and the growing alienation between leaders and rank-and-file members in some of Israel's most prominent worker cooperatives.

Chapter 3 argues that the temptation to profit from an increasing use of hired labor is inherent in the structures of Israeli worker cooperatives, as it is in worker cooperatives in many other parts of the world. The most effective means to counter these temptations have come from external institutional forces, of which the most important have been the efforts of the Histadrut itself. In the later 1960s, however, when the Histadrut gave up its direct control over Israel's worker cooperative movement, these efforts became much less effective, and the proportion of hired workers in the labor force of most Israeli worker cooperatives was left free to soar.

Chapter 4 argues that the increasing differentiation between leaders and rank-and-file members in many Israeli worker cooperatives should not be viewed as a sign of the failure or repudiation of democratic decision making in these cooperatives, but rather as an inevitable consequence of their growing size. From an international comparative perspective, the most remarkable thing about the politics of the larger Israeli worker cooperatives is not how oligarchical they have become, but how democratic they have remained. Nevertheless, the bitter infighting and public scandals that have erupted from time to time within the largest Israeli worker cooperatives have done further harm to their already tarnished reputations and have probably played an additional role in souring the Israeli public on the idea of forming worker cooperatives.

Chapter 5 broadens its perspective to survey some recent crises that in the 1980s affected the other major branches of Israel's labor economy: the kibbutzim, the moshavim, and the industries owned and operated by the Histadrut through its subsidiary, Koor. Whereas in earlier decades, it was only the worker cooperatives whose legitimacy was subjected to serious doubt, by the 1980s, the entire labor economy was facing economic, political, and social challenges. By that time, Israel had become a far different society from what it had been in the 1920s, and whether it could continue to provide a hospitable home for cooperatives or collectively owned workplaces of any kind was now very much in doubt.

Chapter 6 returns to the worker cooperatives to examine their recent history and current prospects and to consider what broader lessons can be extracted from their experiences. In the early 1990s, a new wave of immigration to Israel was stimulating a new wave of births of worker cooperatives; but the response to immigration seemed weaker this time than it had been in the past and did not seem sufficient to reverse the worker cooperatives' long-term decline. The Israeli worker cooperatives seem never to have recovered from their past rough handling by the Histadrut.

It seems that "utopianism" has its limits, even in Israel, and worker cooperatives are one variety of utopianism that never took root there, even though it managed to appear to flourish for a short time. The other major branches of Israel's labor economy acquired a greater practical relevance by being sewn into the fabric of Israel's economy and polity. To this day they remain integrally connected to such major Israeli institutions as the Histadrut, the political parties, and the World Zionist Organization's Jewish National Fund. Israel's worker cooperatives for a time grew rapidly by entering a marriage of convenience with these more powerful social forces, but it was never more than a temporary alliance. In the eyes of the Histadrut leaders, the growth of worker cooperatives was neither conducive to their interests nor consistent with their values. They therefore always showed greater preference for alternative ownership forms, and once the goal of independence had been achieved, they encouraged the Israeli public to reject the worker cooperatives as a dystopian economic form.

If worker cooperatives have been discredited in Israel, are there any constructive lessons that might nevertheless be salvaged from them for other parts of the world? Like worker cooperatives from other times and places, the Israeli worker cooperatives do provide further demonstrations that if you wish to run a business democratically, workplace democracy can indeed be made to work. But like the nineteenth-century worker cooperatives before them, the Israeli worker cooperatives reveal themselves to have an extremely limited ownership form, one that is economically viable only in narrowly circumscribed niches and that has unstable long-term dynamics even in these. Both in Israel and elsewhere, it thus appears, the future expansion of workplace democracy depends on the development of alternative forms of ownership to these.

Before concluding this introduction, I have a few acknowledgments to make. A reader may well ask where an American who does not even speak Hebrew gets the chutzpah to write a book about Israel. The answer is that I had a tremendous amount of help.

Before thanking some of the most important individuals by name, I would like to note that in general I found Israel to be an easy country to do research on. It is small enough geographically that it is feasible to pay a personal visit to just about anyone in the country. Even more amazingly, just about everyone I tried to contact made time to see me. I don't know whether this was due to the country's low population or the friendliness of its people or whether I just had the good fortune to be well connected. Whatever the reason, I felt during my stay in Israel that no doors were closed to me. I was therefore able to speak personally with both leaders and rank-and-file members of most of Israel's major worker cooperatives, the Chevrat Ovdim, and so on.

Of specific debts to specific people, my most fundamental one is to Ephraim Yuchtman-Yaar of Tel Aviv University and to his entire family. "Eppie," as he is called, and his wife, Gila, spent a sabbatical leave at my university in the mid-1980s, and my stay at Tel Aviv University in 1989–90 was inspired in part by a desire to pay a return social call. Eppie had become the dean of Social Sciences at Tel Aviv University by the time I arrived there, which put him in an excellent position to facilitate my visit. Just in case what Brenda Danet (1989) has written about the importance of *protektzia*, or influence, in Israeli society is true, it was always comforting to know that I had connections if I needed them.

One of the first practical services that Eppie Yaar performed for me upon my arrival in Israel was to refer me to Arye Globerson, head of the Golda Meir Institute for Labor and Social Research in the Department of Labor Studies at Tel Aviv University. Professor Globerson in turn referred me to the Merkaz Hakooperatsia, or Cooperative Center, in downtown Tel Aviv.

I feel an enormous debt to Amnon Bar-On, the head of the Merkaz Hakooperatsia, and to the other present and former staff members of the Merkaz who spent many hours with me, including Yekhiel Halperin, Lieber Losh, Moshe Apter, Shimon Rudik, David David, Israel Ziv, and Moshe Greiner. Thanks to Amnon Bar-On and his secretary, Malka Ben-Tov, all the records of the Merkaz Hakooperatsia were made available to me, and the Merkaz staff also helped to arrange my visits to many individual cooperatives, in many cases even coming along with me to act as translators.

I would also like to acknowledge the help I received from many students in the Department of Labor Studies at Tel Aviv University. Asaf Darr was a student in my classes who also quickly became a research assistant and colleague. Asaf took as much personal interest in many aspects of this research as I did myself. Asaf more than anyone else came to act as my eyes and ears where Hebrew sources were involved. Among other things, this means that Asaf transcribed and translated the records of the Cooperative Center and of the Registrar of Cooperatives that provide the basis of the quantitative portions of this study.

Two other graduate students at Tel Aviv University who assisted in this study were Alex Talmor and Julio Fitlik. Alex and Julio were teaching an undergraduate course in workplace democracy in the Department of Labor Studies when I was teaching a graduate course in this same subject. They offered to have their students conduct interviews in Israeli worker cooperatives using a questionnaire that I composed. The results of those interviews were later translated into English by Asaf Darr and now form a part of chapter 4.

I also benefited from interviews and informal conversations conducted with numerous Israeli colleagues. Yehuda Don and Arie Shirom shared with me the benefit of their past research on worker cooperatives in Israel and the United States, respectively. I learned a great deal about current developments on the kibbutz from conversations with and in many cases visits to Menachem Rosner, Michal Palgi, Amir Helman, Uri Leviatan, Stanley Maron, and Amitai Niv. My knowledge of the moshav relies heavily on intense briefings received from Yair Levi, Julia Margulies, and Yossi Yassour. For what I was able to learn about the Chevrat Ovdim I must especially thank Yitzhak Greenberg, Raia Rettig, Dani Rosolio, Michael Shalev, and Amos Yarkoni.

Upon my return to the United States, I have been quite dependent on the collaboration of Robert Hanneman in order to complete the quantitative analyses reported in chapters 2 and 3. In creating and managing our files, we have also relied heavily on the assistance of Neil Hickman, Vered Mirmovich, Orna Al-Yagon, Judith Agassi, and Patricia Hanneman. In completing these analyses we were also greatly helped by the suggestions, comments, and encouragement that we received from Howard Aldrich, Avner Ben-Ner, John Bonin, Art Budros, Raphael Bar-El, Joseph Brada, Glenn Carroll, Michael Conte, Jacques Delacroix, Michael Hannan, Derek Jones, Virginie Perotin, Jeffrey Pliskin, Steve Smith, Udo Staber, Jan Svejnar, and Avi Weiss.

The arguments about the relationship between size and workplace democracy that are presented in chapter 4 were first worked out in presentations I made at the School of Industrial and Labor Relations at Cornell University in March 1993 and at a conference at Givat Haviva in Israel the following month. I would like to thank Tove Hammer, Eric Lindhult, Menachem Rosner, Joyce Rothschild, and Maurice Zeitlin for contributing some very helpful suggestions on how those arguments could be improved.

At State University of New York Press, I would like to thank my editor, Clay Morgan, for sending this manuscript to four perceptive critics for review and for allowing me all of the time I felt that I needed to take their recommendations into account. To those reviewers themselves I am most grateful for their comments. I am also indebted to Menachem Rosner, Gershon Shafir, and Mark Gottdiener for some equally helpful comments on later drafts.

I would like to thank two publishers for granting permission to incorporate portions of previously published materials into this book. The first of these is Sage Publications, which has allowed me to include as part of chapter 1 certain sections from my article, "The Role of Support Organizations in the Development of Cooperatives in Israel," which first appeared in *Economic and Industrial Democracy*, volume 12 (1991), pp. 385–404. Thanks are also due to JAI Press for permission to include in chapter 3 substantial portions of an article coauthored with Robert Hanneman, "The Use of Hired Labor in Israeli Worker Cooperatives, 1933–1989," which appears in *Advances in the Economic Analysis of Participatory and Labor-Managed Firms*, volume 5 (1994).

In the final stages of the preparation of this manuscript, I have also received much helpful encouragement and assistance from many other colleagues and coworkers at the University of California, Riverside, including but not limited to Linda Stearns, Edgar Butler, Jonathan Turner, Austin Turk, Robin Whittington, and Cathy Carlson. Special thanks must also go to Janet Moores and her entire staff in the Interlibrary Loan Department of our campus library, who reached all the way to Israel when necessary to obtain resources needed to bring this research to completion.

I owe some debts of thanks even closer to home. I received a good deal of help from members of my family in the course of conducting this research. For example, my father, mother, and wife all paid me visits during my longest stay in Israel, helping to maintain my morale and to keep me from pining too much for home. As the project was being completed, my mother and my wife were once again pressed into service, this time in the role of proofreaders.

I must express special and very deep gratitude to my wife, Judy Lehr. Judy's principal contribution to this research lies less in services she has performed for the project than in what she has had to put up with—the long disruption of our home life caused by my five-month stay in Israel, the subsequent visits, and the more recent distractions created by the effort to bring this study to an end.

Finally, I wish to acknowledge a debt to a man I never met, Abraham Daniel. For decades before his death in the late 1980s, Daniel was the leading expert on Israel's worker cooperatives. Although he and I never had an opportunity to discuss our common interests face-to-face, I have relied heavily on Daniel's work, particularly in the early phases of this project. It was statistics compiled by Daniel that gave me my first bird's-eye view of the rise and fall of this cooperative population and of the extent to which its members have degenerated over time. It was thus by following a trail blazed by Daniel that I became convinced that this project was both feasible and worth doing. It is therefore to the memory of Abraham Daniel that I dedicate this book.

1. WORKER COOPERATIVES IN ISRAEL'S LABOR ECONOMY

This chapter examines the birth and early development of Israel's worker cooperative movement, in the context of the larger "labor economy" (Daniel, 1976) of which it forms a part. The chapter begins with a general discussion of the processes by which worker cooperatives have historically been formed. This discussion points out a number of general considerations that have helped to make Israel unusually productive of labor-owned workplaces of many types. The chapter's second section looks more specifically at the origins of the various institutions that make up Israel's "labor economy," including the kibbutz, the moshav, the Histadrut, and the Chevrat Ovdim. The third section examines the birth of Israel's urban worker cooperative movement within this preexisting family of labor-owned institutions. This discussion particularly calls attention to certain features that made the relationship between the worker cooperatives and the Histadrut ambivalent from the start and that became the source of much later contention. The final section addresses the later history and dynamics of this uneasy relationship. The chapter concludes that Israel's worker cooperatives were probably never fully accepted as equal partners of Israel's labor economy, and that their incorporation into this institutional environment may ultimately have done these worker cooperatives more harm than good.

WHY DO WORKERS FORM COOPERATIVES?

Both empirical instances of workers' cooperatives and theoretical discussions of the processes that lead to their formation suggest that workers have historically been prompted to form these organizations by a broad range of economic, normative, and political motives.

A cooperative is in the first place a business, and its formation is always to some extent an economic act. Many historical instances of workers' cooperation have been formed by formerly independent workers who joined together to pool their capital, to gain scale economies, and to reap other advantages of size (Russell, 1985b). Nineteenth-century utilitarian reformers like John Stuart Mill anticipated that the pursuit of rational self-interest would eventually lead the vast majority of workers to organize themselves into cooperatives. Mill reasoned first of all that workers would begin to create cooperative ventures in order to "free themselves . . . from the necessity of paying, out of the produce of their industry, a heavy tribute for the use of their capital" (1909, pp. 773–74). Once established, Mill expected cooperative workplaces to reveal an additional competitive advantage over conventionally owned firms, which would come from "the vast stimulus given to productive energies, by placing the labourers . . . in a relation to their work which would make it their principle and their interest . . . to do the utmost, instead of the least possible, in exchange for their remuneration" (1909, p. 789). Mill predicted that "by the very process of their success," the earliest cooperatives would provide "a course of education" to other workers, and that "As associations multiplied, they would tend more and more to absorb all work-people" (1909, p. 791).

Well over a hundred years have passed since Mill first expressed these thoughts. It now appears that workers have been a good deal slower to organize themselves into cooperative workplaces than Mill expected. A major reason for this has been that the economic arguments in favor of cooperation have not been nearly as compelling in practice as Mill imagined them to be. Cooperative workplaces have not been found to outcompete conventionally owned firms and have instead managed no more than to cling tenaciously to the small niches in which they are initially formed. Many economists since Mill have argued that the calculation of individual self-interest gives workers a powerful disincentive against forming a cooperative business, because to do so would expose workers to the risk of losing their jobs and their life savings at the very same time. Thus workers who are rational investors are more likely to allocate their assets in a diversified portfolio of investments not connected with the firm that employs them. And insofar as rational individual workers or groups of workers are motivated to take the risk of creating their own firms, they tend to compensate themselves for these risks by reserving for themselves all of the profits that result from this entrepreneurial activity; they thus avoid structures like worker cooperatives that obligate them to share ownership and profits with workers who are hired after the firm is formed.

In sum, the rational calculation of individual self-interest that was so prized by Mill and other utilitarians has generally done more to discourage the formation of worker cooperatives than to promote it. Insofar as the pursuit of individual self-interest has played a prominent role in the formation of labor-managed workplaces at all, it has been in situations in which this step is driven by economic necessity, because alternative forms of employment are unavailable or unworkable. One instance of this may be the creation of cooperatives by unemployed workers, which some authors have seen as a significant factor in the spread of worker cooperatives (Shirom, 1972; Ben-Ner, 1988a, 1988b). The predominance of group practices in the professions and of cooperatives in other services can also be attributed to economic necessities of this sort. Because these occupations are intensive of human capital, rather than physical capital, the disincentives to the formation of worker-owned businesses are less salient in these fields, and successful firms within them have often found that there is no more effective way to motivate and retain the key members of their labor force than to offer them a share in the ownership of the firm (Russell, 1985b, 1991).

While calculation of individual self-interest may provide the prime motivation for the formation of worker cooperatives under these rare circumstances, in most historical instances of worker cooperatives much more has been involved. For one thing, the formation of cooperatives is almost always a normative as well as economic act; it engages the founders' ideals, as well as their interests. Cooperative founders typically have what Rothschild-Whitt

(1979) refers to as a "social movement orientation." They see the foundation of their firms as taking place not in isolation, but as part of a broader effort to transform capitalism, or at least to reform it. As Mill noted in a discussion of nineteenth-century French worker cooperatives, "It is the declared principle of most of these associations that they do not exist for the mere private benefit of the individual members, but for the promotion of the co-operative cause" (1909, p. 781).

In addition to supplementing economic considerations with values, the formation of worker cooperatives commonly contains an element that is a combination of both. This is a tendency for firm founders to think of themselves not as individuals, but as members of a group, and for them to see their firms as serving the interests not only of themselves as individuals, but also of their entire group. In this respect there is indeed "rationality" in the formation of worker cooperatives, but it is a collective rationality rather than an individual one (Rothschild-Whitt, 1979; DiMaggio and Powell, 1983). This collective rationality typically plays a crucial role in prompting firm founders to share ownership not only among themselves, but also with workers who will later enter their firms.

Potentially, such collective rationality might be derived from the class consciousness and solidarity that firm founders feel with the entire working class, but in practice, it usually has more narrow bases than this. One very common source of it is the homogeneity and sense of community among the practitioners of a common occupation, particularly one whose working hours or work activity isolates them from others. Thus, for example, groups of printers, bakers, truckers, or refuse collectors have often been observed to form cooperatives (Russell, 1985a; Ben-Ner, 1988a). A feature of such cooperatives that both demonstrates their roots in occupational solidarity and illustrates its limits is the fact that membership in such cooperatives is rarely and only slowly extended to clerical employees or other workers who ply different trades within these same firms.

Another important source of group identification consists of ethnic ties among cooperative founders. The best-known and most successful worker cooperatives in the world today are the Mondragon cooperatives in the Basque region of Spain; identification with the Basque cause appears to have played an important role both in the formation of these cooperatives and in the preservation of their structures (Whyte and Whyte, 1988). Other well-known cooperatives have been established by immigrant ethnic groups, including the plywood cooperatives of the American Pacific Northwest and the worker-owned scavenger firms of the San Francisco region. Ethnic solidarity, like occupational solidarity, can act as a double-edged sword, reducing conflicts of interest between members and nonmembers from the same ethnic group, but creating barriers to the admission of members from other ethnic groups (Russell, 1984).

In sum, the formation of worker cooperatives is always to some extent an economic act, but it can almost never be ascribed to the operation of individual self-interest alone. Worker cooperatives are created in order to meet the needs not of individuals, but of groups. And cooperative structures are typically chosen over more conventional capitalist alternatives at least in part because of their consistency with the values of those groups.

This brief discussion can in itself help us to understand why the Jewish settlement (or Yishuv) in Palestine in the early decades of this century was so unusually productive of cooperative and collectively owned workplaces of many types. The answer lies in the fact that this environment provided an unusually strong combination of all of the considerations outlined above. Economically, Jewish immigrants to Palestine were driven to create a new array of worker-owned firms first of all by the absence or unsuitability of conventional alternatives. Palestine in the early part of this century offered scarce opportunities for employment of any kind and even fewer that could allow Jewish laborers to maintain any semblance of the European standard of living that they were accustomed to. Normatively, the early settlers were strongly imbued with anticapitalist values and a social movement orientation. It was their explicit intention to create a new and better society. And above all, these architects of a new society were driven by the pursuit of collective rather than individual goals. Here, for example, is how Aharoni characterized their motivation in a recent history of the Israeli economy:

> The forefathers of Israel were not only revolutionaries but also dreamers, utopians and romantics. They yearned to create a new and just society, anchored in strong values of social justice and equality.
>
> While these zealots were different in many ways, they

all shared at least two basic beliefs. First, that cooperation, based on sentiments of brotherhood, could be made into the dominant mode for social relations. Second, that the needs of the country, of the movement, and of the community were the only criteria for judging the desirability of an operation. These persons did not live for themselves, but for the group, for the ideals, and for the future of the nation . . . p. 149).

These immigrants had thus come to Palestine to benefit not only themselves as individuals, but also the entire Jewish cause, and they therefore created organizations that would be equally broad in their ownership structures and in the purposes they would serve.

THE ORIGINS OF ISRAEL'S LABOR ECONOMY

The Birth of the Kibbutz

A discussion of the origins of Israel's labor economy must begin with the kibbutz, its oldest and most famous element. The first kibbutz, Degania, was established on December 1, 1909, by six founding members. While the time and place of its formation are not in dispute, the literature on the kibbutz offers many contrasting views of the dynamics that led to its creation. Some authors see the kibbutz as Israel's most "utopian" institution and attribute its creation primarily to the Zionist ideologies and socialist values of its founders (e.g., Curtis, 1973; Daniel, 1976). Other scholars, including Preuss (1965), Sussman (1969), and Shafir (1989), have emphasized the extent to which the birth of the kibbutz was a pragmatic response to pressing economic concerns.

For these latter scholars, the most important practical problem that the kibbutz was created to solve was the need to create viable employment opportunities for Jewish immigrants to Palestine. Until the kibbutz was invented, the principal strategy that Zionist philanthropists like Baron Edmond de Rothschild had been promoting was the development of agriculture along capitalist lines. A major problem with this strategy was that each new farm required a great deal of capital to be established, but placed only a single Jewish immigrant in the position of owner. Other Jewish immigrants could seek jobs as hired workers on these capitalist farms, but they faced competition from Arab laborers who were willing to work for lower wages. This competition from Arab labor caused many Jewish workers to be entirely displaced and caused the wages of many others to fall far below the European standard. By the time Kibbutz Degania was being founded, this problem had become so critical that "the overwhelming majority of the immigrants from the earlier years" were either returning to their country of origin or were leaving "for more promising destinations" (Shafir, 1989, p. 75).

The creation of Kibbutz Degania and others like it provided a solution to this problem by creating a form of organization in which only Jewish labor would be employed. Whereas Jewish capitalist employers would always be tempted to hire cheaper Arab labor, cooperative agricultural settlements created by Jewish immigrants would insist on accepting only other Jewish immigrants as members. Shafir uses the vocabulary of Edna Bonacich (1972, 1979) to argue that the creation of the kibbutz "split" the agricultural labor market in Palestine into two segments, one that was both cooperative and Jewish, another that was capitalist and still predominantly Arab. The kibbutz also carried the additional advantage of inducing the Jewish workers to pool the meager resources they had available for consumption, thus making it more possible to recreate some semblance of a European lifestyle on the basis of a still quite modest average wage.

Several historical circumstances surrounding Degania's creation support this economic interpretation of its origins. The founders of Degania had worked previously on a training farm sponsored by the World Zionist Organization at Kinneret, but had left the farm in protest over a plan to hire Arab labor. And the founders of Kibbutz Degania themselves later denied that any but practical considerations governed their actions. Shafir quotes one of them, Joseph Baratz, who insisted in 1923 that the kibbutz "is not the fruit of the international cooperative idea. We did not learn from it, and in the beginning of our path we paid no attention to it. Its origin is in the Eretz Israeli reality" (Shafir, 1989, p. 173).

It is thus clear from the historical record that, as Joseph Tabenkin later noted, "The kibbutz came prior to its idea. It had no preplan" (Kellerman, 1993, p. 50). But it would be a mistake to conclude from the improvisational nature of its origins that the kibbutz was created in response to economic considerations alone. At the very least, it is necessary to note that the kind of economic rationality that led to the creation of the first kibbutz is not individual, but collective. If the founders of the kibbutz had been trying to maximize their own personal incomes, they would have immigrated not to Palestine, but to the United States, a destination that was in general much more popular among the Eastern European Jews of that time. Their personal sacrifices, both in coming to Palestine and in creating the kibbutz, are understandable only against the backdrop of their commitment to the greater Zionist project.

The goal of finding forms of agricultural employment that would be suitable for Jewish labor also cannot be separated from the socialist and Zionist ideology of the Jewish immigrants. As socialists, they sought to create a Jewish working class in the new land, not another Jewish bourgeoisie. As Zionists, they were influenced by ideologists like A. D. Gordon, who saw work on the land as essential to the spiritual rebirth of the Jewish people. This was seen as the only means by which Jews could eradicate the harmful effects on their occupational structure and on their thought that had been brought about by centuries of living as merchants and moneylenders in countries where Jews were forbidden to own land (Winer, 1971).

It thus seems most accurate to say of the origins of the kibbutz that they were neither purely ideological nor purely economic, but were rather a creative combination of the two. In this respect they are an archetypal creation of the Second Aliyah, as the wave of Jewish immigrants to Palestine that arrived between 1904 and 1914 is customarily called. This was the generation that created the Israeli stereotype of the *chalutz*, or "pioneer" (Eisenstadt, 1967, pp. 17–18). These chalutzim prided themselves on their practicality and their readiness to improvise, but they also never strayed far from the Zionist and socialist ideals that had first brought them to Palestine. As Martin Buber pointed out in his *Paths in Utopia*,

> One element . . . has been repeatedly pointed out: that the Jewish Village Commune in Palestine owes its existence not to a doctrine but to a situation, to the needs, the stress, the demands of the situation. . . . But what is called the "ideology"—I personally prefer the old but untarnished word "Ideal"—was not just something to be added afterwards, that would justify the accomplished facts. In the spirit of the members of the first Palestinian Communes ideal motives joined hands with the dictates of the hour; and in the motives

there was a curious mixture of memories of the Russian *Artel*, impressions left over from reading the so-called "utopian" Socialists, and the half-unconscious after-effects of the Bible's teachings about social justice. . . . There were various dreams about the future: they saw themselves as the advance guard of the Workers' Movement, as the direct instrument for the realization of Socialism, as the prototype of the new society; they had as their goal the creation of a new man and a new world (1958, pp. 142–43).

Other writers have seen a similar combination of ideal and practical considerations in the origins of the kibbutz. For Eisenstadt, for example, the kibbutz was created out of a "general attitude . . . of experimentation" (1967, p. 20), but was also tailored to the needs of young people "with strong socialist and nationalist aspirations" (p. 19). Infield sees the creation of the kibbutz as a response to practical necessity (1946, p. 14), but notes also that "From the first, an air of social reform pervaded the colonization work in Palestine" (p. 13).

These authors also note that while the first kibbutz was created in an act of improvisation, its later spread owed much to its ability to appeal to the ideals of later generations of Jewish immigrants to Palestine, beginning with the Third Aliyah. As Shafir puts this point,

Only the Third *Aliya*, arriving between 1918–23, having experienced the Russian Revolution of 1917, painted the kibbutz in its subsequent ideological armor, viewing it as the Eretz Israeli path to socialism.

It was then that inchoate cooperativism was reinterpreted as ideologically grounded collectivism (1989, p. 184).

Eisenstadt agrees with Shafir that "It was later, during the third aliya, that the more sacrosanct attitudes to the kibbutz . . . tended to develop" (1967, p. 20). Shapiro notes similarly that, "In order to survive, laborers organized these self-governed settlements. The self-government, which had started by necessity, became an attractive element in the new organizations for many newcomers" (1976, p. 13). Infield is particularly eloquent in describing how the kibbutz came increasingly to capture the imagination of idealist young Jews in the Diaspora:

Of all the messages from Palestine . . . that of the kvutza [kib-butz] had a special appeal. Here, there were not merely revival and refreshment; here a new life was being created, fashioned by social justice. Preparing for the "ascent" to Palestine, as emigration was happily termed, came to mean preparation for joining a kvutza. . . .

At this juncture, there is a semblance of truth in com-paring the kvutza, as Charles Gide did, with communities founded on a utopian philosophy (1946, p. 16).

The same mix of ideal and practical considerations that con-tributed so much to the origin and early spread of the kibbutz was also important in the reception given to the kibbutz by the World Zionist Organization. The role of this organization in the develop-ment of the kibbutz should not be underestimated, as the WZO made extremely important material and institutional contribu-tions to Kibbutz Degania and all later kibbutzim. Most important is the fact that through its subsidiary, the Jewish National Fund, the WZO owned the land on which most kibbutzim and later moshavim would be established. The WZO and JNF have made a crucial contribution to the kibbutzim and moshavim, first of all by giving them free use of this land. And they may have made a second contribution of equal or greater importance by retaining the title to this property. By keeping the title to kibbutz and moshav property in public hands, they have underlined the institutional re-quirement that the economic activity in these organizations should be directed toward the pursuit of national goals. This arrangement has also removed from the life of these cooperatives what has elsewhere been one of the most important incentives be-hind the degeneration of worker-owned firms, the unrestrained ap-preciation of workers' capital stakes.

The WZO's support for cooperative settlements on collec-tively owned land had developed for reasons similar to those that motivated the Jewish immigrants in Israel. Zionist philanthropists like Baron Rothschild had begun by supporting capitalist agricul-ture, but were increasingly disappointed in the results. Capitalist planters hired Arab laborers to work their farms and often ended up having little direct contact with the land that they owned. Moreover, the Eastern European Jewish immigrants of the Second Aliyah were simply too poor to establish capitalist farms on their own. They needed to be supplied with land, and it became the mission of the WZO to get it for them. But it was impractical for the WZO just to sign the land over to them, as the immigrant farmers also needed training and equipment. So the WZO soon began establishing training farms in Palestine, such as the one at Kinneret that became a forerunner of Degania. The WZO also began to be influenced by ideologies that made a virtue of these necessities. The WZO was led to think in increasingly idealistic terms about the ownership of land in Palestine in part in its role as custodian of the Jewish National Fund. Here is how Infield summarizes the kind of hopes that were expressed for this fund when it was first established in 1901:

> The land was never to be made private property; further, it was not only national property, but he who acquired it had to serve higher purposes than that of personal profit. It was never to be defiled by speculation or by the exploitation of others in its working (1946, p. 12).

The convergence of ideological and practical considerations that would make the WZO the chief patron of the nascent kibbutz movement came to a head as the first decade of the century was coming to a close. At its Eighth and Ninth Congresses, the WZO adopted the plans of Franz Oppenheimer, a cooperative theorist, who called for WZO training farms in Palestine gradually to transform themselves into cooperative settlements (Shafir, 1989, p. 157). When Degania's founders approached Arthur Ruppin, the WZO's representative in Palestine, to request support for their new settlement, he was happy to oblige. Infield reports that Ruppin agreed that "the immigrants had no choice. At the time, at least, it meant, 'either settlement in groups or no settlement at all'" (1946, p. 14). Infield adds that "Cooperative farming was thus forced upon those responsible for the survival of Jewish agricultural settlement and was not a consequence of any preconceived idea" (p. 14). Thus for the WZO, as for its founders, the kibbutz was born in an act of pragmatic improvisation; but in the WZO, as among the kibbutz founders, the kibbutz also struck a responsive ideological chord. This point is well illustrated by a quotation Yonathan Shapiro extracts from a Hebrew source, which notes that for WZO leader Chaim Weizmann, "every new settlement was for him an additional string in the violin of Zionist propaganda in the Diaspora" (1976, p. 74).

In giving birth to the kibbutz, that small group at Degania had thus created an institution that had a remarkable ability to meet both the practical and the ideological needs of Zionists both in Palestine and in the Diaspora. But the work of creating a new Jewish economy in Palestine had scarcely begun. As Buber has noted, the "pioneers" who created the first kibbutzim were "an elite," and the kibbutz was "the form of life that befitted this elite" (p. 143). The question left unanswered by the creation of the kibbutz, therefore, was the question of what forms of organization would provide employment and living accommodations for the many thousands of Jewish immigrants who were about to arrive in Palestine who were not ready to join this moral elite—immigrants who in most cases were also committed Zionists, but who were not prepared for the extremes of self-sacrifice and asceticism that were required by the life on the kibbutzim of that era. It was the effort to answer this question that led to the creation of the other major portions of Israel's labor economy, including the Histadrut and the Chevrat Ovdim.

From Elite to Mass Institutions

The story of the birth of the Histadrut and the Chevrat Ovdim is well told by Yonathan Shapiro in his 1976 book, *The Formative Years of the Israeli Labour Party*. Shapiro portrays the formation of these institutions as an outgrowth of the political activity of David Ben-Gurion and his circle. They set out to found a party and a nation, but soon found that they could not accomplish either goal without first becoming founders of an economic empire. Only after they had created and established firm control over this economic foundation did their later political hegemony become assured.

The forerunner of what we now know as the Israeli Labor Party was founded under the name Achdut Haavodah (Labor Unity) in 1919. As was true of the kibbutz, its founders were members of the Second Aliyah whose ideological fervor was now mixed with pragmatism and a readiness to improvise under the impact of previous failures. Most of these men had already devoted more than a decade to political work in Palestine and had little to show for their efforts. Shapiro estimates that the two major pre-war workers' parties, Hapoel Hatzair and Poalei Zion, together could count as members only four hundred to five hundred of the five thousand Jewish laborers in Palestine in 1918 (1976, p. 14). Now in 1919, under the impact of the Balfour Declaration and the establishment of the British Mandate, Jewish immigrants were pouring into Palestine as never before, but it remained to be seen whether any political party would be able to divert their attention from their pressing economic needs.

Shapiro makes several points about the founding of Achdut Haavodah that provide important insights into the strategies that they would later pursue. First, like the Bolsheviks, Achdut's founders were products of the Russian socialist political culture, and they felt a good deal of affinity with the goals and tactics of their counterparts in Moscow; but they were also well aware that the situation in Palestine required a different strategy. They were socialists without a state, so it would be their mission to create one. Until that goal was achieved, they would be forced to rely on moral methods, not coercive ones. They would need to persuade, rather than force, Jewish workers into joining them, and they would need to coax financial resources out of the WZO as well. In Shapiro's words, "Their lack of coercive power . . . forced them to put great emphasis on achieving a high degree of consensus in the Jewish community in order to legitimize their authority" (1976, p. 4).

This point is an important one. While some accounts of the origins of Israel's labor economy place most of the burden on Zionist and socialist values and others emphasize the role of economic interests, Shapiro incorporates both and proves an important connection between the two. For Shapiro, the two come together through the intermediation of the Achdut Haavodah leaders, who forged a link between them in pursuit of their own organizational interests. Thus in Shapiro's treatment, value consensus within the Jewish settlement is not taken as a given, but is instead treated as the consequence of a deliberate political strategy pursued by the Achdut Haavodah leaders. For Shapiro, it was "the ability of the Achdut Haavodah leaders to use ideology . . . pragmatically" (1976, p. 69) that provided the basis of both its moral and political hegemony. Aharoni offers a similar interpretation, observing that

> there was a great need among Jewish settlers to develop means of enforcement without enjoying the sanctions available to a government of a sovereign state. The Jewish Yishuv was able to achieve a far flung level of discipline and coherence by developing a political culture based largely on consensus as a basis of legitimacy (1991, p. 151).

The first consequence of this strategy for the Achdut Haavodah organizers was that they made a conscious effort to do everything possible to achieve the broadest possible appeal to the new
immigrants who were then streaming into Palestine. One way to
do this was to blur their ideological stance; they identified their
philosophy as "social Zionism" rather than "socialist Zionism"
because they did not want to deter workers who were not socialists
from joining. Aharoni notes of such formulations:

> The politics of the Yishuv period were characterized by the
> enormous importance of ideas, beliefs and hair splitting, but
> also by the ability of the dominant party to achieve coherence
> around a wide consensus after a long process of debates, of
> convincing, and of compromises (1991, p. 152).

The Achdut Haavodah leaders also recognized that their organizing
efforts would have to take on a more economic than political character, as the immigrants' most pressing problems were being created by the Palestinian economy, not the British Mandatory government.

Among the Jewish immigrants' economic needs, jobs remained the highest priority. Jewish workers' parties in Palestine
had recognized this as early as 1905, when Hapoel Hatzair made
"the conquest of labor" a part of its platform (Shafir, 1989, pp.
124–25). To assist the immigrants in finding jobs, Achdut Haavodah established a network of labor exchanges, pressured Jewish
employers to hire only Jewish labor, and sought funding from the
WZO and the international Poalei Zion movement for projects that
would create more jobs for Jewish workers in Palestine.

These were tactics that would later be pursued with great
success by the Histadrut, but by its own efforts alone the Achdut
Haavodah achieved only disappointing results. One reason for this
is that the Hapoel Hatzair party refused either to merge with
Achdut Haavodah or to participate in its programs and instead created its own competing network of labor exchanges and projects. In
1920 the WZO approved funding for a Workers' Bank in Palestine,
but when both the Achdut Haavodah and Hapoel Hatzair sought
control over it, the WZO refused to release the funds to either one.
Most of the new immigrants who were then flooding into
Palestine, in the meantime, remained indifferent to the political
activities of either party and showed little inclination to join either

one. One group from Russia under the leadership of Joseph Trumpeldor explicitly advised its adherents not to join any existing party and urged them to fight instead for "a united federation of labour which would provide work, housing, medical insurance, etc." (Shapira, 1984, p. 64).

The leaders of both parties increasingly saw the wisdom of merging their separate economic programs into a nonpartisan General Federation of Jewish Labor in Palestine. They formally took this step in December of 1920. The organization they established, known ever since as the Histadrut, is officially a trade union, but its decision making has been dominated since its formation by the political parties that created it. To ensure this result, the Histadrut's founders gave it a constitution that calls for its central bodies to be elected directly by the membership in national elections, rather than by the union organizations that make up the federation. Thus Histadrut politics have tended to operate like national politics: each party puts up its own slate of candidates, and Histadrut offices are later allocated among the leaders of the winning coalition in much the same way in which cabinet positions now get shared out among the winning parties in Israeli national elections.

According to Shapiro, this party domination of the Histadrut served a number of political purposes. For the long term, it was intended to prevent the Histadrut from transforming itself into a narrowly focused labor union, which could become so protective of its members' employment prospects that it might turn hostile to further immigration (Shapiro, 1976, pp. 52, 68). And more immediately, "it served the leaders of the Second *Aliya* as the tool for the cooptation of the third wave (1918–23) of immigrants" (p. 193). With this new structure, the Achdut Haavodah leaders rapidly extended their influence. Shapiro estimates that by 1922, the Histadrut had enlisted half of the Jewish laborers in Palestine; by 1926, the proportion who were members had risen to 70 percent (p. 78).

Once the Histadrut had been created, the attention of its organizers shifted to the creation and organization of subsidiaries that could provide its members with employment. Many Histadrut members were employed in building and public works projects that were organized by a subsidiary that later came to be known as Solel Boneh. Many others received funding or employment from the Workers' Bank, known in Hebrew as the Bank Hapoalim. Each

of these organizations quickly became a large and semiautonomous bureaucracy in its own right. In order to establish more effective centralized coordination over these activities, the Histadrut
put all of them under the control of a new economic subsidiary,
the Chevrat Ovdim, in February of 1923.

The formation of the Chevrat Ovdim was not only a response
to internal control problems within the Histadrut, but also reflected
a political and ideological preference by many Achdut Haavodah
leaders for collective and centralized forms of ownership. This preference was encouraged by the Russian Jewish immigrants who
comprised the bulk of the Third Aliyah, and whose socialist fervor
had been stirred by the Russian Revolution of October 1917
(Shapira, 1984, 1989). Upon returning to Palestine from a trip to
Russia in 1921, Ben-Gurion himself called for "the creation of a
general commune with military discipline of all laborers in Eretz
Israel" (Shapiro, 1976, p. 58). Ben-Gurion explained at the time,

> If we decide just on paper that the public must obey our or-
> ders, it will remain ineffective so long as the economic state
> of affairs does not bind the people . . . and this will be possible
> only if we create one collective economy. . . . How else are we
> going to enforce discipline unless we control the economy
> (Shapiro, 1976, p. 57)?

This goal of imposing military discipline throughout the
economy was taken literally by a group of Third Aliyah immigrants that organized itself as the Gedud Haavodah, or Labor
Battalion, in August of 1920. These new immigrants from Russia
were followers of Joseph Trumpeldor, a former soldier who had
served with distinction in both the Czarist and British armies.
Although Trumpeldor himself had died in defense of the settlement at Tel Hai in February of 1920, the new labor battalion was
named in his honor. The Gedud's founders were looking for organizational models that could both absorb mass immigration and
make an immediate contribution to the building of socialism in
Palestine, and the idea of forming "labor battalions" appeared to
meet their needs on both counts (Shapira, 1984).

In the beginning the members of the Gedud supported themselves with contracts for road building work. They were able to increase the scale and importance of their activities dramatically
when the Zionist Congress authorized the establishment of the

largest kibbutz yet attempted on newly acquired land in the Jezreel Valley in 1921. The collective agricultural settlements that had been organized until that time were small, intimate, and selective groups known in Hebrew as kvutzot, or communes. The new "large kvutzah" that the Gedud would establish at Ein Harod was seen as a key to the further growth of the kibbutz as an institution and to the absorption of mass immigration. It was hoped that the new large kvutzah would have many economic advantages over the smaller kvutzot, including economies of scale and the ability to combine both agricultural and industrial activities in the same undertaking; but the main attraction, according to Shapira, "would lie in its non-selective absorption of immigrants" (1984, p. 67).

In 1921 and 1922, the Gedud's struggle to create large kvutzot at Ein Harod and in nearby Tel Yosef "enjoyed great prestige in the labour movement and was recognized as its vanguard" (Shapira, 1984, p. 68). Its leaders threatened to displace the Achdut Haavodah as the most important political force in the Histadrut. While the Achdut Haavodah managed to retain control of the Histadrut, Shapiro reports that the power struggle between the Histadrut and the Gedud "was the main event in the life of the labor movement in Palestine during 1922 and 1923" (1976, p. 105).

By co-opting part of the Gedud's program, and aggressively attacking the rest, the Achdut Haavodah leadership gradually managed to beat back its challenge. At its Second Convention in 1923, the Histadrut formally approved the formation of labor battalions, but at the same time authorized the formation of the Chevrat Ovdim. The Chevrat Ovdim supplanted the Gedud as a collective organizer of road building, construction, and other such work, without attempting to pay all workers equally out of the "common purse," as was advocated by the Gedud and the many smaller urban workers' communes of that time (Sussman, 1969; Shapira, 1984). In 1923, the Gedud leaders were persuaded to allow Kibbutz Ein Harod to leave the Gedud, while the neighboring Kibbutz Tel Yosef remained in the Gedud. Under the leadership of Joseph Tabenkin, the kibbutz at Ein Harod quickly gained the Achdut Haavodah's blessing as the nucleus of a new movement of larger, more centralized, and more closely federated kibbutzim.

While the assets of the kibbutzim at Ein Harod and Tel Yosef were being divided, an incident occurred that was to acquire great significance because of what it symbolized about the new political economy that was then emerging in the Yishuv. Although the

Gedud loyalists in Tel Yosef outnumbered the departing members going to Ein Harod by better than two to one, the formal terms of the separation agreement called for an equal division of assets between the two. Many members of Tel Yosef considered this unfair and began to help themselves to all the livestock and farm equipment at Ein Harod that they could get their hands on. On June 6, 1923, the Histadrut sent Tel Yosef an ultimatum, threatening that all Histadrut institutions would immediately "sever" their relations with Tel Yosef if the disputed property was not immediately returned. When the Tel Yosef assembly sent an equivocal reply, Ben-Gurion sent out letters to all Histadrut institutions on June 10 instructing them to break their ties with Tel Yosef. This left Tel Yosef without flour for its kitchen, without cash or credit, and potentially without access to the medical services provided by the Histadrut's Kupat Cholim, or Sick Fund. While these orders were soon rescinded, they sent a shock throughout the Yishuv. Ben-Gurion's biographer Shabtai Teveth writes that for Ben-Gurion personally, this affair would make his reputation as "a man of force" (1987, p. 219). Shapiro agrees that "During their fight with the Gedud, the Histadrut leaders acquired an image of tough leaders who demanded obedience and would not hesitate to use their economic power to secure compliance" (1976, p. 119).

To make the Histadrut's control over the labor economy more complete, new arrangements were soon sought that could more effectively subordinate the agricultural settlements to the Chevrat Ovdim. These included not only the kibbutzim, but also the more individualistic moshavim. The first moshavim were formed only in 1921, but already by 1922, their population exceeded that of the kibbutzim (Shapiro, 1976, p. 102). As had been the case with the kibbutzim, the birth of the moshavim reflected a mix of ideology and improvisation. Many of the first moshavniks had been influenced by the individualistic philosophy of Eliezer Jaffe of the nonsocialist workers' party Hapoel Hatzair; others were former kibbutzniks who, as Kellerman (1993, p. 52) has noted, merely sought a "socially less challenging" way of life than the kibbutz had permitted, with more scope for personal independence and autonomous family life.

The individual members of the kibbutzim and moshavim had been accepted as members of the Histadrut from the time of its formation; the cooperative nature of these settlements permitted the Histadrut to think of their members as workers rather than as capitalist farmers. But many Achdut Haavodah leaders remained wary of the farmers' independence. Ben-Gurion was concerned, for example, that "The settlers of a moshav . . . pursue their own interests instead of being guided by an overall national plan" (Shapiro, 1976, p. 56). He felt that even the kibbutzim, if left to themselves, would end up "in each being 'ruled by itself and for itself'" (Shapiro, 1976, p. 56).

Shapiro reports that Ben-Gurion was convinced that the Histadrut could not continue to rely indefinitely on "moral precepts" to preserve the unity of the workers' movement: "One also needs legal authority to force traitors" (1976, p. 134). The solution adopted in the case of the kibbutzim and moshavim was the creation of another Chevrat Ovdim subsidiary, Nir, that would become the legal owner of all of these settlements. Thus while the Jewish National Fund would continue to own the land on which the settlements were located, Nir would become the owner of their movable assets and would also become the sole conduit for all future aid from the WZO.

It was not easy to persuade all the settlers to sign over all their assets to this new Histadrut body. After lengthy negotiations, it was agreed that the Histadrut Central Committee would receive only 41 percent of the founder shares in the Nir cooperative, not the 50 percent that the Histadrut had initially proposed. But with this change, the Organization of Agricultural Laborers approved the proposal at its convention that met early in 1926. According to Shapiro, it was the Histadrut leaders' appeals to the values and ideology of the agricultural workers that were decisive in inducing them to take this step: "The principal of the collectivity over the egoistic wishes of individuals, of public over private interest, was most persuasive" (1976, p. 133).

Such ideological appeals were also useful to the Histadrut leadership in their dealings with the WZO. The creators of the Histadrut and the Chevrat Ovdim were extremely dependent on the WZO not only for funding, but also for keeping up the flow of new immigrants into their projects, as the League of Nations had given to the WZO control over the certificates that permitted entry into Palestine. Shapiro reports that "To enlist the support of the WZO, the labor leaders had to impress upon the Zionist leaders that by helping the laborers, they helped the Zionist cause. This use of Zionist ideology was known as 'the appeal to the national conscience'" (1976, p. 74).

The WZO was responsive to such appeals, because its goal was immigration, and it could see that the Histadrut was both representing the interests and capturing the imaginations of the idealistic young immigrants. Shapiro reports that "The leaders of the Zionist movement slowly accepted the claim of the laborers that only their interests were in accord with the national interest, while the economic interests of private property were in conflict with the national interest" (1976, p. 13). The Jewish capitalist farmers' tendencies to hire Arab labor had tarnished their image not only among the Jewish workers, but in the eyes of the WZO as well: "The immediate need to supply work to the laborers, and the farmers' refusal to employ them, was considered a selfish act and a neglect of their Zionist duties" (Shapiro, 1976, p. 13). Thus many WZO leaders themselves began to see merits in the Histadrut's preference for collectively owned projects. Here, for example, is how Chaim Weizmann defended it:

> The halutz must know that when he builds the Rutleberg project [the new electric power plants] or the roads, that he will build it in such a way that not a ha'penny goes into the pocket of a private person, but into the pocket of the nation (Shapiro, 1976, p. 73).

Not all the WZO leaders were as enthusiastic in their support for the labor-owned economy as Weizmann. Some, like Louis Brandeis of the United States, continued to advocate support for more capitalist projects (Kimmerling, 1983, pp. 19–20). To avoid a breach in the movement and to ensure an uninterrupted flow of aid, the Histadrut leaders had to permit the continued development of a Jewish capitalist sector, which is the root of the mixed economy that one finds in Israel today. So relations between the Histadrut and the WZO required compromises on both sides. Michael Shalev has pithily characterized their relationship as an alliance between "a settlement movement without settlers" and "a workers' movement without work" (1990, p. 89).

This alliance between the WZO and the labor leaders in Palestine was further cemented in the 1930s, after Achdut Haavodah and Hapoel Hatzair had merged to form the Labor Party, or Mapai, in 1930. This Labor Party would dominate the politics of Jewish Palestine and later Israel for more than forty years, until the Likud electoral victory of 1977. With the help of its overseas allies, by 1933 it had also become the dominant political force within the WZO. In 1935 the Labor victory within the WZO was made complete, when Ben-Gurion was elected chairman of the Zionist Executive.

The net result of this alliance between the Histadrut and the WZO in Palestine was to "split" both the rural and urban labor markets into Jewish and Arab segments (Bonacich, 1972, 1979; Shalev, 1989, 1992; Grinberg, 1991). Shafir notes that the Jewish National Fund and the Histadrut worked together to "circumvent the land and labor markets respectively" (1989, p. 20). One sign of the importance of the Chevrat Ovdim to this new Jewish labor market is the fact that in 1926 most of the Histadrut's members were employed in constituent enterprises of the Chevrat Ovdim (Shapiro, 1976, p. 18).

Through these historical developments, the economic and social motivations identified somewhat abstractly in the first part of this chapter came to be concretized and institutionalized in the unique political economy of Jewish Palestine. Here is how Shalev has summarized the combination of ideological and pragmatic considerations that produced it:

> The Zionism in "labour Zionism" cannot be separated from the pressing need of the original propertyless settlers to combat their economic vulnerability and, at a subsequent stage, from the labour movement's desire to advance its organizational and political interests. The ideology which the pioneers brought with them is therefore most appropriately viewed as a repertoire which predisposed rather than predetermined action. . . . Jewish labour's nationalism, like its collectivism, was primarily forged in Palestine, on the anvil of political exchange (1992, p. 68).

In this political economy, the sentiments and loyalties discussed earlier in this chapter were now combined with potent mechanisms of enforcement that had the power to impose collective organizational solutions even on immigrants who did not share these commitments. As Aharoni notes,

> The pressures for conformism, for obedience and for putting the individual at the disposal of the community and the mission of building a new society were enormous. . . .

Individuals' subservience to the common good and to the community needs was based to a large extent on ideological belief and strong socialization. In addition, those who did not conform were faced with a loss of social esteem but also of place of work and source of income. The political economic system made individuals extremely dependent on the organization (1991, pp. 152–53).

It was into this unique and powerful political economy that Israel's urban worker cooperative movement would be born.

THE FORMATION AND LATER GROWTH
OF ISRAEL'S WORKER COOPERATIVE POPULATION

Worker cooperatives were being established in the cities of Palestine throughout the period in which the other parts of Israel's labor economy simultaneously were taking shape. As early as 1908, there are records of cooperatives of seamstresses, of tailors, and of teamsters being organized in Jaffa and another cooperative of seamstresses being formed in Jerusalem. The oldest still in existence as this study began was the cooperative printing press Achdut, which was organized in 1910 and included David Ben-Gurion among its founders. A census of the worker cooperatives conducted by the Histadrut in 1926 identified a total of seventy-six organizations with a combined labor force of 835 employees (Viteles, 1968, p. 12).

A number of factors identified in the first part of this chapter appear to have contributed to the early dynamism of this cooperative sector. The underdeveloped state of the Palestinian economy created both an opportunity and a need for cooperative businesses, as it meant both that competition from conventional enterprises was relatively lacking and that new immigrants were often forced to pool their resources to start new businesses if they wanted to find any work at all in their trades. Many founders may also have been inclined to give cooperative structures to their new businesses, because both their Zionism and their socialism gave them a preference for structures that would be collectively owned.

A 1938 report by the Registrar of Cooperatives argued that both "economic and social factors" were responsible for the unusually rapid development of the worker cooperatives in Jewish

Palestine in the first years of the Mandate. Economically, the Registrar felt that the worker cooperatives had benefited from the absence of competition from large or heavy industries. He gave even more attention, however, to "social factors," noting that

> The Jewish labour movement in Palestine aimed from the outset at creating a new social order and at establishing . . . independent undertakings managed by the workers themselves. These two factors led to the spread of cooperation among labour (p. 106).

A Histadrut-sponsored study published in the early 1930s saw a similar mix of economic and ideological considerations as leading to the formation of worker cooperatives among the Jewish immigrants, but in its view, it was the pragmatic motivations that were paramount in most cases:

> Only a few of the cooperatives were founded because of the intention to create new economic forms, . . . to be managed . . . without outside control and without the imposition of an owner's or his assistants' will. A number of cooperatives— perhaps most of them—were established out of the desire to create permanent places of work by a joint effort. . . . There is a third group of cooperatives, mostly in the services, where the objective conditions of work compelled those engaged in it to turn to the cooperative form of organization (Cooperative Center, 1933, translated and quoted by Daniel, 1976, vol. 1, pp. 213–14).

Some of these early cooperatives may also have been induced to adopt cooperative structures because this facilitated the receipt of aid. Since 1912, an international party of socialist Zionists, Poalei Zion, had been offering financial assistance to worker cooperatives through its Palestine Workers' Fund, known in Hebrew as Kapai. After World War I, this fund gave assistance to two cooperatives of carpenters and of metal workers in Haifa, to another cooperative of carpenters in Jaffa, and to several other organizations. In some cases these organizations were so thoroughly dependent on funding from Kapai that they scarcely deserved to be considered cooperatives at all. Here is how one Histadrut source later described their relationship to this fund:

independence was most restricted, almost to the point where the cooperators were not responsible for their common property, their business, their work, management, and so forth. The investment, all of which was made by the Palestine Workers' Fund, resulted in the cost of loss of interest on the part of the members, who considered themselves to some degree hired employees of the fund (quoted in Daniel, 1976, vol. 1, p. 206).

In the early 1920s, as Ben-Gurion and his colleagues began their campaign to establish centralized coordination over all economic aid to Palestine, they sought control of this fund. In 1920, control of Kapai was transferred from Poalei Zion to the Achdut Haavodah party, which was its Palestinian affiliate (Shapiro, 1976, p. 36). In 1923, Kapai was still receiving funds from Poalei Zion, but the responsibility for administering it was then taken over by the Histadrut (Shapiro, 1976, pp. 92–98).

As the Histadrut leaders acquired control of this funding, they had to decide what to do with it. When Poalei Zion suggested the formation of a cooperative center, Ben-Gurion and his associates initially rejected the idea (Shapiro, 1976, p. 35). Ben-Gurion pointed out to his Achdut Haavodah colleagues in December of 1921 that there was a "tendency in the whole world for cooperatives to turn into private enterprises." As a result, he "did not wish the Histadrut to aid them—since it would not be able to control them" (Shapiro, 1976, p. 56). Ben-Gurion was concerned that all private enterprises, including cooperatives, were likely to become increasingly diverted from the goal of attracting immigrants to Palestine and providing them with work. In Ben-Gurion's eyes, "The only solution was for all economic units to be united under the control of the Histadrut" (Shapiro, 1976, p. 56). At the Second Histadrut Congress in 1923, therefore, Ben-Gurion spoke in favor of the formation of the Chevrat Ovdim, and asked only the following difficult questions about the future of the independent worker cooperatives:

How will we preserve the social, class, and Zionist character of our economic enterprises? . . . We are founding cooperatives. . . . What is to guarantee that the workers in these enterprises will not become owners who employ hired labor, as happened in other countries in a number of producer cooperatives after they were economically successful? What is to guarantee that institutions founded by the workers and at their initiative will actually be used for the benefit of the workers' community (Daniel, 1976, vol. 1, pp. 208–209)?

A number of subsequent developments would force the Histadrut leadership to reconsider their policies toward worker cooperatives before another Histadrut Congress would meet. One of these was economic problems among the enterprises owned by the Chevrat Ovdim, which culminated in the bankruptcy of Solel Boneh in 1927. This showed the limitations of basing employment policies too exclusively on organizations owned directly by the Histadrut. The worker cooperatives, in the meantime, experienced similar problems. Of the seventy-eight worker cooperatives that the Histadrut had determined to be in existence at the end of 1926, fifty-three had closed their doors by the end of 1928. Although twenty-seven new worker cooperatives were established over these same two years, this high rate of mortality suggested that the entire worker cooperative population was in immanent danger of dying out in the absence of outside help (Viteles, 1929, p. 115).

Another even more far-reaching development during this period was the arrival of a new wave of immigration, the Fourth Aliyah of 1924–31. Whereas members of the Second and Third Aliyot had been "pulled" to Palestine by their commitment to Zionism, many members of the Fourth Aliyah came because they were "pushed" by the rising tide of anti-Semitism in Poland and other parts of Europe. The Fourth Aliyah was larger than the two previous waves combined, and was characterized by a much more "middle-class, individualistic outlook" (Shapiro, 1976, pp. 18–19). Many of these immigrants were of a type who in earlier years might have chosen to go the United States, but with the passage in 1924 of the highly restrictive Johnson-Lodge Immigration Act, they now had nowhere to go but Palestine.

Unlike the chalutzim of the previous waves of immigration, who saw it as their moral duty to work the land and populate the countryside, the Fourth Aliyah stimulated the development of an urban and capitalist Jewish economy in Palestine. In the process, it destroyed forever the Histadrut's dream of becoming the only significant employer in the Yishuv. And because these new capitalist employers were less reluctant than enterprises owned by the Chevrat Ovdim to make use of Arab labor, renewed competition between Jewish and Arab workers quickly began to exert downward pressure on the wages of Jewish immigrants (Sussman, 1969, 1973).

The arrival of the Fourth Aliyah and its impact on the economy of the Yishuv thus forced the Histadrut to seek ways to co-opt or control indirectly economic enterprises that it could not directly own. The Histadrut employed this strategy successfully with the rural cooperatives when it persuaded the kibbutzim and moshavim to subordinate themselves to Nir in 1926. In 1927, it resolved to try to do the same with worker cooperatives in the cities.

The Third Histadrut Congress voted to organize the worker cooperatives into a Merkaz Hakooperatsia, or Cooperative Center, on July 22, 1927. This new body began to function in February 1928 and held an organizing congress that attracted thirty-seven worker cooperative members in 1930.

While membership in the Merkaz Hakooperatsia was and remains voluntary, worker cooperatives have had strong incentives for joining it. The Merkaz performs many auditing functions for its members that since the time of the Mandate have been required by law. Affiliation with the Merkaz also establishes membership in the Histadrut, which is in turn a passport to such important benefits as access to the medical care provided by the Chevrat Ovdim's medical subsidiary, the Kupat Cholim. The Third Histadrut Congress also directed two other Chevrat Ovdim-owned institutions to pay special attention to the needs of the worker cooperatives. Bank Hapoalim was asked to create a special fund that would be devoted to the needs of the producer cooperatives, and Hamashbir, the Chevrat Ovdim-owned marketing organization, was asked to make a special effort to sell the cooperatives' products and to purchase raw materials for them (Daniel, 1976, vol. 1, pp. 216–17).

In practice the Merkaz has tended to attract virtually all of the producer, service, and transportation cooperatives in Jewish Palestine and later Israel. The only cooperatives that have remained outside of its umbrella are a small number of Arab cooperatives, which have a separate audit union (Daniel, 1972; 1976, vol. 1, pp. 277–94); cooperatives organized by religious organizations, like Hapoel Hamizrachi; a number of secondary cooperatives, such as the transportation subsidiaries created by groups of kibbutzim; and a few taxi cooperatives that in Israel as in other countries have shown no interest in being affiliated with any cooperative "movement" as such.

In its first years the Merkaz was primarily preoccupied with efforts to establish both itself and its members on a firm legal footing and to keep its members alive. The British Mandatory Government had promulgated its first Cooperative Societies Ordinance in 1920, but many worker cooperatives were slow to register themselves as the law required (Daniel, 1976, vol. 1, p. 206). The Merkaz assisted in the preparation of the new Cooperative Societies Ordinance of 1933, which gave cooperatives the option of organizing themselves into audit unions to conduct the audits that were required to be submitted annually to the Registrar of Cooperative Societies. In addition the Merkaz was soon holding seminars in accounting, marketing, and management, arranging bulk purchases for its members of gasoline and other raw materials, arbitrating disputes between members and their cooperatives, and maintaining a cooperative pension fund.

For many years after the formation of the Merkaz, the worker cooperatives attached to it grew in number and in size and in their importance to the Jewish settlement (table 1.1). In the 1930s and 1940s, the prestige of cooperatives in both the countryside and the cities rose in recognition of the role they played in the struggle for independence. Among the rural cooperatives, it was the kibbutzim that stood out, both by virtue of their tenacious efforts at self-defense and because of their disproportionate contributions to the emerging state's army and its officer corps. Among the cooperatives associated with the Merkaz, it was the intercity bus drivers who played the most heroic role, running great personal risks to maintain a lifeline to isolated settlements both during the Arab uprising of the later 1930s and again during the War of Independence (Preuss, 1960, p. 204).

The cooperatives experienced their most rapid growth in the years immediately after 1948, when independence brought unprecedented numbers of immigrants to Israeli shores. Established cooperatives were asked to offer employment to as many of these immigrants as they could, and the Merkaz was asked to assist in the creation of new cooperatives as rapidly as it possibly could. Many of the new immigrants were directed to newly created "development towns," and the Merkaz set up cooperative workshops, bakeries, and so on in many of these areas.

TABLE 1.1
Cooperatives Represented at Congresses of the Cooperative Center,
1930–1985[a]

Congress	Year	Number of Cooperatives	Total Labor Force
First	1930	37	700
Second	1933	39	1,100
Third	1934	74	2,200
Fourth	1938	73	3,000
Fifth	1949	128	5,000
Sixth	1962	205	14,500
Seventh	1968	180	15,500
Eighth	1973	150	18,500
Ninth	1981	102	21,352
Tenth	1985	90	20,843

[a]Daniel (1989, p. 151).

The distributions of worker cooperatives and of cooperative employment by industry for selected years are shown in table 1.2 and table 1.3. Many of these cooperatives involve occupations like printing, baking, and transportation that have been highly productive of worker cooperatives in many other parts of the world (Russell, 1985a, 1985b; Ben-Ner, 1988a). Many are also in industries in which worker cooperatives could benefit from special ties to the Histadrut, the Chevrat Ovdim, and the Israeli state. For example, those that produce building materials, sand, and cement were in a position to act as subcontractors for Solel Boneh. The formation and consolidation of cooperatives in transportation was encouraged in the 1920s and 1930s as a way to present a united front in negotiations with British suppliers designed to bring down the price of fuel; in the 1940s and 1950s, similar policies were pursued because of the contribution that a centrally coordinated transportation industry could make to defense. The spread of cooperative bakeries in development towns in the 1950s was linked to Israeli state policies that governed the allocation of subsidized wheat and that conferred de facto monopolies on the bakeries in each area. A cooperative manufacturer like Haargaz, which makes the bodies for the buses driven by Egged and Dan, benefited from Israeli governmental import policies that banned the import of completed buses but authorized the import of chassis and engines. In the sphere of culture, cooperative conservatories of music have continued to be formed well into the 1980s, at least in part because the Ministry of Education prefers to reserve its support for what it considers to be "public bodies," rather than individually owned private firms.

The combined efforts of the Merkaz Hakooperatsia, the Histadrut, and the Israeli government to promote the formation of worker cooperatives reached their climax in the early 1950s. The

TABLE 1.2
Worker Cooperatives by Sector and Industry, Selected Years[a]

Industry	1926	1933	1949	1959	1976	1984	1989
Transportation	6	15	24	27	22	10	10
Passenger Transport	.	11	7	4	3	3	3
Motor Freight	.	3	17	23	19	7	7
Service	9	14	19	46	39	24	25
Meat, Ice, Oil	.	2	.	12	7	5	4
Restaurants, Hotels	3	4	4	3	6	3	3
Schools, Theaters	.	.	.	8	7	3	5
Laundries	4	2	.	5	3	2	2
Port, Sailing, Fishing	.	.	.	5	.	.	3
Garages	.	.	.	4	.	.	.
Refuse Collection	.	.	.	4	.	.	.
Other Service	2	6	15	5	16	11	5
Production	54	23	78	146	81	46	37
Baking	3	3	12	47	23	8	5
Woodworking	8	5	11	16	12	9	8
Printing, Paper	3	3	6	13	12	8	8
Metal, Electrical	22	5	12	19	10	8	6
Building Materials	6	5	13	7	6	5	6
Sand, Cement, Drill	.	.	.	8	8	5	2
Textiles	6	0	6	6	6	1	1
Food Processing	0	1	0	7	0	2	1
Leather, Shoes	6	0	0	8	0	0	.
Chemicals	0	0	0	4	0	0	.
Other Production	0	1	18	11	4	0	0

[a]1926: Dickenstein (1989, p. 148); 1933: Cooperative Center (1933); 1949: Dickenstein (1989, p. 149); 1959: Losh (1960, p. 26); 1976: Losh (1979, p. 86); 1984: Daniel (1989, p. 72); 1989: Cooperative Center.

TABLE 1.3
Employment in Worker Cooperatives by Sector and Industry,
Selected Years[a]

Industry	1926	1933	1949	1959	1976	1984	1989
Transportation	230	527	2,824	8,403	14,500	14,635	12,132
Passenger Transport	.	450	2,217	7,153	13,000	13,776	11,477
Motor Freight	.	55	607	1,250	1,500	859	655
Service	44	179	576	1,250	2,185	2,345	2,037
Meat, Ice, Oil	0	27	0	400	175	107	75
Restaurants, Hotels	7	67	229	231	250	187	27
Schools, Theaters	0	0	0	140	135	68	124
Laundries	18	15	0	85	75	41	58
Port, Sailing, Fishing	.	0	0	138	0	.	113
Garages	0	0	.	84	0	0	0
Refuse Collection	.	.	.	51	0	0	0
Other Service	19	70	347	122	1,550	1,942	1,640
Production	540	264	1,955	3,687	3,040	2,522	2,089
Baking	14	16	144	609	650	463	387
Woodworking	144	40	348	350	435	191	183
Printing, Paper	112	86	178	386	310	205	172
Metal, Electrical	146	80	342	920	955	1,040	811
Building Materials	56	34	265	131	230	328	325
Sand, Cement, Drill	.	.	0	301	200	252	126
Textiles	32	0	137	86	150	8	6
Food Processing	.	4	0	97	0	45	79
Leather, Shoes	36	0	0	179	0	0	0
Chemicals	0	0	0	47	0	0	0
Other Production	0	4	541	581	110	0	0

[a]1926: Dickenstein (1989, p. 148); 1933: Cooperative Center (1933); 1949: Dickenstein (1989, p. 149); 1959: Losh (1960, p. 26); 1976: Losh (1979, p. 86); 1984: Daniel (1989, p. 72); 1989: Cooperative Center.

number of cooperatives affiliated with the Merkaz Hakooperatsia attained its all-time peak in 1951, at 393. An official of the International Cooperative Alliance who visited the Merkaz cooperatives in 1957 produced a rapturous report about what he had seen:

Amongst the inhabitants of Israel . . . Cooperation is looked upon as a definite moral standard, a way of life. It is the inspiration of the nation's laws as well as of individual behavior. In short, we are face to face with the "Cooperative State" . . .

The new State, it might be said, is one with the Workers' Productive Cooperatives, to which it gave life, and from which it took life (Mondini, 1957, p. 15).

While enthusiastic reports like this were being published abroad, severe demoralization was setting in within the Merkaz. Many of the cooperatives that had been organized so hastily in the first years after statehood quickly failed, and the rate of formation of new cooperatives rapidly declined. By the late 1950s, it had become common for people both inside and outside the Merkaz to remark that the Israeli cooperatives were no longer, or had never been, a "movement." An influential article by Zeev Schiff in Haaretz in 1960 flatly proclaimed "The Bankruptcy of the Co-operative Movement" (Viteles, 1968, p. 348).

These were indeed prophetic words, as since the 1950s the Israeli cooperatives have shown many symptoms of decline. Employment within Israeli worker cooperatives did not begin to fall in absolute terms until 1980–81, when it reached an all-time peak of 21,352 (figure 1.1.), but its relative decline began much earlier. The Israeli government did not begin issuing figures on the size of the national labor force until 1955. The employment in Merkaz cooperatives as a percent of this figure peaked back in 1956, at slightly less than 2 percent of the labor force, and by 1988 had fallen to just under 1.1 percent (figure 1.2). By 1988, moreover, more than two thirds of this cooperative employment was being accounted for by just the two large bus cooperatives, Egged and Dan. Employment in worker cooperatives in manufacturing and in services, on the other hand, had fallen sharply (tables 1.2 and 1.3), to a little more than two thousand workers per sector (2,207 in production, 2,223 in services), of whom more than 80 percent in each sector were hired workers (see chapter 3).

Transportation appears to be the only sector in which Israeli worker cooperatives have achieved any noteworthy success, either in creating employment or in keeping the use of hired labor below the psychologically important barrier of 50 percent. And yet paradoxically, it is in this sector that Israeli worker cooperatives have suffered the greatest decline in their public image in the years since statehood was achieved.

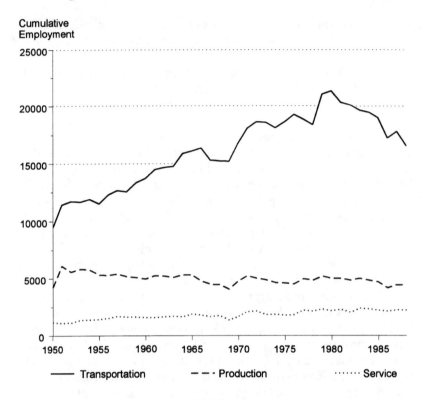

FIGURE 1.1
Cooperative Employment by Sector, 1950–1988[a]

[a]1950–1958: Cooperative Center (1960); 1959 calculated from Viteles (1968); 1960–1985: Daniel (1989); 1986–1988: Registrar of Cooperative Societies (1988, 1989a, 1989b).

In the first years of the new Israeli state, when intercity bus drivers were viewed as heroes by Israelis, the government encouraged the bus cooperatives to consolidate and conferred a de facto monopoly on them. The thinking was that, in return for this monopoly, the bus companies would maintain unprofitable routes to sparsely settled areas and would also stand ready to assist the army in future wars.

Soon after independence, however, government leaders began to accuse the bus cooperatives of violating the public trust, leveling charges that have been repeated many times since. Many of

FIGURE 1.2
Percentage of Labor Force in Worker Cooperatives, 1955–1988[a]

[a]1950–1959: Viteles (1968); 1960–1985: Daniel (1989); 1986–1988: Registrar of Cooperative Societies (1988, 1989a, 1989b). Size of Israeli labor force taken from the *Statistical Abstract of Israel 1990*, supplemented as needed by the 1986 and 1977 volumes of this series. For years in which two figures are reported because of changes in calculation methods, the figure given last is always used.

these complaints seem to be related to the bus cooperatives' status as regulated monopolies, which must obtain government approval for rate increases. There have been a number of cases in which bus cooperatives have requested rate increases, the government has denied them, and the cooperatives involved have declared a strike or a curtailment of service until the increases are approved.

On these occasions, criticisms leveled at the bus cooperatives have not been limited to the size of their wage packages and allegations of inefficiency, but have in some cases been directly related to the bus companies' cooperative character. For example, the cooperatives frequently stand accused of exploiting their hired laborers, of charging excessively high prices for memberships, and of unfairly showing a preference for the sons and sons-in-law of members in the creation of new memberships. As a result of these complaints, the proportion of hired labor and the prices charged for new memberships have often been incorporated into the three-way rounds of bargaining that frequently take place among the cooperatives, the government, and the Histadrut. These pressures have helped to keep the share of nonmember labor lower in the bus cooperatives than it is in most of the Merkaz cooperatives; but they have not prevented the public from forming an image of the bus companies as formerly pioneering cooperatives that have now come to be dominated by their members' greed. Here, for example, is how Preuss has described the decline in their public image in the first decade after independence:

> The employment of hired workers, and all other problems which had been latent before, concerning the distribution of surplus profits by the Co-operatives, have become aggravated. . . . Fixing transport fares is a kindred problem, and due to the taxing conditions of public transport throughout the country the general public takes a burning interest in all these issues. A further point which has provoked controversy is the high cash amount . . . required of new members. . . . The behaviour of drivers in dealing with the public, their investing large sums in luxurious apartments and other undesirable phenomena in the Co-operatives have led to increasing tension between them and the Government and *Histadrut,* culminating in 1956 in a prolonged strike by the Bus Co-operatives. The strike aligned the public, the Labour organizations and the Government in one solid front against the Co-operatives, a constellation which provoked violent debate also in the Knesset (Parliament) (1960, pp. 205–206).

The Merkaz Hakooperatsia and the Histadrut

While statistics on the numbers and formation rates of the Israeli worker cooperatives might suggest that their popularity had peaked in the early 1950s and that their decline began only thereafter, the roots of their decline must actually be sought in a much earlier period. They go back to the time when the Merkaz Hakooperatsia was initially being formed under Histadrut sponsorship in the 1920s.

The Histadrut leadership was from the beginning deeply suspicious of the independence and capitalistic tendencies of the worker cooperatives and established the Merkaz Hakooperatsia more in order to control the producers' cooperatives than to promote them. To make this control more effective, the management board of the Merkaz was made to consist of three representatives appointed by the Histadrut and only two appointed by the member cooperatives. The Histadrut also gave itself special veto powers over actions taken by the Merkaz, and the Merkaz received similar rights over actions taken by its member cooperatives. Although the Merkaz cooperatives requested the right to establish their own journal in 1938 (Viteles, 1968, p. 41), the Histadrut did not authorize them to have one until 1948.

Another sign of the Histadrut's lack of enthusiasm for the worker cooperatives is the fact that, despite promises to the contrary, the Merkaz and its cooperatives were largely left to supply their own financing. The Merkaz was supported by a tax on its members, and its Kupat Hakooperatsia, or Cooperative Fund, was also left to rely largely on members' deposits for funding.

The Histadrut's failure to supply significant funding not only communicates much about the labor leaders' true feelings toward the Merkaz cooperatives, but also signifies an important limit on its ability to control them. As Shapiro notes about their relationship in the 1920s, "cooperatives in the cities were not as heavily subsidized by the WZO as were the agricultural settlements. This may have made their life more difficult, but it also made them less dependent on the Histadrut" (1976, p. 138).

Other limitations on the Histadrut's ability to control the Merkaz cooperatives were inherent in their legal structure. Each cooperative retained title to its own assets, unlike the arrangement between the rural cooperatives and Nir. The Merkaz Hakooperatsia and through it the Histadrut would be entitled to receive 25 percent of the assets of its member cooperatives in the event of their dissolution, but so long as they remained in business they owned and controlled their own property and operated autonomously.

This was, as later events would show, a recipe for acrimony. The members of the Merkaz Hakooperatsia had no control over "their" Cooperative Center, and the Center had no control over its member cooperatives. The Histadrut was eager to assert its authority over the Merkaz cooperatives, but in practice it had little to offer them but exhortation and reproach.

Records remaining from the early years of the Merkaz make it clear that its relationship to its member cooperatives acquired a contentious character virtually from the start. At the First Congress of the Merkaz cooperatives in June of 1930 complaints were already heard of "conflicts . . . with the Histadrut." A resolution adopted at that meeting called for the "human material" in the cooperatives to be more carefully screened and recommended that "trouble makers should be expelled" (Viteles, 1968, p. 13).

By the Fourth Congress of the Merkaz cooperatives in June of 1938, it was clear that relations between the cooperatives and the Histadrut had seriously soured. The perspective of the Histadrut was expressed by a member of the Merkaz Central Committee, who felt that the cooperatives still lacked a proper cooperative consciousness:

> I do not feel that the co-operative ideal has resounded (rung) in their midst. The *petit bourgeoisie* tie is too strong. It seems to me that as the economic aspect strengthens, the social aspects are mutilated by the same degree . . . social and idealistic motives . . . [are] missing (Viteles, 1968, p. 35).

A speaker for the members, on the other hand, described the role taken by the Histadrut toward the cooperatives as that of a "policeman" (Viteles, 1968, p. 82). In one revealing exchange, a Histadrut spokesman acknowledged that relations between the Histadrut and the cooperatives had chilled, but blamed the members of the cooperatives for this estrangement: they "had withdrawn from the daily life of the Histadrut and were rarely seen in the crafts union," and they "did not provide workers for the Histadrut-sponsored public activities." A member of a Tel Aviv bus cooperative retorted,

> If we admit that we sinned and also that we are to blame for the wall between ourselves and the labour councils, this, however, does not free the Histadrut governing organs, and more especially its Council, from the responsibility of breaking down this wall. The lack of understanding, I do not want to say hatred, shown by the labour councils, is inexcusable (Viteles, 1968, p. 81).

Another participant at this same Congress offered a more dispassionate analysis of the sources of this conflict:

The Histadrut's focal goal is to own and/or control factories and other economic undertakings. Therefore, it is not much less interested in changing wage workers into owners than in changing the owners of the WPSTS [Workers' Production, Service and Transportation Societies] into wage workers in the Histadrut-sponsored undertakings which serve the interests of all workers (Viteles, 1968, p. 83).

The focal point of these growing hostilities between the cooperatives and the Histadrut was the increasing use of hired labor. At the instigation of the Histadrut, the Merkaz had formally banned this practice as early as 1934, and several cooperatives were expelled from the movement for breaches of this rule. Nevertheless the use of hired labor continued to expand and led the Histadrut to conduct a major investigation of the cooperatives in the mid-1940s. The Sixth Congress of the Histadrut in 1945 urged its leadership to do everything in its power to bring this practice to an end.

The growing tensions between the cooperatives and the Histadrut were temporarily forgotten in the euphoria that followed independence. In a period in which the "private sector complained that it was discriminated against" (Aharoni, 1991, p. 194), the worker cooperatives were not left out in the allocation of raw materials and development funds. But even in this case, the helping hand extended to cooperatives was more apparent than real. Priority was placed on the need to create short-term job opportunities for recent immigrants, not on the long-term health of the cooperative sector. Many new cooperatives were created on paper only, as crucial equipment that had been promised by the government was never received. New cooperatives were placed in direct competition with each other and with established ones, without making any effort to find out beforehand whether their products would be in demand. When development planning was placed on a more rational footing in the later 1950s, two-thirds of the industrial cooperatives affiliated with the Merkaz were declared ineligible for funding, because they produced goods like shoes and clothing that were now understood to be in oversupply (Viteles, 1968, p. 113). Histadrut-owned institutions tended to be favored over the cooperatives in applications for foreign currency allocations as well as for grants, and they made their own plans without any regard for the needs of the cooperatives. The cooperative bakeries were particularly upset, for example, when the Histadrut-sponsored consumer cooperatives began to build their own in-house baking plants instead of marketing the baked goods produced by the bakers' cooperatives.

As producers' cooperatives succumbed in droves to these defects in planning, the relationship between the Histadrut and the bus cooperatives took center stage. As the Histadrut took part in rate-setting negotiations between the bus cooperatives and the government, it increasingly tended to take the government's side. Viteles quotes one source as commenting that "The Histadrut has come to play the key role as the representative of the public interest in supervising the bus cooperatives" (1968, p. 161). Histadrut General Secretary Namir is reputed to have told the bus cooperatives "that co-operatives are becoming more hated than capitalism and that 'you are the principal cause' for this" (Viteles, 1968, p. 173).

Embattled on all sides, members of both these and other cooperatives began to complain bitterly over the paltry help they were receiving from the Merkaz. In 1953, a member of a bus cooperative referred to the Merkaz in the press as a "prostrate body" and added:

> I think the leaders of this body . . . have always undermined us. . . . Among the rank and file there is a feeling that this body, Merkaz Haco-operatzia, creates dissension, antagonism, and strife instead of serving as a coordinating and unifying centre (Viteles, 1968, p. 181).

Five years later, upon the thirtieth anniversary of the founding of the Merkaz, the center's own journal carried an unsigned article complaining of the Histadrut's unfriendly attitude and "broken promises of financial help." The article alleged that since the time when it was founded,

> the Merkaz Haco-operatzia has marched alone in the path of affliction, without encouragement and assistance. The Workers Bank did *not* [original underlined] create the special fund for the needs of the WPSTS; the Histadrut Executive Committee did not make the annual allotments out of the funds collected abroad . . . Hamashbir Hamerkazi did not pay any special attention to the marketing of the produce of

WPSTS . . . and during the last decade the Government Treasury persistently said no [to the requests of the Merkaz Haco-operatzia] (Viteles, 1968: 364).

In the late 1950s and early 1960s, relations between the cooperatives and the Histadrut appear to have reached their lowest ebb. On January 15, 1958, the Chevrat Ovdim approved a plan to reorganize the Merkaz into three autonomous divisions, within each one of which Histadrut appointees were to carry the decisive vote. The Central Committee of the Merkaz gave its approval to the plan on January 28, without even bothering to consult its member cooperatives (Viteles, 1968, pp. 57–60). Over the next two years, the government entertained proposals to transfer the bus cooperatives to public ownership and removed its development department from the offices of the Merkaz (Viteles, 1968, pp. 109–10). During the first half of 1960, the Histadrut Executive Committee refused to permit the planned Sixth Congress of the Merkaz cooperatives to take place, because the meeting was going to consider a proposal to reduce the voting power of Histadrut representatives in the governing bodies of the Merkaz. In the early 1960s, the funds of the Kupat Hakooperatsia became severely depleted as a result of a series of bad loans that had been made at the urging of the Histadrut; by 1968, the little that remained of this fund was completely taken over by the Bank Hapoalim.

The worker cooperatives were not alone in being treated highhandedly by the Histadrut during this period. Between 1953 and 1958, the government proposed revisions in the Cooperative Societies Ordinance that would have greatly increased the Histadrut's enforcement powers over all its member cooperatives (Viteles, 1966, pp. 95–119). As these efforts were frustrated by opposition from the kibbutzim and moshavim, the Histadrut shifted to a policy of "decooperatization" in its dealings with many of its affiliated cooperatives, including especially the housing and credit cooperatives (Preuss, 1965; Viteles, 1966; Greenberg, 1986). Viteles reports, for example, that twenty-two credit cooperatives were fused into the Bank Hapoalim in this period against the wishes of their members (1966, pp. 149–50). In all of these cases, the Histadrut was showing an increasing preference for organizations that it owned directly, like Hamashbir, the Bank Hapoalim, and Solel Boneh, over cooperative organizations that it found more difficult to control.

These centralizing tendencies within the Histadrut reflected some weaknesses in the Histadrut as well as strengths, as the Histadrut was itself increasingly subject to attacks during this period from both above and below (Grinberg, 1991, pp. 50–53; Shalev, 1992, pp. 211–14). From below, committees of rank-and-file workers, aided and abetted by leftist parties, were demanding that the Histadrut open up its decision-making process and become a more effective spokesman for workers' interests. From the top, Labor leaders like Ben-Gurion were suggesting that it was now time for the Israeli state to take over many of the Histadrut's traditional quasi-governmental functions, allowing the Histadrut to become a more conventional and more democratic trade union. In 1959, the Histadrut's labor exchanges were nationalized in one reflection of this policy (Aharoni, 1991, pp. 70, 133). Disputes over the extent of such reforms later led to a split in the Labor Party between the Histadrut loyalists, who retained control of the party, and a pro-state faction that left to form a new party called Rafi, under the leadership of Ben-Gurion, Shimon Peres, and Moshe Dayan. In the Knesset the Rafi leaders were joined by Menachem Begin and other future Likud leaders in calling for "depoliticization and internal democratization of the Histadrut" and "transfer of its non-union functions to the state" (Shalev, 1992, p. 214).

By the middle of the 1960s, it was apparent to many observers that Israel's entire cooperative movement was seriously sick or even dying and that the Histadrut itself was in need of reform. The Registrar of Cooperatives remarked in 1962, "There is no doubt that if our co-operative movement is interested in continuity . . . it needs an ideological regeneration, reincarnation and reorganization" (Viteles, 1966, p. 155).

In 1967, the Histadrut established an investigative committee under the leadership of Knesset member S. Shoresh to examine the problems of the worker cooperatives and their relationship to the Histadrut. The Shoresh Committee's report in March of 1968 once again noted "the flaws and distortions existing in the producers-services cooperatives," but in general took a much more conciliatory tone than the Histadrut had previously taken in its dealings with the Merkaz cooperatives, noting that they are "an integral part of the labour economy" and "emphatically" recommending their "preservation and development" (Registrar of Cooperative Societies, 1968, pp. 84–86). At the congress of the Merkaz cooperatives that met in December of that year, the slogan was "cooperation for the cooperatives," and for the first time, a representative of one of its member cooperatives (Israel Ziv of Dan) was elected to lead the Merkaz.

Since that time, the Merkaz appears to have had little additional interference from the Histadrut, but also very little help. And as the Israeli cooperative movement has shrunk to include little more than Egged and Dan, so has the Merkaz. The leadership of the Merkaz now consists entirely of members of Egged and Dan, whose services are donated by these cooperatives, because the Merkaz itself is now too poor to afford more than a small clerical staff. An article published to commemorate the fiftieth anniversary of the Merkaz offered the following dismal assessment of the recent state of the movement: "the contribution of co-operation to present socio-economic developments is diminishing," and cooperation in Israel now "finds itself . . . everywhere . . . ignored" (Losh, 1979, p. 90).

CONCLUSIONS

Workers have been led to organize themselves into worker cooperatives for a wide range of reasons, in Israel as elsewhere. The formation of worker cooperatives is rarely either a purely self-interested act or a purely ideological one. Its occurrence becomes particularly likely when cooperation is perceived as the best means of serving the interests of a *group* of some sort, whether the group is defined by occupation, by ethnicity, or by class. In all such cases, the creation of cooperatives expresses a collective rationality, not an individual one.

In the mix of motivations that produced Israel's unique "labor economy," normative considerations were in general stronger in the countryside than they were in the towns. It was the country that attracted the idealistic young chalutzim, who were responding to the call of A. D. Gordon and others who felt that it was time for Jews to cleanse themselves of their Diaspora mentality through manual labor on the land. Even here, the cooperative structures they created had an important economic base in the search for exclusively Jewish forms of employment and in the Jewish National Fund's ownership of the land; but the appeal and dynamism and success of the kibbutz can never be reduced solely to economic considerations of this sort.

It was a different story, however, for those who, in Shapiro's words, "preferred the easier life in the cities" (1976, p. 139). There, cooperation was almost never an end in itself and almost always a marriage of convenience between groups of workers who needed help and a Histadrut-dominated Zionist establishment that preferred to reserve its assistance for collectively owned organizational forms. The Histadrut leaders never liked the worker cooperatives or fully accepted them, but were willing to deal with them if they could help expand the economic sector in which Jewish immigrants had privileged access to high-paying jobs. As Ben-Gurion said in 1922 to an Achdut Haavodah colleague who felt that the bourgeois and capitalist character of the moshavim and urban cooperatives made them incompatible with the working class and socialist identity of the rest of the Zionist labor movement, "the one and only task that dominates our thoughts and deeds is to conquer the country and build it up with the aid of large immigration. All the rest is trivia and rhetoric" (Shapiro, 1976, p. 69).

Even in the cities, however, it would be a mistake to attribute the formation of cooperatives to economic considerations alone. This is true first of all because the cooperatives in Israel's cities, like those in its countryside, were intended to serve the needs not of individuals, but of entire groups—most importantly, the displaced Jews of the Diaspora, for whom new homes had to be prepared in the Land of Israel. And for the Histadrut and Zionist leadership, the goal of providing jobs and a European living standard to Jewish immigrants was not a purely economic act, but also a holy mission, a sacred duty. The Israeli worker cooperatives were born into an institutional context in which the state, the leading political parties, the labor movement, and the public philanthropic bodies all agreed in defining the creation of decent jobs for immigrants as the principal task and in identifying the formation of worker cooperatives as both a practical and socially acceptable means of accomplishing that task.

It is because the need to create good jobs for immigrants was seen not only as an economic but also as a moral task, that Histadrut and government leaders have been so quick to denounce self-interested behavior by the cooperatives as not just an economic threat, but as a betrayal of Zionist ideals. If the Israeli worker cooperatives had been viewed solely as economic entities, created to maximize their members' incomes, then no one would have been in a position to express shock or moral outrage when worker cooperatives began to make use of hired labor and when the bus cooperatives began to press for higher rates. But in the Israeli institutional context, both were treated as clear violations of the public trust.

The moralizing tone that the Histadrut has adopted in its dealings with the worker cooperatives is rooted in these Zionist values, but also reflects the power relationship between the two groups. The Histadrut was forced to use "the appeal to the national conscience" in its dealings with the worker cooperatives, as it had earlier with the WZO, because it had no more effective stick to beat them with. It has relied on moral arguments and public opinion, because, as Daniel has noted, its structural relationship with the worker cooperatives left it in fact "helpless" (1986, p. 22; 1989, p. 96), without any more direct means to influence their behavior.

Once statehood had been achieved, and the resulting initial influx of immigrants had been absorbed, the labor leaders had less need for the worker cooperatives and grew openly contemptuous toward them. In the later 1960s, when their movement was already moribund, the worker cooperatives were set free to go their own way. But even then, the worker cooperatives did not leave the Histadrut, and their relationship was never allowed to reach the point of an open breach. Both groups have continued to rely on one another for legitimation and political support. For example, the Histadrut and the Israeli government have used the Israeli cooperative movement to cultivate diplomatic ties with Third World nations. Managers from Egged and Dan have in many cases spent years in Latin America, providing technical assistance on transportation matters in that region. Such acts of public service are helpful to Egged and Dan in their rate negotiations with the government, because they support their claim to be not just profit-seeking businesses, but also leaders of a cooperative movement and an important national resource.

Subsequent chapters will show that the Histadrut by no means deserves all of the blame for the decline of Israel's worker cooperative movement. The worker cooperatives' own behavior has certainly done a great deal of harm to their reputations in the eyes of the Israeli public. And both the worker cooperatives and the entire Chevrat Ovdim have suffered alike from changes in Israeli society that neither one had the power to prevent or to control. These include the development of a dynamic private capitalist economy in Israel and the transformation of the nation into a much more individualistic and materialistic society in recent decades than it had been in the time of the Mandate.

While the Histadrut cannot be held responsible for these broader and later transformations, it was clearly the Histadrut that struck the first blow against the cooperatives of the Merkaz. The earliest and most damaging criticisms of the worker cooperatives came from the organization that had appointed itself as their patron and guardian. The charges of selfishness and greed that it leveled against the worker cooperatives would have made little sense and had little impact in an individualistic and capitalistic society like that of the United States, where no one is expected to behave in any other way. But in the time and place in which these accusations were first made, they had a tremendous impact, because they were seen as a betrayal of the Zionist and socialist ideals on which the nascent Jewish state and society of Israel were based.

2. The Formation and Dissolution of Worker Cooperatives in Israel, 1924–1992

with Robert Hanneman

This chapter turns from the qualitative account of the history of the Israeli worker cooperative movement that was offered in chapter 1 to a more quantitative analysis of their growth and decline. It provides a more detailed investigation of the processes that have caused Israeli worker cooperatives to be formed and that have affected the speed with which they die.

A theme common to the previous chapter and the present one is the perception that the Israeli institutional environment has changed and that the Israeli worker cooperative population has been declining because its institutional environment is less conducive to the formation of worker cooperatives today than it was in the past. Both chapters provide indications that many formerly important sources of institutional support for the formation of worker cooperatives in Israel are much weaker today than they once were, as the Histadrut, the Israeli government, and the Israeli public all seem to perceive worker cooperatives as less desirable today than they did in previous years. Whereas the Israeli worker cooperatives at one time appeared to derive important legitimation from all three of these sources, all seem to have contributed more recently to an increasing delegitimation of the worker cooperative as an organizational form.

The chapter begins by examining how the legitimation and later delegitimation of worker cooperatives in Israel were affected by some demographic processes that are inherent in this pattern of early growth and later decline. This analysis demonstrates that in the early years, the expansion of the Israeli worker cooperative population had a tendency to feed on itself. The example set by the formation of worker cooperatives in one year in itself stimulated the formation of still more worker cooperatives in the next. As such sociologists as DiMaggio and Powell (1983), Hannan and Freeman (1987), and Carroll and Hannan (1989) have argued, organizational populations of any kind have a tendency to "legitimate" themselves, by virtue of their very existence and expansion. The more that organizations of any given type are seen by members of their society to exist and to proliferate, the more they succeed in demonstrating to the public that they are a viable and appropriate means of solving social and economic problems.

In later years, however, these demographic processes can begin to produce quite different effects. As deaths begin to outnumber new births, as has been true among the Israeli worker cooperatives since the mid-1950s, these deaths can have a delegitimating effect that discourages the formation of new organizations and causes potential organizational founders to question the viability of the entire organizational form. Reductions in birthrates and population size have similar discouraging effects. The result is that the entire process is thrown into reverse. Whereas early success and population growth had a tendency to feed on themselves, failure now feeds on failure, and the entire population falls into a spiral of decline.

The analyses in this chapter begin by examining processes of this sort, because their effects are seen as fundamental and must therefore be taken into account before considering the effects of other influences that are external to the population itself. In the next portions of this investigation, we take up the examination of the external environmental influences. We show that, in addition to the tendencies for the growth and decline of this population to feed on themselves, they were also strongly affected by changes in Israeli society as a whole. Among these environmental influences the most important was rates of immigration. Evidence will also be presented that suggests that the Israeli worker cooperatives were affected by other changes that have occurred in the Israeli social and political environment over the life of this population, such as the gradual decline of the Labor Party and its defeat by the Likud in the election of 1977. An examination of the influence of economic conditions, such as unemployment and economic growth, will in contrast disclose a generally weaker and less consistent pattern of effects, providing little support for the widespread impression that such factors are the primary causes driving the formation of worker cooperatives (e.g., Shirom, 1972; Buchanan, 1978; Ben-Ner, 1988a, 1988b).

The final portion of this chapter examines factors that have affected the mortality of Israeli worker cooperatives. It begins with an analysis of the extent to which the mortality of these organizations is influenced by their age. This investigation examines the extent to which Israel's worker cooperatives have been influenced by such hazards as liabilities of "newness" (Freeman, Carroll, and Hannan, 1983) and "adolescence" (Bruederl and Schuessler, 1990; Fichman and Levinthal, 1991), as well as liabilities of "maturity" (Aldrich, et al., 1990) or "obsolescence" (Baum and House, 1990). The evidence on these issues indicates that the years of greatest risk for the Israeli worker cooperatives occur early in their life spans, although not necessarily in the very first year. Later portions of this analysis report how the mortality of Israeli worker cooperatives has been affected by the industry in which they operate and the city or region in which they are located. These data disclose further evidence of the harm that was done to the Israeli worker cooperatives by the subordination of their movement to the Histadrut and Israeli government's goal of nation building, as worker cooperatives that were formed in outlying areas show significantly shorter life spans than those that were located in more developed urban areas.

The theories used in the examinations of both the formation and dissolution of the Israeli worker cooperatives are derived from the so-called "population ecology of organizations." Although these theories were developed with quite different organizations in mind, they have recently begun to be applied to worker cooperatives as well (e.g., Staber, 1989a, 1989b; Russell, 1993). In addition to whatever light it can shed on the history of worker cooperatives in Israel, this chapter therefore also seeks to contribute to the emerging population ecology of worker cooperatives.

Data and Measures

Data for these analyses were obtained from two primary sources. Since 1924, all Israeli cooperatives have been required to register with the Registrar of Cooperative Societies in Jerusalem. The Registrar also requires all cooperatives to submit to regular audits, conducted either directly by the Registrar, or by an independent audit union. Since the late 1920s, the overwhelming majority of Israeli worker cooperatives have had their audits conducted by the Merkaz Hakooperatsia, or Cooperative Center. The records of the Registrar and of the Merkaz Hakooperatsia therefore served as the two sources of data for these analyses.

Putting together these two sources, and eliminating duplications, we were able to obtain at least partial records on a total of 1,475 worker cooperatives. The principal requirement for the analyses that follow was to obtain data on the year of formation and the year of dissolution, where applicable, of each cooperative in this population. One or both of these two pieces of information was missing for a total of 149 cases, which were therefore deleted from our sample. We do not consider the loss of these cases to be a serious omission, because they constitute only about a tenth of all recorded births. Moreover, since these cases with incomplete information appear for the most part to be unusually short-lived cooperatives, we suspect that our data underestimate by no more than 5 percent the number of Israeli worker cooperatives that were alive at any given time.

Of the two sources we used to identify our total sample of 1,326 usable cases, it was the Registrar's records that proved to be more complete, as the Merkaz Hakooperatsia did not begin to maintain a systematic roster of all its member cooperatives until the mid-1940s. Even after that time its records omitted information about unaffiliated cooperatives. We were able to find slightly more than half of our cases (681) on both lists. For 687 cases we have information from the Registrar alone, and 107 cases are known to us only from information supplied by the Merkaz Hakooperatsia. It was somewhat surprising to find more than a hundred worker cooperatives that are unknown to the Registrar. Some of these appear to be extremely short-lived organizations that went out of business before they could complete the process of being registered. A report by the Registrar published in 1938 noted that many worker cooperatives were going through a trial phase of one or two years before formally registering; while technically against the law, this practice was being tolerated by the Mandatory officials (Registrar of Cooperative Societies, 1938, pp. 106, 108). The absence of other cooperatives from the Registrar's records is less easy to explain, but they appear to be valid cases, as this group includes several living cases such as Egged. Since Egged was created as a merger of several existing cooperatives, it seems likely that its official registration is in one of these extinct names.

For the 682 cooperatives for which we had two sets of records, we compared the two dates of formation and two dates of dissolution, and when they differed, we always took the earlier date. Like Don (1968), who used similar data, we were concerned that the Registrar or the Merkaz Hakooperatsia might have incurred delays in receiving or recording information about cooperative births and deaths. In general we found that the two sets of estimates were reasonably close. Where the two sets of estimates differed by more than two years, we attempted to resolve the discrepancy by consulting the complete listings of the Merkaz Hakooperatsia's membership that were available to us for a total of six years (1931, 1949, 1960, 1975, 1988, and 1989).

Annual counts of births, deaths, and the total number of cooperatives within this sample of worker cooperatives are shown in figure 2.1. The figure indicates that there were significant spurts in cooperative births in the middle 1930s, late 1940s, and early 1950s. More minor periods of new formations occurred in the late 1950s, early 1960s, and early 1970s, but these were not sufficient to reverse the almost steady decline in the worker cooperative population that began in 1952, as deaths of existing cooperatives outnumbered formations of new ones in almost every year after that date.

The distribution of our Israeli worker cooperatives among industries is shown in table 2.1. The annual incidence of births and deaths differs significantly by sector, as shown in figure 2.2. The pattern of rapid growth in the early 1950s, followed by an equally precipitous decline, is most applicable to the production cooperatives, which constitute more than half of this population. The formation of cooperatives in transportation reached its peak much earlier, in the 1930s. By the 1950s, this sector had already come to be dominated by such giants as Egged and Dan, and few new entrants emerged in this period with ambitions to take them on. Service cooperatives, on the other hand, were generally a later development. The formation of these cooperatives shows neither a sharp spike in the early 1950s nor a sharp decline thereafter.

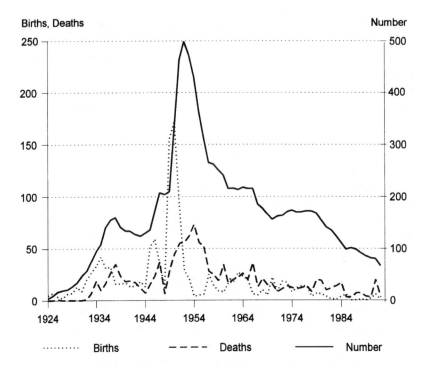

FIGURE 2.1
Births, Deaths, and Number of Worker Cooperatives, 1924–1992[a]

[a]Births and deaths are during the year shown; population is at the beginning of the year shown. Excludes cases with missing data on dates of birth
or death.

The distribution of births, deaths, and total numbers of cooperatives by city and region are shown in table 2.2 and figure 2.3.
Well over a third of the worker cooperatives in our sample, or 501
in all, were located in and around Tel Aviv, which Kellerman has
described as "the organizational center of Labor Zionism" (1993, p.
187). Tel Aviv is defined here as metropolitan Tel Aviv, or Gush
Dan as it is known in Hebrew, and includes such adjacent cities as
Ramat Gan, Petach Tikvah, and Holon. After Tel Aviv, the next
most popular location for the formation of worker cooperatives in
Israel has been the city of Haifa. Haifa, or "the red city" as it is
sometimes called (Kellerman, 1993, p. 227), is a working-class industrial city that has long served as a major center of Histadrut and

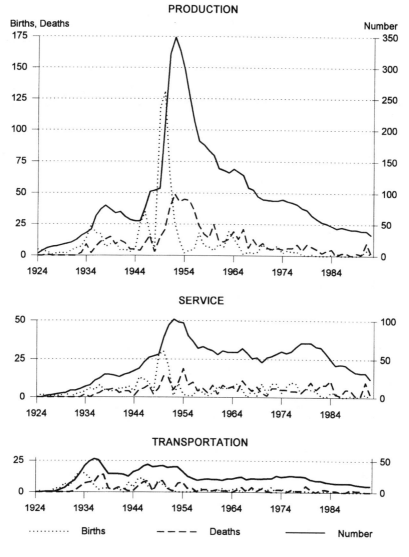

Figure 2.2
Births, Deaths, and Number of Worker Cooperatives by Sector,
1924–1992[a]

[a]Births and deaths are during the year shown; population is at the beginning of the year shown. Excludes cases with missing data on dates of birth or death.

TABLE 2.1
Births, Deaths, and Number of Worker Cooperatives
by Sector and Industry[a]

Industry	Number 1924	Initial Year	Total Births	Total Deaths	Final Year	Number 1992	Mean
Transportation	0	1925	192	182	1992	10	24.1
Passenger Transport	0	1928	45	42	1992	3	7.3
Motor Freight	0	1925	61	54	1992	7	11.1
Other Transportation	0	1929	86	86	1991	0	6.6
Service	0	1925	352	331	1992	21	46.9
Meat, Ice, Oil	0	1931	48	43	1992	5	8.3
Restaurants, Hotels	0	1928	31	29	1992	2	5.1
Schools, Theaters	0	1926	49	44	1992	5	7.3
Laundries	0	1930	18	17	1992	1	4.6
Port, Sailing, Fishing	0	1934	23	23	1982	0	3.5
Garages	0	1933	13	13	1974	0	1.9
Refuse Collection	0	1946	9	9	1970	0	1.3
Other Service	0	1925	161	153	1992	8	18.8
Production	4	1924	750	723	1992	31	93.0
Baking	0	1932	99	95	1992	4	23.6
Woodworking	0	1925	74	68	1992	6	10.0
Printing, Paper	1	1924	52	46	1992	7	9.3
Metal, Electrical	2	1925	86	84	1992	4	12.0
Building Materials	1	1924	132	127	1992	6	12.7
Sand, Cement, Drill	0	1931	31	29	1992	2	3.9
Textiles	0	1928	77	76	1992	1	7.3
Food Processing	0	1936	55	54	1992	1	6.1
Leather, Shoes	0	1925	34	34	1977	0	5.1
Chemicals	0	1935	19	19	1970	0	3.5
Diamonds	0	1943	18	18	1970	0	4.3
Other Production	0	1926	73	73	1982	0	7.3
Sector Unknown	1	1924	27	28	1965	0	4.4
Total	5	1924	1321	1264	1992	62	163.7

[a]Statistics are calculated from the first year in which organizations existed
in the sector or industry (or from 1924, whichever is later). Initial numbers
are for the year shown. Total numbers of births and deaths are through
year-end of 1992. The mean is the average of annual number from initial
to final year.

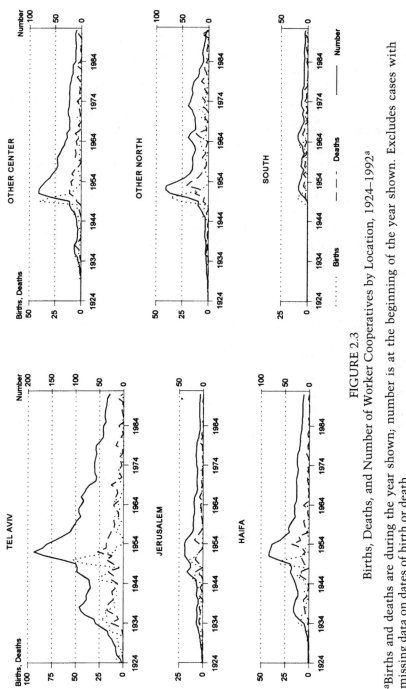

FIGURE 2.3

Births, Deaths, and Number of Worker Cooperatives by Location, 1924–1992[a]

[a]Births and deaths are during the year shown; number is at the beginning of the year shown. Excludes cases with missing data on dates of birth or death.

Labor Party strength, so it is not surprising to find that the worker cooperative movement is also well represented there. The more traditional and religious city of Jerusalem, on the other hand, has been the birthplace of disproportionately fewer worker cooperatives. The pattern of births in this city also lacks the steep growth spurts that occurred in Tel Aviv and in Haifa in the early 1930s and early 1950s. Since Jerusalem was an embattled and isolated enclave in the years between 1948 and 1967, it is not surprising that its worker cooperatives did not experience the same growth in this period as that shown by the cooperatives of these more secure cities to the west and north. Outside these three major cities, in Israel's North, Center, and South, most formations of worker cooperatives did not occur until the development boom that followed the War of Independence. This is particularly true of the South, where no births of worker cooperatives at all were recorded until 1949.

TABLE 2.2

Births, Deaths, and Number of Worker Cooperatives by Location[a]

Location	Number 1924	Initial Year	Total Births	Total Deaths	Final Year	Number 1992	Mean
Tel Aviv	4	1924	498	476	1992	26	67.1
Jerusalem	0	1924	129	122	1992	7	15.2
Haifa	1	1929	181	170	1992	12	26.6
Other Center	0	1930	166	156	1992	10	24.5
Other North	0	1926	212	209	1992	3	21.2
South	0	1949	71	67	1992	4	9.7
Unknown	0	1931	64	64	1992	0	6.3
Total	5	1924	1321	1264	1992	62	164.6

[a]Statistics are calculated from the first year in which organizations existed in the location (1924 or initial year). Initial numbers are for the beginning of the year shown. Total number of births and deaths are to the year-end, 1992. The mean is the average of annual number from initial to final year.

EFFECTS OF DENSITY DEPENDENCE AND POPULATION DYNAMICS ON COOPERATIVE BIRTHS

Density Dependence

According to Carroll and Hannan's (1989) theory of density dependance, the number of new formations in any population of organizations in any time period is a positive but curvilinear function of the density or size of the population at the beginning of that period. The effect of density is curvilinear because population increases have different consequences for competition and legitimation, depending on whether density is low or high. When density is low, even small additions to the population can have a strong legitimating effect, demonstrating the viability of a new form of business and offering concrete examples to imitate. Competitive pressures, in the meantime, remain low at this point. When density is high, on the other hand, further additions to the population no longer carry a significant legitimating effect, as the virtues of the given organization form are already widely known. At these high population levels, however, further increments to the population do cause competitive pressures to become increasingly problematic, and these pressures have the effect of discouraging additional births.

This theory of density dependence has now been successfully tested on a number of diverse populations (Hannan and Freeman, 1987; Carroll and Hannan, 1989; Singh and Lumsden, 1990). Before testing it in this population, however, it is first necessary to ask whether the assumptions of the theory are in fact applicable here. The set of all worker cooperatives in a single country may not qualify as a "population" in the conventional sense of the term. Its members are heterogeneous with respect to industry, or economic "niche," and in most cases they constitute only a small fraction of the firms in any single industrial branch. Is it reasonable to expect the formation of cooperatives in one industry to stimulate the formation of cooperatives in another? Can one validly speak about competitive pressures among firms that together account for only a small portion of the total output of any given industrial field?

We believe that the answer to both of these questions is yes. It is our impression that in a country as small as Israel, if not elsewhere, the various members of the worker cooperative movement do constitute a single population, in at least some senses of this term. They keep a close watch on one another and stimulate each other's development. And they do compete for many of the same resources, even when they operate in different fields. For example, they have competed in the past for the financial resources and technical assistance that have occasionally been made available to worker cooperatives by such sources as the Jewish Agency, the Israeli government, and the Merkaz Hakooperatsia. Perhaps above all, they compete for the limited supply of workers who wish to help found cooperative organizations, about which we will have more to say below.

The results of our effort to test the predictions of the theory of density dependence with data on the full population of Israeli worker cooperatives are shown in the first column of table 2.3. As predicted by the theory, the linear form of density has a statistically significant positive effect on cooperative births. The squared form of density appears here to have a negative or discouraging effect on births, as predicted by the theory, but in this case the effect falls short of statistical significance.

Population Dynamics

An alternative view of organizational formations is the population dynamics theory of Delacroix and Carroll (1983) and Carroll and Huo (1986). This model looks at the effects on organizational founding rates not of population size or density, but of the two component processes that make it up: organizational births and organizational deaths.

In the simplest version of population dynamics, also known as rate dependence, the number of new organizational births in any given time period is posited to be a positive but curvilinear function of the number of births in the previous period. Unlike the theory of density dependence, the population dynamics theory gives no consideration to the consequences of population changes for processes of legitimation; it confines its attention to their implications for processes of competition alone. Thus small increases in the number of births are seen as stimulating additional births, because they act as "signals" of a hospitable competitive environment. As in the theory of density dependence, however, large numbers of births are seen as discouraging additional births, because they cause competitive pressures to set in.

The neglect of legitimation processes is not serious in this

TABLE 2.3
Effects of Demographic Processes on the Formation of Worker Cooperatives, 1924–1992[a]

	I		II		III		IV		V	
	b	S.E.	b	S.E.	b	S.E.	b	S.E.	b	S.E.
Intercept	1.592**	(.526)	1.967**	(.218)	2.148**	(.280)	2.113**	(.224)	1.091**	(.474)
Density	0.010**	(.005)							0.016**	(.004)
Density Squared[b]	-0.012	(.010)							-0.028**	(.009)
Recent Births			0.052**	(.021)	0.055**	(.021)	0.054**	(.021)	0.055**	(.015)
Recent Births Squared[b]			-0.218	(.175)	-0.225	(.194)	-0.218	(.197)	-0.207**	(.096)
Recent Deaths					-0.017	(.033)	-0.010*	(.066)	-0.079**	(.024)
Recent Deaths Squared[b]					0.113	(.567)			0.915**	(.433)
Dispersion	0.933**	(.191)	0.714**	(.113)	0.686**	(.118)	0.687**	(.115)	0.496**	(.121)
Log Likelihood	-265.61		-256.69		-255.58		-255.63		-245.93	
Baseline Log Likelihood	-274.20									

*p < .10, **p < .05

[a]Estimates of parameters are calculated by maximum likelihood under the assumptions of a negative binomial process generating log (births), using LIMDEP. The model is equivalent to exponential Poisson regression with the exception that overdispersion is modeled parametrically. Overdispersion is often interpreted as serial correlation within observations, or positive contagion.

[b]In thousands

case, because taking them into account has no other consequence than to uncover additional reasons for making the same prediction. As in the theory of density dependence, small numbers of births can be expected to increase legitimation by demonstrating the viability of a new form of organization and offering a set of examples to imitate. As births proliferate, on the other hand, additional births would yield increasingly diminishing returns, as the potential demonstration effect attributable to each new population member would gradually be exhausted. This reduction in the positive mimetic effect of births at higher values would produce a negative coefficient for the square of births along with a positive coefficient for the linear form of births, as the theory predicts on the basis of reasoning about competitive processes alone.

For both of these sets of reasons, we join the population dynamics theorists in expecting the number of new formations of Israeli worker cooperatives in any given year to be a positive but curvilinear function of the number of new formations in the previous year. This prediction is tested in the second column of table 2.3. The results shown there are once again supportive. As expected, the linear form of recent births of worker cooperatives has a significantly positive effect on births in the current year. As in the case of density, the squared term once again appears to have the predicted negative effect, but this effect falls short of statistical significance.

The population dynamics theory views the rate dependence of current births on recent births as a baseline against which the effects of all additional influences on organizational formations are to be measured and judged. Within the population dynamics theory, the next most important of these additional influences is the frequency of recent dissolutions or organizational "deaths." As in the case of the effect of recent births on current births, the number of current births within a population is posited to be a positive but curvilinear function of the number of recent deaths.

The reasoning for this is once again based solely on a consideration of the consequences for competition of organizational deaths. According to Delacroix and Carroll (1983), a small number of recent deaths creates competitive opportunities, in the form of former customers of defunct firms whose demands are no longer being met and idle factories and equipment that a later entrant to the field might readily put to use. Large numbers of recent deaths, on the other hand, signal that something has gone wrong with an environment as a whole.

This prediction from population ecology has received less consistent empirical confirmation than have the theories of density dependence and rate dependence. While the findings of a number of studies have been confirmatory (Singh and Lumsden, 1990), those of others have been unsupportive, including the findings of Carroll and Huo (1986). In a study of foundings of state bar associations, Halliday, Powell, and Granfors (1987) predicted and found a linear negative effect of prior failures on current foundings, arguing that even small numbers of failures can signal environmental adversity. Similar linear negative effects of prior failures on current foundings have been reported by Barnett and Amburgey (1990), by Olzak and West (1991), and by Budros (1992). In Staber's study of worker cooperatives in Atlantic Canada (1989b), recent failures among worker cooperatives had the predicted positive but curvilinear effect on current foundings, but among consumer cooperatives a linear negative effect was observed.

This frequent incidence of disconfirmatory results becomes more understandable when the consequences of recent failures for legitimation are taken into account. While the consequences of recent deaths for competition have been conceived by various authors to be either positive or negative and possibly dependent on their levels, their consequences for legitimation are unambiguously and uniformly negative. From the point of view of legitimation, recent deaths should decrease rather than increase the current rate of births, because they would discourage potential organizational founders and cast doubt on the viability of an organizational form. And there is no reason to expect this negative effect of recent deaths on the perceived legitimacy of any form of organization to be reduced at higher values, as deaths that reach epidemic proportions might have a delegitimating effect that is still greater than that caused by small accumulations of individual dissolutions.

We consider a negative and linear effect for recent deaths on current births to be especially likely in the present case, because this is a population in which the negative effects of dissolutions on legitimation can be expected to outweigh whatever favorable consequences they may have for processes of competition. Cooperatives in general seem particularly vulnerable to concerns about their legitimacy, given the long history of skepticism about their viability as an economic form. The population dynamics theorists' arguments about competition, on the other hand, seem less relevant to the present case. Given the heterogeneity of this population with respect to industry, it is hard to see how the death of a cooperative in one industry could stimulate the formation of new cooperatives in another. Even within a single industry, the death of a cooperative might indeed free up resources, but the availability of alternative ownership models within the same industry makes it highly likely that it will be a noncooperative organization that makes use of the idle equipment and that satisfies the unmet demand.

Population dynamics models that test these two alternative formulations of the effects of recent deaths are shown in the third and fourth columns of table 2.3. The third column tests for the positive and curvilinear effect of recent deaths, as posited by Delacroix and Carroll (1983). The prediction is not confirmed, as neither the linear nor the squared form of recent deaths has a significant effect, and the signs of both coefficients are in directions opposite to that predicted by the theory. The fourth column tests for a linear negative effect of recent deaths as reported by Halliday, Powell, and Granfors (1987), Budros (1992), and other researchers. In this case, the presence of such an effect is supported.

In the final column of table 2.3, the terms of these population dynamics models are brought together with the terms of the density dependence model to test a more comprehensive model of the population ecology of the formation of worker cooperatives in Israel. When introduced simultaneously, all six terms retain the signs that were observed in the previous analyses, but in this case all also attain statistical significance. The effects of population density and recent births are confirmed here to be both positive and curvilinear, as predicted by these theories. The effect of the linear form of recent deaths is significantly negative, in keeping with the findings of Halliday, Powell, and Granfors (1987) and Budros (1992), and with the arguments that were introduced here. The only unexpected finding in this final column is the significantly positive coefficient associated with the squared form of recent deaths. While such an effect is not anticipated in any other of our sources, it does appear to be interpretable. It implies that the negative effect of recent deaths, like the positive effects of density and recent births, is most sensitive to changes occurring at lower values and has a tendency to taper off at higher numbers. It suggests that in a country as small as Israel, even small numbers of recent dissolutions are sufficiently widely communicated and are sufficiently discouraging in their effects, that further additions to the number of dying cooperatives add relatively little to this delegitimating effect.

EFFECTS OF THE SOCIAL AND POLITICAL ENVIRONMENT
ON THE FORMATION OF WORKER COOPERATIVES

While the population ecology of organizations emphasizes the influence on individual organizations of the experiences of similar organizations, it also directs attention at influences of the environment in which a population is embedded. In table 2.4, we test the effects of a number of characteristics of the Israeli social and political environment on the formation of worker cooperatives in Israel over the period of this study.

Of the factors within Israeli society that seemed most likely to influence the number of new worker cooperatives that were created in each year, we gave pride of place to the number of new immigrants that had arrived in the country in the previous year. As was indicated in chapter 1, the formation of worker cooperatives has long been viewed in Israel as a particularly appropriate technique for the absorption of new immigrants—by many of the immigrants themselves, by the Histadrut and international Zionist philanthropic organizations, and by the Israeli government.

To test the effects of immigration on the formation of worker cooperatives in this study, we obtained data on the annual number of new immigrants entering Israel between 1948 and 1991 from the *Statistical Abstract of Israel 1992*. Information about the years 1924–47 was obtained from Janowsky (1959). In the analyses that follow, we examine the effect on the number of cooperatives formed in a given year of the number of immigrants who arrived in the previous year. We conceive the effect of immigration as a lagged effect on the grounds that new immigrants must spend a certain amount of time learning a new language and establishing contacts before they can proceed to the establishment of a new firm.

The effect of the number of immigrants in the immediately previous year on the number of worker cooperatives formed in the current year is shown in the first column of table 2.4. The coefficient is positive, as predicted, but not statistically significant. This result is surprising. It is inconsistent with the findings of two previous studies reported by Don (1968) and Russell and Hanneman (1992b). Don's study dealt with the formation of production cooperatives over the period 1950–63 using data obtained from the Registrar. Russell and Hanneman examined the formation of all three kinds of cooperatives over the period 1951–88 using data

TABLE 2.4
Effects of the Social and Political Environment on the Formation of Worker Cooperatives, 1924–1992[a]

	I b	I S.E.	II b	II S.E.	III b	III S.E.	IV b	IV S.E.	V b	V S.E.	VI b	VI S.E.
Intercept	1.111**	(.446)	2.668**	(.453)	2.767**	(.360)	2.440**	(.494)	2.645**	(.377)	2.139**	(.505)
Density	.014**	(.004)	.025**	(.003)	.023**	(.003)	.025**	(.003)	.021**	(.003)	.023**	(.004)
Density Squared[b]	-.025**	(.009)	-.033**	(.007)	-.032**	(.006)	-.032**	(.006)	-.028**	(.006)	-.029**	(.006)
Recent Births	.055**	(.015)	.010	(.013)	.007	(.010)	-.001	(.013)	.008	(.010)	-.002	(.013)
Recent Births Squared[b]	-.224**	(.086)	-.006	(.127)	-.024	(.057)	.008	(.068)	-.027	(.057)	.016	(.066)
Recent Deaths	-.071**	(.024)	-.048**	(.021)	-.038*	(.022)	-.040*	(.021)	-.037*	(.022)	-.039**	(.020)
Recent Deaths Squared[b]	.844**	(.428)	.076	(.374)	-.011	(.376)	-.013	(.348)	-.017	(.371)	-.030	(.337)
Immigration[b]	.003	(.002)			.006**	(.002)	.008**	(.003)	.006**	(.002)	.008**	(.003)
Year			-.041**	(.005)	-.044**	(.006)	-.036**	(.010)	-.037**	(.009)	-.022*	(.013)
Statehood							-.569	(.575)			-.793	(.562)
Likud									-.452	(.394)	-.643	(.384)
Dispersion	.483**	(.125)	.222**	(.065)	.188**	(.061)	.176**	(.062)	.180**	(.058)	.161**	(.060)
Log Likelihood	-245.36		-224.52		-219.98		-218.91		-218.97		-216.96	

*$p < .10$, **$p < .05$

[a]See note a to table 2.3

[b]In thousands

obtained from the Merkaz Hakooperatsia. Both studies reported significantly positive associations between immigration and births of new cooperatives. Both also indicated that immigration appeared to have both immediate and lagged effects. Russell and Hanneman found that the unlagged form of immigration had effects on the formation of worker cooperatives that were similar to but slightly weaker than the effects obtained with a one-year lag. That study also indicated that immigration in a given year continued to raise the annual count of new cooperatives for several years after it occurred.

The initial analyses for this study, which uses data obtained both from the Merkaz Hakooperatsia and from the Registrar, also indicated that there was a statistically significant and positive association between immigration and cooperative formations. It was only after figures on immigration in 1991 and cooperative formations in the year 1992 became available and were incorporated into this analysis that the effect of immigration lost its statistical significance. The meaning of this change in results is clear: immigration is not having the same effect in the 1990s that it had apparently exerted in earlier years. The numbers of new immigrants arriving in Israel in 1990 (199,516) and 1991 (176,096) were far greater than the annual totals for any previous year except for the 239,954 recorded in 1949. While the number of new worker cooperatives formed in Israel in each year did indeed increase in the 1990s (see figures 2.1 and 2.2 and appendix), this new growth spurt was much weaker than those that had occurred in response to immigration in such previous decades as the 1930s, 1950s, and 1960s. Since, in a time series analysis like this one, observations from the beginning or end of the period tend to have a disproportionately large effect on estimates, it seems very likely that the failure of this recent large immigration to stimulate a strong new wave of cooperative formations is responsible for this new result.

This apparent change in the effect of immigration over time adds significance to the second and third columns of table 2.4, which attempt to take into account the entire set of changes that have taken place in Israeli society between 1924 and the present. Israel strikes many observers today (e.g., Eisenstadt, 1985; Chafets, 1986) as being a much more individualistic and materialistic society than it was in the days of the labor Zionist pioneers. Eisenstadt perceives a complete "disintegration of the initial institutional mould of Israeli society" and complains of "a weakening of the pioneering elitist orientation stressing duties, commitment and standards of performance," now increasingly replaced in his view by an emphasis on entitlement (1985, pp. 403, 409). In addition to such broad social changes, Israeli worker cooperatives appear to have been more directly affected by other changes that have taken place in the Israeli economy and polity. Not only worker cooperatives, but cooperatives of all kinds seem to have suffered from decline in both their economic rationale and their ideological appeal. Jewish Israelis no longer see as great a need as they once did to share the entrepreneurial risk of starting a new business in order to secure employment. Cooperatives now not only seem less necessary economically, but also less prestigious and less closely connected in the public mind with meeting the nation's needs. Members of bus cooperatives like Egged, who had once been hailed as heroes of the War of Independence, are now more commonly viewed as price-gouging monopolists and exploiters of hired labor.

Thus Israeli society seems in many ways to be a less conducive environment for the formation of worker cooperatives today than it was in the past. For this reason, we introduce a term for "year" in the second and third columns of table 2.4. The second column indicates that, as predicted, the passage of time has indeed had a significantly negative impact on the formation of worker cooperatives in Israeli society. The third column shows that this effect of year is independent of the effects of changing patterns of immigration. Even more importantly, this model shows that when the negative effects of year have been taken into account, immigration is once again revealed to have a significantly positive effect on cooperative births.

These two columns of table 2.4 also indicate that when this control for the effect of year is introduced, the coefficients for the linear and squared forms of recent births are greatly reduced in size and lose their statistical significance. This suggests that the strong associations between recent births and current births that were reported in the earlier section may have been due in large part to the effects of unmeasured third variables that are covariates of time, such as the changes in the institutional environment and perceived legitimacy of worker cooperatives referred to above. In the face of this long-term trend of declining societal legitimacy, recent births apparently lack the capacity to be a sufficiently potent legitimating force on their own. The effects of density and density squared appear to be sharpened by the inclusion of this control for the effects of changing years and are strongly significant throughout the remaining analyses in table 2.4. The effects of recent deaths are also substantially reduced by the inclusion of these additional variables. The effects of recent deaths are significantly negative in all six models. The effect is linearly negative as we previously predicted in five of the six models. It appears to have a significantly curvilinear effect only in the first model, in which the effects of year are not controlled. Since recent deaths were high in approximately the same time periods in which births were high, the positive effect associated with recent deaths squared in the first column of table 2.4 is probably a statistical artifact produced by the fact that annual counts of both births and deaths reached their highest values in earlier years.

In the final three columns of table 2.4, we test the extent to which the effects of the past six and a half decades of Israeli history can be attributed to two discrete historical events: the attainment of independence in 1948 and the ascent of the Likud bloc to power in 1977. Our expectation regarding independence is that it would have a negative impact on the formation of cooperatives in Israel in the long run, despite the fact that annual birth counts soared to their highest levels ever in the first two or three years after statehood was attained. The spike in cooperative formations in 1949–51, we suspect, was more an effect of immigration than of statehood. We expect the impact of statehood itself on cooperative births to be negative, because it deprived the Israeli cooperative movement of much of its rationale. In the period before statehood, the Israeli labor economy and cooperative movement in their many forms served the Labor Party leaders as their main weapons in the struggle for independence. After statehood was achieved, this struggle had been won; for Israelis who still wished to serve their country, the principal threats were now external, and the path to public service led into the army or the government, not the cooperative movement.

We also expected that the Likud victory in 1977 would prove to have been another major blow to the Israeli cooperative movement. This prediction was based in part on the fact that the ascent of Likud meant a loss of political patronage, as cooperative institutions like the kibbutzim and the Merkaz Hakooperatsia would no longer receive from the Likud government the kinds of preferential treatment they had enjoyed from more left-leaning governments in the past. More importantly, we view the Likud victory as significant because of the sea change it symbolized in Israeli society as well as in Israeli politics. Many observers have noted that the actual impact of the Likud victory on government policies toward the labor economy was far less than had been expected (Ben-Porath, 1983; Aharoni, 1991, pp. 191–94; Shalev, 1992, p. 263); but the significance of the sudden ascendence of the social forces that the Likud represented (Shalev, 1990) for many Israelis remains profound. Socially and politically, it signalled the decisive end of the era of the labor Zionist pioneer, or chalutz, and the rise to prominence of a diverse new set of voices and spokesmen whom Chafets has characterized as *Heroes and Hustlers, Hard Hats and Holy Men* (1986).

These expectations are tested in the final three columns of table 2.4. The estimates suggest that statehood indeed appears to have had a depressing effect on the formation of worker cooperatives in Israel, but that this effect falls short of statistical significance. The same is true for the effect of the Likud victory, which also appears negative, but lacks statistical significance. Russell and Hanneman (1922b), using data obtained only from the Merkaz Hakooperatsia and covering the period 1951–88, found a statistically significant negative effect for Likud, and the analyses for the present study showed a significantly negative effect for Likud in the final model of table 2.4 until the year 1992 was added. We therefore suspect that the substantial numbers of worker cooperatives that were established in Arab communities in the 1980s and 1990s (see appendix), as well as the resurgence in the formation of cooperatives by the Merkaz Hakooperatsia in the 1990s, account for the failure of the negative effect of the Likud victory to attain statistical significance in these results.

Another noteworthy feature of the last three columns of table 2.4 is the fact that neither statehood nor the Likud victory nor the two in combination can fully account for the negative effect that was previously estimated for year. This variable continues to exert a negative and statistically significant effect on the formation of worker cooperatives in Israel, even after the effects of these two distinct historical events have been taken into account. We interpret the residual negative influence of this variable as capturing the cumulative effects of numerous smaller and unmeasured changes in Israeli society that have helped to make it a less conducive environment for the formation of worker cooperatives over time.

EFFECTS OF THE ECONOMIC ENVIRONMENT

The formation of worker cooperatives has often been attributed not to the social and institutional influences that we have been examining here, but to more narrowly economic considerations. In particular, many researchers and theorists have seen workers' decisions to form worker cooperatives as a response to economic changes that reduce the availability or attractiveness of alternative forms of employment.

This in turn leads to the expectation that worker cooperatives are formed in a countercyclical pattern, with higher formation rates in bad times than in good. Shirom (1972), for example, discerns such a pattern in the history of U.S. producer cooperatives and attributes it to the formation of cooperatives by unemployed workers. For Buchanan (1978), it is the effect of economic stagnation on wages that accounts for this pattern, as workers develop aspirations for industrial democracy in response to the failure of their wages to rise. Ben-Ner (1988a, 1988b) notes that nationwide recessions as well as declines in individual industries also increase cooperative birthrates by facilitating the transformation of conventionally owned firms into worker-owned firms.

While theoretical arguments that can account for the reputed countercyclical nature of cooperative formations are thus well developed, empirical research on the issue has lagged far behind, and what little has been done to date has not been supportive of these ideas. In a reanalysis of Shirom's conclusions regarding past U.S. producer cooperatives, Conte and Jones (1985) found that confirmation of the countercyclical hypothesis depended on the inclusion of Depression-era "self-help cooperatives" (Jones and Schneider, 1984) that the authors were uncertain about classifying as cooperatives. Without those cases, unemployment rates had a statistically insignificant but apparently negative effect on cooperative formations. The authors also could find no support for Buchanan's arguments regarding a countercyclical response to trends in economic growth. More recent studies by Staber (1989b, 1993) of the formation of worker cooperatives in Atlantic Canada also could find no statistically significant effects on cooperative foundings for either recessions or unemployment rates.

An early effort to test the relationship between economic conditions and the formation of worker cooperatives in Israel was reported by Don (1968). Over the years 1950–63, Don found unemployment to have a procyclical, negative correlation with annual counts of new production cooperatives, rather than the predicted countercyclical effect.

The effects of unemployment and other economic conditions on the formation of Israeli worker cooperatives from 1951 through 1991 are shown in table 2.5. The economic measures are derived from the *Statistical Abstract of Israel 1992*. Unemployment rates for the full Israeli labor force have been published regularly only since 1955. Daily averages of the number of unemployed seeking assistance from adult labor exchanges, on the other hand, are available all the way back to 1949, with the help of previous volumes. We consider this latter measure to be the more appropriate one to use, in any case, because the literature implies that it is the actual number of unemployed workers, not the unemployment rate, that leads most directly to the creation of new cooperatives.

In table 2.5, we again treat the demographic model from the right hand column of table 2.3 as a baseline that provides the most appropriate backdrop against which to view the effects of all other variables. The first column of table 2.3 examines how this model itself behaves over the truncated time period (1951–91) over which all of our economic measures are available. This is an important step to take, because the literature on density dependence warns that the model can yield invalid coefficients if it is tested over only a short portion of a population's life span (Carroll and Hannan, 1989; Singh and Lumsden, 1990). In this column, however, we once again observe a significantly positive coefficient for the linear measure of density and a significantly negative coefficient for the squared form of this variable. The effects of the linear and squared forms of both recent births and recent deaths, in contrast, lose their statistical significance in this smaller sample of years.

The effect of the average number of unemployed workers on the annual total of new cooperative formations is shown in the second column of table 2.5. As in Don (1968), we observe nothing countercyclical in the response of Israeli worker cooperatives to unemployment, as this variable has no significant effect in this model.

The effect of another important measure of short-term economic performance, annual percentage change in the per capita gross domestic product, is shown in the third column of table 2.5. Both in this column and the next one, GDP is measured in constant

TABLE 2.5

Effects of the Economic Environment on the Formation of Worker Cooperatives, 1951–1991[a]

	I		II		III		IV		V	
	b	S.E.	b	S.E.	b	S.E.	b	S.E.	b	S.E.
Intercept	-.806	(.704)	-.676	(1.007)	-.833	(.710)	.108	(2.723)	1.565	(3.487)
Density	.020**	(.010)	.019*	(.011)	.021**	(.010)	.018	(.012)	.013	(.015)
Density Squared[b]	-.029*	(.017)	-.027*	(.016)	-.030*	(.016)	-.026*	(.016)	-.021	(.018)
Recent Births	.023	(.069)	.023	(.052)	.023	(.065)	.025	(.047)	.023	(.037)
Recent Births Squared[b]	-.062	(2.461)	-.060	(1.612)	-.059	(2.326)	-.067	(1.247)	-.052	(.413)
Recent Deaths	.019	(.043)	.019	(.041)	.018	(.044)	.011	(.050)	-.011	(.057)
Recent Deaths Squared[b]	-.477	(.620)	-.473	(.618)	-.462	(.630)	-.376	(.703)	-.191	(.824)
Unemployed[b]			-.002	(.010)					-.009	(.011)
Percent Change GDP					-.004	(.030)			-.016	(.032)
GDP							-.028	(.083)	-.060	(.096)
Dispersion	.265**	(.115)	.262**	(.114)	.265**	(.116)	.264**	(.114)	.250**	(.113)
Log Likelihood	-125.07		-125.05		-125.05		-124.97		-124.74	

*p < .10, **p < .05

[a]See note a to table 2.3

[b]In thousands

prices, so that variations in annual rates of inflation would have no effect on these analyses. Change in GDP is measured as the rise (or fall) in GDP from the previous year to the current one, expressed as a percentage of the previous year's GDP. Because figures on GDP go back only to 1950, the measure of change in GDP could be calculated only for the years 1951–91, which is why all the models tested in table 2.5 are limited to this range. The third column of table 2.5 suggests that GDP growth, like unemployment, has no significant effect on the formation of worker cooperatives in Israel during these years.

While the two previous columns tested the effects of short-term economic conditions, the fourth column tests the effects of long-term changes in GDP. Ben-Ner (1988a, 1988b) argues that there are two contradictory relationships between the state of an economy and the formation of worker cooperatives: a countercyclical response to short-term conditions and a procyclical response to long-term economic growth. The fourth column of table 2.5 suggests, however, that a measure of the overall level of GDP, like our measure of annual changes in GDP, has no statistically significant effect on the formation of worker cooperatives in Israel over this period.

In the final column of table 2.5, we test a model into which all three of these economic variables have been incorporated at the same time. In this model, the effects of all three variables remain insignificant.

In analyses not shown here, we tested other versions of these models, in order to make sure that we were not being too quick to dismiss explanations that attribute the formation of worker cooperatives to economic conditions. Attempts to combine the economic variable simultaneously with both demographic variables from table 2.3 and the social and political variables from table 2.4 proved unsuccessful, as these models had dangerously high numbers of independent variables for the modest number of years involved and produced coefficients on the demographic variable that could not be accepted as valid baselines from which to proceed to the examination of the effects of other variables. Models that combined the economic variables solely with the social and political variables from table 2.4 also raised concerns that more independent variables were being included than the small number of years available could permit us to differentiate.

The first four columns of table 2.6 show the coefficients estimated for the economic variables in models in which these variables

TABLE 2.6
Effects of the Economic Environment on the Formation of Worker Cooperatives,
Excluding Demographic Processes, 1951–1991[a]

	I		II		III		IV		V		VI	
	b	S.E.	b	S.E.	b	S.E.	b	S.E.	b	S.E.	b	S.E.
Intercept	2.782**	(.446)	2.261**	(.201)	4.058**	(.331)	4.059**	(.604)	12.955**	(2.512)	15.182**	(4.021)
Unemployment[b]	-.034**	(.012)					-.023**	(.008)			.013	(.012)
Percent Change GDP			.056**	(.027)			.003	(.039)			-.014	(.039)
GDP					-.119**	(.023)	-.106**	(.032)	.338**	(.153)	.438**	(.214)
Year									-.223**	(.066)	-.276**	(.110)
Dispersion	.801**	(.186)	.879**	(.212)	.541**	(.182)	.453**	(.153)	.304**	(.104)	.305**	(.119)
Log Likelihood	-141.81		-143.58		-134.86		-132.48		-126.40		-125.83	

*p < .10, **p < .05

[a]See note a to table 2.3

[b]In thousands

alone are included, first alone and then in combination. The coefficients shown in the first three columns are in each case contrary to the two-part theory of Ben-Ner. The effects of unemployment are significantly negative, or procyclical, and the significant positive coefficient associated with annual changes in GDP indicates that the effect of this variable, too, is if anything procyclical. Only the long-term measure, GDP level, shows a statistically significant effect that can be viewed as countercyclical, and this is the one economic variable to which Ben-Ner attributed a procyclical effect.

Because Israel's per capita GDP has risen fairly consistently over time, we were concerned that the effects associated with GDP in the previously tested models might be contaminated by other covariates of time, such as the social and political changes whose effects were discussed above. For this reason, we have inserted the effects of year into the last two columns of table 2.6. We see in those columns that when the negative effects of unmeasured social and political changes have been taken into account, a measure of overall level of economic development such as per capita GDP does indeed appear to have a significantly positive effect on the formation of worker cooperatives as Ben-Ner predicts. Also noteworthy is the fact that the negative effect of year that was initially reported in table 2.4 remains negative when a measure of GDP is introduced. This supports the interpretation that the changes in Israeli society that have done most to discourage the formation of new worker cooperatives since independence have been social and political developments, not economic ones.

The short-term measures of economic conditions, in the meantime, continue to perform weakly in both of the combined models shown in columns four and six of table 2.6. The effects of annual changes in GDP are not significant in either model. The effects of unemployment appear significantly negative in one combined model, nonsignificantly positive in the other. In either case the main point is that signs of these estimates are erratic, and their significance levels are unstable, primarily because whatever effects they may exert barely touch the threshold of statistical significance. In other analyses not reported here (Russell and Hanneman, 1992b), we tested other strategies for estimating the effects of these and other measures of economic conditions and produced a similar pattern of weak and mixed results.

The countercyclical interpretation of cooperative formation does not work well in Israel, but that does not necessarily imply that this model cannot validly be applied to other cooperatives in other times and places; it may mean only that researchers will need to be more careful in the future in specifying that it applies only to some cooperatives and not to others, or only to certain times and places and not to others. In Ben-Ner's (1988b) theory, for example, countercyclical patterns of formation are explicitly associated only with cooperatives that are created as transformations of preexisting conventional firms. Since the vast majority of Israel's worker cooperatives were not established as transformation cooperatives but as wholly new enterprises, the countercyclical interpretation should perhaps never have been expected to be applicable to them. In so far as it can be related to economic conditions at all, their growth seems more procyclical than countercyclical, but in general the rise and fall of this population seem to have been more strongly and more consistently affected by the demographic, social, and political changes that we have examined above.

THE AGE DEPENDENCE OF MORTALITY

Liabilities of "Newness" and "Adolescence"

An issue that has recently received increasing attention from sociologists is the age dependence of organizational death rates. Once again, most of the credit for calling attention to this issue goes to the population ecologists. Following Stinchcombe (1965), Freeman, Carroll, and Hannan (1983) began by positing a "liability of newness," in which the risk of business failure is assumed to peak in the first year and to decline in subsequent years. Bruederl and Schuessler (1990) and Fichman and Levinthal (1991) later proposed that the age dependence of organizational death rates may more accurately be described as a "liability of adolescence," in which organizational mortality peaks not in the first year, but several years later. In addition to these hazards of "newness" or "adolescence," some researchers have also suggested that organizations may be vulnerable to liabilities of "maturity" (Aldrich, et al., 1990) or "obsolescence" (Baum and House 1990). Support for the latter notions was recently offered by Ranger-Moore (1991), who found in a sample of New York life insurance companies that when the size of these organizations was taken into account, their death rates increased rather than decreased with age.

As these ideas are applied to worker cooperatives, it is also necessary to consider whether the age dependence of mortality takes a different shape in populations of worker cooperatives than it does in organizations of other types. Aldrich, et al. (1990) have suggested, for example, that cooperatives, like trade associations, are "minimalist" organizations (Halliday, Powell, and Granfors, 1987), which are capable of surviving on relatively low overhead and maintenance costs and can if necessary borrow money from their members in times of hardship. If true, this implies that their mortality is more likely to conform to an adolescence pattern. One would also anticipate the adolescence pattern if worker cooperatives are founded with larger labor forces than conventional organizations, because larger organizational size has also been associated with the adolescence pattern (Bruederl and Schuessler, 1990).

The duration dependence of the hazard of mortality of Israeli producer cooperatives that were established between 1924 and 1990 is examined in figure 2.4. The figure plots the hazard under five contrasting sets of theoretical assumptions. The Kaplan-Meier model assumes that the hazard in each year is unique to that year, and thus simply tracks the empirically observed form of the hazard. The Exponential model hypothesizes a constant hazard. The Weibull formulation is consistent with the hypothesis of a "liability of newness," in which the risk of business failure is assumed to peak in the first year and to decline in subsequent years. The Log Normal and Log Logistic models, in contrast, test two forms of the "liability of adolescence" reasoning advanced by Bruederl and Schuessler (1990) and Fichman and Levinthal (1991).

Our expectation here was that the mortality of Israeli cooperatives would conform more to an "adolescence" pattern than to one of "newness." We thought this first of all because of the evidence offered by Bruederl and Schuessler regarding the connection between mortality and organization size. Their data indicate that the "newness" model is most appropriate to self-employed individuals or to organizations with only two to four employees per firm. Since, under Israeli law, an organization must have at least seven members to be registered as a cooperative, we expected their mortality to fit the "adolescence" pattern that Bruederl and Schuessler associate with larger firms. In addition, we were also influenced by the argument of Aldrich, et al. (1990) that the "minimalist" nature of cooperative organizations should also lead us to expect to find an "adolescence" pattern in the deaths of these firms.

Measures of the goodness of fit of these various models are re-

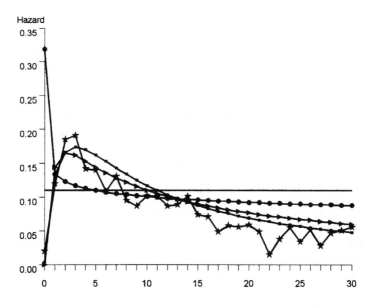

Figure 2.4
Estimated Hazard by Duration under Alternative Models

		Log Likelihood	Survival Quartiles		
			75%	50%	25%
★	Kaplan-Meier	–3891.6	2.0	4.0	10.0
—	Exponential	–4063.7	2.6	6.3	12.6
●	Weibull	–4041.4	2.1	5.6	12.4
▶	Log Normal	–3882.8	2.3	4.9	10.4
■	Log Logistic	–3891.4	2.3	4.6	9.5

ported at the bottom of figure 2.4. While these measures are not directly comparable across all of these models due to differences in the way they are calculated, both these measures and a visual inspection of the figure indicate that the liability of the "adolescence" model does indeed do a better job of fitting these data than the simpler "newness" model does. In particular, it is evident from the empirical or Kaplan-Meier pattern shown in the figure that the peak hazard of mortality within this population occurs not in the first year but in the third. It is necessary to add, however, that the measured "adolescence" of this population occurs very early. Given inherent delays in the administrative and accounting processes associated with organizational failures (Don, 1968), the difference between the "newness" and "adolescence" models may be more statistically than substantively important in this population.

Studies of several other populations of worker cooperatives have indicated a more pronounced "adolescence" pattern in the age dependence of deaths. In a study of 1,526 worker cooperatives formed in the United Kingdom between 1974 and 1986, Ben-Ner (1988a) found that peak hazard of death in this population occurred at about age three. Perotin (1987) reports that the mortality rate for French worker cooperatives peaks at from three to five years.Staber (1989) found that mortality in his sample of worker cooperatives in Atlantic Canada did not peak until the fifth year.

Also of interest is the question of whether worker cooperatives are more or less prone to liabilities of "maturity" or "obsolescence" than organizations of other types, particularly in light of claims that these organizations have trouble raising capital for new investments (Berman and Berman, 1989) and that their democratic structures tend to degenerate over time. Staber's (1989a) data are intriguing in this regard. He finds that hazard rates of his Canadian worker cooperatives decline after the fifth year, but then rise again during a period of "mid-life crisis" that lasts from about age fifteen to age thirty.

Among Israeli worker cooperatives, it is hard to discern evidence for any such "mid-life crisis" in the Kaplan-Meier pattern shown in figure 2.4. The most dangerous time in the life of the Israeli worker cooperatives is clearly the period of adolescence. The hazard of mortality declines steadily in almost every year after the third one. There appear to be local minima in the hazard at ages seventeen and twenty-two, and slightly higher hazards at the ages around these years, but these appear to be minor and random fluctuations, not evidence of mid-life crises.

Another noteworthy feature in figure 2.4 is what it says not only about the years in which peak hazards occur, but also about median survival times. Both the empirical Kaplan-Meier estimates and the Log Normal model, which was the theoretical model with the best overall goodness-of-fit, indicate that worker cooperatives in this population have a median life expectancy of under five years. This result contrasts strikingly with the findings of Staber's

(1989a) study, as his Canadian worker cooperatives had a median life expectancy of nearly eighteen years. Staber cites data on the mortality of worker cooperatives in the United Kingdom that look more similar to our Israeli results. He concludes that it is his Canadian worker cooperatives that stand out as unique and adds that "the question of why the failure rates of cooperatives in Atlantic Canada are lower than those in Great Britain deserves further study" (1989a, p. 71).

Differences in Mortality by Industry and Sector

It has often been noted that producer cooperatives and similar organizations appear to do better in some industries than in others. For example, cooperative printshops, bakeries, and trucking firms are common not only in Israel, but in many other parts of the world (Ben-Ner, 1988a). Among worker cooperatives in Atlantic Canada, Staber (1989a) found cooperatives in services and in a second group of industries that included transportation to be significantly longer-lived than those in manufacturing or in resource extraction. A number of theoretical perspectives have also been invoked in order to help explain why such patterns should hold. For example, Russell (1985a, 1985b, 1991) has used both transaction cost theory and agency theory to predict that producer cooperatives should be both more common and more successful in service and transportation industries than they generally are in manufacturing.

Differences among Israeli worker cooperatives in survival times by sector and industry are shown in table 2.7. Looking first at sectoral differences, the data are consistent with Staber's findings and Russell's arguments about the superior survival prospects of worker cooperatives in the services compared to those in manufacturing. The best performers in this group are the cooperative laundries, delivery services, restaurants, and cultural pursuits, such as conservatories of music. It is a bit puzzling to find the refuse collection cooperatives to be the shortest-lived cooperatives in this sector, as Russell (1985a, 1985b, 1991) describes a population of worker-owned refuse collection companies in the San Francisco Bay area, most of whose members survived for many decades. Given the small number (eight) of Israeli worker cooperatives engaged in such activities, it is possible that the results shown in table 2.7 for this group are due to chance.

TABLE 2.7
Survival of Worker Cooperatives Founded 1924–1992 by
Sector and Industry[a]

	N	Duration at Survival Quartile (years)			Mean Survival (years)
		75 Percent	50 Percent	25 Percent	
Transportation	193	2	4	10	7.8
Passenger Transport	43	3	6	13	9.7
Motor Freight	61	3	6	14	10.6
Other Transportation	89	2	3	6	4.7
Service	352	2	4	11	9.6
Meat, Ice, Oil	46	2	5	15	10.5
Restaurants, Hotels	32	2	3	18	10.1
Schools, Theaters	49	2	4	19	10.8
Laundries	18	4	11	27	16.0
Port, Sailing, Fishing	23	2	4	11	7.4
Garages	13	2	4	10	6.0
Refuse Collection	8	2	3	5	4.3
Other Service	163	2	4	10	8.5
Production	757	2	4	10	9.1
Baking	100	4	11	21	14.7
Woodworking	74	2	5	9	9.5
Printing, Paper	53	2	6	11	12.0
Metal, Electrical	86	3	5	11	10.4
Building Materials	134	2	3	6	6.7
Sand, Cement, Drill	32	2	3	7	5.0
Textiles	77	2	3	7	6.2
Food Processing	56	2	4	7	6.1
Leather, Shoes	35	2	5	9	7.7
Chemicals	19	3	4	9	6.5
Diamonds	18	3	5	7	6.4
Other Production	73	2	4	8	6.4
Sector Unknown	28	2	5	12	6.6
Total	1330	2	4	10	9.2

[a]Kaplan-Meier estimation

Another surprise in table 2.7 is the relatively low mean survival time (7.8 years) within the transportation sector. This contradicts not only Staber and Russell, but also everything we know about the success of Egged and Dan. Looking within the transportation sector, table 2.7 suggests that it is not the bus cooperatives or the trucking cooperatives that show low survival times, but the large number of cooperatives listed under miscellaneous "other transportation." Cooperatives that clearly specialized in either passenger transport or in the hauling of motor freight show above-average survival times, which is more consistent with the findings of Staber and the arguments of Russell. One should not attach too much significance to this classification of transportation cooperatives by type. In the time of the Mandate, the Registrar often failed to note the specific form of transportation provided. While the category of "other transportation" includes some cooperatives that provided both forms of transportation, it appears to consist primarily of cooperatives whose specialization is simply unknown to us. Because we were in a better position to ascertain the specialty of transportation cooperatives that are still operating or merged into living cases, this may have caused the "other transportation" category to consist disproportionately of short-lived cooperatives and therefore biases comparisons among these three types. A more important point to be made on behalf of the transportation cooperatives is that by far the largest numbers of recorded mergers occurred in this sector (see appendix). Our files contain records of twenty transportation cooperatives that dissolved by merging into the ten living cases or their antecedents. If one acknowledges that the cooperatives that went into the formation of such contemporary transportation giants as Egged and Dan are in at least some sense still in operation, then the performance of worker cooperatives in this sector does not seem so weak relative to that of those in other sectors.

Among the production cooperatives, we find cooperative bakeries and printshops living longer than others, and cooperatives in sand and cement, food processing, and textiles being significantly shorter-lived. We are tempted to offer ex post facto theoretical interpretations of some of these industry differences. Food processing and textiles may be instances of the kind of capital-intensive, unskilled activities in which Russell argued that worker cooperatives might be at a disadvantage in competition with conventionally owned firms. The work of bakers and printers may involve some of the special skills and governance problems that Russell pointed to as secrets behind the success of many varieties of worker-owned firms. But we hesitate to go very far along this path, given the absence of any real data on the nature of work in any of these organizations and in light of various idiosyncrasies of the Israeli case. The success of Israel's cooperative bakeries, for example, cannot be discussed without reference to the fact that in the 1950s and 1960s the baking of bread in Israel was a closely regulated activity, in which the price of both flour and bread was set by the government and supplies of both were distributed on the basis of allocation rather than market competition.

Effects of City and Region

Differences in the survival of Israeli worker cooperatives by city and region are shown in table 2.8. The table indicates that worker cooperatives have survived longer in Haifa and in Tel Aviv, two secular cities that are traditional centers of the labor Zionist movement (Kellerman, 1993), than they have in Jerusalem. The life spans of worker cooperatives have been shortest in the South. The high mortality of worker cooperatives in this region illustrates the price that has been paid by many of Israel's worker cooperatives for their incorporation into official programs designed to help settle the less developed parts of the country.

TABLE 2.8
Survival of Worker Cooperatives Founded 1924–1992 by Location[a]

		Duration at Survival Quartile (years)			Mean Survival (years)
	N	75 Percent	50 Percent	25 Percent	
Tel Aviv	504	2	5	12	10.3
Jerusalem	129	2	5	9	7.9
Haifa	182	2	5	13	10.6
Other Center	214	2	3	7	6.6
Other North	165	3	5	12	9.6
South	71	1	3	5	6.1
Unknown	65	3	6	8	6.0
Total	1330	2	4	10	9.2

[a]Kaplan-Meier estimation

CONCLUSIONS

In its quantitative analysis of the history of this population of worker cooperatives, this chapter has joined the previous qualitative one in seeing institutional processes as being most responsible for bringing about the pattern of growth and decline. The early dynamism of this population seems in the first place attributable to its unusually supportive institutional environment. In later years, key institutional sponsors like the Labor Party and the Histadrut became less supportive in two ways: (1) their own attitudes toward the worker cooperatives gradually shifted from patronizing friendship to open hostility; and (2) both the Histadrut and the Labor Party suffered increasingly from internal divisions and were further weakened by splits, scandals, and the emergence of new social and economic forces and constituencies in Israel over which they had little control.

Although we have no direct evidence, Israeli public opinion as a whole appears also to have turned against the worker cooperatives even before the Labor Party was swept from power in 1977. According to Israeli observers like Preuss, Schiff, and Viteles, it had happened already by 1960. The last straw for many Israelis was the Egged bus strike of 1956. In widely condemning the Egged drivers for their avarice, Israelis were of course doing no more than following the example that had already been set for them by the Histadrut, the Labor Party, and the government. The moralizing tone taken by virtually all these parties in their characterizations of the bus drivers even today seems to be a lingering vestige of the heyday of labor Zionism, an illustration of the continuing importance in Israel of what the labor leaders used to refer to as "the appeal to the national conscience" (Shapiro, 1976, p. 74).

It thus seems that the Histadrut, the Israeli government, and the Israeli public all view worker cooperatives as less legitimate today than they once did, and as less worthy of public encouragement and support. These institutional circumstances appear to account better than any others for the decline of this population after its once promising start. More narrowly economic considerations, in contrast, seem less relevant to this story. The widely popular "business cycle" interpretations of the formation of worker cooperatives, for example, do not fit these Israeli data. The response of Israeli worker cooperatives to short-term economic conditions is, if anything, more procyclical than countercyclical, but it would be more accurate to say that they show no systematic response to short-term economic conditions at all. The effect of long-term economic growth on the formation of worker cooperatives, on the other hand, is, if anything, positive, according to both the theory of Ben-Ner (1988b) and our estimation. This in turn implies that the decline of worker cooperatives in Israel cannot be dismissed as a simple consequence of economic growth and leads us back to the institutional explanations that have already been featured here.

Insofar as any variable in their resource environment has had an important effect on the formation of worker cooperatives in Israel, the most crucial resource has been the number of new immigrants pouring into the country each year. Immigration was clearly the most important external engine driving the formation of worker cooperatives in Israel over most of this period. Immigration in the pre-state period and in the years immediately following independence was the most important cause of the formation of new worker cooperatives that occurred during those years, and the more modest immigration flows in later years did much to account for their later decline.

That immigration should have such effects, however, was due to some unique institutional reasons. And the effects of immigration appear to be changing, as these institutional circumstances themselves have changed. The immigrants arriving in Israel today are different in many ways from the immigrants of the past, and the society that they are entering is even more different. The new wave of immigration of the 1990s has shown no sign so far of stimulating anything like the number of new cooperative formations that such large numbers of new immigrants could have been expected to produce in the past.

The processes of density dependence and population dynamics discussed at the beginning of this chapter appear to have amplified the effects of these other conditions, accelerating the growth of Israel's worker cooperative population in the years of greatest dynamism and further depressing it at other times. They suggest that in the first few decades, the growth of this population was fueled in part by its own success. Births of new cooperatives in one year led to further births in the next, and increases in the size of the total population in one year stimulated more increases in the next. But since the mid-1950s, these processes have worked in reverse. Lack of births in one year has led to lack of births in the next; population decline in one year has contributed to population decline in the next.

It is in this context in which failure fed on failure that we find it unsurprising to observe that failures of worker cooperatives also discouraged further births, rather than having the stimulating effect on population growth predicted by Delacroix and Carroll (1983) and also reported by Staber (1989b). The difference between our results on this point and those of Staber requires special comment, because Staber's study, like this one, deals with a sample of worker cooperatives—in his case, 205 worker cooperatives in Atlantic Canada over the period 1940–87. We suspect that the striking difference in survival times between his Canadian worker cooperatives and our Israeli sample may be the key to explaining the difference in the apparent effects of recent deaths reported in these two studies. The median worker cooperatives in Staber's sample survived for nearly eighteen years, while those in Israel lived for less than five. This makes it easier to understand how the failures of Staber's worker cooperatives could have had a stimulating effect, as cooperatives that had lived that long are indeed likely to have left many useful resources behind. Worker cooperatives as short-lived as those in Israel, on the other hand, are likely to have left no other legacy than the example of their failures, which thereby served only to increase the fears of those who might otherwise have followed in their footsteps and thus helped to convince potential cooperative founders that they would be better advised not to take this risk.

In this chapter and the previous one, emphasis has been placed on the extent to which worker cooperatives in Israel were at first passive beneficiaries and later passive victims of institutional transformations that lay largely beyond their control. The next two chapters, in contrast, will focus on the extent to which the worker cooperatives' own behavior has contributed to their decline. In particular, they will take a closer look at two internal practices of the worker cooperatives that have done more than any others to tarnish their image in the eyes of the Israeli public: their tendencies to make increasing use of hired labor (chapter 3) and the high degree of oligarchy and of instability that have often been noted in their ostensibly democratic internal politics (chapter 4).

3. THE USE OF HIRED LABOR IN ISRAELI WORKER COOPERATIVES, 1933–1989

with Robert Hanneman

Nothing has done more to sour the relationship between the Israeli worker cooperatives and the Histadrut, or to damage their public image, than their increasing use of hired labor. Given the tremendous importance that these cooperatives' critics have attached to this practice, this chapter will look more closely at it. The chapter will provide more detailed information about the extent to which the Israeli worker cooperatives have employed hired laborers and about the degree to which their use of hired laborers has changed over time. It will also attempt to identify the causal factors that have played the greatest role in making these cooperatives increasingly dependent on the labor of nonmembers.

Since the nineteenth century, worker cooperatives have repeatedly been accused of becoming less cooperative in character as they grow older, larger, and more successful (e.g., Blumberg, 1968; Russell, 1985a; see also Cornforth et al., 1988). John Stuart Mill may have been the first to describe this as a tendency to "degenerate" over time (1909, p. 790). Some treatments of this alleged "degeneration" of worker cooperatives call special attention to gradual changes in the way these organizations make decisions;

they point to instances of the transformation of direct democracy into increasingly representative, oligarchical, and/or technocratic patterns (Webb and Webb, 1920; Shirom, 1972; Meister, 1984). The applicability of these processes to the Israeli worker cooperatives will be discussed in chapter 4. For other critics, the main theme in this story of degeneration is the growing use of hired nonmember labor (Holyoake, 1906; Mill, 1909; Gunn, 1984; Russell, 1985a; Craig and Pencavel, 1992; Estrin and Jones, 1992). It is with this type of degeneration that the present chapter will be concerned.

In Israel, the idea that worker cooperatives make increasing use of hired labor is often attributed to the German sociologist Franz Oppenheimer, who in 1896 discussed the problem in a book that explored the potential role of cooperatives in agricultural settlement. Oppenheimer thought that agricultural cooperatives had a promising future, but minced no words in expressing his pessimistic assessment of the prospects for worker cooperatives in most other fields: "It is extremely seldom that a Producers' Cooperative reaches a flourishing state. When it reaches that state, it ceases to be a Producers' Co-operative" (Oppenheimer, 1896, p. 44, translated in Preuss, 1960, p. 195). For Oppenheimer, the reluctance of producers' cooperatives to admit new members, and their eventual transformation into closed groups, were "the natural consequence of a law, the *Law of Transformation*" (Oppenheimer, 1896, p. 44, translated in Preuss, 1960, p. 196).

Oppenheimer's views became particularly influential in Israel, because his proposals in favor of cooperative agricultural settlements were widely discussed in the World Zionist Organization and helped make the WZO more receptive to later innovations like the kibbutz. Shafir notes that "Oppenheimer's influence on the Zionist movement was tremendous, and in 1903 Herzl, on the floor of the Sixth Congress, characterized his affiliation as one of the greatest conquests of Zionism" (1989, p. 151). When the Eleventh Congress of the WZO asked the Jewish National Fund to work out a system of labor for the land owned by the fund, it was Oppenheimer who wrote the JNF's endorsement of cooperative forms of settlement (Oppenheimer, 1917).

The notion that worker cooperatives inevitably transform themselves into conventional capitalist undertakings was in wide circulation in Jewish Palestine by the 1920s. As has been shown in chapter 1, the founders of the Labor Party and the Histadrut had their own reasons for disliking the worker cooperatives: their individualistic ownership structures made them less attractive from both a socialist and a Zionist point of view, and the Labor leaders were generally wary of any organizations over which they had no direct control. But the accusation that worker cooperatives gradually differentiate themselves into a class of managers and a class of hired hands was a charge that had great impact on a broad range of public opinion, both within the Labor Party and outside of it, both in Palestine and abroad. Hired labor too readily became Arab labor, as the experience with agricultural settlements had already shown. This led the WZO to join the Labor Party and the Histadrut in insisting on a strict ban against the use of hired labor in the agricultural cooperatives. None of these parties saw any reason to make an exception to this policy for the urban worker cooperatives, because all viewed "self-labor," rather than hired labor, as not only an economic necessity, but also a Zionist ideal. Only by performing their own manual labor, it was widely felt, could Jews purge themselves of the one-sided commercialism and intellectuality of Diaspora life and once again make themselves spiritually whole (see, for example, Winer, 1971).

Insofar as worker cooperatives have a tendency to rely increasingly on hired labor, this has also been troubling to the worker cooperatives' own leading advocates and defenders. If worker cooperatives inevitably transform themselves back into conventional capitalist firms, why should anyone go to the trouble of trying to help them? This is an argument that was occasionally invoked by the Merkaz Hakooperatsia's own members in efforts to urge the members of other worker cooperatives to join them in searching for more effective solutions to this problem. For example, at a critical meeting of Merkaz Council in March of 1958, a member of Israel's oldest cooperative, the Achdut Press, suggested that "there was no useful purpose in organizing additional WPSTS [Workers' Production, Service and Transportation Societies] since the continuity of the existing WPSTS is very doubtful because they were closed co-operatives" (Viteles, 1968, p. 109).

The use of hired labor within this population for all the years for which it is available is reported in table 3.1. The table indicates that worker cooperatives in Israel, like those in many other countries, do indeed make increasing use of nonmember labor over time. The proportion hired begins in 1933 at about a modest fifth of the cooperative labor force, but then nearly doubles in less than a decade. It falls in the early 1940s, but then resumes its rise, climbing above 40 percent in the 1950s. It reached 50

TABLE 3.1

Hired Laborers in Worker Cooperatives, 1933–1988[a]

Year	Labor Force	Members	Hired Laborers	Hired Laborers as Percent of Labor Force
1933	992	788	204	20.6
1938	3,061	1,931	1,130	36.9
1939	3,050	1,973	1,077	35.3
1940	3,073	1,981	1,092	35.5
1941	3,452	2,086	1,366	39.6
1943	5,346	4,186	1,160	21.7
1945	4,625	3,267	1,358	29.3
1948	5,564	3,733	1,831	32.9
1949	6,970	4,689	2,281	32.7
1950	9,527	6,021	3,506	36.8
1951	11,478	6,380	5,098	44.4
1952	11,721	6,136	5,585	47.7
1953	10,678	5,737	4,941	42.7
1954	11,910	6,973	4,937	41.5
1955	11,518	6,480	5,038	43.7
1956	12,283	6,689	5,594	45.5
1957	12,669	6,655	6,014	47.5
1958	12,555	6,674	5,881	46.8
1959	13,341	6,879	6,462	48.4
1960	13,724	7,073	6,651	48.5
1961	14,496	7,446	7,050	48.6
1962	14,689	7,741	6,948	47.3
1963	14,767	7,863	6,904	46.8
1964	15,907	7,949	7,961	50.0
1965	16,059	8.219	7,840	48.8
1966	16,374	8,780	7,594	46.4
1967	15,326	9,263	6,063	39.6
1968	15,247	9,021	6,226	40.8
1969	15,201	8,814	6,387	42.0
1970	16,819	9,089	7,730	46.0
1971	18,090	9,922	8,168	45.2
1972	18,658	10,509	8,149	43.7
1973	18,598	10,708	7,890	42.4
1974	18,128	10,751	7,377	40.7
1975	18,660	10,551	8,109	43.5
1976	19,292	10,233	9,059	47.0
1977	18,885	9,728	9,157	48.5
1978	18,399	9,818	8,581	46.6
1979	21,044			
1980	21,352			
1981	20,350	9,704	10,646	52.3
1982	19,933			
1983	19,661	9,284	10,377	52.8
1984	19,480	9,077	10,403	53.4
1985	18,996	8,892	10,104	53.2
1986	17,255	8,288	8,967	52.0
1987	17,829	8,032	9,797	54.9
1988	16,562	7,407	9,155	55.3

[a]1933: Cooperative Center (1933); 1938–1945: Cooperative Center (1949); 1948–1959; Viteles (1968); 1960–1985: Daniel (1989); 1986–1988: Registrar of Cooperative Societies (1988, 1989a, 1989b)

percent for the first time in 1964, and has not fallen below that level since 1978.

Growth in the use of hired labor in these cooperatives becomes even more striking when one sorts Israeli worker cooperatives by sector, as shown in table 3.2. The transportation sector, which accounts for the lion's share of cooperative employment, is also the only sector in which the reliance on hired labor has never exceeded 50 percent. In the other two sectors, that threshold was crossed many years ago, and the share of labor that is hired currently exceeds 80 percent.

This chapter examines the growing use of hired labor in Israeli worker cooperatives that is documented in these tables in some detail, in an effort to identify the specific factors that have done the most both to promote and to retard it. To this end, we direct our attention not only to the long-term trend, about which there is little question, but also to the ups and downs of this transformation, its changing pace, its limits and exceptions. Why, for example, did the use of hired labor in these cooperatives rise rapidly in the 1930s, but then fall in the 1940s? Why did the use of hired labor in the production and service sectors remain essentially flat for most of the 1950s and 1960s, but then rise rapidly after 1968? Why is transportation such an exception? Are there any other industries or niches in which the use of hired labor in Israeli worker cooperatives remains unusually low?

In the discussion that follows, we offer answers to all of these questions. We begin by demonstrating that Israeli worker cooperatives, like similar cooperatives in many other parts of the world, have powerful incentives to employ nonmember labor inherent in their structures. We then examine the role played by institutional forces such as the Histadrut and the Merkaz Hakooperatsia, which appear to have served as the most important force acting to delay the operation of these incentives. Later sections explore the effects of industry and sector and of characteristics of individual cooperatives, including their size, age, and capital requirements.

INCENTIVES TO EMPLOY NONMEMBERS

Such contemporary economists as Ben-Ner (1984) and Miyazaki (1984) have recently argued that a temptation to make increasing use of hired labor is inherent in any cooperative in which members pay themselves the equivalent of a market wage plus some premium that reflects the cooperative's profits. In such situations, members wishing to maximize their individual incomes will seek to minimize the number of members, in order to have "fewer ways to cut up the pie."

TABLE 3.2
Labor Force and Percent Hired in Worker Cooperatives by Sector, 1960–1988[a]

Year	Transportation		Service		Production	
	Labor Force	Percent Hired	Labor Force	Percent Hired	Labor Force	Percent Hired
1960	8,758	46.0	1,572	43.1	3,394	57.3
1961	9,240	44.8	1,568	43.9	3,688	60.2
1962	9,465	43.2	1,656	45.0	3,568	59.2
1963	9,660	41.8	1,691	49.7	3,416	59.4
1964	10,589	46.2	1,651	46.7	3,667	62.6
1965	10,800	45.3	1,822	46.3	3,437	61.3
1966	11,580	44.9	1,797	38.9	2,997	56.5
1967	10,833	35.8	1,655	36.2	2,838	55.8
1968	10,777	37.0	1,736	42.5	2,734	55.0
1969	11,144	39.8	1,354	32.3	2,703	56.0
1970	12,047	41.4	1,640	50.9	3,132	60.8
1971	12,871	39.3	2,089	55.9	3,130	62.0
1972	13,628	37.5	2,136	59.8	2,894	60.9
1973	13,721	35.8	1,826	54.8	3,051	64.6
1974	13,478	33.2	1,844	56.9	2,806	65.8
1975	14,052	36.4	1,785	58.9	2,823	68.6
1976	14,767	41.6	1,811	62.7	2,714	65.8
1977	13,924	40.8	2,235	71.3	2,726	69.0
1978	13,548	39.4	2,140	65.4	2,711	68.1
1979						
1980						
1981	15,321	44.5	2,295	78.3	2,734	74.2
1982						
1983	14,656	43.8	2,396	82.1	2,609	76.6
1984	14,635	44.6	2,338	84.1	2,507	76.0
1985	14,306	44.9	2,225	82.3	2,465	75.2
1986	13,087	43.2	2,143	80.4	2,025	78.3
1987	13,390	44.9	2,252	88.5	2,187	81.8
1988	12,132	44.2	2,223	88.5	2,207	82.9

[a]1960–1985: Daniel (1989); 1986–1988: Registrar of Cooperative Societies (1988, 1989a, 1989b)

While this inherent temptation to make use of hired labor has only recently received attention in the contemporary economic literature, it has actually been well understood in Israel since the time when worker cooperatives were first being organized among the Jewish workers in Palestine. Here, for example, is how the Mandate's Registrar of Cooperative Societies described this process in his 1938 report:

> The facts are that co-partnerships of labour are exposed to a temptation not present in other forms of cooperation. In a consumers' or marketing society . . . for instance, it is to the interest of members to enlarge membership, for each new member increases the business of the society. The increased volume of business in turn reduces the percentage of overhead expenses and increases the savings made in the business and therefore, also the benefits accruing to each member. In co-partnerships of labour the situation is reversed. Every additional member increases the number of those who share in the profits, though not necessarily increasing the business done or the amount of profits to be shared. Each new member, therefore, is likely to be looked upon as reducing the profits of the others. More especially if the society achieves business success, an increasing tendency may develop among the members to limit their number so as to retain all the savings from the business for themselves, and, if additional workers are needed, to take them on as employees, not as members (Registrar of Cooperative Societies, 1938, p. 1080.

For Franz Oppenheimer, the tendency to seek to increase members' profits by making increasing use of hired labor was not only a temptation, but an economic necessity. Restricting the number of profit-sharers was needed both to keep the members' entrepreneurial motivation from being diluted and also to enable members to raise the capital that would be needed to finance technological innovations (Preuss, 1960, p. 196).

In Israel, as in many other countries, these inherent temptations to employ nonmembers are exacerbated by the capital structures of worker cooperatives. As Israeli worker cooperatives accumulate capital, prospective members must raise increasingly formidable amounts of cash in order to pay for an equal share of the capital stock. By the 1980s, the capital invested in some Israeli worker cooperatives had risen to values of over $100,000 per member. Few if any of these cooperatives have developed sufficient financial sophistication to collect capital contributions in installments or to provide financing for the purchase of memberships. One reason for this is that many cooperatives' liquid assets are constantly drained by the need to cash out retiring members. In Egged and Dan, this problem has on some occasions become so severe that both cooperatives have needed to maintain waiting lists of members who wish to retire but who cannot be permitted to until their cooperative raises more cash. More chronically, these antiquated capital structures have served as major obstacles in the paths of hired laborers who wish to become members in these cooperatives.

Another powerful impediment to the admission of new members in many Israeli worker cooperatives is the common practice of paying equal wages to all members. This practice seems traceable to the egalitarian ideology that was common in the pre-state period throughout the Histadrut (Sussman, 1969). Members of many contemporary Israeli worker cooperatives argue now that it is attributable more to an important pragmatic consideration. Using arguments similar to those of Hansmann (1990), they insist that this policy saves them from much internal discord and is the only politically viable wage policy for a democratic workplace. A consequence of this policy of wage equality, however, is that Israeli worker cooperatives are forced to employ nonmembers whenever they wish to pay someone either substantially more or substantially less than members are customarily paid. This in turn promotes the familiar situation in which cooperative membership is limited to a homogeneous group of skilled workers who share a knowledge of some trade, while unskilled laborers as well as clerical and professional staff have no possibility of becoming members.

With incentives and structures such as these, skeptics like Oppenheimer and Ben-Gurion may have been correct in thinking that a tendency toward the growing use of hired labor was inevitable in these cooperatives. There remained to be determined only the pace and timing of this transformation and the existence of possible limits and exceptions.

THE ROLE OF THE HISTADRUT IN DISCOURAGING
THE USE OF HIRED LABOR

Of factors that have acted to retard the spread of hired labor in Israeli worker cooperatives, pride of place must go to the Histadrut and to its allies in the Merkaz Hakooperatsia and in the Israeli government. As was discussed in chapter 1, the Histadrut was a staunch opponent of this practice and made repeated efforts to discourage its use. Unfortunately, neither the Histadrut nor the Merkaz ever discovered any constructive means for dealing with this problem, with the result that the only effective weapons at their disposal were coercion and reproach. These blunt instruments did for a time succeed in achieving some limited results, but they did so at great cost, as they played a major role in demoralizing Israel's nascent worker cooperative movement.

For decades, it was the policy of both the Histadrut and the Merkaz Hakooperatsia to take an unsympathetic attitude toward any worker cooperatives that made use of hired labor, regardless of the excuses that they might offer for this practice, such as the claim that they denied memberships to new employees only during the period when they were learning their new trades. In 1932, a committee that the Histadrut had appointed to seek solutions to this problem recommended the imposition of "harsh restrictions" and in general took the position that the problem could best be dealt with by "intensifying the authority and influence of the Chevrat Ovdim" (Daniel, 1968). At the Third Congress of the Merkaz cooperatives in 1934, the use of nonmember labor was totally outlawed, and three worker cooperatives were expelled from the movement for refusing to agree to abide by this rule. This punishment was meted out on subsequent occasions as well (Viteles, 1968, pp. 303, 308). Stories are also told of worker cooperatives that reluctantly agreed to admit new members in response to such pressures and were later destroyed by conflicts between old and new members (e.g., Mondini, 1957, p. 18).

The Histadrut conducted a major inquiry into the use of hired labor in worker cooperatives under the leadership of Golda Meir in the mid-1940s and passed a resolution urging its governing council to do everything in its power to discourage this practice at the Sixth Histadrut Congress in 1945. At the Fifth Congress of the Merkaz cooperatives in 1949, the worker cooperatives formally adopted a set of "seven articles" that had been proposed by the Histadrut for discouraging the use of hired labor. Some of these seven articles were of little more than symbolic significance (for example, one appointed another committee, another reaffirmed the role of the Histadrut in determining the wages of hired workers), but one provision gave Histadrut representatives the right to participate in meetings of the management of Merkaz cooperatives, in addition to the right they already had to participate in meetings of the rank-and-file members.

From 1949 through 1952, the Histadrut's pressures on the Merkaz Hakooperatsia to reduce the use of hired labor appear to have been relaxed, as both bodies gave their full attention to the creation of new cooperatives that could help absorb the great new wave of immigration that arrived on the heels of independence. In the mid-1950s, the Histadrut's former efforts were resumed, but the labor leaders for a time pursued new tactics, focusing on the weapons they had acquired through the Labor Party's political hegemony in the new state. Thus both in 1953 and again in the period 1956–68 the government proposed revisions to the Cooperative Societies Ordinance that would have increased the Histadrut's power to discipline cooperatives that make excessive use of hired labor (Viteles, 1966). When these efforts failed because of opposition from the kibbutzim and moshavim, the Histadrut concentrated on using the leverage it had acquired over the most prominent worker cooperatives, the bus companies, through the government's role in approving periodic rate increases. At Histadrut insistence, reductions in the proportion of hired labor have often become a quid pro quo for the bus cooperatives to have their proposals for rate increases approved (Viteles, 1968).

By the late 1950s, the Histadrut was once again seeking to impose a more direct and centralized control over all of its member cooperatives, including those affiliated with the Merkaz. In 1960, the Histadrut launched a new campaign to root out the use of hired labor in the worker cooperatives. Once again, it began by appointing a special committee to look into the problem. The committee was headed by Yerucham Meshel, a future head of the Histadrut, and its recommendations signaled that the Histadrut was about to take an aggressive new stance. The committee ordered that all hired workers with more than three years' seniority must immediately be accepted as members. It also forbade the bus cooperatives to continue their practice of freely admitting the sons of members as new members until the status of the other hired workers had been resolved.

The harsh new tone of the Histadrut came as a shock even to its own appointee, Y. Ritov, who for many years had headed the Merkaz. Ritov complained that "forcing cooperatives to accept members does not take place in any cooperatives in the world, does not take place in the [other] cooperatives in Israel, and cannot be accepted in our cooperatives" (Daniel, 1968, p. 98). But when the Merkaz cooperatives were finally permitted to hold their long-delayed Sixth Congress in 1962, their leaders meekly went along with the Histadrut program. The convention resulted in a call for "more intensive" efforts to limit the use of hired labor, and warned that in the case of cooperatives that make no efforts to reduce their dependence on hired labor, "all financial and organizational help of the institutions of the Histadrut will be taken from them" (Daniel, 1968, p. 102).

For many Israeli worker cooperatives, these threats and fiats were the last straw in their relationship with the Histadrut and made them determined to break free. Many of them had rankled under the Histadrut's authority for decades. In the 1940s, for example, during a previous Histadrut campaign to reduce the use of hired labor, many of the transportation cooperatives stopped paying dues to the Histadrut. At that time some initiated steps to reregister with the Registrar as different kinds of cooperatives, outside the authority of the Merkaz Hakooperatsia and the Histadrut. In the 1960s, as complaints about the Histadrut's high-handedness were once again increasing, independence from the Histadrut again began to look attractive. But before the worker cooperatives attempted to bolt from the Histadrut again, the Histadrut's own Shoresh Committee in 1968 recommended that the Merkaz cooperatives be granted their independence, or at least much greater autonomy than they had ever known before.

After representatives of the worker cooperatives were permitted to assume leadership of their own movement in 1968, both the Histadrut and the Merkaz Hakooperatsia appear to have largely abandoned their formerly punitive tactics for discouraging the use of hired labor. In practice, this left Israeli worker cooperatives in the production and service sectors with nothing to prevent an almost steady increase in the use of hired labor within them, as shown in table 3.2. Only in transportation, where the bus cooperatives Dan and Egged remain subject to government regulation, has the proportion of the labor force accounted for by hired labor remained below the symbolically important level of 50 percent.

These figures suggest that despite its structural weaknesses, the Histadrut's efforts to restrict the use of hired labor in Israeli worker cooperatives were indeed the most effective barrier against this practice from the time when the Merkaz Hakooperatsia was created through 1968. But the Histadrut does not deserve all of the credit for the reductions in the use of hired labor that occurred during this period. According to the figures in table 3.1, for example, the two most important declines in the share of hired labor in Israeli worker cooperatives occurred between 1941 and 1943, when the proportion hired dropped from 39.6 percent to 21.7 percent, and between 1964 and 1967, when it fell from 50 percent to 39.6 percent. While both of these declines coincide with major Histadrut campaigns to discourage this practice, it is not certain that the Histadrut is entirely responsible for the results that were achieved. In particular, it seems very likely that changes in the Israeli economy as a whole during these two periods contributed significantly to the reductions in the use of hired labor that occurred in these years.

The rise in cooperative memberships between 1941 and 1943, for example, may have been influenced by war-induced labor shortages, with memberships being offered to hired laborers as inducements to keep them from leaving their firms. Russell (1985a) notes that a similar process appears to have occurred among worker-owned refuse collection companies in the San Francisco region during this period. According to Shalev (1992, p. 43), "boom conditions" also prevailed in Palestine during World War II, and this situation appears to have improved the bargaining position of Jewish workers throughout the Mandatory economy.

Between 1964 and 1967, changing macroeconomic conditions may once again have played an important role in bringing about the decline in the use of hired labor that is shown in table 3.1. Total employment in the Israeli economy boomed in 1965 and early 1966, to be followed by a severe recession that lasted until the Six Day War of June 1967 (Fisher, 1988; Shalev, 1984, 1992). During the boom period, memberships may have been offered to hired workers as an extra inducement to keep them from leaving for other jobs, as seems to have occurred during World War II; and during the period of declining employment, the proportion of hired labor in Israeli worker cooperatives seems to have declined largely because the employment of hired workers was reduced at a greater rate than that of members.

Support for this interpretation is provided by Daniel, who examined influences on the use of hired labor in Israeli worker cooperatives in works published in 1968 and 1989. In 1968, Daniel emphasized the institutional pressures that were then coming from the Histadrut and seemed to share the perception of the Merkaz leaders that these pressures were becoming intolerably strong. From the perspective of the 1980s, however, Daniel concluded that reductions in the number of hired workers, not increases in the number of members, had been the most important cause of the decline in the proportion of hired labor that occurred in the years 1965–67. Daniel blamed this on the nationwide recession. He also noted that in the manufacturing sector, in particular, "the use of hired labor expands and contracts according to changing economic conditions" (1989, p. 97).

Russell and Hanneman (1992a) conducted several quantitative tests of the responsiveness of worker cooperative employment to changing economic conditions in Israel over the period 1956–88. These analyses yielded several results that are relevant to these arguments. They confirmed that, in general, the employment of hired labor in worker cooperatives is more variable than the employment of members. Since security of employment is often assumed to be a major goal of membership in a cooperative (e.g., Domar, 1966; Miyazaki and Neary, 1983; Bonin, 1984; Dow, 1986; Berman and Berman, 1989; Kahana and Nitzan, 1989), it would have been very surprising if these analyses had produced a different result. The study also joined Daniel (1989) in finding employment to be more variable in manufacturing than in the other two sectors. Employment was most stable in the transportation sector, but it was also in transportation that the variations in employment that did occur were most closely associated with changes in national rates of unemployment. Given that the two bus cooperatives are among Israelis' major means of commuting, it is not surprising to see that the bus cooperatives' total ridership and total employment are strongly associated with national totals of people employed. But contrary to expectations, Russell and Hanneman found no significant effect for unemployment on the share of hired labor in Israeli worker cooperatives over this period. Only in transportation did unemployment appear to be having statistically significant effects on the employment of either members or hired laborers, and in that sector it reduced both categories of employment and therefore had no significant effects on the ratio between the two.

While one must therefore be cautious in generalizing to other economic downturns that occurred in other time periods, the figures in table 3.2 in themselves support the interpretation that the rapid transition from boom to bust that occurred between 1965 and 1967 did indeed have a strong influence on the proportion of hired labor in Israeli worker cooperatives in those years. Among service cooperatives, for example, employment was rising in 1965, so the decrease in the share of hired labor recorded in that year signifies that memberships at that time were increasing more rapidly than hired positions. In the next two recession years, however, service cooperative employment was falling, and the decline in hired labor signifies that positions for hired laborers were being eliminated more rapidly than jobs for members. In the production cooperatives, employment was falling throughout this three-year period, so the three declines recorded in the proportion of hired labor in that sector all imply a similar preference for preserving the jobs of members while eliminating those of hired workers. In transportation, employment rose in 1965 and 1966, but fell substantially in 1967. The sharp decrease in the share of hired labor recorded in the latter year was due in part to an increase of 575 in the number of memberships, from 6,377 to 6,952, but owed even more to a reduction of hired positions from 5,203 to 3,881, a total decline of 1,322. Of these lost positions for hired workers, fewer than half can be accounted for by hired workers who became members. Most of the remaining hired workers either must have been laid off or left voluntarily without being replaced.

All of this suggests that changing economic conditions may have played a greater role than Histadrut pressure in bringing about the two most important reductions in the use of hired labor that occurred during the period of Histadrut's domination of Israel's worker cooperative movement. This in turn implies that the Histadrut's punitive policies toward the use of hired labor in the worker cooperatives were far less effective than they might at first glance appear to be. Their results seem particularly meager when one takes into account the tremendous harm these policies seem to have done to the morale of the Israeli worker cooperatives and to their national reputations.

Both the Histadrut and the Merkaz Hakooperatsia have also occasionally made efforts to find more constructive solutions to the problem of hired labor in the worker cooperatives, but these sporadic initiatives have yielded even more disappointing results. One of the Histadrut's first efforts in this regard was a recommendation in 1934 that if worker cooperatives found it indispensable to have at least some hired positions—for example, because they employed apprentices or had a lot of seasonal work—they should at least establish a profit-sharing program for their nonmember workers. While this was on the face of it a laudable recommendation], in its remoteness from any likelihood of immediate implementation it was symptomatic of the lack of communication between the Histadrut and the Merkaz cooperatives of that time. Lacking either backing from the members or the force of law, this recommendation amounted to no more than an exhortation to the worker cooperatives from the Histadrut that they should be more generous to their hired employees.

Some more constructive efforts by the Histadrut and the Merkaz have been aimed at making it easier for nonmembers to raise the capital required to purchase memberships. Between 1946 and 1949, the Chevrat Ovdim purchased a half interest in seven worker cooperatives in an effort to cut in half the price of a membership share (Daniel, 1968). In 1975, it made similar investments in order to help lower the price of memberships in the Achdut Bakery of Tel Aviv and the butchers' cooperative, Ichud (Daniel, 1989). In the 1950s and 1960s, the Histadrut and the Merkaz encouraged several of its member cooperatives to reduce the price of an initial membership by dividing their share capital into voting and nonvoting shares, limiting members to one voting share each, but allowing veteran members to own larger numbers of nonvoting shares. Israel's largest production cooperative, Haargaz, experimented with this system in the 1960s, but it did not catch on, and as early as 1959 the vast majority of Merkaz cooperatives had gone on record as saying they "do not accept" this proposal (Viteles, 1968, p. 324). After the worker cooperatives took affairs into their own hands at the Seventh Congress of the Merkaz cooperatives in December 1968, they set up a fund that would make loans to hired laborers to assist them in purchasing their shares; but this fund was closed not long after having been established in 1969, because of a lack of capital (Daniel, 1989).

These efforts indicate that on at least some occasions, both the Histadrut and the Merkaz were earnestly seeking solutions to the problem of hired labor in the worker cooperatives and were prepared to commit significant sums of money to this search. But none of them did more than to temporarily delay the rise of hired labor in the cooperatives involved. And for at least two reasons, these efforts were inevitably destined to fail. First, insofar as appreciating share prices were the root of this problem, these programs served only to ameliorate the symptoms and did not eradicate the cause; they facilitated the purchase of memberships in the short term, but did nothing to prevent their price from growing out of reach in the future. Second, the use of hired labor in Israeli worker cooperatives has rarely been attributable to the dynamics of capital alone, and financial measures alone have therefore rarely been sufficient to prevent it. In 1955, for example, a study by the Merkaz concluded that in only 9 percent of its member cooperatives were the capital requirements for membership "the decisive reason" behind the denial of memberships to hired laborers (Viteles, 1968, p. 318).

The story of the Histadrut's failure to prevent the increasing use of hired labor in Israeli worker cooperatives is thus similar in many ways to the findings of Sussman (1969, 1973) regarding the Histadrut's efforts to determine the wages of Jewish workers in the pre-state period. In both cases, egalitarian policies inspired by the Histadrut's ideology and organizational interests were defeated by economic motivations and market forces that were beyond the Histadrut's control. But here, as in Sussman, the point is not that at all times and in all places institutional forces are powerless to resist the inexorable effects of economic processes. The more appropriate conclusion is that in this place and in this form, the Histadrut's institutional efforts were ineffective. Here, as in Sussman, it is organizational weaknesses in the Histadrut, and specific limits to its control of the Palestinian and Israeli labor markets, that are most responsible for the Histadrut's defeat.

The need to examine variations in the strength of institutional resistance to market pressures is illustrated by the contrast between the Histadrut's failure to deal effectively with the problem of hired labor in the worker cooperatives and the relative success that has been achieved by the kibbutzim in dealing with this problem. The kibbutzim have also been tempted to make use of hired labor (Viteles, 1967; Daniel, 1975; Leviatan, 1980; Ben-Ner and Neuberger, 1982; Rosner and Tannenbaum, 1987) and have also incurred the wrath of the Histadrut when they have done so.

But the members of the kibbutzim have always been more strongly committed to labor Zionism than have the members of the worker cooperatives, and the kibbutzim therefore have a resistance to the use of hired labor that is deeply rooted and home-grown, rather than emanating solely or even primarily from the Histadrut. Because their movement is older and more prestigious than the Histadrut, the kibbutzim have also never been dominated by it; in fact, the path of influence has generally run the other way around, as the kibbutzim have tended to be overrepresented, rather than underrepresented, in the highest councils of the Histadrut (Perlmutter, 1957, 1970). The kibbutzim, most importantly, have produced their own set of autonomous and powerful federations, and these federations rather than the Histadrut have played the leading role in keeping down the use of hired labor on the kibbutzim (Leviatan, 1980; Rosner and Tannenbaum, 1987).

In addition to having a stronger home-grown consensus that use of hired labor must be restrained, the kibbutzim have also benefited from having an ownership structure that minimizes the temptation to make use of hired labor and that gives their federations real teeth. The ownership rights that the kibbutz members signed over to the Chevrat Ovdim subsidiary Nir in 1926 have in practice been exercised by the kibbutz federations (Rosner, 1991b). The importance of conferring such leverage on these central regulatory authorities was well recognized by the kibbutz movement's leaders, at the time when they were agreeing to transfer their assets to Nir. Shaul Avigur of Kibbutz Kinneret wrote in 1926 that until the assets of the kibbutzim would be reassigned to such central bodies,

> the social and Zionist principles of our settlements were not imbued in their economic structure. They depend only on the personal loyalty and moral conviction of the members. As long as we do not imprint these social principles on the economic structure of our settlements, the danger will remain (Shapiro, 1976, pp. 133–34).

In the absence of any structural mechanisms comparable to those that tie the kibbutzim to the Chevrat Ovdim through Nir, the Histadrut's efforts to discourage the use of hired labor in the worker cooperatives have been forced to rely largely, in Avigur's words, "on the personal loyalty and moral conviction of the members" and on whatever influence the Histadrut could exert upon them. If the Histadrut is correct in its claims that the dedication of the members of the worker cooperatives to the ideal of cooperation was never particularly great, then the most remarkable fact about the figures in tables 3.1 and 3.2 may be not that the proportion of nonmember labor is currently so high, but that it remained relatively low for so long. This in turn suggests that the "human capital" in the worker cooperatives may never have been quite so unsuitable as the Histadrut perceived it to be. But the temptation to profit from the increasing use of hired labor continued to grow, and the structural relationship between the Histadrut and the Merkaz cooperatives in the end left it "helpless," as Daniel notes (1986, p. 22; 1989, p. 96), to prevent them from giving in to it.

That cooperatives in transportation have not joined in this trend appears to be due to another important institutional circumstance. Daniel notes that since the mid-1960s, "most efforts to limit hired labor were applied to this branch" (1989, p. 96). The Histadrut's efforts have focused on the bus cooperatives not only because they are the largest and most visible part of Israel's worker cooperative population, but also because this is the sector in which these efforts have had the greatest chance of success. Unlike the worker cooperatives in other fields, Israel's two giant but cooperatives continue to operate in a highly regulated environment and must continue to seek governmental approval for all rate increases. At the Histadrut's insistence, government negotiators have continued to take an interest in the proportion of hired labor within these cooperatives, keeping it at all times below the politically sensitive threshold of 50 percent.

This regulatory situation may also have had an impact on the bus cooperatives themselves that made them more receptive to these forms of pressure. The bus cooperatives are insulated by the rate-setting system from one of the most important incentives to use hired labor that operates in other cooperatives. Since, in the bus cooperatives, members' incomes are not determined by market mechanisms, but are instead set at the highest levels that regulators will tolerate, they are less influenced by the number of workers who share claims on the cooperatives' income, thus leaving members with weaker incentives to substitute nonmembers for members. In this respect the Israeli bus cooperatives are in a situation similar to that of the worker-owned scavenger companies of the San Francisco Bay area, which showed a similar tendency to maintain low proportions of hired labor for long periods of time (Russell, 1985a).

Their long association with the Histadrut has had one additional effect on all Israeli worker cooperatives that may now be acting to maintain high proportions of hired labor within these cooperatives instead of reducing them. The regulations of the Merkaz Hakooperatsia and its member cooperatives declare the Histadrut to be a part owner of all Israeli worker cooperatives, entitled to 25 percent of their assets in the event that a cooperative is dissolved. To avoid paying this penalty, many old Israeli cooperatives cling to their status as cooperatives, even though they have long since ceased to be cooperatives in all but name. Of the seventy-two cooperatives belonging to the Merkaz Hakooperatsia in 1989, for example, thirty-five lacked even the minimum of seven members required for initial registration as a cooperative under Israeli law. In the absence of Histadrut's capital stake in these cooperatives, many of them might long since have transformed themselves into conventionally owned firms and would thus already have been purged as they probably should have been from the cooperative rolls.

EFFECTS OF INDUSTRY AND SECTOR

While the influences just addressed are clearly of fundamental importance, there are also good reasons to ask whether the nature of work performed in a cooperative exerts an additional effect on the extent to which hired labor is used or the rapidity with which it is introduced. It has often been noted, for example, that labor-managed workplaces are much more widespread in some industries than in others. Russell (1985a, 1985b, 1991, 1993) has argued that the information costs, transaction costs, and agency costs associated with various work activities are important determinants not only of the prevalence and relative success of worker cooperatives in various industries, but also of the ease or difficulty with which hired labor can be introduced in them. The argument is that where labor activities can readily be controlled by conventional means, it is relatively easy to substitute hired labor for the work of members, and the performance of the cooperative will not suffer as a result. Where work is difficult to supervise and involves rare skills, on the other hand, membership in a cooperative may be the most effective way to motivate and retain a labor force, and hired labor can be introduced only at a significant cost in performance.

In Israel, similar points have been used by Oppenheimer (1896), Preuss (1960), and others to argue that cooperative production is inherently better suited to agriculture than to industry. The reason for this, in the words of Preuss, is that

> agricultural enterprises can be expanded only by dint of intensified labour. In industrial plants, on the other hand, including Co-operatives, expansion and a position on the market are achieved mainly by mechanization and rationalization and other methods which are intrinsically "anti-Cooperative." Now, an enterprise based on "intensive" labour has greater chances of preserving its Co-operative character than a plant growing by extensive methods, intrinsically conflicting with Co-operative ways (1960, p. 198).

Efforts to test such notions in this study are hampered by a lack of direct information about the specific work activities performed in each Israeli cooperative. We do, however, have data about the distribution of cooperatives across major industrial groups. We have located information about the average use of hired labor within each industrial category for the years 1958 and 1984, and have data about industrial affiliation and the use of hired labor within each individual cooperative in the population for the years 1933 and 1989. The means and variability of the use of hired labor by industry in these years are shown in tables 3.3 and 3.4.

In general, the results in these tables provide little support for the expectation that the speed and prevalence with which hired labor is introduced are significantly different from one industry to another. They do far more to suggest that the forces inducing these cooperatives to make use of hired labor have been virtually universal and have affected almost all of these cooperatives in about the same way.

A few exceptions to this generalization deserve some additional comments. The industry group that most stands out as significantly different from the others by virtue of its relatively low use of hired labor is passenger transport. In 1989, this group consisted of the two bus cooperatives plus a taxi cooperative in Jerusalem called Nesher Tours. Egged had 4,692 members and 3,400 nonmembers; Dan employed 1,811 members and 1,508 hired laborers; and Nesher Tours had 58 members and only 8 hired workers. This group thus constitutes the only significant category

TABLE 3.3

Use of Hired Laborers by Sector and Industry, 1933, 1958, 1984, and 1989[a]

Industry	1933			1958			1984			1989		
	Co-ops	Labor Force	Percent Hired	Co-ops	Labor Force	Percent Hired	Co-ops	Labor Force	Percent Hired	Co-ops	Labor Force	Percent Hired
Transportation	15	527	13.5	3	6,463	45.8	10	14,635	44.6	10	12,132	44.2
Passenger Transport	11	450	11.5	3	6,463	45.8	3	13,776	43.0	3	11,477	42.8
Motor Freight	3	55	12.7				7	859	70.5	7	655	67.5
Service	14	179	27.4	48	1,268	42.0	24	2,345	83.8	25[b]	2,037	92.4
Meat, Ice, Oil	2	27	12.0	12	418	12.9	5	107	58.9	4[b]	75	52.0
Restaurants, Hotels	4	67	23.9	4	250	72.4	3	187	85.6	3[b]	27	63.0
Schools, Theaters				8	118	39.8	3	68	58.8	5	124	69.4
Laundries				6	99	57.6	2	41	85.4	2	58	89.7
Port, Sailing, Fishing	2	15	0.0	3	102	47.1				3	113	78.8
Garages				3	73	63.0						
Refuse Collection				4	43	27.9						
Other Service	6	70	42.9	8	165	52.7	11	1,942	85.9	5[b]	1,640	97.6
Production	23	264	25.0	150	3,613	51.1	46	2,522	75.6	37[b]	2,089	83.7
Baking	3	16	8.0	48	606	31.8	8	463	74.9	5[b]	387	87.9
Woodworking	5	40	5.0	16	325	56.0	9	191	61.3	8[b]	183	76.5
Printing, Paper	3	86	16.3	12	335	54.6	8	205	77.1	8	172	79.7
Metal, Electrical	5	80	46.3	22	989	68.3	8	1,040	81.7	6	811	82.7
Building Materials	5	34	14.7	6	144	45.1	5	328	80.2	6	325	84.9
Sand, Cement, Drill				8	299	31.8	5	252	52.8	2	126	85.7
Textiles				7	79	39.2	1	8	37.5	1	6	33.3
Food Processing	1	4	25.0	8	74	29.7	2	45	77.8	1	79	94.9
Leather, Shoes				9	165	52.7						
Chemicals				4	47	40.0						
Other Production	1	4	0.0	10	550	53.8						

[a] 1933: Cooperative Center (1933); 1958: Cooperative Center (1960); 1984: Daniel (1989); 1989: Cooperative Center.

[b] The number of cooperatives reporting labor force statistics for 1989 are: Service Sector (20); Meat, Ice, Oil (3); Restaurants, Hotels (2); Other Services (3); Production Sector (35); Baking (4); Woodworking (7).

TABLE 3.4

Variability in Use of Hired Laborers by Sector and Industry, 1933 and 1989[a]

Industry	1933					1989				
	Co-ops	Minimum	Maximum	Mean	Median	Co-ops	Minimum	Maximum	Mean	Median
Transportation	15	0.0	54.5	13.5	11.1	10	12.1	83.5	44.2	49.7
Passenger Transport	11	0.0	53.3	11.5	10.4	3	12.1	45.4	42.8	42.0
Motor Freight	3	7.1	33.3	12.7	11.1	7	26.1	83.5	67.5	71.4
Service	14	0.0	64.3	27.4	25.8	25[b]	33.3	99.4	92.4	73.0
Meat, Ice, Oil	2	4.8	33.3	12.0	19.0	4[b]	33.3	72.7	52.0	44.7
Restaurants, Hotels	4	18.8	26.7	23.9	24.0	3[b]	41.7	80.0	63.0	60.8
Schools, Theaters	0					5	36.4	90.5	69.4	69.4
Laundries	2	0.0	0.0	0.0	0.0	2	88.2	91.7	89.7	90.9
Port, Sailing, Fishing	0					3	37.5	84.4	78.8	78.7
Other Service	6	0.0	64.3	42.9	45.9	8[b]	52.0	99.4	97.6	96.0
Production	23	0.0	75.0	25.0	9.1	37[b]	14.3	94.9	83.7	72.7
Baking	3	0.0	0.0	0.0	0.0	5[b]	66.7	93.8	87.9	86.7
Woodworking	5	0.0	16.7	5.0	0.0	8[b]	38.5	88.9	76.5	66.7
Printing, Paper	3	8.1	26.3	16.3	9.1	8	42.9	87.5	79.7	73.9
Metal, Electrical	5	42.9	75.0	46.3	44.8	8	25.0	90.9	82.7	70.2
Building Materials	5	0.0	33.3	14.7	14.3	6	40.0	90.9	84.9	71.7
Sand, Cement, Drill	0					6	14.3	89.9	85.7	52.1
Textiles	0					2	33.3	33.3	33.3	33.3
Food Processing	1	25.0	25.0	25.0	25.0	1	94.9	94.9	94.9	94.9
Other Production	1	0.0	0.0	0.0	0.0					
Total	55	0.0	75.0	19.1	16.7	72[b]	12.1	99.4	55.3	71.4

[a]1933: Cooperative Center (1933); 1989: Cooperative Center.

[b]The Number of cooperatives reporting labor force statistics for 1989 are: All Sectors (65); Service Sector (20); Meat, Ice, Oil (3); Restaurants, Hotels (2); Other Services (3); Production Sector (35); Baking (4); Woodworking (7).

in which the proportion of hired labor remains below 50 percent in every cooperative.

There are good reasons for thinking that this may indeed be a "nature of work" effect. In their classic article on information costs, Alchian and Demsetz (1972) mentioned vehicle drivers as an archetypal case of an occupation whose work is difficult to monitor and who therefore often own their own equipment due to the failure of conventional ownership arrangements to control their work effectively. In studies of worker-owned scavenger firms and taxi cooperatives, Russell (1985a) noted that dealing with the public beyond the watchful eyes of employers is another work activity that is difficult to control by conventional means and that gives competitive advantages to firms that rely on worker ownership to control their labor force.

These arguments are attractive, but should not be pushed too far. In the case of the bus cooperatives, we still suspect that the institutional constraints to which they have been subjected have played the greater role in keeping their use of hired labor down. Also, if the operation of vehicles always keeps the proportion of hired labor down, this effect should show up in other industries in which this is the predominant work. In the trucking cooperatives, however, the use of hired labor is substantially higher than it is in the bus cooperatives, although it remains lower than the average for cooperatives in other fields.

Cooperatives that deliver meat, ice, and oil or that specialize in sand and cement are other groups of cooperatives in which workers operate vehicles and may deal directly with customers and in which the use of hired labor is unusually low; but the cooperatives in these groups are so few and so diverse that we hesitate to generalize about them. The cooperatives that deliver meat, for example, are made up primarily of butchers, not truck drivers. Visits to two of these cooperatives (Ichud-Igud and Raanan) in early 1990 suggested that in these organizations, the activity that makes it most important for workers to be members is the cutting away of a hide. Many workers may handle a carcass before the skin is completely removed, and if one of them puts a nick in the hide, its resale value as shoe leather is greatly reduced. Since a good hide at that time was worth as much as 120 NIS, while poor hides were yielding as little as 70 to 80 NIS each, this fact alone made the butchers consider it prudent for everyone who did this work to be motivated by a share of the profits. They also noted that the meat itself and internal organs had to be handled with nearly equal care.

One man at Ichud-Igud added that the work of his cooperative was inherently "group work" that therefore required group incentives. As he explained this point,

> When I start the work, I hand it over to another. I depend on the person before me to do the work well, and the person after me. It's not like [the Charles Chaplin film] *Modern Times.* Here it's not measures. . . . No one cow is the same as another. You have to do a certain kind of job that goes with this cow. Sometimes you can't make the same cuts. It's like a football team. You can't take twenty-six individuals, that would lead to chaos. We hired a skilled professional, but he couldn't work with the team. With our group, everyone knows the other one, including the weak points of each.

These remarks are of course very consistent with the arguments of Alchian and Demsetz and others who claim that difficulties in the metering of team production are among the most important causes of such group-based incentives as profit sharing and professional partnerships (Alchian and Demsetz, 1972; Williamson, 1981).

Turning to industries in which the introduction of hired labor was particularly rapid or pronounced, only the cooperatives that manufacture metal and electrical products stand out. The use of hired labor in these cooperatives was substantially higher than in other cooperatives in both 1933 and 1958. Only in the 1980s did the other cooperatives catch up to them in the extent to which they engage in this practice. It is tempting to infer from this record that these metal fabricating cooperatives came closest to Preuss's (1960) image of factory production, in which work is more intensive of capital than of labor effort and in which the workplace is readily controlled in a centralized manner by machinery and supervisors.

Variations among Organizations

In analyses not shown here, but reported in Russell and Hanneman (1994), we used data about individual firms in 1933 and 1989 to explore the extent to which the use of hired labor within Israeli cooperatives is affected by characteristics of individual cooperatives, such as their size, age, and capital requirements. The expectations that guided this study were that the relative share of hired labor within a cooperative would be a positive function of each of these three influences.

The idea that increases in firm size should be associated with an increasing use of hired labor could be derived from the work of a number of theorists, including Ben-Ner (1984) and Miyazaki (1984). One of the oldest bodies of theory that points toward this conclusion is the work of Max Weber. In his classic discussions of the preconditions for "direct democracy," Weber insisted that such a form of decision making could only be shared among a "limited . . . number of members" and that a "social alienation of the members . . . occurs when the group grows beyond a certain size" (1968, pp. 949, 951). Additional reasons why increasing size might lead to a growing use of hired labor can be derived from other portions of Weber's work. For Weber, the broadest and most general consequence of size in organizations of all types is that it promotes bureaucratization. A fundamental part of this process of bureaucratization is the development of an ever more elaborate division of labor. The constant proliferation of new and more specialized work activities can be expected to promote the increasing use of hired labor in any cooperative organizations in which memberships are reserved for practitioners of a single occupation or a narrow range of jobs. As we have already seen, this is the case in most Israeli worker cooperatives, as a result of their practice of compensating members with equal pay and of employing as nonmembers workers who possess greater or lesser skills.

The idea that the advancing age of cooperative organizations also contributes to the restriction of memberships within them can be associated with so-called "life-cycle" models of cooperative degeneration, such as those of Batstone (1983) and Meister (1984). Common to these models is the notion that these organizations have tendencies to lose their ideological fervor over time, gradually routinize their internal practices, and come more and more to imitate the structures of the more conventional organizations that surround them.

In considering the effects of advancing age on worker cooperatives, one must take into account not only the age of the organization itself, but also the ages of its individual members. Many worker cooperatives are founded by youthful members who in the beginning perform all of the manual labor themselves. As the founders age, they often move into managerial positions and feel they have ever less in common with the younger hired laborers who now perform all of the manual work. Older members are also likely to become increasingly preoccupied with the need to make preparations for retirement, to reap gains from their past capital investments in their firms, and in general to earn as much income as possible from their membership before they have to give them up.

Empirical evidence that worker cooperatives have a tendency to make increasing use of nonmember labor as they advance in age has been reported by Russell (1985a) for taxi cooperatives and worker-owned scavenger firms and by Craig and Pencavel (1992) for the plywood cooperatives of the Pacific Northwest. A study of French worker cooperatives by Estrin and Jones (1992) also reported that the proportion of hired labor increased with age, but this was found to be true only over the first forty-five years of a cooperative's existence; thereafter, the proportion of hired labor fell in response to further increases in age. This latter finding is consistent with Batstone's (1983) model of the effects of age on worker cooperatives, which holds that the increasing degeneration of democratic workplaces eventually gives rise to periods of "regeneration." Because both Batstone and Estrin and Jones were basing their conclusions on studies of French worker cooperatives, however, it is possible that the curvilinear effect of age observed by these researchers might be due to unique features of the history, structures, or institutional environment of these French worker cooperatives. Among the Israeli worker cooperatives, Russell and Hanneman (1994) tested only for linear effects of age. This was due primarily to the limited number of cases with which these predictions could be tested; but given the fact that, as late as 1989, the median age of the Israeli worker cooperatives was only 38.5 years, it also seems unlikely that these alleged curvilinear effects of age would have had enough time to make themselves felt, even if there had been a sufficient number of cases to make it possible to test for them.

Russell and Hanneman (1994) also made an effort to measure the effects of capital on the use of hired labor in these cooperatives. Capital accumulation has long been viewed as a major contributor to the use of hired labor in worker cooperatives, for reasons that have already been discussed. Increases in the amount of capital per member have been alleged to create additional incentives to seek to profit from hired labor and to make it more difficult for hired workers to finance purchases of memberships. Oppenheimer, Preuss, Russell, and others have also viewed growing capital intensity as promoting changes in the work of a cooperative that facilitate centralized supervision and thereby make it less necessary for workers to be members.

Attempts to measure the effects of capital among the Israeli worker cooperatives suffered from limits in the availability of data. For both 1933 and 1989, data on capital per member could be located for only a minority of the cooperatives. For 1933, data on capital per member were available for only seventeen out of fifty-five cooperatives. In that year, this measure ranged from a low of just 80 IL in a service cooperative to a high of 4,000 IL in one of the bus cooperatives; the median value was 675 IL. For the 1989 sample, the nearest year for which data on capital could be located was 1984. These data were taken from an appendix to the initial draft of Daniel (1989) that was not included in the published version of this work. This source provided information on capital per member for nineteen of the seventy-two cooperatives described in table 3.4. These later figures on capital were given in U.S. dollars, and ranged from a low $5,000 in the cooperative Hatik that produced cardboard cartons in Haifa to a high of $100,000 in the cooperative Hagal that provided port services in that same city.

Despite these limits in sample sizes and the availability of data, Russell and Hanneman obtained results that were generally consistent with the predictions that increases in the size, age, or capital of a worker cooperative make that cooperative more likely to make use of hired labor. Differences in size among Israeli worker cooperatives appeared to be having only weak and mixed effects on the use of hired labor in 1933, but had strongly positive and statistically significant effects in a wide range of industries in 1989. That the effects of size were stronger and more consistent in 1989 than in 1933 seemed attributable to the fact that there was a much greater variation in size among Israeli worker cooperatives in 1989 than in 1933. The effects of a cooperative's age on the tendency to use hired labor was significantly positive in both the manufacturing and service sectors in 1933 and in the service sector only in 1989. In the other sectors, the effects of age also appeared to be positive, but fell short of statistical significance. Capital per member had no significant effects on the use of hired labor in 1933, but in 1989 it did appear to be exerting the expected positive effect. This positive effect of capital in 1989 was statistically significant both in the transportation sector and in the full sample.

While the effects of size, age, and capital were as predicted in almost all cases in which they were statistically significant, the failure of these effects to attain statistical significance in many instances is a sign of the relative weakness of these effects. Tables 3.2 through 3.4 in themselves also suggest that all of these individual differences among worker cooperatives were of far less importance in determining the share of hired labor within them than changes that took place between 1933 and 1989 in the Israeli worker cooperative population as a whole. If one searches for a single piece of information that would make it possible to predict with greatest accuracy the proportion of hired labor in any Israeli worker cooperative, the most important issue would be not which cooperative, but which era in the history of this population. Almost all Israeli worker cooperatives made little use of hired labor in the 1920s and early 1930s, and almost all of them had predominantly hired labor forces in the 1970s and 1980s. These facts thus underline the importance of the institutional influences that received their organizational expression in the changing relationship between the Merkaz Hakooperatsia and the Histadrut.

Similar lessons emerged from a study by Rosner and Tannenbaum (1987) of the effects of organizational characteristics on several measures of the degeneration of workplace democracy in a sample of forty-nine kibbutzim. The dependent variables in that study included the degree of member participation in assemblies and the frequency of leadership turnover, as well as the use of hired labor within the factories operated by these kibbutzim. Independent variables included both the size and age of each kibbutz and the percent of each kibbutz's income that it derived from industry. The authors found that rotation of leaders was significantly reduced by all three independent variables. Participation in assemblies also appeared to be negatively affected by each of the three variables, although these effects were statistically significant only in the case of age and industrialization. In the case of the use of hired labor, however, the authors found a significant effect for only one of these variables, a positive association between the use of hired labor and the extent of industrialization. This finding is consistent with Oppenheimer's views about the greater suitability of agriculture than industry for cooperative production. But the authors found that the use of hired labor within the factories of these kibbutzim was being more strongly affected by a different variable, the federation that each kibbutz was affiliated with. Kibbutzim associated with Kibbutz Artzi (the National Kibbutz federation) were significantly less likely to use hired labor in their factories than were the kibbutzim aligned with two other federations, Kibbutz Meuchad (the United Kibbutz federation) and Ichud Hakvutzot Vehakibbutzim (Union of Kvutzot and Kibbutzim).

In a similar study, Leviatan (1980) examined data for all kibbutzim in all three of these federations in the late 1980s, the same time period in which Rosner and Tannenbaum's (1987) data were collected. Those more complete data indicate that the use of hired labor in the factories of kibbutzim in the Meuchad federation was actually rather similar to that of the factories of Kibbutz Artzi. It was the kibbutzim of the looser and more decentralized Ichud federation that stood out most from both. In 1978, for example, the percentage of hired labor was 16 percent in Kibbutz Artzi, 21 percent in Kibbutz Meuchad, and 59 percent in Ichud. All three federations appeared at the time to be conducting aggressive campaigns to discourage the use of hired labor, with the result that the percentage of hired labor had been falling in all three federations in almost every year since 1970. Leviatan therefore joined Rosner and Tannenbaum in concluding that the ideologically inspired resistance put up by each kibbutz federation against the use of hired labor was a much stronger influence in fighting this practice than any individual organizational characteristics that were measured in either of these studies.

CONCLUSIONS

Many elements of the story told in this chapter are already quite familiar to most Israelis. That Israeli worker cooperatives have a tendency to make increasing use of hired labor is one of their best-known features. It is also well known that both the Histadrut and the government have often reproached the worker cooperatives for this practice and that the worker cooperatives have been less successful than the kibbutzim in keeping their dependence on hired labor in check.

There are important ways, however, in which the analysis provided here contradicts perceptions of this phenomenon that are widely shared in Israel. For example, although the bus cooperatives have received more persistent criticism for the use of hired labor than any other Israeli worker cooperatives, we have shown here that they actually make less use of hired labor than all but a few others. Their relative success in limiting the use of hired labor is even more remarkable when the large size and advanced age of these cooperatives are taken into account.

Another way in which this account departs from many widespread impressions is in the causes to which the increasing use of hired labor is ascribed. Both the Histadrut and many other critics have often been most inclined to attribute the worker cooperatives' growing dependence on hired labor to a moral weakness among their members. In the Histadrut's view, for example, the moral fiber of the cooperatives' founders was deficient from the start; if they had been more strongly committed to the goals of Zionism and of socialism, they would have avoided these petit bourgeois structures entirely and would instead have either sought employment in a Chevrat Ovdim-owned enterprise or gone to work on a kibbutz. Then over time, the cooperators' weak loyalties to Zionism and socialism were allegedly further eroded by the dependence on capitalist profits, with the result that the cooperators gradually transformed themselves into a full-fledged exploiting class.

This is a common assessment of the Israeli worker cooperatives, not only within the Histadrut, but among the Israeli public. But it is most unfair to the members of these worker cooperatives, because it attaches far too much importance to their moral character. It contains within it a profoundly utopian and voluntaristic view of the bases of socialism, equality, workplace democracy, and all similar aims. It implies that if we would all just be good enough, we could somehow wish ourselves to an ideal economic state.

In our view, the more important failing that is reflected in this story was in making the fate of these cooperatives so highly dependent on their members' moral character in the first place. Cooperation can never survive if it is based on altruism alone. Cooperative structures cannot hold out indefinitely in defiance of their members' own self-interest. This lesson has been incorporated into the structures of the kibbutzim, which vest the ownership of kibbutz assets in the kibbutz federations as a whole, in the Chevrat Ovdim through Nir, and in the Jewish National Fund. If the kibbutz, that most morally elite of institutions, does not make the mistake of basing itself on its members' altruism alone, how could Israel's worker cooperative movement have been expected to succeed with such a strategy?

We thus share the view of Franz Oppenheimer that as worker cooperatives are most commonly structured, the increasing use of hired labor within them "is not a moral transgression, but rather

. . . the natural consequence of a law" (1896, p. 44, translated in Preuss, 1960, p. 196). But it would also be a great oversimplification to attribute the increasing use of hired labor in the Israeli worker cooperatives solely to the economic motivations that are featured in the work of Oppenheimer, Ben-Ner, and other theorists whose views were discussed above. Economic incentives and internal structures cannot be asked to do all the work of explaining this transformation, as they differ little from one time period to another. They apply persistent pressures toward the use of hired labor throughout the time span under review and therefore cannot help us to understand why the Israeli worker cooperatives should have been more successful at resisting these pressures in one period than another.

Changes in economic conditions, similarly, appear to have had an important influence on the use of hired labor in at least some time periods, but also cannot help to answer the question of why the use of hired labor should be so much greater in recent years than it was in the time of the Mandate. In the case of this economic influence, the problem is not that it has been uniform, but that it has fluctuated throughout the period under review and therefore provides no net trend.

The key to the transformation that occurred in the Israeli worker cooperatives over this period must be sought in something that changed between the early and late portions of this time span. This underlines the importance once again of the worker cooperatives' relationship to the Histadrut. It is this factor that changed more than any other during the period under review and whose influence is most clearly perceptible in the statistical record shown in tables 3.1 and 3.2. It was the Histadrut that left the worker cooperatives so heavily dependent on the ideological commitment of their members, when it decided to withhold financial support from them and when it chose moral suasion as its chief instrument for dealing with them. From this light, the most remarkable thing about the relationship between the worker cooperatives and the Histadrut is not that these moral weapons ultimately failed, but that they succeeded for so long. And they might have achieved even greater results had the Histadrut not lost interest in the worker cooperatives in the 1960s and left them to their fate.

In sum, the tendency of worker cooperatives to use hired labor should be viewed not as a moral failing, but as a result of a number of economic and sociological processes that we are increasingly able to understand and in at least some cases to resist. But the inability of the Histadrut either to understand or to prevent this practice served as a constant irritant in its relationship to the worker cooperatives and eventually became the most prominent cause of the delegitimation of these cooperatives, both in the eyes of the Histadrut and of the society at large.

In this context, the growing use of hired labor in the Israeli worker cooperatives can be taken as a barometer of the institutional decline not only of the worker cooperatives in particular, but of the Histadrut's entire labor economy in general. Indirect evidence for this was provided in chapter 2, and more will be said about this theme in chapter 5. But much can be inferred from the evidence of this chapter alone. The Histadrut may never have understood the use of hired labor in worker cooperatives very well, but in the early decades of this history it had both the will and the means to keep the practice in check. In later decades, on the other hand, it lost the stomach to keep up this fight. The Histadrut's surrender on this issue is probably due in part to the Histadrut's loss of interest in the worker cooperatives as they shrank into insignificance, but it also seems at least partly attributable to a gradual decline in the Histadrut's own moral influence, economic power, and political clout. Insofar as a failure of commitment is at work here, it can be charged as much to the Histadrut as to the worker cooperatives themselves.

The story told here is thus similar in a number of ways to Sussman's (1969, 1973) analysis of the failure of the Histadrut's efforts to maintain minimum standards for the wages of Jewish workers in the time of the Yishuv. In both cases, the Histadrut's institutional initiatives were overwhelmed by market forces, and in both cases, specific weaknesses in the organizational weapons available to the Histadrut in battling these market forces appear to bear a good part of the blame. But the histories of these policies seem different in one important respect. In Sussman's account, it is market forces that were ultimately triumphant and that determined the final outcome. Here, it appears to have been a change in the Histadrut's own attitudes and priorities that did most to give market forces free reign.

The interplay of economic and institutional forces that we have observed in both chapter 2 and chapter 3 thus serves to underline how truly "utopian" has been the effort to create and preserve a population of worker cooperatives in Israel. It is inherently utopian to seek to impose value-based organizational solutions on economic choices. That attempt in itself creates a heavy dependence on institutional forces. The effort worked for a time, when the Jewish settlement in Palestine was literally "utopia," or "nowhere"—a land without capitalism, without much of an economy of any kind. But as this "nowhere" became "somewhere," as capitalism has developed in Israel and has come to play a role there more similar to the one it plays in other lands, institutional support for alternatives to capitalism in that country has correspondingly declined. As both the Histadrut and the Israeli public have alike grown less interested in the formation and preservation of worker cooperatives, the birthrates of worker cooperatives have declined, and the use of hired labor in the remaining worker cooperatives has increased.

4. DEMOCRACY AND OLIGARCHY IN ISRAELI WORKER COOPERATIVES

After the use of hired labor, the issue that has done most to damage the reputations of the Israeli worker cooperatives has been the relationship between their elected leaders and the rank-and-file members. This has been especially true of the two bus cooperatives, Egged and Dan. The very size and prominence of these organizations might in themselves have attracted the frequent attention of the press; but Israel's bus cooperatives have drawn much more than their fair share of notoriety by allowing their internal politics to erupt into scandalous headlines on numerous occasions. In-groups and out-groups have filed lawsuits and made charges of criminal conduct, as successive sets of present, former, or would-be leaders have accused their rivals of incompetence, corruption, and abuses of power.

These internal problems of the most prominent Israeli cooperatives raise old and general questions about whether democratic workplaces can govern themselves at all, and whether democratic management, if achievable even for a short term, can be made to last. England's Fabian socialists Sidney and Beatrice Webb, for example, gave emphatically negative answers to both of these questions. After researching the history of worker cooperatives in nineteenth-century Britain, they offered the following pessimistic conclusion:

The relationship set up between a manager who has to give orders all day to his staff, and the members of that staff who, sitting as a committee of management, criticize his actions in the evening, has been found by experience to be an impossible one (1920, p. 72).

The Webbs also asserted flatly that "All such associations of producers that start as alternatives to the capitalist system either fail or cease to be democracies of producers" (1920, p. 29).

For many theorists, such discouraging assessments of the long-term prospects for democracy in modern workplaces have been linked to more broadly pessimistic views about the future of democracy in any form. For Michels (1962), the inevitable demise of democracy was preordained by his famous "iron law of oligarchy," which results from the increasing differentiation of leaders from rank-and-file members in any democratic organization. "Who says organization," wrote Michels, "says oligarchy" (1962, p. 365). Weber expressed similar views in his discussion of the processes that cause "direct democratic administration" to turn into "rule by notables" (1968, pp. 950–52). Meister (1984, chapter 7) has posited a four-stage model of the degeneration of democracy in organizations, which he sees as applicable to democratic associations of all types, including worker cooperatives in France, Israeli kibbutzim and moshavim, and Yugoslav self-managed firms.

Empirical support for such pessimistic views has come from studies of workplace democracy in many contexts. Tendencies toward increasingly oligarchical decision making have been observed in workers' council in Yugoslavia and Western Europe (Rus, 1970; Obradovic, 1975; Hartmann, 1979), in Israeli kibbutzim (Etzioni, 1958; Ben-Rafael, 1976, 1988), and in worker cooperatives (Shirom, 1972; Russell, 1985a). In his survey of the history of industrial cooperatives in the United States, Shirom concluded that "a relatively permanent managerial stratum emerged in almost every cooperative shop which endured long enough for this inevitable process to take place" (1972, p. 545).

Many empirical researchers join Weber in attributing the perceived oligarchical tendencies of democratic workplaces to organizational size and to the increasingly elaborate division of labor that organizational growth gives rise to. Some observers of labor unions have reported, for example, that decision making in these organizations appears to become more oligarchical as these organizations grow in size (e.g., Pierson, 1948; Marcus, 1966). Studies of professional group practices in the United States have reported similarly that as these firms become larger, they tend to develop more hierarchical authority structures and are increasingly inclined to delegate authority for many key decisions to specialized offices or committees (Kralewski, Pitt, and Shatin, 1985; Tolbert and Stern, 1991a, 1991b).

This growing accumulation of arguments and evidence regarding the inevitability of increasing oligarchy in democratic workplaces has not gone entirely unchallenged. On the general issue of the feasibility of democracy in contemporary societies, the political scientist Robert Dahl (1961) has suggested that "pluralism" is the term that best describes the kind of decision making that is practiced in modern democracies. In Dahl's "pluralist" model of democratic decision making, a growing differentiation between leaders and followers is not necessarily incompatible with democracy, provided that there is meaningful competition between aspiring elites and democratic participation in the choice of elites. Among organizational theorists, Tannenbaum (1968) has contributed the notion that decision making in organizations is not always a zero-sum game; participation by specialized managers and by rank-and-file workers need not be in conflict, as both can be incorporated into a larger and more comprehensive decision-making process. In an effort to craft a general theory of "membership-controlled organizations," Collins (1975, pp. 329–40) suggests that the opposition between democracy and oligarchy in these organizations should be viewed not as a dichotomy, but as a continuum. In Collins's view, such influences as growing size and advancing age are acknowledged to increase the influence of leaders over rank-and-file members in any membership-controlled organization, but are not seen as causing these organizations to lose their democratic character entirely.

Empirical studies of democracy in the workplace have also occasionally cast additional doubt on the inevitability of Michels's (1962) "iron law," by identifying limits and exceptions to it. The best known of these studies is Lipset, Trow, and Coleman's (1956) classic analysis of the International Typographical Union (ITU). These authors emphasized two factors that appeared to help make the democratic character of this union unusually long-lived. The first was the nature of work performed by these printers. The work itself made the membership of this union unusually well-read, while their unconventional working hours isolated them from others, thereby helping to create a distinct occupational community that promoted a rich and vocal public opinion within the union. The second major factor that helped to maintain democracy in the ITU was the presence of a two-party system within the union. This guaranteed that the rank-and-file membership always contained a dissident minority of past and future leaders who had both the motivation and the skills required to mount effective challenges to the authority of any existing leadership group.

This search for exceptions to the iron law of oligarchy has born fruit within the literature on worker cooperatives as well. In a study of worker cooperatives in France, Batstone (1983) observed that while oligarchical tendencies certainly do arise in these firms, they are often countered by reactions from the rank and file, which reassert the democratic nature of these firms and which may also lead to the creation of new institutions that put democracy in these workplaces on a stronger footing than it had known before. Similar instances of rank-and-file revolts have been observed in a variety of democratic workplaces located in the United States (Russell, 1985a). In democratic workplaces, as in labor unions (e.g., Nyden, 1985), these rank-and-file revolts are often reform movements, which not only result in leadership turnover, but also reinterpret and revitalize the democratic traditions of the firm.

The purpose of the present chapter is to assess the applicability of Michels's iron law and of the pessimistic views of the Webbs to the worker cooperatives of contemporary Israel. It is based on interviews and archival materials obtained from fifteen of these organizations (table 4.1). This constitutes about a fifth of the population of worker cooperatives in Israel in 1990, the year in which these data were collected. Sampling for this survey was not random, but systematic, as special efforts were made to include all of the largest (Egged and Dan) and most historic (Haargaz, Dfus Achdut) cooperatives in this population. Other cooperatives were selected in order to provide coverage of a broad range of industries, sizes, and ages. For convenience in data collection, all but one of these cooperatives (Namlit) were located within the vicinity of Tel Aviv. Data from seven cooperatives (Egged, Dan, Haargaz, Ichud-Igud,

Namlit, Shor, and Raanan) I collected myself, conducting interviews either in English or in Hebrew with the help of a translator.
Interviews at the remaining eight cooperatives were conducted in
Hebrew by students in labor studies at Tel Aviv University and
were later translated into English by Asaf Darr.

This analysis of the politics of these worker cooperatives will
disclose many signs of oligarchical degeneration in the overwhelming majority of them; but there is much in the behavior of
these cooperatives that is reminiscent of the work of Lipset, Trow,
and Coleman and of Batstone as well. Even in cooperatives in
which leaders hold their positions for long periods of time, they
often seem to do so only by being highly attentive to the wishes of
their rank-and-file constituents, not by disregarding them. And
while there are indeed critics who complain that there is too little
workplace democracy in the Israeli worker cooperatives, there are
others who feel that they have too much.

TABLE 4.1
Israeli Worker Cooperatives Included in Decision-Making Study

Cooperative	Activity	Year Formed	Members (1988)	Hired (1988)
Egged	Bus Service	1933	4,692	3,400
Dan	Bus Service	1945	1,811	1,508
Haargaz	Manufacture buses, office equipment	1933	120	600
Ichud-Igud	Slaughterhouse	1939	26	21
Mafiyah Achdut	Bakery	1934	24	170
Namlit	Tiles	1931	21	170
Hakoach	Trucking	1947	17	86
Kalid	Repair office equipment	1971	12	13
Shor	Music conservatory	1976	12	8
Retsef	Panels, building materials	1961	8	10
Dfus Achdut	Printer	1910	7	40
Raanan	Slaughterhouse	1962	6	16
Chomah	Building materials	1950	6	4
Galei Aviv	Laundry	1948	4	30
Dfus Klali	Printer	1958	4	5

THE POLITICS OF EGGED

By far the largest and most prominent of the Israeli worker cooperatives is the bus cooperative Egged, which provides most bus transportation in contemporary Israel. At the end of 1988, this single cooperative had 4,692 members and another 3,400 hired employees. The size, age, and complexity of this cooperative have helped to give it a rich and varied political life, and its importance to the country has caused its internal politics to be closely followed in the Israeli press. The evolution of the relationship between the leaders and rank-and-file members in this cooperative can best be understood by dividing its history into three major periods: a period of rising oligarchy, from the 1950s to the 1970s; a period of challenge to the traditional leadership and short-lived victory by an "alternative" leadership group in the mid-1970s; and a so-called period of "turnabout" (*mifne*), in which the previous leadership was returned to power.

The Rise of Oligarchy in Egged (1950s–1970s)

Egged became the giant it is today as a result of mergers among more than a dozen small to midsize cooperatives, some of which have roots that go back to the 1920s. The first company called Egged was formed in 1933, as a merger of four intercity bus cooperatives headquartered in and around Tel Aviv. In that same year, another group of cooperatives in the area immediately north of Tel Aviv came together to form the bus company United Sharon, which in 1942 was joined with Egged. Through a similar series of successive mergers in the 1940s in the North, five bus companies in the Haifa area were consolidated into the cooperative Shachar, which in 1951 was merged into Egged along with the Drom Yehuda cooperative from the South. Egged's final major acquisition was Hamekasher, in Jerusalem, which merged with Egged in 1961.

Already by the 1950s, this series of mergers had made Egged an extremely large company, and size itself helped to make the company's leadership increasingly remote from the rank-and-file members. It was no longer feasible for the membership even to come together to meet with or elect the leaders in one single place. Voting in Egged is conducted within geographical divisions, which continue to resemble the regional entities that had once operated independently (for example, Egged's five divisions at present cover Haifa and the North, the Sharon area, Tel Aviv, Jerusalem, and the

South). In Egged elections, voters meet within regions not to elect company leaders directly, but only to elect representatives to the governing council (vaad). By 1975, this council had swelled to 168 members. The primary function of this body was to elect a "management" (hanhalah) of forty-six members, which in turn selected a nine-man "secretariat" (maskirut).

It was this secretariat that actually governed Egged, and already by the middle of the 1950s, it had become a purely managerial body. Each of its nine members held a managerial job. Three were in charge of operations in the North, Center, and South; five handled such specialties as finance, maintenance, traffic, tourism, and external affairs; and the last was general manager of the company.

In the 1950s, there was still significant turnover in these positions, as a younger group who called themselves the Progressives contested the leadership of the company's pioneers and gradually replaced them. Once the Progressives' victory was complete, however, the company's managers tended to hold their offices for ever longer periods of time. This transition was not only de facto, but de jure as well, as the length of time between elections, which had at one time been as little as a single year, was increased first to two years and then to four.

Officers who spent years in office could generally count on reelection not only because of their experience and expertise, but also because of the favors they had dispensed. Michael Harrison, a political scientist at Bar-Ilan University, later wrote that Egged in this period had developed "a well-developed system of political patronage . . . in which an individual driver who was unhappy with his route assignments or vacation leave would feel free to take his grievance directly to the head of the cooperative or to some other member of the national administration" (1981, p. 5). Harrison also noted that another aspect of this patronage system was for victorious officeholders to reward "supporters and campaign activists with positions providing greater influence and financial reward" (1981, p. 3). In an interview given to the *Jerusalem Post* in 1972, the Chevrat Ovdim official responsible for relations with the bus cooperatives agreed that Egged members frequently pressured the management to give them white-collar jobs, with the result that there was "too much padding of administrative positions." This official added that "I just do not understand why so many of them want jobs. They prefer to do anything, even if it's only being a toilet inspector, rather than continue at the wheel" (Segel, 1972, p. B7).

That same *Jerusalem Post* article carried the charge that these processes had led the Egged leadership to become increasingly differentiated from the membership not only politically, but socially as well. The words of its author, Mark Segel, are worth quoting at length.

> When Egged was a relatively small business, there was a direct relationship between elected managers and members. Today, with the management sitting in the building on Derekh Petah Tikva, there is a sense among members that a managerial class is emerging. This is especially so because elections are held less frequently than they used to be. There are complaints of members of the Secretariat drawing away from the ordinary members, of a too high living standard, with telephones paid for, expense accounts and private cars.
>
> As one member put it, "They get out of touch with the rank and file. They mix with others in the managerial class in Israel. They start drinking whiskey, they drop Time cigarettes and move on to Marlboros. All we now have is a bureaucratic contact with our secretaries" (1972, p. B6).

The Challenge from an "Alternative" Leadership Group

These quotations from the *Jerusalem Post* are signs not only that there was a growing perception of oligarchy in Egged in 1972, but also that this perceived growth of oligarchy was in turn giving rise to dissent. Adding to the political significance of this dissent was the fact that Egged had a party system, as in Lipset, Trow, and Coleman's ITU (1956). And while the ITU had just two political parties, Egged in the 1970s had three factions (Kidum, Oz, and Shinui) that stood ready to capitalize on any errors that the Progressives might make. By 1975, these three factions had joined together in an alliance that called itself "The Alternative to Govern."

These parties within Egged had no formal connection to any national political movements and received no official recognition within Egged itself. Elections within Egged were organized as competitions among individual candidates and made no use of party lists. But in order to be a candidate for any office, it was necessary for a nomination to bear the signatures of forty or fifty other members, and it was around this process of nomination that factions tended to form.

Another noteworthy feature of Egged politics is that the governance and management of the company were sufficiently large and complex to provide experience in leadership to present and future dissidents, as well as to hard-core loyalists of the governing group. A veteran of Egged's internal struggles of the 1970s later commented to me that "a driver does not become top man without preparation; 'the revolution' does not come to people without experience."

The first rounds in Egged's impending "revolution" were fired in January of 1973, when leaders of the opposition published two circulars outlining their platform. They demanded higher wages, a shorter workweek, and increased fringe benefits. They also asserted that the company should stop spending so much money on perquisites for management, such as "expensive cars for company officers" (Oked, 1973).

By 1974 the opposition had begun to make allegations of corruption and mismanagement, and by 1975 they made an issue of the company's very structure itself. On the one hand, they felt that the company should be made more democratic and therefore demanded that elections should be held at least every two years and that terms of office should be limited. On the other hand, they wanted the administrative structure of the company to be made more professional and less an object of political patronage. They therefore advocated a greater use of outside consultants, of employee training programs, and of formalized criteria for selection and advancement.

Between 1974 and 1976, the leaders of the Progressives and of the Alternative waged a bitter struggle for the control of Egged. In 1972, the Progressives had been accused of trying to weaken the opposition by bringing several of its leaders into the national management and the secretariat itself. If this was indeed an effort at cooptation, it did not work, as in October 1974 two leaders of Kidum were summarily expelled from the secretariat after demanding an investigation of alleged corruption in the building of an Egged parking lot. These two leaders were also brought up on charges before an Egged internal court, having been accused of acting "in a disorderly fashion" in the office of the chairman. A number of other opposition leaders were suspended or hauled before Egged internal courts at about this same time for such infractions as "holding a press conference without permission" (Jerusalem Post, 1974a, 1974b).

In its efforts to counter these blows, the opposition sought help from outside, not only from the press, but also from the courts and the government. A court ruled in late October that the expulsion of two opposition leaders from the secretariat had been illegal, because the signatures of eight members of the management had not been obtained in order to call the special meeting at which this action had been taken; within days thereafter, they were expelled again at a legally called meeting. The opposition also took its complaints of corruption to such authorities as the police, the attorney general, and the controller of road transport. These appeals for outside intervention ultimately bore fruit, as in June of 1975 two Egged leaders were indicted for having bribed two Transport Ministry officials in 1971.

The opposition was also very energetic in this period in mobilizing the rank and file within Egged. A series of wildcat strikes led the leadership to hold early elections in May of 1975 and to preempt opposition demands for reform by offering its own plan for the reorganization of Egged. The Egged governing council was reduced in size from 168 to 120 members, and the management was cut from 46 to 30 members. The vote in that May election was very close, and for a time it appeared that the Alternative faction had narrowly won control of a split secretariat. Before long, however, the Oz faction had joined the Progressives in another narrow coalition, and Kidum was back in opposition. In January of 1976, opposition leaders obtained the signatures of nearly half of Egged's members on a petition that objected to a planned transfer of certain assets from the members back to the company so that they might be sold. They also encouraged complaints in that same month about the company's tardiness in paying December paychecks to members and employees.

For most of 1976, Egged was in such a state of political paralysis that it was virtually impossible to govern. In April of that year, the company's leaders resigned in disgust and asked the government to try to run the cooperative. At governmental insistence, a coalition of Progressive, Oz, and Kidum leaders was reluctantly formed, but this did not bring an end to the internal wrangling. In August of 1976, the governing council voted overwhelmingly to try to break this political deadlock by calling new elections. In that fall's elections, the Kidum faction gained undisputed leadership in Egged and was at last free to implement its program.

Some of the Kidum leaders' first steps were efforts to put Egged's finances on a more secure footing. They closed down unprofitable routes, ended the policy of giving free rides to soldiers, negotiated a new loan from the government, and paid the import taxes on some new buses that had been impounded for failure to pay these duties.

The Kidum leaders also implemented many of the reforms that had been major platforms in their campaign. The period between elections was shortened from four years to two. They established a variety of training programs and brought in consultants to help them improve the company's administration. One reform that resulted was a decentralization of line responsibility for routing, scheduling, and maintenance to the managers of three major geographic divisions (North, South, and Jerusalem). Another major initiative was a formalization of procedures for making route assignments, approving transfers, leaves, and expenditures, and selecting and promoting personnel. Harrison, who was one of the consultants the company hired during this period, later commented that as a result of these personnel reforms, "For the first time in the cooperative's history, positions were allocated primarily on the basis of the suitability of the candidate as judged by objective criteria, rather than as rewards for political loyalty or personal ties" (1981, p. 7).

Is "Turnabout" Fair Play?

Despite these energetic efforts to reinvigorate the politics of Egged and reform the company's management, the Kidum victory would prove to be short-lived. The former Progressive leadership remained in the company and soon reorganized their faction under a new name. They now called their movement Mifne, which can be translated as Turning Point, or Turnabout. In the election held on November 21, 1978, Mifne candidates won a majority among the delegates to the governing council that were elected in the North and also won control of the companywide control commission. In December of 1980, Mifne candidates won sixty-seven seats on the governing council to only forty for Kidum and acquired similarly decisive majorities at all other levels of government.

Mifne's highly effective campaign to regain the leadership of Egged rested in part on a number of specific criticisms that it made of the Kidum leadership. In 1978, for example, Mifne chastised the Kidum leaders for their failure to buy new buses and for failing to move more quickly to pursue a possible merger with Dan. In 1980, Mifne candidates accused the leadership of taking out too many high-interest loans and complained that the company's manpower was increasing while its ridership was falling.

In addition to these specific charges, Mifne made use of a more general theme that had earlier played an important role in Kidum's own campaign. Now that the former Progressive leaders had returned to the rank and file and were driving buses themselves, it was their turn to wage class warfare against the company's managers. One former Progressive and current Mifne leader confided somewhat cynically:

> It is easy to appear before the driver population and make them jealous of management. . . . You wake every morning at 4:00, get to work at 5:00, maybe stay at work til midnight, serve with the armed forces; the manager has a car, a telephone, an office, and a secretary who washes his car. . . . I know this creature from all sides.

Mifne not only made use of this general theme, but also utilized a number of specific tactics that go along with it. Now it was Mifne's turn to play the outraged innocents who demanded an immediate investigation of alleged managerial corruption. Upon gaining control of Egged's internal control commission in 1978, Mifne announced an intention to hire a detective agency and an accountant to investigate the national secretariat and "clean up" Egged (Friedler, 1978). In June of 1979, Mifne stole another weapon from Kidum's bag of tricks and organized a series of wildcat strikes.

Kidum was slow and ineffective in responding to this challenge, in part because it had been disarmed by its own program and ideology. By attempting to destroy the company's system of political patronage, Kidum had left itself with no way to punish its enemies or to reward its loyal supporters. The only favors Kidum was willing to dispense were those that could be distributed equally throughout the company. In June of 1978, for example, the leadership purchased Omega watches for all of the members; this gift was later denounced not only within Egged, but even in the Knesset, as a transparent "bribe" intended to influence the upcoming Egged elections. While this was an embarrassment, Kidum was hurt even more by its inability or unwillingness to play the old game of dispensing favors to individual members who asked for them. It antagonized many of its own supporters by depriving them of power, limiting their discretion, or rejecting their petitions. As Harrison described these dynamics, some influential national regional managers who were affiliated with the winning party became open or covert opponents of the reform when their own interests were threatened. . . . Some rank and file members, frustrated by the formalization of communication and decision making and nostalgic for disrupted relationships of patronage, concluded that the management no longer cared about its simple members. Particularly embittered were members whose sons were denied membership in the cooperative under the new selection procedures. On one particularly dramatic occasion a delegation of aggrieved fathers appeared before the national Secretariat at Egged headquarters and in lengthy speeches evoked the glories of the cooperative past and the requirement of steadfast loyalty and mutual support among members of the "Egged family" (1981, p. 13).

In sum, it would appear that Kidum was hoist on its own petard. Its own previous charges and tactics had been flung back in its face, and its own program had rendered it incapable of countering them. It was also at their own initiative that Kidum's leaders were forced to stand for reelection every two years. A popular saying in English holds that "turnabout is fair play." A "turnabout" is exactly what Kidum got, whether fair or not.

After its victory in 1980, Mifne once again lengthened the period between elections from two years to four; in this case the change was attributed to "a Transport Ministry demand." The opposition reorganized itself under a new name, Ya'ad, but was "all but wiped out" in the 1984 election, winning not a single seat on the governing council and only one out of seven positions on the internal control committee (Jerusalem Post, 1984). In 1985, the head of the internal control committee accused the Egged chairman, Shlomo Amar, of illegally recording his telephone conversations. Amar denied the allegations but resigned his position, ostensibly in order to devote himself full time to his duties as a member of the Knesset. A year later, Amar was accused of paying a bribe to avoid his periodic service in the army reserves. Amar blamed the accusation on "wars inside Egged," calling it "the work of his opponents in the Egged power struggle." The Jerusalem Post noted at the time that "power struggles in Egged are noted for their ferocity" (Isacowitz, 1986).

DAN

The politics of Israel's second major bus cooperative are similar in many ways to those of Egged. Dan, too, has a party system. Like Egged, Dan has known periods of dramatic leadership change. And while Dan was until recently led by a man who before his recent retirement had held his position for more than twenty years, he seems to have achieved this longevity by coping successfully with many of the same political issues that drive the politics of Egged.

Dan's roots, like those of Egged, go back to the 1920s, and it too was put together through a similar succession of mergers of small companies. In 1928, the first of these mergers combined Galei Aviv, which served north Tel Aviv, with Hamaavir, which provided bus service between Tel Aviv and Jaffa. A suburban merger in 1932 linked Regev, serving Ramat Gan, with Ichud, which served Petach Tikvah. In 1945, Ichud-Regev combined with Hamaavir to form Dan.

As in Egged, Dan's more than 1,800 members do not elect their leaders directly. The members vote only for delegates who serve on a thirty-nine-member council (*moatzah*). The council in turn elects a management, or executive (*hanhalah*), of fifteen members, and the management then selects a secretariat (*mazkirut*) of about eight members, which actually runs the company.

In the 1960s, Dan is said to have gone through a period of about six years in which the leaders changed at each election, which at that time was every two years. Looking back on that period, one veteran Dan member commented that company leaders appear to be most vulnerable to rejection by the members the first time they stand for reelection. The thinking seems to be "We tried a new guy last time, so why shouldn't we do the same thing now?" But after a new leader has proved himself and shown that he can "make the trains run on time," it becomes more and more difficult to unseat him.

In May of 1969, Dan experienced a leadership change that was particularly dramatic, because the company head, David Assa, was dismissed from office before the completion of his term. A number of factors appear to have contributed to Assa's fall. One was a general perception both inside the company and without that it was not being well managed at the time. For example, an article in the *Jerusalem Post* in February of that year cited figures that made Dan appear less efficient and less profitable that Egged and reported that many of Dan's passengers "are frankly dissatisfied with the service, complaining of rude drivers, dirty and crowded buses, disdain for time schedules, and a lack of sense of direction" (Dean, 1969). Within Dan, members were becoming particularly restive about incomes that were significantly lower than those of members of Egged and also developed a feeling that their officers were living too much better than they. One participant in the revolt that occurred at that time noted that officers in that administration were making personal use of company cars, but "we stopped that." The company's internal control commission began asking Assa how he had acquired the money to buy his new large house; he is said to have answered that a person in his position "receives a lot of gifts." The final blow occurred when it came to light that the company was taking out loans and failing to register them in a manner prescribed by law. At a meeting of the management that took place early in May, both Assa and the finance director Mordechai Atzmon were dismissed from their positions by a 13 to 2 vote (*Jerusalem Post*, 1969).

Assa was replaced by Yosef Horowitz, who subsequently held his leadership position for more than twenty years. When one inquires into the factors that have contributed to this leader's long tenure, most accounts begin with the fact that he satisfied the members' demands for better pay, newer buses, and shorter workweeks. He also seems to have done his best to be responsive to individual requests for small favors as well.

Even members of the opposition acknowledge that Yossi Horowitz was an extremely skillful politician, who used his office to be helpful to his political opponents as well as to his allies. "It's not Bolivia," one of them commented; there was no penalty for voting against Horowitz or for speaking against him at meetings. This informant saw a good deal of wisdom in this policy, because a member of the opposition who is punished for his dissidence is likely to become a permanent enemy of the leader and to vote against him again; defeated opponents who are embraced by the leadership, on the other hand, are much more likely to change sides.

The Horowitz administration was gracious in victory not only to individual supporters of the opposition, but to the parties of opposition leaders as well. In a typical Dan election, candidates from the ruling Progressive party receive two-thirds or more of the popular vote and more than thirty seats on the council. This gives them enough voting strength to monopolize all the positions in the management and secretariat, but they customarily give some seats on each body to opposition candidates, preferring a coalition government to one-party rule. When asked why the Progressive leaders have been so eager to co-opt the opposition parties, one former opposition leader responded that it is "impossible to govern the cooperative without them."

These policies of defusing and co-opting opposition appear to have been extremely effective. They have enabled the Progressives to retain the leadership of Dan for many decades in succession, while the opposition party is constantly in a period of reorganization, changing its name and its composition after virtually each election. But the opposition never completely dies out. There are always individuals and networks within the company who feel that their interests could be better served by a different group of leaders. For those who feel this way, there also remains a clear sentiment that "you must have a group, you must have a party" in order to make your voice heard.

While keeping the membership generally satisfied with their rule, Horowitz's Progressives also gradually introduced many reforms in Dan's management similar to those that were advocated in Egged by Kidum. For example, a manager in Dan's traffic department reported that in the past, the top jobs in many Dan departments were purely political appointments, but since 1969, there has been a greater tendency to treat managers like civil servants, to send them to special courses and the like. The company has also rationalized its division of labor and now makes greater use of nonmember specialists, such as engineers. A coworker who overheard these remarks added that it would be inaccurate to think that the old ways are now completely gone. Rather, he suggested that there is now a "dual system" of decision making in Dan—a "political system" and "a system of consultants."

LEADERSHIP CHANGE IN MIDSIZED COOPERATIVES

No other worker cooperative in Israel has even one-tenth the number of members of either Egged or Dan, and no other of these cooperatives has a political life that even approaches theirs in complexity. In no other Israeli worker cooperatives did we find a system of political parties, and nowhere else did we encounter such a pattern of repeatedly contested elections.

We did observe some echoes of the large cooperatives' politics within cooperatives of intermediate size, ranging between about twenty-five and one hundred members. Such cooperatives are large enough to have leadership circles that are clearly differentiated from the rest of the membership, and of the four cooperatives falling in or near this size class that were included in this study, we heard stories of rank-and-file rebellions against the leadership in three.

Haargaz

When the research for this work was being conducted, Haargaz was the third largest worker cooperative in Israel and the third best known. Its name was familiar to many Israelis, because it manufactured the bodies of most of the buses used by Egged and Dan. Haargaz means "the box," reflecting the fact that the company started out as a maker of wooden orange crates in 1932. In 1990, the company operated four plants, only one of which made buses. The others were devoted to the manufacture of prefabricated housing and mobile homes, desks and shelving made from both metal and veneer, and a variety of other forms of office furniture and supplies.

When we visited the offices of Haargaz in early February of 1990, we learned that the company had experienced a quite sudden change in its management only a few weeks before. The man who had led the company for a number of years was suddenly voted out in December, with more than two-thirds of the membership voting against him. When asked why this had happened, our main informant was initially reluctant to give reasons. "It's a family matter," was all he would say at first.

After a little more questioning, we uncovered at least some of the circumstances that had led to this leader's fall. They begin with the fact that the structure of Haargaz was unusually democratic, with the entire five-man management (hanhalah) standing for reelection every year, in contrast to the two-and four-year terms of office that are customary in other cooperatives. This management is typically composed of three heads of administrative departments and two members who "work on the line." The member who spoke to us suggested that after successfully standing for reelection a number of times, "a person in position seven, eight, or nine years becomes overconfident." But if the company's economic results begin to go sour, the manager suddenly finds himself having "to explain more and more." Late in 1989, there was much for the membership to become disgruntled about, as the company was doing so poorly that there was no money available to pay bonuses, to buy work clothes for the members, or to provide other perquisites that the members had come to expect from the cooperative.

If these economic problems were primarily responsible for the replacement of this leader, his dismissal did little to reverse the company's decline. The company's finances continued to deteriorate to a point at which the Histadrut felt compelled to step in. This central trade union federation had purchased a half interest in Haargaz as early as 1945, and in 1992 Haargaz was completely absorbed into the Chevrat Ovdim.

Ichud-Igud

The cooperative slaughterhouse known as Ichud-Igud takes pride in being one of the most democratic cooperatives in Israel today. Our informant there boasted that "we are the only cooperative in the land today." By this he meant that Ichud-Igud is the only cooperative whose members do not earn a fixed wage, but are paid instead an amount exactly proportional to the actual income of the cooperative. Ichud-Igud was also one of the few Israeli worker cooperatives in which the members greatly outnumber the hired laborers, by a score of twenty-six to five in 1990 according to this informant. The cooperative is also quite democratic in its structure, with nine of its twenty-six members serving as elected officeholders (three managers, three controllers, and three judges), and all of them standing for reelection every year. And if all that is not enough, the cooperative's current leader also boasted that "we had a revolution two years ago."

The target of this revolution was a leader who had allegedly "dominated" the cooperative for more than ten years. When asked for details as to how this single individual had succeeded in "dominating" his twenty-five colleagues, his successor responded that this man had been good at manipulating people and pitting one against another. But later, this informant called attention to an additional factor that also seems to have played a role in the politics of Egged and Dan—namely, that there is power in incumbency, that political success in a cooperative has a tendency to feed on itself. In the past of this cooperative, there have been some leaders who have lasted as little as a year or even just a month, but there have been others who have also served for long periods of time. In general, it seemed to this respondent, if a leader "survives for two or three years," it is likely that he "will survive for ten or fifteen years."

When asked how so "dominant" a leader could have lost his political support, the answers given suggest a now familiar pattern of growing resentment of the privileges of management by a jealous rank and file. This president "was the only one who didn't work." "That was one of the symptoms," this informant believed. This leader also decided that every member of management should get one day off a week. "Now we don't do that," the successful revolutionary informed us.

Asking how Ichud-Igud is governed since its "revolution" took place, we were told that "today we go to the other side; we are like Eastern Europe." Now, management is more collegial, and two signatures are required on every large check. Like some past reform-minded administrations in Egged and Dan, Ichud-Igud's new management has also attempted to formalize the organization's procedures and to codify its rules—"We did a lot of things to stop the anarchy, and are putting things in the rule book."

Our informant felt that Ichud-Igud's democracy drew some of its vitality from the work its members' performed. Removing skins from animal carcasses is both arduous and highly skilled work. Most of the workers are members, because if someone "is a good worker, we will do everything to keep him here." The twenty-six current members know their work so well that "every one is more clever than the other; every one has a better idea of how to do it." This reminded our informant of a joke that was then very popular in Israel. "Why do Israelis not make love in the street?" the joke inquires; "because too many people would give them advice on how to do it," is the well-known reply.

Namlit

By virtue of both its current size (seventeen members in 1990) and its recently stable politics, the tile-making cooperative Namlit belongs more in the next section, dealing with small cooperatives, than in the present one. But in the past, this cooperative was significantly larger in size (with as many as forty-two members at its peak) and also knew greater political turmoil.

Namlit's current members still recall an occasion in the late 1950s when a manager who became unpopular with the members was voted out of office. The members took particular delight in emphasizing that this unseated manager had then been "sent to work on a lorry." Since that incident, however, Namlit members report that there have been "no big politics here."

DECISION MAKING IN SMALL WORKER COOPERATIVES

In all of the small worker cooperatives we visited, we heard no reports of recent leadership changes of any kind. In some instances, this may be due merely to oversights or other lapses in our process of data collection; it is possible that if we had asked a few more questions of a few more respondents, we might have uncovered evidence of greater turmoil in these cooperatives than was evident at our first visit. In most cases, however, we saw clear evidence that managers in these cooperatives were tending to hold their offices without serious challenges for long periods of time. Chomah and Galei Aviv, for example, had each been led by the same single individual for more than thirty years. At Kalid, the director and treasurer had held their positions since 1974. The manager of the Achdut bakery of Tel Aviv had been in office for an estimated fifteen years, and the head of the Achdut printing press had occupied his position since 1980. At Retsef, we were told that "the same three management [hanhalah] members have held their posts for many years, and the elections are only a formality."

Some unique structural features of these smaller cooperatives may have contributed to this apparent tendency for their leaders to remain in office for long periods of time. For one thing, their simpler social structures seem to promote greater solidarity between leaders and the rank and file. They lack the incipient class antagonisms between workers and bosses that have so frequently been made an issue in the politics of larger cooperatives like Egged and Dan. In these smaller cooperatives, it is more common to find either that nearly every member is a worker (as in Chomah, Shor, Retsef, and Kalid) or that every member is a boss (as in Galei Aviv, the Achdut printing press, and the Achdut bakery). The latter cooperatives are organizations that are "small" only in their number of members, but not in the total size of the firm. These cooperatives are in such an advanced state of "degeneration" that they currently employ five or more hired laborers for each of their members. Under these circumstances, every cooperative member tends to be a de facto supervisor or foreman, whether his job title actually defines him as such or not.

Lacking sharp divisions between leaders and rank and file, these organizations also lack intermediate strata that might produce potential rivals who could someday compete with company leaders for the top jobs. It takes a relatively rare combination of ability, experience, and motivation to produce a member or group of members capable of mounting a successful challenge against the leadership of one of these firms. In the smaller cooperatives, such potential challengers are particularly difficult to find. A more typical complaint in these cooperatives is the perception by managers that they are the only ones who really care about the problems of their cooperatives, the only ones who come faithfully to meetings, and so on.

Social solidarity between leaders and rank and file in these cooperatives is promoted not only by the lack of differentiation between them, but also by the organization's small size. Even where their daily work roles differ, managers and other members remain in face-to-face contact and experience a high degree of communication and cooperation with one another on the job. Thus we were told at Retsef that "the members express their opinions not at the general assembly, but on the production line."

This leads directly to a final point worth making about the smaller cooperatives, which is that it would be a mistake to conclude from the low rate of managerial turnover in these organizations that decision making within them is entirely undemocratic. As the above quotation indicates, members in these cooperatives have many opportunities to communicate their wishes directly to their leaders in the course of their frequent informal contacts with them. At Galei Aviv we were told similarly that "All the members share in decision making. The office of head of the cooperative is only a formal one."

SIZE AND DEMOCRACY IN ISRAELI WORKER COOPERATIVES

The apparent finding of this survey, that the possibility and actuality of leadership turnover are higher in large worker cooperatives in Israel than in small ones, is a surprising result, as it is the direct opposite of what the work of authors like Michels and Weber would lead us to expect. For Michels, oligarchy comes from organization, and the more elaborate the organization, the greater the degree of oligarchy. Weber is equally explicit in asserting that

> The growing complexity of the administrative tasks and the sheer expansion of their scope increasingly result in the technical superiority of those who have had training and experience, and will thus inevitably favor the continuity of at least some of the functionaries (1968, pp. 951–52).

While the present findings appear to run directly counter to assertions like this, it may be possible to reconcile them. There are clearly two kinds of democracy at work in these cooperatives, and size appears to have different consequences for each one. One form of democracy is the "direct" form of democracy described by Weber and advocated by such classic thinkers as Rousseau (Margolis, 1979) and by such contemporary authors as Mansbridge (1980) and Sale (1980). This direct form of democracy is based on homogeneity, communication, and consensus between leaders and followers, all of which are indeed likely to be undermined by increases in size. The other form of democracy illustrated in these cases is the liberal, "representative" form of democracy embraced by such theorists as James Madison and J. S. Mill (Margolis, 1979). While the conditions for attaining direct or consensual democracy are undermined by increases in size, conditions for realizing the more representative form of democracy are improved by them (Margolis, 1979). In particular, in organizations like these that begin with no norms requiring the rotation of management, the conditions for leadership turnover may actually be enhanced rather than diminished as an organization grows in size.

One reason for this, these cases suggest, is that size creates increasing social differentiation and social distance between leaders and rank-and-file members. These differences in turn feed a growing resentment of the leaders by the rank and file, who become increasingly jealous of the leaders' privileges and unique lifestyles. Such antagonisms and resentments are a potent political force. They have served as the basic ingredient of many rank-and-file revolts, not only at Egged and Ichud-Igud, but also in the French worker cooperatives described by Batstone (1983) and in the worker-owned firms in the United States described by Russell (1985a).

While these growing resentments provide the fuel that fires

later rank-and-file revolts, a second consequence of growing size produces the match that actually causes the flame to ignite. This is the fact that growing size promotes the emergence of rivals for the leadership, who have the ability, experience, and motivation needed to mount a successful challenge to the leader. Such potential candidates grow more numerous as the numbers of members holding jobs in middle and top management increase. The emergence of such rivals reaches its peak of development when an organization grows large enough for this opposition to crystallize in the formation of semipermanent parties, as in Lipset, Trow and Coleman's ITU (1956) or in the Israeli bus cooperatives Egged and Dan.

While these potentially favorable effects of size on democracy have not previously been associated with worker cooperatives, they have occasionally been identified in discussions of democracy in other contexts. In a general discussion of the implications of size for democracy in communities and nation-states, for example, Dahl and Tufte (1973) offer a number of relevant arguments. They hypothesize, for example, that "The greater the number of members in a democratic political system, the greater the chance that a dissenter will find enough allies to pass the threshold for dissent." This thinking contributes to a related hypothesis, that "As the number of members in a democratic political system increases, the likelihood of persistent and overt opposition to majority views also increases" (1973, p. 91).

Of more direct relevance to worker cooperatives are the results of two studies of the effects of size on democracy in labor unions reported in the 1970s. The assumption or impression that size has harmful consequences for union democracy has often been reported in the literature on union governance (e.g., Pierson, 1948, pp. 594-95; Lipset, Trow, and Coleman, 1956, pp. 13-14; Strauss, 1977, pp. 232-33), but this notion has rarely been tested empirically. Among the first authors to conduct a quantitative investigation of the association between size and union democracy were Edelstein and Warner (1976) in a comparative study of the effectiveness of opposition in British and American unions. The authors' overall empirical conclusion was that "our data on effectiveness of opposition offer no support for the common notion that large national unions tend to be more oligarchic" (1976, p. 98). This conclusion in turn rested on two sets of findings. Among fifty-one American unions, all of which had more than fifty-thousand members, the effectiveness of opposition showed no correlation at all with size. Among the sixteen British unions in their sample that held periodic elections, some of which were also significantly smaller in size, the authors reported a positive correlation of .53 between size and the closeness of elections (1976, p. 97).

In attempting to understand how size might have neutral or even positive consequences for the effectiveness of opposition within a union, Edelstein and Warner pointed to processes that are broadly similar to those identified here. In general, those authors argued that the effectiveness of opposition within a union is a positive function of the number and the autonomy of union officials of intermediate rank (1976, pp. 68–72). They felt that size could be expected to enhance the effectiveness of opposition, insofar as it promotes the development of these intermediate sources of power. That size was not found consistently to have this effect in their study appeared to be due in large part to the limited range of sizes among the unions that were included in their samples (1976, p. 112).

Other relevant findings were reported by Anderson (1978) in a study of democracy in ninety-five local unions in Canada. Anderson found that size was indeed associated with reduced direct democracy in local unions, as measured by the participation and perceived influence of rank-and-file members in the governance of their locals; but size appeared to have a positive effect on the closeness of presidential elections. One reason for this was that, as argued here, organizational size appeared to increase the number of candidates for president.

Taken together, these arguments and findings suggest that direct and representative democracy may bear the same relationship to size that Emile Durkheim (1933) posited for the two major forms of social solidarity, "mechanical" and "organic." Durkheim argued that as societies grow in size, they inevitably transform themselves from a form of solidarity that is based on intimacy, homogeneity, and simplicity, to one that is more appropriate for a large and diverse society with an elaborate division of labor. It appears here that what is true of social solidarity in general is also true of the forms of democracy achievable in modern organizations in particular.

For those who join Sale in insisting that "The only true democracy . . . is direct democracy" (1980, p. 493), these conclusions will bring little comfort. If we expect of democratic workplaces the kinds of consensual unity and face-to-face intimacy that are characteristic of families, peer groups, and town meetings, then we must acknowledge that size indeed makes these forms of democracy more difficult to achieve. But if one expects no more democracy in modern workplaces than the representative government that we currently encounter in our cities and nation-states, then growing organizational size may actually enhance rather than eliminate the possibility of attaining it. The loss of the first form of democracy creates the conditions for the second, including the discontent and alienation of rank-and-file members and intermediate-level leaders that provide powerful political bases for successful oppositional movements.

Among the Israeli worker cooperatives, these considerations go far toward explaining why the analysis of decision making in these organizations pointed more toward positive than negative effects of size. Neither the large Israeli worker cooperatives nor the small ones make any serious claims or efforts to realize Weber's model of direct democracy, with its frequent assemblies and rotated leadership, and it is not clear that any of them ever did at any point in their histories. In this regard it is important to differentiate the Israeli worker cooperatives from Israel's kibbutzim. While the kibbutzim have shown strong dedication to the norm of rotated management (Rosner and Cohen, 1983) and fight to preserve it even now (Rosner, 1993), the worker cooperatives in Israel's cities have never embraced this ideal. These organizations have typically started out by having one of their members assume the leadership and have permitted that individual to retain that position for as long as the members perceive him or her to be doing a competent job. In democratic workplaces that start out with structures and customs such as these, the effects of size on leadership turnover may be the exact opposite of what Michels and Weber would predict.

The explanation offered here also helps to make it more understandable why Egged should have experienced such noticeably stormier politics over the past three decades than Dan. Egged is much larger than Dan and has a more complex structure. Egged's central leaders have also had to contend with influential regional subunits, all of which functioned at some time in the past as one or more independent entities.

Looking outside of Israel, this discussion implies that workplace democracy may have a much greater potential scope in contemporary Western economies than has generally been recognized. Although in many countries, it is hard to find democratic

workplaces in which more than a few hundred employees participate in the election of the leadership, the examples of Egged and
Dan suggest that workplace democracy is not inherently limited to
organizations of this size. Rather, they indicate that it is possible
to maintain democratic decision making for long periods of time
even among many thousands of workers in one firm. These organizations have long since abandoned direct democracy, if indeed they
ever practiced it; but to say that they are not still practicing some
form of workplace democracy one must first join Rousseau and
Sale in saying that representative democracy is no democracy at
all. It seems more consistent with general usage to join Mansbridge
(1980) in describing the form of democracy practiced in Egged and
Dan and in our nation-states as an "adversarial democracy," but as
"democracy" nonetheless. For all of its faults, this is in the contemporary world the most important form of democracy we know.

DEMOCRACY AND EFFICIENCY:
ARE ISRAELI WORKER COOPERATIVES TOO DEMOCRATIC?

The preceding survey and analysis have concluded that while
the form and nature of workplace democracy differ considerably
from one Israeli worker cooperative to another, there is a substantial degree of democracy in the decision-making practices of all of
them. This means in turn that these organizations provide a rare
opportunity to examine the validity of a number of widely held
views about the impact of workplace democracy on decision
making in a firm.
    From the time of Weber (1968, pp. 137–38) and the Webbs
(1920), through the work of contemporary economists like
Williamson (1975, 1985) and Jensen and Meckling (1979), an impressive array of social scientists has ascribed a large number of
crippling economic weaknesses to democratic firms. This pessimism about the economic consequences of workplace democracy
that is so widespread in European and American sources has also
been echoed in Israeli discussions since the time when Israel's
worker cooperatives were first being formed.
    Preuss tells us that for the WZO's Oppenheimer, "lack of cap-
ital, lack of markets and lack of discipline are the obstacles that
bring industrial Producers' Co-operatives to their inevitable fall"
(1960, p. 195). Speaking apparently for himself, Preuss adds that

worker cooperatives suffer from "the difficulties hampering dynamic management in a democratic body compared to the autocratic ease in a private enterprise" and "the danger of controversy and dispute among members, often requiring potential negotiation before they can be solved" (1960, p. 196). Since Preuss was one of Histadrut's leading spokesmen in the 1920s in its campaign to establish the Merkaz Hakooperatsia (Darr, 1993a), it is significant that he held these views.

Also active in writing about the Israeli worker cooperatives in this period was Viteles. In 1929, Viteles quoted with approval the findings of a 1926 U.S. Department of Labor study, which saw the democratic management of producers' cooperatives as leading to "difficulties in discipline, as the worker-member is apt to feel that he is as good as the manager . . . and to resent taking orders from him " (p. 120). In 1932, Viteles again cited the experiences of "similar enterprises in other countries" as a basis for reporting that "inefficient management" contributes to the apparently "large mortality rate" of workers' productive societies (p. 132).

The Mandatory government's Registrar of Cooperative Societies, in his 1938 report, took an equally dim view of the quality of decision making in "co-partnerships of labour." He believed in particular that the democratic nature of these organizations causes them to pay out too much of their incomes in the form of wages and to set aside too little for depreciation and reserves (1938, pp. 106–107).

One problem with both the Israeli and international literatures on this topic is that in both, a priory arguments and general impressions greatly outnumber empirical results. In this study, we sought to redress this imbalance between theory and observation by asking members of these cooperatives themselves what they considered to be the greatest strengths and greatest weaknesses of their decision-making practices.

We found that many members of Israeli worker cooperatives are quite ready to volunteer criticisms of their structures. There also seem to be some fairly widely shared opinions about what the principal weaknesses of their decision-making practices appear to be.

One criticism that we heard in many cooperatives is that democratic decision making takes up too much time. This was the chief complaint we heard, for example, at the Achdut bakery, where we were told that "sometimes decision making takes more time in the cooperative than . . . in capitalist firms." At Galei Aviv, this had also been perceived as a problem in the past, but was seen as less troublesome now that the cooperative had shrunk from its peak of about a dozen members to its current size of just four. Our informant there commented that

> In the past, when the number of members was higher, we had a problem with joint decision making. Now the cooperative form of organization doesn't slow down decision making, because of the small number of people involved.

At Haargaz, delays in decision making caused by the need for wide consultation among the members were seen as harming the cooperative's international competitiveness. A manager in the Haagaz office pointed out that in this age of the computer, the telex, and the fax, "everyone in the world wants an answer *now*, not tomorrow . . . sometimes you have to make decisions in *minutes*, not in hours or days." Quoting prices for products and bidding for special orders typically require quick decisions of this type. This manager felt that the need to be able to make more rapid decisions would increase over time and that this liability of cooperative decision making would become an even more serious problem in the future than it was at the present time. "In three, five, or seven years," he said,

> we will need to make decisions in minutes or *seconds*. We can't consult a board and a partner [Chevrat Ovdim]. From 1992 we will be a part of Europe. We will need to be able to make the kind of decisions that they make. We can't say that we are a democratic organization and we have to have a meeting.

Our informant at Ichud-Igud also considered decision making in his organization to be unnecessarily time consuming and expensive. "It takes us four hours to buy a pen!" he exclaimed in clear exasperation. What made this problem particularly galling for this manager was that it appeared to be rooted in a lack of trust by the members in their leaders. For example, the members will not let a leader go alone to make a large purchase, because they are suspicious that he might accept a bribe and agree to pay too high a price. Three members typically go together to get estimates for vehicle repairs. For purchases of work clothes, it is necessary to buy from well-known reputable sellers, like Hamashbir, because members are particularly suspicious of transactions with unfamiliar sellers. The manager summarized that "It is not enough to do things right, it must be visible to the members that it has been done right."

In addition to these complaints that democratic decision making consumes too much time and energy, we also frequently heard charges that cooperative organization makes managers more responsive to the needs and wishes of members than is healthy from the point of view of the firm. At Haargaz, for example, we were told that members often ask managers to loan them small sums of money as advances on their pay. These advances are eventually paid back, but until that happens, they can leave the firm dangerously short of cash.

At Dan, I asked whether the desire of the leaders to grant requests and appeals from members weakens the organization's ability to discipline its members. "It's very, very true what you said," was the initial response. But this member went on to say that this does not completely cripple the organization's ability to maintain standards, because it is people outside the management (hanhalah) who bear primary responsibility for maintaining discipline. In all Israeli worker cooperatives, the election of internal judges is kept separate from the election of managers, and this seems to help to insulate the cooperatives' disciplinary machinery from their internal politics.

Both in Dan and Egged, a problem that was more frequently attributed to the managers' excessive responsiveness to the members was a perception that too many managerial positions had been created just so another member could have the pleasure of holding a white-collar job. The opinion of a Chevrat Ovdim official that there was "too much padding of administrative positions" at Egged in 1972 has already been quoted. I heard similar complaints about Dan when I visited its headquarters in 1990. One office worker commented, for example, that the company has "too many people in offices not doing anything."

The specific content of members' requests thus seems to differ considerably from one cooperative to another. In one cooperative members may be after loans, in another they may seek leniency or a white-collar job. But in addition to these specific demands, two themes showed up again and again in our discussions about these requests.

One persistent theme in discussions of demands that emanate

from the membership in these cooperatives is the members' insistence that benefits received by any one member should be made available to all. This insistence on equality may be a reflection of the egalitarian ideology that is widespread in Israel's labor economy (Sussman, 1969, 1973). Some members also join Hansmann (1990) in seeing it as the most efficient way to minimize internal wrangling in a democratic firm. But there are voices within the Israeli worker cooperatives who see this policy as harmful in its practical effects. One computer specialist in Dan, for example, volunteered the opinion that "from a management point of view, a cooperative is not a good idea." To illustrate this point, he offered the example that if an office worker tells the management that his or her office needs a new phone line, the management will answer that "if it gives one to you it must give one to all."

The members' insistence on equality in the Israeli worker cooperatives is most evident in their preference for equal pay among members. This policy, too, appears to carry important costs. For example, it contributes to the use of nonmember labor in Israeli worker cooperatives, because these cooperatives have no other way to incorporate the labor of workers whose skills are normally compensated with wages that are either much higher or much lower than what the members receive. The demand that members should receive equal pay, when coupled with the requirement that managers should be members, may also retard the professionalization of management in these cooperatives and deprive the cooperatives of needed managerial skills.

In addition to both the specific and the general content of the members' demands, one must also consider the consequences of the sheer volume of their requests. The manager we spoke with at Haargaz commented that perhaps the most unique thing about managing a cooperative like his is the fact that "everyone wants you to listen to his problems." It is hard to turn a deaf ear to such requests, because "no one in management can forget that in a few months he has to stand for reelection." As a result of this political fact, the members "can open every door."

Harrison (1981) made similar observations in his analysis of the politics of Egged. He concluded that the politics of this cooperative were systematically turning the attention of its leaders inward toward the membership and away from the customers and market conditions that ought to have been their chief preoccupation. In his words, the concentration of the top managers on the needs of the membership and their proximity to the members in outlook and background would seem to have diminished their capacity for dealing decisively and imaginatively with the need to increase public support and with changing economic and ecological conditions (1981,p. 12).

In addition to its politics causing the leaders of the cooperative to look inward rather than outward, Harrison also felt that its politics encouraged leaders to take a short-term orientation toward their cooperatives' problems and to neglect long-term strategic planning. He noted that

Egged only seems to have begun to respond to . . . internal and external threats when they reached crisis proportions. The institution of electing the managers from among the rank-and-file members, most of whom are bus drivers, may have further reinforced the tendency to handle problems through "fire-fighting," rather than through planning and the development of routine solutions to recurring problems. Individuals who rose from the rank of bus driver to supervisory or managerial positions typically had little or no professional, academic, or managerial training. Moreover, their peer culture placed a premium on quick and vigorous responses to personal, technical, and organizational challenges rather than on systematic analysis and problem solving (1981, p. 9).

While all members of Israeli worker cooperatives might not agree with all of these criticisms, most we spoke with did seem to feel that their organizations were paying a price in efficiency for their democratic institutions. But the predominant sentiment that we encountered appeared to be that the benefits of these institutions outweighed their costs.

In Haargaz, for example, our informant within the management acknowledged that while the cooperative's managers often complain that its decision-making apparatus is cumbersome and inconvenient, the rank-and-file members were generally quite satisfied with it. This was not based on a mere estimate of rank-and-file opinions, but a difference in perspectives that had come up frequently at meetings. Whenever the membership had discussed the possibility of selling the firm, the management had been much more open to this possibility than the rank-and-file membership. Our informant felt this difference in opinions was rooted in objective differences between the managers and rank-and-file members in what each had to gain or lose from a change in ownership. The managers felt that they would receive higher salaries from conventional owners than they earned as members of the cooperative. The rank-and-file members believed that they received higher wages as members of a cooperative than they would receive from a conventional employer, and they also enjoyed the greater access to managers and equality with them that they experienced as members of a cooperative.

At Egged and Dan, we heard even stronger expressions of fidelity to the ideal of workplace democracy, both from rank-and-file members and from leaders as well. For example, Shlomo Levine, the current leader of Egged, while acknowledging many of the defects in his cooperative's decision-making system, insisted that its democratic practices continue to have wide and deep roots. Some of these roots are in the nonrational side of the cooperative's members, in their values and emotions. But "democracy," he asserted, also "has its own cleverness, rationale, or reason; the nation will not vote for people who will not suit; the voter has some common sense."

What Levine considered to be true of democracy in his nation, he implied was also true of democracy in his firm. Having reviewed the history of the dramatic struggles for power in Egged and in Dan in the 1960s and 1970s, we see a good deal of truth in his remarks. Both Egged and Dan seem to have been strengthened rather than weakened by their rank-and-file revolts of this period. These uprisings by the membership led to many badly needed reforms in these cooperatives' administrations, including an increasing professionalization of their managements. By all accounts these movements were a success, as outside experts who have some knowledge of the two bus cooperatives have generally laudatory things to say about the quality of their managements, and quantitative analyses of their cost structures suggest that they are no less efficient than comparable bus systems located in other parts of the world (Berechman, 1987).

While the democratic managements of Egged and Dan have not prevented these organizations from being judged a success, the performance of Israel's other worker cooperatives has not been as impressive. As was noted in chapter 2, the median Israeli worker cooperative over the period 1924–92 was dissolved less than five years after being formed. Although we lack the comparable data on the mortality of alternative forms of organization that would be needed to provide a precise answer to the question whether or not this makes the Israeli worker cooperatives unusually short-lived, the Israeli literature on worker cooperatives has judged these organizations to be especially prone to failure since the period in which they were first being formed. Viteles, for example, reported in 1932 that "There has been a larger number of official and unofficial liquidations of both small and large Workers' Production Societies than of any other type of cooperative societies" (p. 132). Preuss joined Viteles in describing the worker cooperatives as suffering from "a comparatively high 'death rate'" (1965, p. 200). Thus leading Israeli commentators on worker cooperatives like Oppenheimer, Preuss, and Viteles have been virtually unanimous in seeing these organizations as being uniquely short-lived and in identifying the democratic nature of their decision making as one of their principal economic handicaps. In the absence of more prominent successes like Egged and Dan to refute such pessimistic views, they appear to have gone largely unchallenged.

CONCLUSIONS

As this study was initially being planned in the late 1980s, leadership problems and internal discord in the Israeli bus cooperatives were continuing to produce an almost steady stream of scandalous headlines. Egged, in particular, continued to attract more than its share of unfavorable publicity. In 1985, when Egged's chairman, Shlomo Amar, was accused of illegally wiretapping and recording telephone conversations made by a political opponent, the affair became a national issue. Because Amar was then serving in the Knesset, he was immune from prosecution; but the government's attorney general asked the Knesset to lift his immunity, and a good deal of attention was devoted to the affair until the Knesset House Committee refused this request in July. In September, Egged announced that Amar had resigned his position and was being replaced by Shlomo Levine (Oked, 1985). But the scandal wouldn't die, and in 1986 a new charge was added against Amar: that he had bribed someone to perform his army reserve service in his place (Isacowitz, 1986). A year later, the press carried reports of "an intensifying power struggle in advance of the cooperative's March elections" (Karp, 1987) under headlines like "Dissident Egged Members Cause Uproar at Meeting" (Schachter, 1987).

The press coverage in this period also intimated that the government was becoming increasingly critical of Egged's democratic management. In 1984, the *Jerusalem Post* noted that Egged's ruling Mifne party had changed the period between elections back to every four years from the two-year period initiated by Kidum "according to a Transport Ministry demand." In 1987, the government's comptroller complained that Egged had failed to submit adequate financial documentation and also charged that the cooperative was overpaying some of the professionals in its employment (Schachter, 1987).

Press stories about Egged have thus continued to portray decision making within this bus cooperative as oligarchical, divisive, often corrupt, and inefficient. And since Egged is the only worker cooperative to which the Israeli press gives such systematic attention, the reputation of this entire organizational form in Israel has been increasingly dependent on the public image of this company and its management.

The analysis offered here has differed from these popular impressions in a number of ways. The record of the Israeli worker cooperatives, both in preserving their democratic institutions and in governing themselves effectively with them, appears from this analysis to be no worse than mixed. Egged and Dan and some of the other worker cooperatives have indeed had plenty of scandals and have known both corrupt and ineffective leaders, but no clear evidence has yet been produced that the quality of leadership in these organizations has on balance been either any worse or any better than it would have been in more conventionally organized firms.

The scandals within these worker cooperatives also seem in many instances to have been widely misunderstood. Rather than being taken as signs of the failure of workplace democracy, or of its oligarchical degeneration, many of them can be best interpreted as signs of democracy's continued vitality and strength. The noisy and vituperative transitions that have occasionally erupted within Egged and Dan and other worker cooperatives have caused embarrassment for some leaders, but have also given evidence that the democratic process within these organizations is still at work. From the point of view of the work of Michels, Weber, the Webbs, and other such theorists, the most remarkable thing about these large and venerable worker cooperatives is not how oligarchical they have become, but how democratic they remain.

But this is not how these events have been perceived or interpreted in Israel. The tendency of these and other democracies to wash their dirty linen in public has given these organizations a great deal of bad press. The frequent charges of mismanagement and corruption that have emerged from these organizations have clearly done further harm to their already tarnished public images and have played an additional role in delegitimating the worker cooperatives in the eyes of the Israeli public.

5. Israel's Labor Economy between Crisis and Collapse

As all of the preceding four chapters have indicated, Israel's population of worker cooperatives had entered a prolonged period of decline many decades before this study began. Their relationship to the Histadrut had long since soured; deaths of existing worker cooperatives had outnumbered births of new ones in almost every year since the 1950s; and the worker cooperatives' use of hired labor and rancorous internal politics had been bringing them little but bad publicity for years.

By the late 1980s, however, Israel's worker cooperatives were no longer alone in looking like organizations whose best days were behind them. Israel's entire labor-owned economy was undergoing a period of economic hardship, contraction, and self-doubt. Factories owned by the Chevrat Ovdim subsidiary Koor were laying off workers, being divested, or closing their doors. Moshavim faced widespread bankruptcy, and even the once-proud kibbutzim were petitioning the government for help in relieving their mounting burden of debt.

Defenders of one or more portions of the labor economy insisted that their problems were not of their own making, but originated in a series of external political and economic events. The most important of these was a dramatic shift in the economic policies of the Israeli government in the mid-1980s. In the late 1970s and early 1980s, credit was made readily available on easy terms. All segments of the labor economy took advantage of this easy credit to borrow heavily in this period, obtaining financing for numerous ambitious investments. By August of 1985, however, runaway inflation led the government to reverse this policy. Access to credit was suddenly tightened. Interest rates were set at high nominal values and indexed to the rate of inflation as well. Economic contraction made it even harder to earn enough income to make the payments on debt that had been accumulated in earlier years. Thus new borrowing was constantly needed in order to pay old debts, at ever higher real interest rates.

In the eyes of Israelis who were inclined to be critical of the labor economy, these external events had contributed to the economic difficulties of the kibbutz, the moshav, and the factories owned by the Chevrat Ovdim, but they were not their ultimate cause. The more fundamental causes, many critics felt, were poor management and faulty incentives. Better managers might not have expanded their businesses so recklessly. The managers of these labor-owned enterprises might have behaved more prudently if it was their own personal wealth that they were placing at risk and if they could be held personally responsible for paying back these debts.

By the late 1980s, thoughts like these were being expressed not only outside the various segments of Israel's labor economy, but within them as well. There was widespread acknowledgment that these organizations had expanded carelessly, readily accepting the government's offers of cheap credit and trusting that the government would bail them out if they went too far. But the government since 1977 had been dominated by Likud, not by Labor, and with hindsight it appeared foolish to have expected the same indulgence from a Likud government that a Labor government might have offered. There was also widespread soul-searching within these organizations about whether their democratic structures remained consistent with the economic realities of contemporary Israel. Were they placing the best-qualified managers at the head of each enterprise, and were they motivating them properly?

Questions like these soon contributed to calls for reform and a search for new models within all of these movements. This in

turn made the late 1980s and early 1990s a time not only of economic hardship, but also of intellectual ferment. Wherever one
turned in Israel's labor economy, in kibbutzim, in moshavim, and
in Koor, one encountered serious discussions about the desirability
of various reforms.

The present chapter reports on the impact of the economic
crisis of the 1980s within each of the three major components of
the labor economy of contemporary Israel—the kibbutz, the
moshav, and Koor. In each of these three spheres, information is
provided about the magnitude of the crisis, about causal factors
that may have contributed to it, and about structural reforms that
have been introduced or proposed in response to it.

While these developments are of interest in themselves, they
are examined here especially for help they might offer in evalu-
ating the current health and future prospects of Israel's dwindling
population of worker cooperatives. Does the recent decline of these
more prominent institutions imply that all forms of cooperative or
collective ownership in Israel are now thoroughly passe? Do the reforms being proposed within these spheres have the potential to revitalize not only the branch of the labor economy that gave rise to
them, but Israel's moribund worker cooperatives as well? These
questions are asked implicitly throughout this chapter and are addressed explicitly in the concluding one, which examines the state
of worker cooperatives in Israel today.

BETWEEN THE OLD AND THE NEW KIBBUTZ

In 1989 and 1990, news about the kibbutz was dominated by
stories devoted to the mounting problem of kibbutz debt (Brinkley,
1989; Williams, 1989; Brooks, 1989; Brod, 1990). Collectively
Israel's 270 kibbutzim owed the government 7.2 billion NIS, or
close to $4 billion, and were engaged in delicate negotiations to re-
finance this debt. Shimon Peres of the Labor Party made no secret
of the fact that one of his prime motivations for participation in a
coalition government with Likud was to gain the post of finance
minister for himself and to use this position to assist the kibbutzim in rescheduling their debts (Brilliant, 1989).

These negotiations produced an agreement in December
1989. The government contributed 1.65 billion NIS in debt forgive-
ness and new grants and offered favorable terms for repayment of
the remaining debt. The kibbutzim agreed in return to sell off

some assets, to send at least 11 percent of their members to work outside the kibbutz, and to lower their standard of living by at least seven percent (Brilliant, 1989; Maltz, 1989b).

I visited more than a dozen kibbutzim during the time I spent in Israel between 1989 and 1993, and signs of the belt-tightening that was made necessary by this financial crisis were evident in virtually all of them. It was most evident in their dining halls. Meals without meat had become very common. In Kibbutz Maayan Zvi, expensive rolls were no longer available at breakfast. Kibbutz Nir David had had to dismiss the cook who had been hired to improve the quality of its meals and was back to making due with the efforts of amateurs.

The kibbutzim were cutting back on a number of other expenses as well. Funds for travel abroad had been greatly curtailed. And kibbutzim that had formerly had three or four members maintaining their grounds could now afford to allocate no more than one person to such work. So suddenly, overgrown gardens and leaking faucets had become common sights.

Something that was as striking as the belt-tightening on all of these kibbutzim was an attitudinal change. The kibbutzniks appeared to have lost the cockiness that they had been noted for in the past. They were no longer so confident of being a model for the future and a national elite. People talked about how the economic crisis had produced "psychological pressure," "trauma," and "panic." Eliezer Ben-Rafael has noted that the kibbutz model suddenly found itself "losing much of its legitimacy in the eyes of many kibbutzniks themselves" (1991, p. 77). One quite disillusioned veteran of more than forty years of kibbutz life told me sadly, "We left a capitalist society, we thought we would make a new man and a new society, but it didn't work." Most other kibbutz members I encountered appeared to be taking things more calmly than this, but everywhere I turned there was talk of change: changes that had already been made; changes that were currently being considered; and changes that could not be permitted without destroying the unique identity of the kibbutz.

In its preoccupation with crisis and with change, this current era of kibbutz history was not entirely unique. The kibbutzim had been described as being in a state of "crisis" many times before (e.g., Spiro, 1956) and had been seen both by their members and by outsiders to be undergoing profound changes for years (e.g., Cohen, 1983; Ben-Ner, 1987). Fundamental changes had been occasioned by efforts to rear and to retain the first and second generations of kibbutz-born children (Rosner et al., 1990). Children born on the kibbutzim were not as ascetic and self-sacrificing as their parents, and many compromises had been made in order to keep them interested in kibbutz life. By the 1980s, almost all kibbutzim had abandoned their past practices of collective child-rearing and had instead given in to persistent demands to allow children to sleep in their parents' apartments. Whereas the kibbutzim had initially viewed college degrees as luxuries that were irrelevant to kibbutz life, they had gradually stopped placing barriers in the way of their children's desires for higher education. The kibbutzim had also been industrializing their economies for several decades, both in order to expand their sources of income and raise their standard of living and as a way to create additional and more interesting job opportunities for their increasingly educated youth. By 1990, the typical kibbutz operated one or two factories in addition to carrying out its traditional farmwork.

These internal changes had exacerbated conflicts between individualism and collectivism that are perhaps inherent in kibbutz life. As the kibbutz economy grew increasingly diverse, the gap between the most and least rewarding jobs constantly widened. In the beginning, all kibbutz work had been arduous, but the kibbutzniks had found meaning in the dirt and sweat that they shared. As I was told by one kibbutznik, "You worked where you were told before. The issue of whether you wanted to didn't come up." Increasingly, however, the kibbutzniks demanded work that allowed them to use their educations, or provided opportunities for self-expression. Unpopular tasks, on the other hands, were given to hired workers or to volunteers from abroad (see Mittelberg, 1988) or to the remaining few dedicated members, who now often felt that they were being taken advantage of by the more selfish members. "Have you learned the word 'freier' [sucker]?" I was asked. "That's a person who gets up at 4:00 AM to milk the cows for no reward."

Both the diversity and greater affluence made possible by kibbutz industrialization have had divisive consequences on many kibbutzim, as members have struggled over job assignments, access to better housing, air conditioners, cars, and other luxuries. One disgruntled kibbutznik told me, "Today, if you don't shout a bit and bang on the table, you don't get anything. You have to worry about your own interests, the kibbutz doesn't look after you." A spokesman for the kibbutz movement seemed to refer to similar problems when he observed, "On a continuum of collective, as opposed to individualistic orientation, kibbutz members have tended to move towards the latter extreme and have adopted a selfish kind of individualism that fails to serve the community" (Avrahami, 1989, p. 32).

While these changes had been occurring and these tensions had been growing for decades, they acquired a new significance under the stimulus of the economic crisis. The relationship between work and reward and the distribution of consumer goods were no longer viewed primarily from the point of view of the social fabric of the kibbutz; of equal or greater interest now was their impact on the economic bottom line.

This change was most apparent in the approval that was suddenly given to members working outside the kibbutz. Kibbutz members have been working outside their kibbutzim for decades—in the army, in the government, in the kibbutz federations, in universities, and elsewhere. But these arrangements were always accepted with great reluctance and always treated as either temporary or very exceptional. University professors and other professionals who are members of kibbutzim require special permission to hold these jobs. When such outside employment has been permitted, it has typically carried a price. I am acquainted with one professor on a kibbutz who spends her sabbatical leaves in the kitchen, while another spends his weekends in the guard house; a lawyer spends her weekends washing dishes, while a psychologist works extra shifts in a factory. It has often seemed that the other kibbutz members resent these professionals' privileged lifestyles and are taking steps to make sure they don't enjoy them too much.

Many of these attitudes are still very common, but there is an important new element in the way the kibbutz views outside employment. These arrangements have suddenly come to be highly appreciated because of the income that they provide. Members who work outside a kibbutz are required to turn over all of this outside income to the kibbutz. When the income they can earn on the outside is large, the kibbutz is now inclined to encourage this outside work.

The psychologist I know on one kibbutz is happy to have this new freedom to pursue his profession, but is not entirely pleased about the change in attitude that brought it about. He is a bit resentful of the fact that when the issue of his working hours was presented as a matter of his professional development and personal self-expression, his kibbutz did nothing but place obstacles in his path. But now he is encouraged to work all the hours he can, solely because his kibbutz now "sees everything through the hole of a grush" (i.e., views all issues in monetary terms).

A similarly calculating attitude is now taken toward work performed inside a kibbutz as well as outside. One now encounters a greater range of jobs inside the kibbutzim than ever before. While the story of kibbutz industrialization was already old news, by the late 1980s and early 1990s it was also clear that the postindustrial revolution had finally come to the kibbutz. Suddenly service and professional occupations were the fastest growing categories of employment. Three kibbutzim had their own law firms, Kibbutz El-Rom was putting subtitles on foreign films, and many more kibbutz members than ever before were earning incomes as artists or photographers or in other creative pursuits.

These were occupations that the kibbutzim had been slow to open up to, as their ideology continued to attach the highest value to agricultural labor. It had not been too difficult to broaden this outlook to include manufacturing work, but most kibbutzniks have retained the socialist's traditional disdain for white-collar work. It has been economic necessity, rather than an ideological change of heart, that has gradually led the kibbutzim to become more receptive to service work. Hardest to embrace have been jobs that the kibbutzniks consider to be servile or mercenary; but dozens of kibbutzim now operate guest houses or other facilities for tourists (Kramer, 1984), and I was told of one kibbutz that now operates a convenience store.

The new openness of the kibbutzim toward artistic occupations is driven less by their need for money than by their members' desire for self-expression; but decisions about how much time an artist will actually be permitted to spend on such work are once again subjected to economic calculation. To devote up to one or two days per week to art, it is enough to be recognized as an artist by the Kibbutz Artists' Organization; but to give more time than this to artistic pursuits requires an economic justification. The practice now on many kibbutzim is to calculate the average daily income derived from the most typical economic activities of that kibbutz, and then to compare the income to be obtained from any proposed alternative use of a member's time against that standard. The kibbutzim have not become quite so mercenary as to require that the income derivable from an artistic pursuit must always be equal to or greater than what could be earned from farm or factory work; it is considered sufficient if this income comes close. In sum, it is OK to work as a painter on a kibbutz today, provided that you actually sell a painting now and then.

This new spirit of economic calculation applies not only to the work of individuals, but also to each enterprise and each household. In all three of these areas, the kibbutzim now seem to rely less on collective decision making and to permit greater autonomy, subject only to the discipline of market-based constraints. For enterprises, this means that the "profit-center" concept is now very much in vogue. In many kibbutzim, capital-intensive operations like factories have now been organized as independent subsidiaries with their own boards of directors. These boards are now free to set policies for their enterprises without interference from the kibbutz assembly, provided that they continue to run these ventures profitably.

Households within the kibbutz have also been placed on an increasingly monetary footing. Because in virtually all kibbutzim children now sleep in their parents' apartments, and many kibbutz families now eat their meals in private rather than in the common dining hall, kibbutz households have become larger and better appointed than they were in the past. A major contributor to the current kibbutz debt burden was borrowing that went not to increase economic production, but to increase the average size of kibbutz housing. With red-tile roofs, attractive landscaping, and comfortable interiors, many kibbutz apartments now look like California condominiums, and kibbutz families now spend their evenings together with televisions, VCRs, and stereos, like middle-class families in many other parts of the world.

This kind of lifestyle can be expensive, of course, so the kibbutzim have had to place each household on a budget. Kibbutz families now receive a complex set of cash and noncash allowances to cover expenses like food, clothes, entertainment, travel, furniture, and energy. Many things that kibbutzim formerly distributed as free goods are now being metered and charged for. These range from energy, telephones, and the use of kibbutz-owned vehicles, to such small but symbolic items as toilet paper and tickets for concerts. The net effect of all this new accounting is that each family has had its overall budget cut, but has also gained more autonomy in the choice of which luxuries will actually be the first to go. With meters being installed in each apartment to monitor their energy use, kibbutz households have acquired still another set of new incentives to economize on resources that had previously been made available to them without any personal cost.

Here and there, one hears about even more radical changes that have been introduced or at least discussed on one or more kibbutzim that have been particularly hard-hit by the crisis. One such case is Kibbutz Bet Oren. This kibbutz fell into severe economic difficulties by 1986, as a result of which many of its members left and many of its housing units stood empty. A reformer named Dodik Rothenberg led a new group into the kibbutz with some startling new ideas about how to save it. By 1987, Bet Oren had become a major center of change. It extended the concept of individual family budgets to such formerly taboo areas as meals in the dining hall and the allocation of housing. On this kibbutz, an individual or family that wanted to move to a larger apartment could do so immediately, but would have to pay for the larger space. Nonmembers would also be permitted to reside on the kibbutz and to eat in its dining hall, provided that they paid rent for their apartments and another fee for their meals.

An even more radical proposal to emerge from Bet Oren was a suggestion that kibbutz members should be given an incentive to work overtime that would take the form of extra pay for the extra work. To an outsider, the proposal might have appeared to be only a modest change. Kibbutzniks would still receive no compensation for their standard five-day workweek; a monetary reward would be offered only for members who were willing to work a sixth day. A variation on this proposal had already long been common practice on many kibbutzim, as kibbutz teenagers often raise money for special purchases or for summer travel in Europe by hiring out their labor on weekends to neighboring kibbutzim.

Nevertheless, this last proposal was seen as heresy on many kibbutzim, because it seemed to contradict a fundamental principle on which the kibbutz is based—the principle "From each according to his ability, to each according to his needs." Kibbutzniks have also long prided themselves on working only for moral and ideological incentives, not monetary ones. So this proposal to introduce even a modest form of payment for work within the kibbutz was roundly criticized, and the United Kibbutz Movement (Takam) refused to permit Bet Oren to take this radical step.

Smaller changes in their traditional structures, in the meantime, continued to be introduced on many kibbutzim. In 1988,

Yehuda Harel brought many of these changes together into a coherent image of what he called "the new kibbutz." Harel's new kibbutz was to be a much freer, more individualistic, and more economically rational entity than the one that had preceded it. Each kibbutz member would be paid a salary, while the centralized distribution of need-based and free goods would almost completely disappear. Each factory or enterprise would be autonomous from the kibbutz general assembly and would have control over its own labor and capital inputs, rather than being required to provide work to any individuals simply because of their membership in the kibbutz.

Harel's "new kibbutz" was significant both because of the elements it contained and because of the identity of the man who was proposing them. Harel was at the time the leader of Yad Tabenkin, which served as the intellectual center of the largest kibbutz federation, Takam. Harel's proposals were also quickly taken up by other influential spokesmen. For example, Amir Helman (1989) and other faculty at the Ruppin Institute expressed similar views. While Yad Tabenkin can be thought of as the kibbutz movement's major think tank, the Ruppin Institute is its business school, and at any given time, hundreds of kibbutz members are enrolled in its courses. Other voices calling for systematic reform of the kibbutz included Reuven Shapira (1990), who felt that the rotation of managers in kibbutz factories deprives these enterprises of the services of their most skilled and successful leaders, and Gideon Kressel (1991), who felt that the collective ownership and decision-making practices of the kibbutz leave managers insufficiently accountable for their errors.

While the "new kibbutz" had many vocal backers, it soon revealed itself to have an even more powerful set of enemies. Leaders of the two major kibbutz federations gave it a cold reception. Influential kibbutz theorists denounced the model as well (e.g., Rosner, 1988), and Harel was asked to leave Yad Tabenkin. Harel appealed to the rank and file of the United Kibbutz Movement for support, but was soundly defeated in a bid to become the leader of Takam.

During the visits that I paid to Israeli kibbutzim between 1989 and 1993, there was a sense everywhere that the kibbutzim were changing, but there was also widespread discussion about the limits beyond which these changes would not or could not be allowed to go. Surveys conducted within the kibbutz movement indicated that some changes had already been widely accepted, but that others remained virtually taboo. A 1992 survey of 194 kibbutzim affiliated with the two largest federations, Takam and Kibbutz Artzi, found that the reforms that had been most frequently adopted were those that affected the budgets of individual households. Monetary budgets for each household were by then in use in 66 percent of these kibbutzim, and 57 percent had incorporated the home use of electricity into the household budget. Increasing the autonomy of kibbutz enterprises was also growing in popularity, as 51 percent of the kibbutzim surveyed had created boards of directors for their factories, and 39 percent were treating economic units as "profit centers." But many other proposed reforms were having trouble catching on. A modest sixteen percent of these kibbutzim had discontinued the kibbutz tradition of rotating even highly successful enterprise managers out of their posts. Only 6 percent had followed the example of Kibbutz Bet Oren in requiring members to pay for meals they eat in the central dining hall, and only 6 percent had adopted the controversial practice of offering payment for additional hours worked (Getz, 1992; Getz and Rosner, 1993; Rosner, 1993).

As the kibbutzim entered the 1990s, the cumulative import of all these changes remained unclear. The "old kibbutz" was unquestionably in trouble and undergoing many changes, but efforts to advance a coherent model of a radically new kibbutz had been widely rejected as well. Here and there, on the fringes of the kibbutz movement, economically troubled kibbutzim such as Kibbutz Ein Zivan in the northern Golan Heights continued to experiment with differential pay (e.g., Odenheimer, 1992/93). But in the center of the kibbutz movements, within the federations and at Yad Tabenkin, most voices condemned such sharp departures from kibbutz traditions and struggled to define what the future kibbutz orthodoxy should be (Magid, 1991; Karmon, 1991; Ben-Rafael, 1991; Rosner, 1993). The net effect of all these diverse suggestions and opinions was to leave the kibbutz in a kind of limbo. The kibbutz seemed stuck in a twilight zone between the old kibbutz and the new. The identity crisis that had for many years afflicted the kibbutz seemed likely to continue, either until these debates had been resolved, or at least until the former prosperity of the kibbutzim had been restored (Rosolio, 1993; Getz and Rosner, 1993).

MOUNTING PROBLEMS AND WANING HOPES
ON THE MOSHAVIM

Although the economic crisis of the 1980s had exerted profound effects on the kibbutzim, these problems appeared trifling when compared to the disastrous effects of the crisis on Israel's moshavim. While these economic difficulties had caused many kibbutzim to reduce their consumption and reorganize their production, very few kibbutzim had been forced into dissolution. The total number of kibbutzim declined from about 270 in the early 1980s to about 260 in 1992. Of the few kibbutzim that had closed their doors, most had done so because of social and demographic problems, not because of insolvency. Among the moshavim, on the other hand, by 1990 it was no longer sufficient to describe their situation as a "crisis", one instead increasingly heard the moshavim described as being in a complete state of "collapse." Bankruptcies of moshavim were rampant. By 1992, more than two-thirds of Israel's 450 moshavim either already had been or were in the process of being completely disbanded (Sadan, 1992).

Overviews of the causes of this widespread collapse of the moshavim have been offered by Kislev, Lerman, and Zusman (1989), by Levi (1990), and by Zusman (1990). As was the case with the kibbutzim, the moshavim were seduced by the easy credit of the late 1970s and early 1980s. In some of these years, nominal rates of interest lagged behind the rate of inflation, producing negative real rates. Both Kislev, Lerman, and Zusman (1989) and Levi (1990) note that "the crisis was aggravated by the feeling . . . that should financial problems arise for farmers and their organizations, they will be invariably rescued by a political system that always accorded a preferential treatment to the rural cooperative sector" (Levi, 1990, p. 144). This expectation was disappointed after the institution of an economic stabilization program in August 1985, however, when the debt of the moshavim began to rise rapidly in real terms, and the government did little to help them cope with it.

While these problems were common to both the kibbutzim and the moshavim, certain structural features of the moshavim did much to exacerbate them. Even after all the recent changes, each kibbutz has only one economy, a collective one, and each kibbutznik knows that his or her own economic future depends on the success of the collective enterprise. On a typical moshav, a so-called "moshav ovdim," purchasing and marketing are performed collectively, but each individual household works its own land and earns its own income. Most importantly, members of these moshavim were in the anomalous position of raising capital collectively, and guaranteeing each other's debts, but having little control over the conditions affecting each other's ability to repay. Pinhas Zusman (1988, 1990) is particularly attentive to the "moral hazards" and "free-rider" problems to which this situation can lead. It encouraged many moshav members to take on far too much debt at absurdly high rates of interest, because they did not view the loans as their own personal obligations, but as the cooperative's.

The potential for such behavior was inherent in the structures of most moshavim, but problems were for many years avoided, because the moshavim had moral communities and governance structures of sufficient strength to hold such opportunistic behavior in check. As Zusman pointed out in a book written largely before the collapse of the moshavim had begun,

> in view of the monitoring and enforcement problems, the performance and indeed, the very survival of the moshav, depend on the moral foundation of the community. The existence of appropriate "moshav ethics" reinforced by enlightened self interest is crucial for moshav success (1988, p. 95).

The dependence of the moshavim on shared commitments to cooperative values is illustrated by variations in the success of moshavim, depending on their period of founding and on the ethnic origins of the founders. In general the strongest moshavim have been those formed in the years before 1948, when the moshav movement was fed by people who were similar in backgrounds and values to those who created the kibbutz. The weakest moshavim have been those that were formed in the years following independence as a way to provide housing and jobs for new immigrants. These new immigrants, and especially those from African or Asian countries, typically had no prior knowledge of or interest in cooperatives and were herded into cooperative agricultural settlements simply because the authorities responsible for immigrant absorption had decreed that this should be so. Weintraub and Sadan (1981) estimate that of Israel's 450 moshavim, 100 were formed "from below" either before or after independence by largely European immigrants who had a genuine desire to be members of cooperatives.

The other 350 were "managed" cooperatives created "from above." Sadan calculated in 1992 that of the 100 cooperatives in the first group, only 29 percent were being disbanded, 10 percent because of internal problems and 19 percent because of the bankruptcy of a regional credit cooperative that they were affiliated with. Among the 350 moshavim that had been organized "from above," on the other hand, almost 86 percent were failing, and no more than 14 percent seemed likely to survive (Sadan, 1992).

Yair Levi, another authority on the moshavim, also suggested to me that Israel's forty-nine moshavim shitufim, with more communal structures, have withstood the crisis better than have the moshavim ovdim, the more common moshavim. A moshav shitufi, or collective moshav, pays salaries to its individual members on the basis of the size of their households and other measures of need, but it earns its income through shared economic activities that are similar to those of a kibbutz. Because of their structural and ideological affinities to the kibbutzim, some moshavim shitufim are currently affiliated with the kibbutz federation Takam rather than with organizations of moshavim. As the kibbutzim are increasingly inclined to put their own members on monetary budgets, the line between the kibbutzim and the moshavim shitufim has become increasingly difficult to draw.

While collective norms and collective economic undertakings have helped to protect many moshavim from the centrifugal consequences of excessive individualism, shared commitments throughout the moshav population have increasingly been undermined by a growing differentiation among the members. This differentiation has its roots in a decline in the relative share of agriculture within the Israeli economy that began in the 1950s. The growing industrialization and urbanization of Israel has transformed many moshav members into part-time farmers, while others have become specialists in the production of more lucrative and exotic crops. This growing differentiation of moshav members has made it harder for them to reconcile their conflicting preferences to make decisions about collective investments and has undermined their solidarity as well, making it harder and harder for them to operate as effective moral communities (Levi, 1990).

Increasing differentiation and individuation within the moshavim have contributed to a growing atrophy of cooperative functions, even in moshavim that have not formally been disbanded. In a report based on data collected in 1987, Applebaum

(1990) noted that large numbers of moshavim had long since ceased functioning as the "multi-purpose community coopera- tives" that they were originally conceived as and were now doing little more than acting as the municipal governments for their vil- lages. Thus they continued to perform such functions as providing water and electricity to their members, but they no longer played any role in the growing or marketing of agricultural products.

All of these developments contributed to a widespread dis- couragement and demoralization within the moshav movement. Insofar as anyone had any optimistic thoughts to express about the moshavim in 1989 and 1990, they were directed toward the prospects for moshav industrialization. The moshavim had lagged far behind the kibbutzim in shifting their focus from agriculture to industry (Trattner, 1989), largely because the individualistic struc- tures of the moshavim ovdim made it difficult for their members to pool investments in large-scale enterprises. The more collective structures of the moshavim shitufim, however, were more con- ducive to such efforts, and in the 1980s, a small number of them had begun to test the feasibility of locating some high-tech eco- nomic ventures within moshavim. Several of these high-tech moshavim were located in what is called the Gush Segev, or Segev region, located near the town of Segev in the Galilee (Bar-El, 1987). This region was well suited to be a site for innovative activities on moshavim, as its rocky and hilly terrain made it poorly suited for farming. Having heard many enthusiastic reports about these high- tech moshavim in the Gush Segev, I paid visits to two of them with a colleague from Tel Aviv University in February of 1990.

Our first stop was at Moshav Shorashim, located seven kilo- meters southwest of the development town Karmiel. Shorashim had been founded in 1980 by a group of engineers from the United States and was made up of thirty-one families at the time of our visit. The moshav's best-known product was an EEG machine that had been marketed under the brand name of "Cerebro-trac." The monitor had brought Shorashim a great deal of fame, but had later "had a setback," we were told. The moshav's disappointed hopes for this product had clearly inspired a great deal of postmortem analysis of how and why their plans had gone wrong, and the mem- bership appeared to be in process of extracting some painful lessons from the experience and formulating a more realistic set of expectations for the future.

Shorashim's current general manager, who invited us to call

him Yossi, told us that, with hindsight, the moshav's members could now see that their initial expectations had been too narrow. They began by wanting to do only high-tech work. They increasingly invested too much of their hopes in their most prominent product. When its sales began to decline, they began to spend more and more money on marketing, which turned out to be a case of throwing good money after bad. Looking back on Shorashim's infatuation with that single product, Yossi commented that "we were too impressed by it, and put too much of our energy into it."

By the time of our visit, Shorashim had owned up to these mistakes and was redefining its goals for the future. Shorashim's members don't believe in rotation of management for its own sake, but some of its managers had been asked to give up their positions in the interest of promoting a new approach to its problems. The new philosophy at Shorashim was to be open to many more ways of earning an income than the narrow set of activities it had focused on in the past. It no longer defined itself as a maker of brain wave monitors alone; we were now told that Shorashim's "leading branch" is one that specializes in "collecting, analyzing, and displaying physiological parameters," producing both hardware and software for such purposes. One current product performs analyses of blood; another project deals with the measurement of stress and fatigue in eyes. Altogether, Yossi estimated that the work of this branch constituted 70 percent of Shorashim's activity.

In its search for work to occupy the rest of its capacities, Shorashim had become quite flexible and diverse. Another 10 percent of its current activity consisted of writing technical manuals in English. Much of the remainder Yossi described as "educational tourism," which included renting out their facilities for seminars on such subjects as Arab-Jewish relations, technology today, new settlements in the Galilee, and more. Shorashim's workers have performed a variety of other services. They had recently completed a small subcontracting job for the firm Elbit, assembling cards that served as components in computers to be installed in tanks and planes. Another activity until recently had been the assembly of tens of thousands of "bug zappers" per year for the firm Amcor. That venture had employed twenty to thirty people at its peak, but the work was lost when competition from Taiwan took over the European market.

While pointing out the various activities that Shorashim has been and is currently involved in, Yossi also tried to identify their common themes. One is a shift in emphasis from selling products to selling services. Another is a much broader and also more realistic range of activities that Shorashim's members are prepared to become involved in. "Initially we wanted only to be high-tech," suggested Yossi. "Now we just don't want to pollute." Other things that Shorashim still does not want to do include getting involved in expensive, capital-intensive projects or taking on activities that cannot be handled comfortably on Shorashim's small scale. "It has to be something we can *manage*," Yossi emphasized. "That's our biggest limitation after capital—labor we can supply. It has to be something our people can manage." As an example of an activity that Shorashim now sees as being beyond its reach, Yossi pointed to marketing. That's a lesson that emerged from the experience with the brain wave monitor. Shorashim's members now realize that they want to do the development and the manufacturing of new high-tech products, but let a partner do the marketing.

My colleague and I both sensed from Yossi that these had been painful lessons to learn and that Shorashim had been going through some quite difficult times. But as for the general concept of high tech on the moshav, Yossi insisted that one "can't say it's a completely lost cause." He pointed to the importance of improvements in communication, like the fax machine, that make distance less important and that make it possible to locate activities like those of Shorashim quite far away from their markets and customers.

Moshav Yaad in the Gush Segev is older than Shorashim and better established. It was founded in 1974 by graduates of the Technion who were specialists in computer science and engineering. In February of 1990, these skills continued to form the core of its most profitable activities. Fifteen members and another fifteen outsiders were engaged in the production of computer software for clients like the Digital Equipment Corporation. Nine members and nine nonmembers produced microelectronic systems for agriculture and industry—devices for weighing, feeding, conveying, and production control. Another twenty members and two or three outsiders worked in the moshav's architectural office, the largest in Northern Israel. Six members and six outsiders worked in agricultural activities, which included the growing of houseplants, avocados, and sabra pears. Three members were engaged in unique activities tailored to their own individual skills and needs—one was making jewelry, another was making handicrafts, and a recent immigrant from Belgium was translating technical works from French into English.

Many reforms and philosophies that were only recently being discussed on the kibbutz were already well established in Moshav Yaad. Professional self-development and the attainment of a high standard of living were accepted as explicit goals from the beginning, along with mutual aid. Members are free to choose their own work, but are held to strict accounting. If a member's activity fails to produce a sufficient income, the work will be discontinued or given to a hired labor, and the member will be reassigned to other work. The member making jewelry, for example, is an electronic technician who asked for a chance to try this work. He had been given half a year "to prove himself," but would have to find something else if the effort did not pan out.

While such practices were now becoming widely accepted, even on the kibbutz, other ideas expressed at Moshav Yaad might still be greeted as heretical there. Benji Livnai, the general manager of Moshav Yaad, told us that Yaad had always been a moshav *shitufi* (united), but not *shivioni* (equalized). Although the members of Moshav Yaad have generally received equal salaries, they have also always been free to keep any gifts or other unearned income that they receive from outside the cooperative—inheritances, reparations payments from Germany, and so on. Benji noted that on a kibbutz, "people play tricks" with such outside sources of income, attempting to conceal them in order to keep them, but on Moshav Yaad, members are free to buy cars or go abroad or do anything else with their private wealth derived from the outside.

Moshav Yaad was also not averse to using at least one form of inequality in incomes as a stimulus to additional work. The working hours for male members of Moshav Yaad were set at eight hours per day, and men could not receive extra pay by working overtime; but the workload for women was only five hours per day, and women who worked more hours than this were rewarded with additional income.

More recently, Moshav Yaad had begun to consider some even more radical departures from the principle of equality that the moshavim shitufim have traditionally shared with the kibbutzim. Benji noted the irony that "the kibbutzim keep approaching us, but we keep moving farther away." There had been growing dissension within Moshav Yaad over differences in earning power between branches. Discussions had begun over the possibility of splitting the moshav up into its separate branches. Each firm would then keep its own profits, and each family would earn its own money and pay its own taxes. There was also talk of introducing unequal salaries within branches.

Changes this radical would involve ceasing to be a moshav shitufi, as it is not permitted to pay unequal salaries and still call oneself a moshav shitufi. But Benji said that both he and many of his fellow members were ready to face this possibility. Despite the economic success of Moshav Yaad, Benji felt that "a cooperative is a means, not an end. It's a good way to start, a good way to live for a certain period; but it's against nature, . . . it's not natural any more."

It was a bit of a shock to encounter such a confession of lost faith in what was reputed to be one of the strongest and most hopeful parts of the Israeli moshav movement. But such thoughts were widespread among the Israeli moshavim and their well-wishers in 1989 and 1990. In November of 1989, a moshav expert at the Ruppin Institute expressed the judgment that the moshav "is not for our age." He noted that the pioneers of the moshav were all farmers, all poor, all the same age, all with the same education. Now there is too much differentiation on the moshav for its residents to be united in a single cooperative. Some are farmers and some are lawyers. Some rely on the moshav for a livelihood and some do not. As a result of such problems, "everyone realizes that we need a perestroika here."

In February of 1990, I heard similar views expressed by a specialist in research on the moshav at the Settlement Study Centre. This researcher too felt that Israel's "cooperatives are now a residue of another historical era." They originated in the Zionism of the early settlers, in a socialism that had no state, and in the practical needs of poor people who found it easier to cooperate than to attempt to do everything alone. The major thing that was changed since those times is the Israeli economic structure. The moshavim began as homogeneous entities, but now in the same cooperative one finds "people with different types of farms, different risks, and different chances for success." You can't cooperate, this informant pointed out, when people "have different interests and different risks."

RETRENCHMENT AND RESTRUCTURING AT KOOR

The economic crisis that traumatized the kibbutzim and caused the collapse of the moshavim also had a staggering effect on the industrial plants owned by the Chevrat Ovdim. Known collectively as Koor Industries, this Histadrut-owned sector consisted in 1986 of about three-hundred enterprises, and employed more than thirty-two-thousand workers. Under the impact of the soaring real rates of interest that followed the government's economic stabilization program of August 1985, Koor's balance sheet quickly began to show unprecedented losses. In 1987, it lost $244 million on sales of $2.6 billion (Teitelbaum, 1989). In October of 1988, Koor began to miss payments on its foreign debt, and Bankers' Trust, its largest foreign creditor, petitioned a Tel Aviv court to liquidate the company (Maltz, 1989a).

While Koor negotiated with its creditors to reschedule its debt, it was forced to lay off thousands of workers and to close or sell off many of its subsidiaries. Some of its best-known ventures were completely divested, including the Alliance tire factory, Teva Pharmaceuticals, and Israel Investors Corporation, which published the *Jerusalem Post*. Through such measures, Koor's labor force was reduced to twenty-two-thousand by the fall of 1989.

Such drastic measures were not sufficient to stem the flow of losses, however, leading the Likud government to propose in September of 1989 that the entire company should be sold. As negotiations with domestic and foreign creditors dragged on through the fall of that year, all of Israel debated what would and should become of Koor. On December 25, the Chevrat Ovdim agreed to turn over its shares in Koor to the government and to the banks, in return for debt relief. A few days later, the government announced that it would not accept these offered shares, because it did not wish to be saddled with the responsibility of owning Koor. In January of 1990, Shamrock Holdings of the United States and the Belzberg family of Canada explored the possibility of buying Koor, but both bidders made their offers contingent upon further debt relief. As Koor's employees went on strike to protest the proposed sale, it increasingly became apparent to all concerned that the company was unsellable in its present form. The company, the government, and domestic and foreign creditors realized that there was no other option than to renegotiate the terms for repayment of Koor's debts. A tentative agreement among these parties was announced in early February of 1990.

These economic difficulties were bad enough in themselves, but they had important political and ideological ramifications as well. As one Histadrut source put it, "The political and ideological antagonists of the labour economy greeted the 1987 balance sheet of Koor with glee; here, they claimed, was proof of the inefficiency of the labour economic sector in Israel" (Teitelbaum, 1989, p. 24).

Koor's defenders countered that its recent financial problems were only temporary setbacks. They insisted that Koor had been profitable in the past and would be profitable again. Recent research by Ben-Ner and Estrin (1991) indicates, for example, that from 1969 to 1981, plants owned by Koor were on the average more productive than comparable private firms.

Chevrat Ovdim spokesmen also noted that Koor's recent difficulties were not of its own making and that many firms in Israel's private sector were suffering just as badly as it was in this period. For example, Israel's second largest industrial concern, Clal, also suffered heavy losses on its industrial operations during this period and was able to balance its books only with the aid of profits earned on its financial and commercial activities (Teitelbaum, 1989). Another economic affiliate of the Histadrut, the Bank Hapoalim, actually increased its market share and capitalization from 1986 to 1989, but its performance was of no help to Koor, because they are organized as separate firms (*Jerusalem Post*, 1989).

One factor that caused Koor and other Israeli manufacturers to be especially hard hit by the crisis was the exchange-rate policy of the government after 1985, which held the value of Israel's currency stable at a relatively high level. By keeping a lid on the price of imports, this policy helped to tame inflation, but it also hurt the foreign sales of major exporters like Koor. Koor was also hurt by cutbacks in purchases of weapons systems by the government. Koor's electronics subsidiary, Tadiran, was particularly affected by this change, as its civilian products divisions continued to show profits, while the Tadiran division that made communications products for the military began to accumulate disastrous losses. Teitelbaum summarizes that Koor was "triply harmed" by these recent changes in the Israeli economy: "as an exporter to the dollar area, as a large-scale producer of supplies to the military establishment which had cut back its orders, and finally as a big 'consumer' of investment capital, the cost of which skyrocketed" (1989, p. 24).

Koor also appears to have suffered more directly than either the kibbutzim or the moshavim from the change in the relationship between the Histadrut and the government that followed the Likud victory in 1977. Before that time, relations between these major Israeli institutions had been extremely intimate. Both were dominated by Labor Party leaders, and the Histadrut like the government was more interested in meeting the nation's needs than it was in balancing its books. Koor pursued a policy of locating new plants in underdeveloped parts of Israel, even if these remote locations imposed additional costs. Histadrut also liked to try to find managerial positions in its industrial subsidiaries for officers as they retired from the army. In return, the government assisted Koor in any way it could. One favor upon which Koor became increasingly dependent was a policy that permitted a substantial portion of the pension assets of Histadrut's members to be invested in enterprises owned by the Chevrat Ovdim (Aharoni, 1991, pp. 163–66).

When Likud won its first electoral victory in 1977, it initially pursued a conciliatory policy toward the Histadrut, in the hope of obtaining wage restraint. It therefore continued to honor the easy credit policies that were holdovers from the Labor era. As inflation accelerated, however, the Likud government became increasingly frustrated at Histadrut's reluctance to restrain its members' wage demands. In 1980, Finance Minister Yigal Horowitz punished the Histadrut for this lack of cooperation by cutting off the Chevrat Ovdim's access to workers' pension money (Grinberg, 1991, pp. 79–83, 87–92). Aharoni notes that "Clearly, this arrangement and its discontinuation had a far-reaching impact. . . . The change in the bond arrangements clearly affected the Histadrut enterprises in a significant way" (1991, p. 165). In this period the Bank of Israel also adopted a regulation that restricted lending by the Bank Hapoalim to Koor. Both changes made Koor increasingly dependent on external sources of financing and thus made it especially vulnerable to the dramatic rise in real interest rates that began in August 1985.

In 1988 and 1989, Koor's defenders could point to all of these considerations in their search for factors that mitigated Koor's responsibility for its current economic difficulties. Critics outside the Histadrut were not as kind. Aharoni, for example, notes that the Histadrut's cozy relationship with the government and its privileged access to workers' pension funds "allowed the Histadrut firms to tolerate relatively high levels of featherbedding and inefficiencies" (1991, p. 166). Aharoni also argues that the Histadrut's dual role as both an employer and a trade union gave it a special handicap in responding to a recession, because it made the Chevrat Ovdim-owned enterprises especially reluctant to lay off workers or to reduce wages. For this reason,

Histadrut firms had great difficulty making the necessary adjustments. As a result, several large Histadrut enterprises found themselves near bankruptcy. The first was Solel Boneh, which despite a 50% reduction of construction activities continued to pay its workers a monthly paycheck even though they were really disguising unemployment. Then came Koor. . . . Again, one reason was the continuation of losing activities. Another was an increased level of wages without regard to market conditions (1991, p. 165).

In the face of both mounting losses and mounting criticisms, Koor's creditors insisted that the Chevrat Ovdim must respond with more than excuses; they demanded reforms. Chevrat Ovdim's own leadership was increasingly inclined to acknowledge that Koor's management had not been as good as it could have been, that the pursuit of national, political, and trade union goals had caused Koor to give insufficient attention to the profitability of each venture, and that Koor, in short, now needed its own "perestroika" (Teitelbaum, 1989).

The first set of reforms intended to serve as a response to the crisis was announced by the Chevrat Ovdim leadership in the summer of 1988. The major element contained in this package was a call for increased decentralization of the industrial operations affiliated with the Chevrat Ovdim. The central offices of Koor would continue to be responsible for general financial policies, long-term research and development, and auditing the books of its subsidiaries, but the authority and responsibility for managing each enterprise were to be shifted to lower levels. Each enterprise would have its own board of directors. The manager of each enterprise would be appointed by the board of directors and would be responsible solely to the board and workers of that enterprise.

This program of decentralization was to be coupled with other reforms designed to lend new meaning to Chevrat Ovdim's old but tenuous claim to be in some sense "labor-owned." Legally, the Chevrat Ovdim is a registered cooperative, owned collectively by all of the Histadrut's 1.7 million members. In practice, the employees of Chevrat Ovdim have tended to react to it as if it were either a conventional private employer (Aharoni and Lachman, 1982) or a branch of the government (Reshef and Bemmels, 1989). Since the 1960s, the Histadrut has been experimenting with a variety of mechanisms designed to make its employees feel more like owners. These have included representation for workers on the boards of directors of holding companies like Koor and provisions for the profits of money-making subsidiaries to be shared with employees (Palgi, 1991).

The reforms approved in the summer of 1988 offered the potential to increase workers' participation in the management and profitability of Chevrat Ovdim-owned enterprises in several ways. The program of decentralization would confer important powers on the boards of subsidiary enterprises, on which workers would also be represented. And the program of profit sharing would henceforth be supplemented by a system of direct ownership of stock shares or bonds by individual employees. As this system was described in an English-language publication of the Histadrut, it would contain the following elements:

> Participation of the workers in ownership of Hevrat Ha'Ovdim enterprises will be implemented through the distribution of stock shares or bonds of the firm where the worker is employed. The shares or bonds distributed to workers shall not be subject to trade or transferred to others. This kind of workers' participation shall be put into practice in enterprises of Hevrat Ha'Ovdim, both in firms which have offered stock shares to the general public, and those which had not hitherto issued stock shares. The directors of the Koor concern were charged with working out an operative plan, within three months, for the implementation of participation of workers in ownership, a plan which will also serve as a model for other firms in the labour economy. The government will be urged to grant special income tax exemptions to those employees who purchase partial ownership of the firms in which they work (*Labour in Israel*, 1989, p. 2).

While calls for increased participation for workers in management reflected an old agenda of the Histadrut's left wing, these plans for workers' shareholding derived from some newer and more practical concerns. Koor was desperate for capital and was seeking to raise money in almost any way it could. Since 1987, shares in Koor had begun to be sold on public stock exchanges. Under these circumstances, the sentiment grew within the Histadrut that if profits are now going to be made from owning shares in enterprises of the Chevrat Ovdim, then the workers in these enterprises ought to be given a preferential chance to purchase those shares.

Negotiations between Histadrut and the government to draft a new law governing employee stock purchases quickly bore fruit. This was due in no small measure to the fact that Shimon Peres of the Labor Party represented the government in these negotiations in his capacity as minister of finance. The government also had its own interest in passing such a law, as the government planned to divest some shares it owned in firms like El Al and the Bank Hapoalim, and it wanted to have the option of selling some of these shares to the firms' employees. There was support for the new law within the private sector as well, as several high-tech manufacturers with ties to the United States wanted to follow the American practice of encouraging share ownership by employees. A law promoting employee share ownership in Israel was passed by the Knesset early in 1989. It offered a tax deduction to employees for wages they used for purchases of their employers' stock, up to a maximum of 10 percent of their salaries.

When I arrived in Israel in September of 1989, this law had already been passed, but had not yet been applied, as Israel's tax authorities were still scrutinizing the new statute and drafting the detailed regulations that would guide its actual implementation. In the meantime, a different innovation in the ownership and management of Chevrat Ovdim-owned enterprises was generating a great deal of excitement. This was a small tile-making factory in Beersheba named Chasin Esh that was being hailed by some as the "new hope" of the cooperative movement in Israel.

Chasin Esh had been a Koor subsidiary that employed sixty-seven people at its peak. After the venture had failed and closed its doors, a group of former employees had asked permission to reopen the business as an independent cooperative. Chevrat Ovdim agreed to lease them the facilities, and this small group of workers went on to achieve what appeared to be a spectacular success. The eighteen members of this cooperative, with the help of a hired manager and eight seasonal hired workers, were soon turning out more tiles than the plant had produced before its closure. A Chevrat Ovdim official responsible for the project told me of Chasin Esh that "they are working very hard, and they are very proud."

Chasin Esh struck many observers as a promising new model, not only because of its high productivity, but also because of some unique features of its structure. The fact that Chasin Esh was controlled by its member workers but not owned by them made it Israel's sole example of the model for worker cooperatives that has been advocated by Jaroslav Vanek (1975, 1977). Vanek has long argued that debt financing for such cooperatives is the best way both to motivate the productive use of assets in worker cooperatives and to minimize the use of hired labor within them. When the supply of capital and membership in a cooperative become too closely associated, Vanek warns, this both increases the use of hired labor and causes the cooperative to be starved for capital.

Another feature of Chasin Esh that drew favorable comment in some quarters was the absence of any ties between it and the Merkaz Hakooperatsia. Chasin Esh was registered as a cooperative with the Registrar of Cooperatives in Jerusalem, but had no ties to the Cooperative Center in Tel Aviv. "The Merkaz Hakooperatsia would kill them," I was told by one Chevrat Ovdim insider, and given the moribund status of the Merkaz cooperatives, many other observers were inclined to agree. The Merkaz Hakooperatsia, it was pointed out, is dominated by the two bus cooperatives and is therefore hostile to cooperatives with alternative financial structures. By the Chevrat Ovdim leadership, on the other hand, I was told that "It's a small baby, a very dear one, and we give it special treatment."

It also did not require too much imagination to see in the relationship between Chevrat Ovdim and Chasin Esh a blueprint for an Israeli Mondragon (Whyte and Whyte, 1988). Chevrat Ovdim could provide capital and technical assistance to worker cooperatives in a role analogous to that of Mondragon's Caja Laboral Popular, while Chasin Esh could serve as its first successful venture, the Israeli counterpart to Mondragon's Fagor. Parallels of this sort were in fact on many people's minds, as a delegation of Histadrut and kibbutz movement officials had visited the worker cooperatives of Mondragon in Spain in the mid-1980s, and the example of Mondragon had lain at the heart of the "new model" for worker cooperatives in Israel that had been advanced by Abraham Daniel (1986, 1989).

The success of Chasin Esh encouraged policy makers in left-wing parties like Mapam and the Citizens' Rights Movement to draft bold new proposals for the democratization of Chevrat Ovdim as new Histadrut elections approached in the fall of 1989. Mapam proposed that "The smaller Hevrat Ha'ovdim firms should be turned into cooperatives while workers in the larger factories should be offered some form of worker ownership" (Black, 1989b). Worker ownership in the larger enterprises would provide workers with 26 percent of the stock, and their shares would be made non-tradeable. These two provisions together would ensure that "The stake would be enough to guarantee the workers a say in running the firm, regardless of who held the remaining 74%" (Black, 1989b). In the proposals on Histadrut governance put forward by Dan Jacobson of Tel Aviv University for the CRM, the main emphasis would be placed on furthering shopfloor participation. "This would be accomplished through the creation of autonomous work groups inside the factory, responsible for their own sphere of operations" (Black, 1989a). "In cases where Hevrat Ha-ovdim wants to sell companies," CRM was similar to Mapam in proposing that "the firms' workers should be offered the right of first refusal" (Black, 1989a). Insofar as workers lacked the capital to finance these purchases, Jacobson and the CRM proposed that "the money should be lent to them by the Histadrut's Bank Hapoalim" (Black, 1989a).

When the Histadrut elections actually took place in mid-November of 1989, they came as an anticlimax, as it quickly became apparent that they would bring no such radical changes. Histadrut's leaders from the Labor Party were returned to their offices and continued to govern Histadrut much as they had before, insofar as their creditors left them any discretion at all.

It had also become obvious to knowledgeable insiders even well before the November election that Chasin Esh was a unique experiment that the Chevrat Ovdim leadership had no intention of repeating. The problem with Chasin Esh from the point of view of the Chevrat Ovdim was that it left Koor as the owner of the factory, while what Koor really wanted to do was to divest the plant, recoup its capital investment, and use the proceeds to prop up its remaining enterprises. In its search for a buyer for the Chasin Esh property, Chevrat Ovdim saw two possibilities: it could sell the plant to its workers, or it could find an outside buyer. The Chevrat Ovdim leadership gradually realized that it preferred the latter option to the former one and that the detour through a cooperative might have done nothing but make that sale more difficult. Selling Chasin Esh to the workers faced two major problems. The first was that it would be very expensive for the workers. It is possible that a bank might help them raise the money, but that would only exacerbate the second problem, which was that the factory badly needed an infusion of new investments. If the workers used all the credit available to them just to purchase the existing plant, they would be unable to raise the capital needed to pay for these new investments.

As a result of logic of this sort, the Chevrat Ovdim leadership was becoming increasingly convinced in 1989 that experiments like Chasin Esh would not solve its problems. They saw a much brighter future in such alternative ownership models as joint ventures with local or foreign companies and public offerings of stock. These options were seen as more attractive than sales to workers, because Koor's factories in general were starved for capital, and their workers lacked the resources to meet their capital needs. One Histadrut official also pointed out to me that in Israel, unlike the United States or Sweden, the government lacks the resources to overcome this problem by offering substantial tax subsidies for workers' capital stakes.

In this situation, it appeared increasingly likely that if worker ownership was to play any role at all in the changes taking place in the Chevrat Ovdim, it would be primarily in order to make public stock offerings and complete divestitures of enterprises more palatable to employees. In regard to worker ownership, it was thus becoming more and more difficult to find any real difference between the policies of the Histadrut leadership and the proposals advanced by the Likud party in September of 1989, which had called for the complete divestiture of the Chevrat Ovdim. In neither set of policies could one discern any real conviction that worker shareholding would motivate employees or turn a failing enterprise around. In both, worker ownership appeared to be valued not for its potential impact on workers, but for its ability to legitimate a transfer of ownership to other groups.

On my most recent visit to Israel in the spring of 1993, Koor's economic recovery program was well under way and was already being hailed as a success. The Koor empire was now much reduced in size, but was once again solvent. This return to profitability could not be viewed as a validation of Koor's traditional ownership system, however, because it had clearly been based on a repudiation of it. Koor was now being managed on the basis of conventional business principles, and the Chevrat Ovdim had been enjoined to stay out of Koor's decision making on the insistence of the banks. The period of economic restructuring had left the Chevrat Ovdim as an owner of only 35 percent of the assets of Koor, and that ownership share was expected to fall by at least another 10 percent before the steps outlined for Koor's economic recovery would be complete.

Unique Variations and Common Themes

While the three major branches of Israel's labor economy have all been suffering tremendous recent shocks, there are clearly major differences among them in the causes and extent of their current problems and in their responses. These differences can in turn be linked to some more fundamental differences among these organizations in their economic and institutional structures.

Of these three sets of organizations, those affiliated with Koor are the ones whose ownership is most centralized and collective. They behave more like enterprises that are owned by the government than like cooperatives of any type. Their formation and dissolution have always been matters for negotiation among the Histadrut, political authorities, and external funding agents, and have never depended on the private initiatives of workers, either as individuals or in groups. The causes of and solutions to the recent crisis in Koor have therefore been sought at this same high level—in the relationship of Koor to the government, political parties, and the Histadrut leadership; in the way in which these organizations recruit their managers and obtain their capital; and in the way in which organizational goals and strategies are defined and pursued. Until the recent economic shocks, Koor's managerial appointments were based on political patronage, and its wage and staffing policies reflected an internal political need to protect employment at all costs. Beginning in 1985, Koor finally began to pay a price for the Histadrut's past efforts to be a political movement, a labor union, and an employer, all at the same time. On the insistence of its external creditors, Koor now appears to be solving its own identity crisis by transforming itself into a more conventional private firm.

The kibbutzim and moshavim, in contrast, are more similar to worker cooperatives, in that they are founded and administered by semiautonomous groups, and their survival depends on the continuity of those groups. Both sets of groups now seem to have been seriously weakened by a growing diversity and individualism among their members. The moshav has been affected by these trends far more than the kibbutz, because its highly decentralized structure leaves it much more open to these changes at the grassroots. With the exception of the moshav shitufi, the moshav has always been more individualistic than the kibbutz, both in its ethic and in its structure. The member of the moshavim own their own homes, cars, and businesses, and their increasing tendency to pursue their own individual economic ends has reduced the ostensible "cooperative" nature of their village to a mere vestige.

The kibbutzim have been more successful in resisting these tendencies, because they have much stronger collective structures. This is true not only of the relationship between the individual member and his or her own kibbutz, but also of the relationship of each kibbutz to its own federation and to the holding company, Nir, that owns its assets (Rosner, 1991b). The kibbutz federations have cushioned the impact of the economic crisis by imposing levies on the more prosperous kibbutzim to help the poorer ones stave off bankruptcy. The federations have also formulated and enforced collective decisions about the extent and limits of permissible reforms. On a scale of individualism versus collectivism, the kibbutzim thus belong somewhere between the two extremes represented by the moshavim and Koor (see Rosner, 1991a). Their ability to respond collectively rather than individually has allowed the kibbutzim to cling to a common identity, even while that identity is in the process of being redefined in response to the crisis, and gives them the best prospects for surviving the recent economic difficulties with their movement intact.

Despite the real and important differences among these organizations, there do appear to be a few general conclusions that can be applied to all of them. The broadest is that Israeli society is now far less hospitable to labor-owned institutions of all these types than it was in the 1920s. The economic rationale for these institutions is now largely gone. Individuals and groups no longer see as great a need as they once did to form cooperative organizations in order to create employment opportunities for themselves, and the national leadership sees little need for them as well. The social legitimation that these organizations once enjoyed is also now a thing of the past. Rather than being seen as embodying the highest ideals of the nation, the kibbutzim are now held up as objects of hatred and derision by their Sephardic neighbors in development towns (Eisenstadt, 1985, pp. 421, 498).

Interestingly, the Likud victory in 1977 had less direct impact on the financial health of most of these institutions than it was widely expected to have (Ben-Porath, 1983; Aharoni, 1991, pp. 191–94; Shalev, 1992, chapter 6). Shalev comments, "The Likud took office seemingly determined to savage the Histadrut," but in practice, it "found it prudent to avoid head-on confrontation"

(1992, p. 263). One Likud finance minister announced an intention to increase taxes on the kibbutzim, but dropped the proposal when a commission he appointed concluded that these organizations were already paying more rather than less than comparable private firms (Aharoni, 1991, p. 192). The Likud's restraint in dealing with the labor economy appears to have been due in part to its desire to improve its showing in national and Histadrut elections; but it also reflects the fact that the Likud was itself a coalition of diverse elements and had trouble formulating consistent economic policies of any kind. Aharoni notes that "In reality, there were more differences in the economic policies of the four ministers of finance in the first two time periods of the Likud-led governments than between them and the Labor-led period" (1991, p. 191). Thus only in the case of the Chevrat Ovdim-owned enterprises did the Likud governments take actions that had any direct impact on their finances, and even in that instance, the loss of special access to workers' pension money in 1980 is seen by Aharoni and most others as merely a contributing factor in the later economic crisis and not its most important cause.

While the direct economic impact of the Likud victory was relatively minor, the labor economy was much more strongly affected by the broader changes in Israeli society of which that victory was a symbol and culmination. Whereas both the government and society of Israel had previously offered the labor economy both encouragement and support, both were now increasingly skeptical, and even hostile. It was not only that these specific institutions appeared to have gone out of style, but that the entire value structure that had given rise to them was now seen as having passed. In a book on *The Transformation of Israeli Society* written a few years after the Likud victory, Eisenstadt wrote of a "disintegration of the initial institutional mould of Israeli society" and of an "exhaustion of ideology" (1985, p. 403). In particular he perceived a "weakening of the pioneering elitist orientation stressing duties, commitment and standards of performance" (p. 409) and saw this as giving way to a new emphasis on entitlements (p. 409) and a new "atmosphere of free for all, of enrichissez-vous, of quick grabbing and spending" (p. 528). Eisenstadt attributed these transformations to such economic influences as the individuating consequences of education and social mobility (p. 429), plus the political-historical fact that the basic program of the labor Zionist elites had largely been accomplished and was therefore now ideologically "spent" (p. 489).

Israelis were thus now much more individualistic and less self-sacrificing than they had been in the past and less interested in cooperative or collective ownership of any kind. These changes in attitudes had occurred not only outside the labor economy, but within it as well, and it was these new attitudes that caused the economic crisis of the late 1980s to become a spiritual crisis at the same time. The kibbutzim, moshavim, and Koor were not alone in suffering economic hardships during these times, but only in these institutions did these difficulties become an occasion for such widespread soul-searching and self-doubt. These cooperative and collectively owned institutions were increasingly less likely to be perceived as appropriate solutions to individual or social problems not only by the Israeli public, but by their own members. They were losing legitimacy not only in the eyes of the general public, but also in their own members' eyes.

The crisis of confidence in Israel's labor economy was deep and profound, but it is also evident from these developments that Israel's cooperative movement was not dead. It was clearly down, but not out. In all three of these sets of organizations, new projects were still being attempted, and creative new initiatives were still being launched. The kibbutzim were still establishing new ventures in manufacturing and the services, many of which now took the form of joint ventures with firms in the private sector or with other kibbutzim. New high-tech moshavim were being founded in the Gush Segev and other locations, and the Chevrat Ovdim was experimenting with Chasin Esh and employee shareholding.

While there was thus a widespread perception that the old models no longer worked, a good deal of creativity was now being invested in the search for new models that might take their place. It is in this context that it is now appropriate to turn back to a consideration of the worker cooperatives. They too are down, but perhaps not yet out. It remains to be seen whether they have anything to learn from or to contribute to the current crisis of confidence and search for new models within the other major components of Israel's labor economy.

6. Do Israeli Worker Cooperatives Have a Future as Well as a Past?

Earlier chapters have already noted that the problems of the Israeli worker cooperatives began in the 1930s, 1940s, and 1950s, in the growing rift between them and the rest of the Histadrut, which at that time dominated the Israeli economy and polity. In the 1980s and 1990s, the Histadrut lost its former dominance, its entire labor economy was in serious trouble, and it no longer had much in the way of resources, patronage, or moral support to offer to the worker cooperatives, even if it wished to. By this point, the entire Histadrut empire was suffering from many of the same social changes that had been undermining the worker cooperative movement for decades.

In this environment, it was becoming increasingly difficult to foresee any conditions under which the long-term decline of Israel's worker cooperative population might be reversed. The purpose of the present chapter is to assess the current state and future prospects of this population and to see if any circumstances can be identified under which worker cooperatives might be expected to play as great a role in Israel's future as they have played in its past.

THE MERKAZ HAKOOPERATSIA IN THE 1990S

When I first arrived in Israel in September of 1989, the Merkaz Hakooperatsia had recently experienced a leadership change. Israel Ziv of Dan, who had led the Merkaz since 1968, had retired and been replaced by Amnon Bar-On of Egged. Bar-On had previously served Egged in many capacities, as a bus driver, a manager, and a provider of technical assistance to transportation systems in South America.

Although the Merkaz had operated semiautonomously since 1968, it remained a part of the Histadrut. Bar-On told me that he had talked at length with the Histadrut leadership about the future of the worker cooperatives before he agreed to accept responsibility for the Merkaz. Bar-On had made clear to the Histadrut leaders that he had no interest in presiding over the demise of the Israeli worker cooperative movement. He took the job only with the understanding that he would be helping to create new worker cooperatives, and he expected the Histadrut to assist him in this effort.

At our first meeting and in all of our later conversations, Bar-On always had a number of concrete initiatives in mind that gave practical meaning to his hopes. There was never a time in the period between 1989 and 1993 when the Merkaz Hakooperatsia was not in touch with five, ten, or fifteen groups of workers who were expressing a serious interest in forming new cooperatives. At the beginning of the 1990s, the new flow of immigration coming in from the Soviet Union and its successor states was the focus of much of this hope. If immigration had fueled the formation of worker cooperatives in Israel in the past, here was a great new wave of immigration and therefore a new opportunity to create worker cooperatives on a large scale. About a dozen worker cooperatives were established by new immigrants from the Soviet Union between 1990 and 1992, encouraging hopes that there would be many more to come.

In our later meetings in 1992 and 1993, Bar-On was also encouraged by the establishment of a new cooperative loan fund. The fund consisted of 600,000 NIS, or close to $300,000, which had been put together from three sources—200,000 NIS from the Merkaz, 200,000 from the Chevrat Ovdim, and 200,000 from a Histadrut fund that supports the development of unsettled areas. The money in this fund could potentially be put to many uses. It could support the establishment of new cooperatives, or new capital investments for existing ones, provided that they used the money to facilitate the admission of new members. Loans could also be used to help individual workers purchase memberships in their cooperatives. These loans to individuals could be for amounts up to 10,000 NIS. They would last for a period of five years and would charge no interest, but would be indexed against inflation.

While such initiatives helped Bar-On and other Merkaz staff members to resist the temptation to abandon all hope, it was hard for an outsider to place much faith in them. The capital in this loan fund and the amounts contemplated for each loan seemed awfully small when measured against the needs to which they might be applied. With memberships in some Israeli worker cooperatives valued at more than $100,000, it was hard to see how a loan of 10,000 NIS would be of much help in buying one. And given the unchanged capital structures of the Israeli worker cooperatives, small loan programs of this type could only delay the growing use of hired labor in these cooperatives, but could not prevent it.

The establishment of this loan fund and the creation of a handful of new cooperatives could also not outweigh some other ominous signs of trouble among the Israeli worker cooperatives. Between 1990 and 1992, about a third of the approximately seventy-five worker cooperatives that had been associated with the Merkaz Hakooperatsia in 1989 were dissolved. This group included some of the most prominent of Israel's remaining worker cooperatives. In May of 1992, it was particularly shocking to learn that the venerable bus and furniture-making cooperative Haargaz had recently been taken over by the Chevrat Ovdim and had ceased to exist as a cooperative.

This news came as a shock not only to outside observers, but also to the leadership of the Merkaz. It had been done "behind our backs," I was told. And this was not the only sign that the relationship between the Merkaz Hakooperatsia and the Histadrut continued to suffer from many of the same troubles that had been remarked on in the past. "They are not supporting us," I was told. The Chevrat Ovdim's contribution to the new loan fund had not been its own money, but came from the worker cooperatives themselves. It consisted largely of Chevrat Ovdim's proceeds from the sale of assets formerly owned by the Achdut bakery of Haifa, which had failed in 1990. When an Israeli worker cooperative is dissolved, 25 percent of its assets become the property of Chevrat Ovdim. Since most Israeli worker cooperatives leave only negligible assets behind when they dissolve, this provision had been largely forgotten, but this bakery had owned enough capital to make the Chevrat Ovdim the beneficiary of a 150,000 NIS windfall. A good deal of cajoling had been needed to persuade the Chevrat Ovdim to reinvest this money among the worker cooperatives, and it seemed to have left some hurt feelings on all sides. When I first learned about this fund in 1992, the administration of the new loan fund had not yet been worked out, and delicate negotiations were still taking place to decide who would control the fund and what its investment criteria would be.

While discussions about the Chevrat Ovdim and the new loan fund revealed tensions and frayed nerves, on other subjects I occasionally encountered complete demoralization. When I asked one staff member in 1992 for news about the older cooperatives, "They are dying" was the response. Insofar as these older cooperatives were clinging to life at all, it was because their members did not want to give up the 25 percent of their value that would be owed to the Chevrat Ovdim in the event of their dissolution.

On the subject of the new immigrant cooperatives, this same staff member sounded equally discouraged in interviews that took place in 1992 and 1993. He dismissed the past two or three years of effort on the new immigrants' behalf with the simple words "We failed." "The project began with a lot of noise," he added later, "but failed." One source of this disappointment was the World Zionist Organization's Jewish Agency, which had not funded a number of proposals for new cooperatives that had been submitted to it. This staff member also confided, however, that lack of capital had not been their biggest problem. "At the beginning we thought that the capital problem was number one," he said, "but it's a social problem." This "social problem" is that the new Russian-speaking immigrants have no real interest in cooperation. I was told that the "Russians saw cooperation as a means to other ends," but not as something to be valued in its own right. Another Merkaz staff member said to me that the "Russian immigrants think a cooperative is like a kolkhoz, which means that you work, and the government takes the money; so they don't want it." Many new immigrants who had sought the help of the Merkaz in forming worker cooperatives had apparently viewed this step as but a temporary tactic in the unending struggle for resources between the citizen and the state. They saw the creation of their cooperatives as possible ways to obtain grant money or to save on their taxes, but showed little interest in cooperation itself. As a result I was told that many if not most of the cooperatives of new immigrants that the Merkaz had helped to establish in 1990 and 1991 existed only on paper by the time I inquired about them in 1992.

These widespread failures of both old worker cooperatives and new ones had left this staff member in a very discouraged state when I spoke with him in April of 1992. Of the Merkaz as a whole he declared flatly, "It is dead." "To say you think it has a future," he added, "You have to be a liar."

On my final visit to the offices of the Merkaz Hakooperatsia in April 1993, some fresh faces had joined its staff and brought new enthusiasm to the fight. While the cooperatives that had been organized in 1990 and 1991 were acknowledged to have failed, higher hopes were being expressed for three or four new ones that had started up in 1992 and 1993. The Merkaz had become more selective in choosing ventures to back, by one estimate turning away five or six projects for every one that gets approved. Its staff were optimistic that the new ventures starting up in 1992 and 1993 had reasonably good chances for success. Most were in the building trades, in which, it was noted, many cooperatives had been established in the past. And while the new immigrants from the former Soviet republics had no cooperative ideology or interest in socialism, one Merkaz spokesman asserted that their cooperatives "have a future," because their members "need one another."

Expectations within the Merkaz Hakooperatsia itself in the early 1990s thus ranged all the way from guarded hope to complete despair. To produce an independent assessment, it is helpful to use the information reported in the appendix to see how the formation of cooperatives within the Merkaz Hakooperatsia has compared to the formation of worker cooperatives outside the Merkaz over the years 1949–92. In 1949 and 1950, the Merkaz was responsible for more than a hundred new cooperative registrations in each year, and this constituted more than three-quarters of all registrations of new worker cooperatives recorded in those years. From the mid-1950s to mid-1960s, the annual count of cooperative formations attributable to the Merkaz Hakooperatsia fluctuated between a low of two in 1956 and a high of twenty-five in 1963, but continued to constitute a fairly stable three-fourths of the national total. Annual births of Merkaz cooperatives began to fall in both absolute and relative terms in the late 1960s. By the late 1970s and the 1980s, cooperatives affiliated with the Merkaz Hakooperatsia were being eclipsed in most years either by cooperatives affiliated with the audit union of the Arab Cooperatives of Workers and Farmers (ACWF) or by cooperatives with no affiliation at all.

Increasingly, the unaffiliated category appeared to be the Merkaz Hakooperatsia's most serious rival, as the ACWF was appealing to a quite different, non-Jewish constituency, and many of its affiliates appeared to be forming their cooperatives for reasons quite unique to this population. Many of the electric power cooperatives that the ACWF helped to register in the 1970s and early 1980s, for example, were probably more akin to moshavim than to worker cooperatives. The unaffiliated cooperatives, on the other hand, more typically involved Jewish workers, who were engaged in activities that in other instances had been conducted under the umbrella of the Merkaz.

Over the years, unaffiliated worker cooperatives had been established in virtually every industry. In the 1970s and 1980s, they became especially common in the taxi industry and among hired car services for tourists. One of the best known of these unaffiliated taxi cooperatives is Kastel of Tel Aviv, which registered in 1975. Another unaffiliated taxi cooperative is described by Darr (1993b). The formation and later dynamics of these cooperatives appear to owe nothing to any cooperative ideology or fidelity to the labor Zionist movement, but appear to be rooted instead in characteristics of this occupation that hinder conventional forms of supervision and thereby favor the development of a self-employed labor force (Russell, 1985b, 1991).

In the 1980s, the annual count of new cooperative registrations affiliated with the Merkaz Hakooperatsia fell in many years to zero, leaving the unaffiliated cooperatives as the only organizational category that showed any signs of life at all. In 1991 and 1992, the formation of cooperatives by the new wave of Russian speaking immigrants allowed the Merkaz Hakooperatsia to reassert its historic role as the most important source of new cooperative formations among Jewish workers in Israel. But to an outsider, it was difficult to see how this resurgence could last. When this new wave of immigration subsided, the number of new worker cooperatives being formed in each year could once again be expected to fall. And as it became increasingly apparent to would-be cooperators that the Merkaz Hakooperatsia had few resources and little patronage to offer them, it seemed unlikely that the Merkaz would be able to prevent a growing proportion of the worker cooperatives that are formed in the future from falling into this "unaffiliated" category.

WORKER COOPERATIVES AND LABOR ZIONIST UTOPIANISM

A theme that has been reflected in many chapters of this book is that the ideological and organizational links between the Israeli worker cooperatives and labor Zionism were never as helpful to these cooperatives as they superficially appeared to be. The alliance with labor Zionism was always a double-edged sword, both ideologically and politically. In the short term, it did gain for the worker cooperatives important patronage and protection. In bus transportation, in particular, the official support given by the Merkaz Hakooperatsia, the Histadrut, and the Israeli government to the formation and consolidation of worker cooperatives was instrumental in enabling the bus cooperatives to attain the preeminence that they still enjoy in this field.

But in the long term, the alliance with labor Zionism hurt the Israeli worker cooperatives in many ways. From the perspective of labor Zionism, worker cooperatives were of questionable legitimacy, right from the start. They were suspect first of all because their work was centered in cities and not on the land. Second, they were looked down on because both their ownership structures and their urban locations contributed to making them petit bourgeois and individualistic in their outlook and lifestyle. Finally, their well-known tendency to make increasing use of hired labor was seen as a clear violation of the labor Zionist norm of self-labor. Because of such problems, the Histadrut and the Labor Party were never more than half-hearted and unreliable sources of political and economic support for the worker cooperatives, and they soon became more critics than patrons.

While utopianism played a uniquely important role in the formation of the Israeli economy, that utopianism thus worked more against the Israeli worker cooperatives than in their favor. Israeli utopianism was institutionalized both initially and always predominantly in the kibbutz. It was expressed secondarily and more weakly in such less morally elite institutions as the Histadrut and Chevrat Ovdim. Worker cooperatives, in contrast, were being condemned as dystopias from early in the century. Virtually all influential parties had agreed by the 1920s that they suffered from crippling limitations. The worker cooperatives' critics differed only in whether they saw their use of hired labor, the quality of their management, or other problems as their most serious flaws.

Thus despite the amazingly large number of worker cooperatives that were established in Jewish Palestine and later Israel in the course of this century, these organizations were never promoted out of any real enthusiasm. They have always been more an expression of the pragmatism and opportunism of the labor and Zionist leaders than of their ideological preferences. The Histadrut and labor leaders have used the worker cooperative movement as a way to co-opt a portion of the more petit bourgeois and individualistic immigrants and to keep them affiliated with the Labor Party, the Histadrut, the Chevrat Ovdim, and the Kupat Cholim. In this regard the worker cooperatives did for the Histadrut and Labor Party in the cities something akin to what the moshavim were doing for them in the country. Both helped the Histadrut and Labor leaders claim to the WZO that they spoke for the entire nation and that they were the most appropriate conduits for aid throughout the land. And while the structures of these organizations were not fully consistent with the ideals of labor Zionism, it nevertheless helped that they could at least be said to have superficial similarities with them. After the widespread failures of the urban kvutzot, or communes, affiliated with the Gedud Haavodah (Sussman, 1969; Shapiro, 1976; Shapira, 1984), even the Gedud's sympathizers within the Histadrut had concluded by the mid-1920s that worker cooperatives were the closest approximation of their ideals that was feasible for many occupations in Israel's cities.

Promoting the formation of worker cooperatives served other practical needs of the interpenetrating labor and Zionist leaderships as well. It was an attractive way to dole out economic aid among immigrants who practiced a common trade. It minimized disputes about fairness, and shared out aid among the largest possible number of recipients, while simultaneously facilitating economies of scale. Worker cooperatives could also easily be made to serve development goals. Each new development town, for example, required a source of fresh bread and other baked goods. Establishing a cooperative bakery met that need and also created jobs for some immigrant bakers. It also helped to induce those bakers and their families to come live in the new town, in addition to attracting potential residents and new customers.

After independence had been achieved and the first great wave of immigrants that it attracted had been absorbed, perceptions of the nation's needs began to change, and the unity of the labor Zionist movement was lost. The Histadrut pursued a policy of decooperatization toward the urban credit cooperatives and housing cooperatives and increasingly dissociated itself from the worker cooperatives. But the ties between the worker cooperatives and the Histadrut were never completely severed, because each has continued to look to the other for political and ideological support. Membership in the Histadrut gains for Egged and Dan a powerful ally and helps them claim to be not just profit-seeking businesses, but national institutions and part of a movement. For national, Labor Party, and Histadrut leaders, the bus cooperatives are a military resource, a source of votes, and a way to cultivate closer diplomatic relations with other countries.

When I first arrived in Israel to begin this study in September of 1989, someone described the Merkaz Hakooperatsia to me as a "cooperative movement without cooperatives." Others suggested to me that Israel had "never, never" had a worker cooperative movement and that the worker cooperative movement that it claimed to have had always been a "fiction."

If Israel ever had a worker cooperative movement at all, by 1993 that movement consisted of the two bus cooperatives and little else. And these two large cooperatives were clearly now both the greatest success of the Israeli worker cooperative movement and its greatest limitation.

To an outside observer, the success of the two bus cooperatives seemed far greater than most Israelis were prepared to grant. Although Egged and Dan had regularly been pilloried by the Histadrut and by the public for their use of hired labor, their reliance on nonmembers was in fact far lower than in most of Israel's worker cooperatives. Each had brought the benefits of cooperative membership to thousands of workers, a rare achievement not only in Israel, but also in the world. Despite their internal wrangling and numerous scandals, these two bus cooperatives were also generally regarded as being efficient and reasonably well managed (e.g., Berechman, 1987), while practicing a degree of workplace democracy that was remarkable in light of their large size. By international standards, therefore, Egged, Dan, and their predecessors deserve consideration as some of the most important successful instances of worker ownership and workplace democracy in history.

But in the eyes of the Israeli public, the model of workers' cooperation represented by Egged and Dan has long since been discredited and rejected. And this is because within Israel, these cooperatives have not been judged by comparing their behavior to that of similarly structured organizations located in other countries;

they have instead been judged by comparing them to the other major branches of the Chevrat Ovdim and on the basis of their compatibility with the ideals and practical purposes of labor Zionism. For example, that worker cooperatives with these structures tend to make increasing use of hired labor had previously been reported in many countries and was well known to influential Zionist and labor leaders like Oppenheimer and Ben-Gurion from early in this century. But this knowledge did nothing to increase the Histadrut leadership's understanding or toleration of this practice. The labor leaders continued to be scandalized by the worker cooperatives' employment of hired labor, because this practice was both an affront to their labor Zionist values and a threat to their practical efforts to unite the entire nation in one economic organization (the Chevrat Ovdim) and one working class (as represented by the Histadrut). Hired labor both contradicted the labor Zionist ideal of "self-labor" (Leviatan, 1980) and had the potential to undermine the economic and political goal of "the conquest of labor" (Shafir, 1989). And while both the kibbutzim and moshavim also had tendencies to make use of hired labor, only the worker cooperatives were so quick to embrace it and to impose heavy capital requirements on hired laborers who wished to become members. When compared to institutions like the kibbutz and Koor that were considered the property of the entire nation and had no capital charges or membership fees, the bus cooperatives have always looked like more selfish and therefore inferior alternatives. When it was charged in the 1980s that an Egged leader had grown so corrupt and self-indulgent that he would bribe his way out of his reserve military service, the news was horrifying, but not necessarily surprising; it instead attracted a lot of comment and repetition, because it appeared to illustrate things about Egged that many Israelis were only too ready to believe. It was treated as just a particularly vivid and extreme example of Egged members pursuing their individual interests at the public's expense.

By the 1990s, Israel's waning population of worker cooperatives had shrunk to little more than Egged and Dan. All of the Merkaz leaders were members of bus cooperatives, and their salaries were still paid by them. Merkaz staff now had few successful cases to talk about or take a visitor to see beyond their own bus cooperative. Since on many occasions both bus cooperatives had been targets of negative attention in the press, it was hard to see the efforts of the Merkaz Hakooperatsia as much more than an attempt to improve the public image of the two bus cooperatives and to help to salvage some portion of their declining reputations.

The many decades of struggle between the worker cooperatives and the Histadrut had thus reduced the Merkaz Hakooperatsia to playing a largely defensive and conservative role. And insofar as labor Zionism and Israel's labor economy continue to generate new models of cooperative production, the initiative for these organizational innovations has been located almost entirely outside the Merkaz Hakooperatsia rather than within it. The Chevrat Ovdim is itself officially considered to be a worker cooperative, having registered as one in 1924. The expansion of the Chevrat Ovdim subsidiary Koor during and after World War II represented what was for many years the Histadrut leadership's preferred model of cooperative production. More recently, Koor used an innovative leasing arrangement to spin off an unwanted subsidiary to a worker cooperative in its experiment at Chasin Esh. The moshav movement, which appears to have suffered most from the recent economic shocks, has nevertheless come up with a more interesting notion than anything currently being discussed at the Merkaz Hakooperatsia, in its model of "the high-tech moshav." And the most vital portion of the labor economy, by this measure as by so many others, is once again the kibbutz. While deaths of cooperative factories have exceeded births of such organizations in Israel in almost every year since the early 1950s, cooperative production in other forms has expanded rapidly on the kibbutzim. In 1987, the Kibbutz Industries Association officially recognized approximately four hundred enterprises operated by kibbutzim, including factories, guest houses, and a growing number of service activities (Registrar of Cooperative Societies, 1989a, p. 20). Since in that year there was a total of only 282 kibbutzim (p. 2), there were an average of 1.4 of these nonagricultural ventures on each kibbutz. Because a number of these subsidiaries were joint ventures among two or more kibbutzim, the total number of ventures affiliated with each kibbutz in most cases could be expected to be even higher than this.

While Israel's labor economy thus continues to promote and to practice cooperative production in a number of ways, the official alliance between the Israeli worker cooperatives and organized labor Zionism has not been kind to the worker cooperatives themselves. Even from the point of view of the Histadrut, it is hard to identify any sense in which its policies toward the worker cooperatives can be viewed as a success. If the Histadrut's main purpose in establishing the Merkaz Hakooperatsia was indeed to encourage the formation of worker cooperatives, then its policy was successful for a short time but in the long run a failure. If the Histadrut's real purpose in forming the Merkaz was not to promote the worker cooperatives, but to police them and to prevent them from making increasing use of hired labor, then the Histadrut's record is again one of intermittent short-term successes giving way to another clear long-term failure. Only if the purpose of the Merkaz Hakooperatsia was to reduce the competition for external aid funds from this alternative ownership form can its creation be construed even by the Histadrut as having been any kind of success. But in that case, it was indeed a shrewd move, as it is hard to imagine a more effective organizational strategy for making the worker cooperatives look bad.

UTOPIAN AND NONUTOPIAN FORMS OF WORKPLACE DEMOCRACY

Both at the opening of this manuscript and again near the end, it has been noted that Israel's population of worker cooperatives is only one of many forms that utopianism has taken in the economic history of Jewish Palestine and later Israel. Kibbutzim and moshavim, the Gedud Haavodah and the Chevrat Ovdim have all been even more expressive of Israel's utopian impulses.

To describe a form of economic organization as "utopian" often implies more than one thing. It means in the first place that the economic structure in question is radically different from conventional ones. Since the time of Engels, if not before, the word "utopian" has carried a second meaning as well. In his famous diatribe against Duehring and later in a separate essay (1935, 1939), Engels drew a contrast between earlier reformist approaches to socialism, which he branded as "utopian," and the Marxists' own more politically and economically hard-nosed variety of socialism, which he described as "scientific." Since Engels, the label "utopian" has signified proposals that are not applicable in the economies and societies that most of us live in and that therefore have no practical relevance for the real world.

The many branches of Israel's labor economy are all clearly "utopian" in the first sense of this term. Are they also utopian in the second? For the most part, the answer seems to be yes. This strange family of institutions owes its creation to a unique set of conditions that can no longer be duplicated, even in Israel.

In particular, worker cooperatives with the simple structures we encounter in Israel appear to be of very limited applicability, both in Israel and elsewhere. Even when one makes allowances for the Histadrut's prejudices and the lack of significant forms of financial support, the performance of these organizations has not been impressive. The history of the Israeli worker cooperatives supports rather than challenges widespread impressions that such organizations emerge and succeed only under rare circumstances, and that they become increasingly likely to abandon their cooperative structures the older, larger, and more capital-intensive they become. These organizations thus now tend to be found only in narrowly limited economic niches, in Israel as in other parts of the world.

Elsewhere in the labor economy, the kibbutz, the moshav, and Koor have all shown greater dynamism in the past, but have all been deeply shaken by crises in recent years. Of the three, the kibbutz continues to show the most vitality and resilience, as it has at virtually every phase of Isareli history.

The continued economic viability of the kibbutz seems all the more remarkable when one considers that of the many forms of economic organization one can observe in the labor economy, it is the kibbutz whose structure seems most utopian, in the first sense of this term. While worker cooperatives attempt to occupy an intermediate position between capitalism and socialism and are gradually transformed by the logic of profit seeking and capital accumulation into more fully capitalist institutions, the kibbutzim have a more utopian economic structure to match their more utopian aim. All but a few kibbutzim continue to resist any form of individual material incentives for work. They instead continue to live by the Gedud Haavodah's ideal of meeting all their members' needs out of one common purse. Helman (1980) has shown that the kibbutz preference for sharing incomes rather than using differential incomes to motivate higher productivity applies not only within individual kibbutzim, but also among them. Helman found that the level of consumption on each kibbutz is less closely related to the income of that kibbutz than it is to the prosperity of its entire federation. Both individual kibbutz members and the kibbutzim themselves also continue to renounce any claims to own the land they live and work on or their capital or their homes.

Kibbutz assets continue to become the property of Nir, which in practice places them at the disposal of the kibbutz federations (Rosner, 1991b).

Rosner (1991a, 1993) has argued that the kibbutz has derived a great deal of both moral and economic strength from this consistency in its utopianism. But while the very utopianism of the kibbutz may indeed have helped to make it, in Buber's (1958) words, "an experiment that did not fail," it also sharply limits its exportability to other countries and contexts. Despite the currently comfortable standard of living on the kibbutz, the kibbutz system for managing ownership and incomes is structurally equivalent to a vow of poverty and makes the kibbutzim seem more like monasteries than forms of gainful employment. Even within Israel, the kibbutzim remain now as isolated islands of rural utopianism in an increasingly urban and capitalist sea. The many past efforts to establish kibbutzim in Israel's cities, particularly at the time of the Gedud Haavodah, were all unsuccessful. It proved impossible to reconcile the kibbutz structure with urban patterns of property ownership and income distribution, or to protect kibbutz values against the individualistic and materialistic seductions of the cities' bourgeois lifestyle.

As with the kibbutz, the constructive lessons that can be extracted from the experiences of any other portions of Israel's labor economy are limited by their very "utopianism," which is to say by their continued dependence on the highly exceptional circumstances that initially gave rise to them. It is hard to understand the role played in contemporary Israeli society by either the kibbutz or the Histadrut or the bus cooperatives without knowing something about the rich blend of socialism and Zionism, along with a great deal of economic and political pragmatism, that went into the creation of Israel's diverse set of labor-owned and labor-managed institutions. After these unique contextual circumstances have been given their due, however, there remain at least a few ways in which the experiences of Israel's worker cooperatives point toward generalizations that appear valid for other countries. Some of the more important of these lessons are discussed in detail below.

Viable Models of Democracy in the Workplace

Perhaps the most positive conclusion that the history of the Israeli worker cooperatives clearly points toward is that it is indeed possible to have democracy in modern workplaces, if we want it.

Despite all the pessimism of theorists like Weber and Michels about the inevitable atrophy of democracy in the face of growing bureaucracy and oligarchy, many of Israel's aging worker coopera- tives continue to show no inclination to abandon their democratic traditions.

In the case of such extremely large cooperatives at Egged and Dan, the claim that they provide a viable model of workplace democracy rests ultimately on a question that is not empirical, but definitional. Are the party systems, contested elections, and occa- sional leadership turnover that we observe in these organizations sufficient to qualify their decision making as "democratic?" Or should we reserve the word "democracy" for the more consensual forms of decision making advocated by Rousseau, Mansbridge, and Sale, or for the more egalitarian rotation of leadership positions de- scribed by Weber as "direct" democracy?

The position taken here has been that workplace democracy must indeed be judged to be impossible, or nearly so, if the defini- tion of democracy to be used in deciding the issue is a utopian one. Weber's direct democracy, for example, is not impossible, but it is utopian. It requires conditions that are so stringent and rare that they can be found virtually nowhere. These conditions include small organizational size, simple and stable administration, a norm of rotated leadership, and an egalitarian division of labor that leaves all members equally qualified to participate in decisions and to hold administrative offices. We observe these conditions today only in a few isolated niches, such as university faculties or group practices in the professions.

Perhaps the most far-reaching instance of direct democracy in the world today is the Israeli kibbutz (Rosner and Cohen, 1983; Rosner and Blasi, 1985). Despite the presence of exceptionally fa- vorable circumstances, efforts to realize the ideal of direct democ- racy have achieved only limited success, even in this case. On the one hand, social scientists have been reporting for decades that de- cision making on the kibbutz is becoming more oligarchical (e.g., Etzioni, 1958; Ben-Rafael, 1988). On the other hand, many critics within the kibbutzim have recently been arguing that kibbutz de- cision making is still not oligarchical enough. These critics recom- mend that in the interest of greater economic efficiency, successful kibbutz managers should be encouraged to serve longer terms in their specialized posts (e.g., Helman, 1989; Shapira, 1990).

While the kibbutzim debate the question of how much of

their tradition of direct democracy they wish to retain, and in what form, cooperatives like Egged and Dan practice a form of democracy in their workplaces that is much more familiar to us all and is much easier to attain. This is the representative or adversarial form of democracy. While this form of democracy is inferior in many ways to the more direct and consensual kind, it has the merit of being applicable to organizations that are large in size and professional in their management. In most modern cities and nation-states, this is the only form of democracy that we know. And in many modern workplaces, it may be the only form of democracy that we can have.

While the representative democracy of Egged and Dan seems more widely accessible in contemporary workplaces than the direct democracy of the kibbutz, it would be unwise to underestimate the difficulty of exporting to other workplaces even the modest amounts of democracy that we observe in Egged and Dan. With the exception of their large size, these two bus cooperatives continue to offer many of the conditions that authors like Weber (1968), Lipset, Trow, and Coleman (1956), and Collins (1975) have identified as giving workplace democracy its best chance. These include a relatively stable technology and administration, an egalitarian division of labor, and work activities that make this labor force unusually autonomous, responsible, and articulate. One should also not forget that Egged and Dan were formed through mergers of many smaller cooperatives, rather than as transformations of conventional private firms.

Thus while I began by arguing that we should not be so "utopian" as to reject the bus cooperatives' representative model of workplace democracy out of hand, we should also not take this more familiar form of democracy so much for granted that we fail to see the achievement these cooperatives represent. Democracy in all its forms is a delicate institution, difficult to establish and easily disturbed. But given the challenges it involves, it is helpful to recognize that it comes in more than one form. This strikes me as the chief lesson we learn from an examination of the forms of democracy that are practiced in the Israeli worker cooperatives.

Utopian and Nonutopian Forms of Ownership

While Israel's worker cooperatives thus offer evidence that democracy is attainable in contemporary workplaces, the ownership structure they rely on has proved here as elsewhere to provide an unsuitable basis for workplace democracy in all but a few exceptional niches. Factories owned solely by their workers, each sharing equally in wages, ownership, and profit, are attractive as ideals, but have shown themselves to be utopian in practice. A firm that raises capital from no other source than its own workers soon finds itself starved for capital in all but the most labor-intensive industries. Equality in ownership and wages leaves members with little incentive to contribute additional labor or capital to their firms. These features also become barriers to the admission of new members. This is especially true the more capital expansion is financed by retained earnings, which causes memberships to appreciate in value and become harder for hired laborers to purchase.

These defects of production cooperatives as classically structured have long been recognized in the economic literature, and a number of alternative ownership arrangements have been offered for dealing with them. Vanek (1975, 1977) identified debt financing as the best way to make sure both that capital contributions are properly compensated and accounted for and that memberships do not appreciate in value. Economists like Gui (1984) later recognized the capital structures of the Mondragon cooperatives to be a practical realization of Vanek's debt financing. Although the Mondragon cooperatives do collect modest nonrefundable capital contributions from their workers at the time they become members, they obtain the bulk of their capital from two other sources: loans from the Caja Laboral Popular and retained earnings. Retained earnings, however, are accounted for as loans from the members, earn interest, and are refunded to members when they retire. This system of internal debt financing allows senior workers to recoup large payments for their accumulated capital investments, while keeping the capital contributions required of new members at relatively modest levels. Other versions of Vanek's debt financing can be observed in the leasing of capital to worker cooperatives, as in the relationship between Israel's butcher cooperatives like Ichud-Igud and the municipalities they serve.

Another ownership arrangement that has been offered as a more stable basis for workplace democracy is the "social ownership" that was developed in socialist Yugoslavia. Yugoslav theorists like Edvard Kardelj (1975, 1979, 1981) differentiated "social ownership" from both capitalist ownership and state ownership. They rejected both of these alternative systems of ownership, because each was seen as equally inimical to workers' rights to manage their own workplaces. Capitalism inevitably limits workers' self-management, whether this takes the form of outside capitalists attempting to control the firm, or of an inside group of managers and/or worker-owners who use their ownership as a basis to deny participation in decision making to other workers. Socialism also limits workers' self-management, insofar as it is realized through a system of ownership by the state, in which bloated state bureaucracies attempt to manage the entire economy from the center. The Yugoslav system of "social ownership" hypothetically barred both of these limitations on the autonomy of the Yugoslav "workers' councils," although in practice the League of Communists and the municipal, republican, and federal political authorities continued to have a tremendous de facto influence on their decisions.

In more recent years, the Yugoslav utopia has dissolved into independent republics and civil wars, and capital assets that were once described as being socially owned are being renationalized and often privatized (Uvalic, 1991). But while Yugoslavia's own system of social ownership is in decline, the concept of social ownership itself seems likely to live on, as one can find important examples of it in other countries as well. In many countries, for example, the capital in universities is socially owned. That is, whether this capital came originally from private donors or from the state, university governance systems typically prevent capital suppliers from having a direct say about what is taught in the classroom and reserve for faculty most control over the curriculum.

Rosner (1991b) has argued that kibbutz assets, as well, are socially owned. Like the Yugoslavs, Rosner sees the social ownership of kibbutz assets as playing an important role in strengthening the self-managed institutions of the kibbutzim. But for Rosner, the significance of kibbutz ownership lies less in the economic incentives that it creates than in the role it plays in legitimating close connections between the individual kibbutzim and their central federations.

These successful cases of debt financing and social ownership demonstrate that workplace democracy can indeed be made more durable and more dynamic, if it is rooted in a more conducive ownership structure. Other potentially important forms of ownership are becoming even more widespread in the world today and therefore seem even less utopian in their promise for the future. These include the many varieties of employee shareholding that have recently been spreading in such countries as the United States (Blasi and Kruse, 1991), Japan (Jones and Kato, 1993), Russia (Blasi and Gasaway, 1993) and Poland (Krajewska, 1993). Another significant innovation has been the leasing of assets to a firm's employees, as illustrated by Soviet experimentation with this form in the final years of the USSR (Logue and Bell, 1992) and by the Histadrut's own efforts at Chasin Esh.

Of course, all of these forms of ownership either remain relatively rare or have so far had little to no impact on the extent of workers' participation in decision making in the firms they involve. In this sense the search for viable ownership arrangements that can provide long-term support for workplace democracy remains in a "utopian" phase throughout the world. But so far, the principal contribution of the Israeli worker cooperatives in this case has been to provide an ownership model that clearly does not work in all but a small number of exceptional circumstances.

Support Organizations

Reference has already been made several times to the cooperatives of Mondragon. These cooperatives are remarkable not only for their internal capital structures, but also for the dense network of support organizations that surround them. These include a cooperative bank, which provides funding and technical assistance, a technical school, and a center for research and development (Whyte and Whyte, 1988).

Against the standard that has recently been set by this "worker cooperative complex" (Whyte and Whyte, 1988) in Mondragon, the efforts of the Histadrut and the Merkaz Hakooperatsia cannot help but seem inadequate in comparison. In all time periods, these organizations provided little material assistance and limited organizational know-how. When contrasted to the support structure surrounding the Mondragon cooperatives, the support system that the Histadrut devised for Israeli worker cooperatives was "utopian," in Engels's pejorative sense, in at least two respects.

It was utopian, first of all, to define the use of hired labor in worker cooperatives as a moral problem, to be corrected with strict discipline, education, and "more careful screening" of the human material, rather than as an economic problem, to be solved by developing more appropriate capital structures and incentives. It was also utopian for anyone in the Histadrut or outside of it to think that the interests of the worker cooperatives could best be served or represented by an organization that so thoroughly looked down on them and that had such a clear ideological and political preference for alternative ownership forms.

Both of these policies relied heavily on optimistic notions about the moral perfectability of mankind and ignored the political and economic realities of the relationships involved. To this extent they were indeed utopian in Engels's sense. But in adopting these policies, the Histadrut was not being naive. The Histadrut's utopianism was in this case more of the Marxist-Leninist variety. Like their counterparts in Russia, the Yishuv's labor leaders were prepared to form political alliances with all sorts of related movements and organizations, if such pragmatic compromises in the present might hasten the arrival of the utopia they hoped to establish in the future. By embracing the worker cooperatives, the Histadrut hoped to co-opt a portion of the Fourth Aliyah and of the Yishuv's growing petite bourgeoisie and to retard the development of rival political and ideological movements from these sources.

The Histadrut's goal in creating the Merkaz Hakooperatsia thus seems to have been largely co-optative and preemptive. It reflects an attempt to discredit one utopia (the worker cooperatives) in favor of others (the Jewish state, the Chevrat Ovdim).

By the middle of the 1960s, the Histadrut seems to have realized that the organizational structure that it had designed to co-opt and preempt the Israeli worker cooperative movement had by this point nearly killed it. As they were no longer a threat, and were also no longer so strongly needed for the task of nation building, the Histadrut let the worker cooperatives go their own way. But by this point, the Merkaz Hakooperatsia had been transformed by years of struggles between its members and the Histadrut into little more than a defender of its members against outside attack. So the Merkaz continues to advocate the bus cooperatives' outmoded and utopian form and, like the Histadrut before it, has invested little effort in developing alternative ownership models.

Combining Material and Ideal Interests in Utopian Economic Forms

The introduction and first two chapters of this work argued that the creation of worker cooperatives can rarely be attributed to the self-interest of the founders alone. Individual material incentives are typically supplemented in their formation by a wide range of "institutional" influences, which include the values, ideologies, and group affiliations of the founders, the availability of apparently successful models to imitate, and coercive pressures from funding sources and political bodies (DiMaggio and Powell, 1983).

In the third chapter and the present one, the emphasis in many arguments has shifted to a different point, which is that the Histadrut relied far too heavily on institutional mechanisms to limit the use of hired labor in the Israeli worker cooperatives, without ever finding a way to counter the powerful economic incentives that were doing the most to cause these organizations to make increasing use of nonmember labor. The Histadrut put all its faith in its own coercive power and moral suasion, with results that we have already seen.

Thus we saw in the earlier chapters the power of institutional forces but are reminded of the limitations of these forces in some of the later ones. But the most important common point in all of these discussions was that worker cooperatives are rarely established successfully on the basis either of institutional sources alone or of workers' individual self-interests alone. In worker cooperatives, as in other utopias, utopian ideals cannot be put into practice until forms of economic organization are invented in which workers' material incentives and ideal interests are closely aligned.

It is in its tremendously fertile ability to translate utopian values into practical economic and political structures that Israel's labor Zionist utopianism is most unique. The kibbutz owes much to its founders' ideals, but was created in an act of improvisation, in response to practical economic struggles. The kibbutzim became more ideological under the influence of the Third Aliyah, but even these idealistic pioneers knew that their values could not hold out forever in defiance of their self-interests. The kibbutz members therefore voted in 1926 to assign the ownership of their assets to the holding company Nir, thus removing any temptation to profit personally from the sale of kibbutz assets.

The Chevrat Ovdim also owes its origin to a rich combination of ideological and pragmatic appeals to its members and supporters. It was consistent with the Zionist and socialist aims and values of the labor leaders and immigrants of the Second and Third Aliyot, while also responding to the practical concern of all parties involved (immigrants, labor leaders, and the WZO) that the immigrants must be provided with jobs.

The origins of Israel's Merkaz Hakooperatsia in 1927 also reflect a mix of ideological and practical considerations, but in this case the pragmatism involved was of a more cynical kind. It was a cooperative movement created and led by people who did not believe in cooperatives. The most influential labor and Zionist leaders, like Oppenheimer, Ben-Gurion, and Preuss, had already formed negative impressions of worker cooperatives on the basis of experiences in other countries, before the Merkaz Hakooperatsia was formed. The Histadrut leaders also followed Oppenheimer in seeing the tendency of worker cooperatives to make increasing use of hired labor as being an inevitable result of insoluble defects. Unable even to imagine a constructive solution, they invested little effort in the search for one and instead created the Merkaz Hakooperatsia to coerce the Israeli worker cooperatives into conformity.

Thus while much more promising capital structures were being developed by the industrial cooperatives of Mondragon, the Israeli worker cooperatives retained structures and public images that have roots in the nineteenth century. They are perhaps one of the last vestiges of Europe's nineteenth-century worker cooperative movement. Like many other nineteenth-century cooperatives, Israel's worker cooperatives offer proof that democracy is attainable in modern workplaces, if we want it; they show that workplace democracy can indeed be made to work. But it has also been well known since the nineteenth century that worker cooperatives of this form have tendencies to transform themselves into conventional capitalist firms in all but a small number of narrow economic niches.

In his Inaugural Address written for the First International in 1864, Marx remarked that as demonstrations, "The value of these great social experiments cannot be over-rated." "At the same time," he added,

> the experience of the period from 1848 to 1864 had proved beyond doubt that, however excellent in principle, and however useful in practice, cooperative labor . . . will never be able to arrest the growth in geometric progression of monopoly, to free the masses, nor even to perceptively lighten the burden of their miseries. It is perhaps for this very reason that plausible noblemen, philanthropic middle-class spouters, and even keen political economists, have all at once turned nauseously

complimentary to the very cooperative labour system they had vainly tried to nip in the bud by deriding it as the Utopia of the dreamer, or stigmatizing it as the sacrilege of the Socialist (1972, p. 380).

In this sense, Israel's worker cooperatives may be the most "utopian" portions of its labor economy. It is they that are the most impractical and most limited in their potential range of applicability. One might have expected otherwise. Because their economic structures contain more individualistic elements, and are thus more of a compromise with capitalism, one might have expected them to be more successful at coexisting with capitalism. But because their structures and incentives are misaligned, their structures are unstable and have therefore depended too heavily on the institutionalized utopianism of the Histadrut to preserve their cooperative forms.

Recent developments among the worker cooperatives, and in Israel's entire labor economy, suggest that the utopian period of Israel's history is now long past. This does not mean that the history of worker cooperatives and of other forms of employee ownership and workplace democracy in Israel is coming to an end. Worker cooperatives continue to be formed in Israel and outside of it, and other forms of employee ownership and workers' participation in decision making are becoming even more widespread. So Israel should continue to produce new forms of ownership and workplace democracy in the future, as it has in the past. But in the future, we may be justified in expecting that Israel will produce fewer "utopian" varieties of workers' cooperation, in Engels's pejorative sense, and more practical ones instead.

APPENDIX

Israeli Worker Cooperatives, 1924–1993

Years[1]	Cooperative[2]	Location[3]	Activity[4]/ Product	Org.[5]	Ref[6]
1910–93*	Dfus Achdut	C 1 Tel Aviv	P 43 Printing	M	M&R
1919–45	Alal Haifa	N 3 Haifa	P 44 Machinery	M	M&R
1920–	Cherut	U 9 Unknown	S 20 Water Supply	M	M
1922–36	Aman Matechet	C 1 Tel Aviv	P 44 Metals	M	M&R
1923–26	Adolf Stand	C 1 Tel Aviv	P 45 Building	NR	R
1923–	Hamaarach	U 9 Unknown	U 99 Unknown	M	M
1923–33	Ovdei Haari	C 1 Tel Aviv	U 99 Unknown	NR	R
1924–70	Hapoel Hatsair	C 1 Tel Aviv	P 43 Printing	M	M&R
1924–34	Olim Bonim	C 2 Jerusalem	P 45 Building	NR	R
1924–34	Solel Boneh	C 2 Jerusalem	P 45 Building	NR	R
1925–	Dror	U 9 Unknown	S 20 Water Supply	M	M
1925–34	Hamovil	C 1 Tel Aviv	T 12 Motor Freight	NR	R
1925–34	Hanagarim Jaffa	C 1 Tel Aviv	P 42 Wood	NR	R
1925–34	Hanapach	C 1 Tel Aviv	P 44 Metals	NR	R
1925–34	Hasandalim	C 1 Tel Aviv	P 49 Boots	NR	R
1925–34	Manor	C 1 Tel Aviv	S 20 General Labor	NR	R
1925–45	Midracha	C 1 Tel Aviv	P 45 Panels	M	M&R
1925–45	Zohar	C 1 Tel Aviv	S 20 Electric Power	M	M&R
1926–36	Agudat Hakadarim	C 1 Tel Aviv	P 40 Ceramics	NR	R
1926–36	Charoshet Barzel	N 4 Afula	P 44 Metals	M	M&R
1926–41	Cherut	C 1 Tel Aviv	P 44 Metals	NR	R
1926–	Hatchiah	U 9 Unknown	U 99 Unknown	M	M

(continued)

Years[1]	Cooperative[2]	Location[3]		Activity[4]/ Product		Org.[5]	Ref[6]
1926–34	Ovdei Haopera	C	1 Tel Aviv	S	23 Music	NR	R
1926–	Shichlul Tel Aviv	C	1 Tel Aviv	P	45 Marble	M	M
1927–37	Even	C	2 Jerusalem	S	20 General Labor	NR	R
1927–33	Hanagarim	C	2 Jerusalem	P	42 Wood	NR	R
1927–	Hasharon	U	9 Unknown	P	48 Food	M	M
1928–79	Atid Tel Aviv	C	1 Tel Aviv	P	47 Clothing	M	M&R
1928–	Charoshet-ETS	U	9 Unknown	P	42 Wood	M	M
1928–	Eshed Nes Ziona	U	9 Unknown	P	45 Water Systems	M	M
1928–50	Haichud	C	1 Petach Tikvah	T	11 Passenger Transportation	NR	R
1928–45‡	Hamaavir	C	1 Tel Aviv	T	11 Passenger Transportation	M	M&R
1928–45‡	Hanamal	C	1 Tel Aviv	T	12 Motor Freight	M	M&R
1928–34	Ichud	C	1 Tel Aviv	P	44 Metals	M	M&R
1928–64	Misaada Jerusalem	C	2 Jerusalem	S	22 Restaurant	M	M&R
1928–	Mitbach Hapoalim	U	9 Unknown	S	22 Restaurant	M	M
1929–38	Achdut	C	2 Jerusalem	T	10 Misc. Transportation	NR	R
1929–34	Agudat Hakadarim	C	1 Petach Tikvah	P	40 Ceramics	NR	R
1929–93*	Carmel	N	3 Haifa	P	42 Wood	M	M&R
1929–	Chrisho Amoka	U	9 Unknown	S	20 Tractor Service	M	M
1929–	Ezuz	C	2 Jerusalem	U	99 Unknown	NR	R
1929–69	Habimah	C	1 Tel Aviv	S	23 Theater	NR	R
1929–	Hasharon	U	9 Unknown	P	42 Wood	M	M
1929–34	Hegeh	C	1 Tel Aviv	T	10 Misc. Transportation	NR	R
1929–34	Hygroskopiah	C	1 Tel Aviv	U	99 Unknown	NR	R
1929–40	Merkaz Tveriah	N	4 Tiberias	T	10 Mixed Transportation	M	M&R
1930–	B.R.N.A.	U	9 Unknown	P	40 Fertilizer	M	M
1930–54‡	Drom Yehudah (Hadarom)	C	5 Rehovot	T	11 Passenger Transportation	M	M&R

1930–	Etzion	U	9 Unknown	P	42 Wood	M	M
1930–	Gavish Tel Aviv	C	1 Tel Aviv	P	45 Panels	M	M
1930–	Hachermon	U	9 Unknown	S	20 Misc. Service	M	M
1930–	Hamalaachim	U	9 Unknown	P	44 Metal	M	M
1930–44	Hamovil	C	1 Petach Tikvah	T	10 Misc. Transportation	NR	R
1930–	Hashravrav	U	9 Unknown	S	20 Water Supply	M	M
1930–36‡	Hitachdut Hanehagim	N	4 Hadera	T	10 Mixed Transportation	M	M&R
1930–42‡	Hitachdut Hanehagim (Hasharon Hameuchad)	C	1 Tel Aviv	T	11 Passenger Transportation	NR	R
1930–41	Hovalah	C	2 Jerusalem	T	12 Motor Freight	M	M&R
1930–69	Machbesat Kitor Levanah	C	1 Tel Aviv	S	24 Laundry	M	M&R
1930–40	Misrad Kablani	N	3 Haifa	P	45 Building	NR	R
1930–60	Mitbachei Hapoalim	N	3 Haifa	S	22 Restaurant	M	M&R
1930–41	Omoull Israel	C	1 Tel Aviv	P	43 Printing	NR	R
1930–38	Pharmacy	C	1 Tel Aviv	S	20 Pharmacy	NR	R
1930–32‡	Regev	C	1 Tel Aviv	T	11 Passenger Transportation	NR	R
1930–38	The Orange	C	1 Jaffa	U	99 Unknown	NR	R
1930–38	Yehudah	C	5 Rishon Lezion	T	10 Misc. Transportation	M	R
1931–35	Haarmon	C	5 Raanana	S	21 Produce Ice	NR	R
1931–	Haemek	U	9 Unknown	T	12 Motor Freight	M	M
1931–33‡	Hamahir	U	9 Unknown	T	11 Passenger Transportation	M	M&R
1931–61‡	Hamekasher	C	2 Jerusalem	T	11 Passenger Transportation	M	M&R
1931–43	Hanul	U	9 Unknown	P	47 Textiles	NR	R
1931–	Haorgim	C	1 Petach Tikvah	P	47 Clothing	NR	R
1931–33	Hege‡	C	2 Jerusalem	T	11 Passenger Transportation	M	M&R
1931–38	Nagarie Jaffa	C	1 Jaffa	P	42 Wood	NR	R
1931–93*	Namlit	N	3 Haifa	P	45 Building Materials	M	M&R
1931–33	Sherut Hadar	N	3 Haifa	T	11 Passenger Transportation	NR	R

(continued)

Years[1]	Cooperative[2]	Location[3]	Activity[4]/Product	Org.[5]	Ref[6]
1932–38	Ayecuri	C 1 Jaffa	T 10 Misc. Transportation	NR	R
1932–36	Balat	C 1 Tel Aviv	P 40 Misc. Production	NR	R
1932–47	Bemeg	C 1 Tel Aviv	U 99 Unknown	NR	R
1932–84	Charish	C 1 Tel Aviv	S 20 Misc. Service	M	M
1932–33	Esheol	C 1 Tel Aviv	P 44 Metals	NR	R
1932–34	Hadar Hacarmel	N 3 Haifa	T 10 Mixed Transportation	M	M&R
1932–34	Hamakdim	C 1 Tel Aviv	T 10 Misc. Transportation	NR	R
1932–49	Hanehag	C 1 Tel Aviv	T 10 Misc. Transportation	NR	R
1932–36	Hanamal Haifa	N 3 Haifa	T 10 Misc. Transportation	NR	R
1932–34	Haofeh	C 1 Tel Aviv	P 41 Bakery	NR	R
1932–	Hatsemeg	U 9 Unknown	U 99 Unknown	M	M
1932–39	Hertseliah Raananah	C 1 Tel Aviv	T 11 Passenger Transportation	M	M&R
1932–37	Hitachdut	C 1 Tel Aviv	T 10 Misc. Transportation	NR	R
1932–45‡	Ichud Regev	C 1 Tel Aviv	T 11 Passenger Transportation	M	M
1932–37‡	Kadimah	C 2 Jerusalem	T 11 Passenger Transportation	NR	R
1932–79	Levanon	C 1 Tel Aviv	S 24 Laundry	M	M&R
1932–38	Merets	C 2 Jerusalem	T 10 Mixed Transportation	NR	R
1932–44	Misrad Kablani	C 1 Tel Aviv	P 45 Building	NR	R
1932–58	Yehudah	U 9 Unknown	P 41 Bakery	M	M&R
1932–36	Yehudah	C 1 Tel Aviv	T 10 Misc. Transportation	NR	R
1932–38	Yehudah	C 5 Rehovot	P 41 Bakery	NR	R
1933–34	Al Abbariel	C 1 Jaffa	T 10 Mixed Transportation	NR	R
1933–35	Al Ummal	C 2 Jerusalem	T 10 Mixed Transportation	NR	R
1933–36	Aliya	N 4 Pardes Hanna Karkur	T 10 Mixed Transportation	NR	R
1933–38	Bakaa	C 2 Jerusalem	T 10 Misc. Transportation	NR	R
1933–36	Beit Sefer Letechnicah	N 3 Haifa	S 23 Education	NR	R

1933–38	Binyan	N	3 Haifa	T	10 Mixed Transportation	NR	R
1933–37	Bus Service	C	1 Jaffa	T	10 Mixed Transportation	NR	R
1933–93*	Egged	C	1 Tel Aviv	T	11 Passenger Transportation	M	M
1933–92	Haargaz	C	1 Tel Aviv	P	44 Metals	M	M&R
1933–42	Habinyan	C	1 Tel Aviv	P	40 Misc. Production	NR	R
1933–34	Hagalil	U	9 Unknown	T	10 Mixed Transportation	NR	R
1933–35	Hakesher	C	1 Tel Aviv	T	10 Misc. Transportation	NR	R
1933–36	Hakodeach	C	5 Raanana	P	46 Drilling	NR	R
1933–36	Hakovesh	C	5 Rishon Lezion	T	10 Mixed Transportation	NR	R
1933–34	Hamekashet	C	2 Jerusalem	P	42 Wood	NR	R
1933–39	Hamerets	C	1 Tel Aviv	T	10 Mixed Transportation	NR	R
1933–35	Haoved	C	5 Nes Tsiyonah	T	12 Motor Freight	NR	R
1933–49	Harakevet	C	1 Tel Aviv	P	45 Building	NR	R
1933–39	Hilal	C	5 Tulkarm	T	10 Misc. Transportation	NR	R
1933–	Igra (Eshed Igra)	C	5 Ramatayim	U	99 Unknown	NR	R
1933–45	Keset Achim	C	1 Tel Aviv	U	99 Unknown	NR	R
1933–36	Lapid	N	3 Haifa	S	20 General Labor	NR	R
1933–37	Mechanical	C	1 Jaffa	S	27 Garage	NR	R
1933–47	Misrad Kablani	C	2 Jerusalem	P	45 Building	NR	R
1933–35	Moshavei Ovdim	C	1 Jaffa	T	10 Misc. Transportation	NR	R
1933–36	Rahit	C	1 Petach Tikvah	P	42 Wood	NR	R
1933–37	Salameh	C	1 Tel Aviv	T	10 Mixed Transportation	NR	R
1933–34	Zehirut	C	2 Jerusalem	T	10 Misc. Transportation	NR	R
1934–93*	Achdut Bakery	C	1 Tel Aviv	P	41 Bakery	M	M&R
1934–	Bagalil	N	3 Haifa	P	42 Wood	NR	R
1934–36	Bazelet	C	2 Jerusalem	P	45 Building	NR	R
1934–54	Chever Haifa‡	N	3 Haifa	T	11 Passenger Transportation	M	M&R
1934–37	Eg	C	5 Rishon Lezion	P	42 Wood	NR	R

(continued)

Years[1]	Cooperative[2]	Location[3]	Activity[4]/Product	Org.[5]	Ref[6]
1934–50	Gaza	N 3 Haifa	P 47 Textiles	M	M
1934–42	Habasar	C 1 Petach Tikvah	S 21 Butchers	NR	R
1934–46	Haemek Hashaanan	N 3 Haifa	T 10 Mixed Transportation	NR	R
1934–93*	Hanamal Hachadash	N 3 Haifa	T 12 Motor Freight	M	M&R
1934–	Hanof	C 1 Tel Aviv	T 12 Motor Freight	NR	R
1934–36	Haolam	N 3 Haifa	T 10 Misc. Transportation	NR	R
1934–37	Haoved	C 1 Petach Tikvah	T 10 Misc. Transportation	NR	R
1934–46‡	Har Hacarmel	N 3 Haifa	T 11 Passenger Transportation	NR	R
1934–42	Hashen	U 9 Unknown	P 45 Building	NR	R
1934–37	Hatofrot	C 1 Tel Aviv	P 47 Clothing	NR	R
1934–50	Ligah	N 3 Haifa	P 47 Clothing	NR	R
1934–43	Makolet	C 1 Tel Aviv	S 20 Grocery	NR	R
1934–37	Malbenah	C 1 Tel Aviv	P 45 Building	NR	R
1934–42	Matechet	C 1 Petach Tikvah	P 44 Metals	NR	R
1934–41	Menorah	C 1 Tel Aviv	P 45 Building	NR	R
1934–35	Merkavah	C 1 Tel Aviv	T 10 Misc. Transportation	NR	R
1934–50	Michsei Namal	C 1 Tel Aviv	S 26 Port Service	NR	R
1934–40	Misaadah Cooperativit	C 1 Tel Aviv	S 22 Restaurant	NR	R
1934–37‡	Mishmar Mifrats Haifa	N 3 Haifa	T 11 Passenger Transportation	M	M&R
1934–40	Misrad Kablani	N 3 Haifa	P 45 Building	HPHM	R
1934–49	Misrad Kablani Petach Tikvah	C 1 Petach Tikvah	P 45 Building	NR	R
1934–47	Moniyot Bat Galim	N 3 Haifa	T 1 Passenger Transportation	NR	R
1934–38	Nagarei Hapoel Hamizrachi	C 1 Tel Aviv	P 42 Wood	HPHM	R
1934–37	Nesher	C 1 Tel Aviv	T 11 Passenger Transportation	NR	R
1934–39	Shefer	C 1 Tel Aviv	P 42 Wood	NR	R
1934–37	Yamiyat	N 3 Haifa	T 11 Passenger Transportation	NR	R

1934–35	Yamiyat Al Wihadan	C	2 Jerusalem	T	10 Mixed Transportation	NR	R
1934–37	Yamiyat Ittichad	C	1 Jaffa	T	11 Passenger Transportation	NR	R
1934–35	Yamiyat Liyart	C	2 Jerusalem	T	10 Mixed Transportation	NR	R
1934–37	Yamiyatel Magl	U	9 Unknown	T	11 Passenger Transportation	NR	R
1935–90‡	Achdut Bakery Haifa	N	3 Haifa	P	41 Bakery	M	M&R
1935–39	Agudat Hashochatim	N	3 Haifa	S	21 Butchers	NR	R
1935–35	Al Khalil	C	2 Jerusalem	T	10 Mixed Transportation	NR	R
1935–38	Al Manshiyat	C	1 Jaffa	T	10 Mixed Transportation	NR	R
1935–37	Amer	C	1 Tel Aviv	P	45 Building	NR	R
1935–39	Brosh	C	5 Rehovot	P	42 Wood	NR	R
1935–37	Chimaim	C	1 Tel Aviv	P	50 Chemicals	NR	R
1935–45	Gagit	C	1 Tel Aviv	P	45 Building	NR	R
1935–78	Gimmasiah Bialik	N	3 Haifa	S	23 Education	M	M&R
1935–38	Habasar	C	5 Herzlia	S	21 Food Service	NR	R
1935–35	Habniyah	C	1 Tel Aviv	P	45 Building	NR	R
1935–38	Hachashmal	C	5 Rishon Lezion	P	44 Building Electrical	NR	R
1935–43	Hairgun Lehovalah	C	1 Tel Aviv	T	12 Motor Freight	NR	R
1935–41‡	Hakesher	N	3 Haifa	T	11 Passenger Transportation	NR	R
1935–38	Hakoach	C	1 Petach Tikvah	T	10 Misc. Transportation	NR	R
1935–38	Hamasger	C	1 Tel Aviv	P	45 Building	NR	R
1935–54	Hamatate	C	1 Tel Aviv	S	23 Theater	M	M&R
1935–39	Hamechonen	C	1 Tel Aviv	P	44 Metals	NR	R
1935–39	Hamumcheh	N	3 Haifa	P	45 Building	NR	R
1935–38	Hanaal	C	1 Tel Aviv	P	49 Shoes	NR	R
1935–38	Haraftan	N	3 Haifa	P	45 Building Pitch	NR	R
1935–38	Hasabal Haivri	C	2 Jerusalem	T	12 Motor Freight	NR	R
1935–43	Hasefer	C	1 Tel Aviv	P	43 Printing	NR	R
1935–38	Hashomer	C	1 Tel Aviv	S	20 Guard Service	NR	R

(continued)

Years[1]	Cooperative[2]	Location[3]	Activity[4]/Product	Org.[5]	Ref[6]
1935–49‡	Hatikvah	C 1 Petach Tikvah	T 10 Mixed Transportation	NR	R
1935–40	Hatris	C 1 Tel Aviv	P 42 Wood	NR	R
1935–37	Hes	C 5 Kfar Hes	P 45 Building	NR	R
1935–38	Ichud	C 1 Tel Aviv	P 44 Metals	NR	R
1935–	Ilan	C 1 Tel Aviv	P 42 Wood	M	M&R
1935–64‡	Lechem	C 5 Rishon Lezion	P 41 Bakery	M	M&R
1935–38	Maanit	C 5 Tel Mond	P 46 Deep Hoeing	NR	R
1935–39	Malben	C 1 Tel Aviv	P 45 Building	NR	R
1935–37	Masad	N 3 Haifa	P 45 Building	NR	R
1935–40	Melet	C 1 Tel Aviv	P 45 Building	NR	R
1935–37	Merek	N 4 Hadera	P 42 Wood	NR	R
1935–36	Merkaz Lehovalot	C 1 Tel Aviv	T 12 Motor Freight	NR	R
1935–	Misrad Kablani	C 5 Kfar Saba	P 45 Building	NR	R
1935–36	Nagib	C 2 Jerusalem	T 10 Mixed Transportation	NR	R
1935–54	Ovdei Silicat	C 1 Tel Aviv	P 45 Building	M	M&R
1935–50	Policlinicah	C 1 Tel Aviv	S 20 Physicians	NR	R
1935–37	Rimon	C 1 Tel Aviv	T 10 Mixed Transportation	NR	R
1935–38	Sabalim	N 3 Haifa	T 12 Motor Freight	NR	R
1935–40	Shemesh	C 1 Tel Aviv	S 20 Electric Power	NR	R
1935–38	Zvulun	N 4 Kiryat Ata	T 10 Mixed Transportation	NR	R
1936–93*	Aloniyah	N 3 Haifa	P 42 Wood	M	M&R
1936–39	Arzah	N 3 Haifa	P 42 Wood	NR	R
1936–37	Aviv	N 3 Haifa	T 10 Mixed Transportation	NR	R
1936–	Erez	N 3 Haifa	P 42 Wood	NR	R
1936–49	Habasar	C 5 Kfar Saba	P 48 Meat Products	NR	R
1936–49	Hachulah	N 4 Kfar Giladi	U 99 Unknown	M	M

1936–38	Hagalil Haifa	N	3 Haifa	T	10 Mixed Transportation	NR	R
1936–39	Hahaapalah	C	1 Tel Aviv	P	44 Tinsmiths	NR	R
1936–38	Hakablan	N	3 Haifa	P	45 Building	NR	R
1936–42	Hakorech	C	1 Tel Aviv	P	43 Book Binding	NR	R
1936–37	Hamaafiyah	C	1 Tel Aviv	P	41 Bakery	NR	R
1936–38	Hanagariyah	C	1 Tel Aviv	P	42 Wood	NR	R
1936–37	Hanul	C	2 Jerusalem	P	47 Clothing	NR	R
1936–39	Hasapan	C	1 Tel Aviv	S	26 Port Workers	NR	R
1936–37	Hatsabaim	C	1 Tel Aviv	P	45 Building	NR	R
1936–38	Hayarkon	C	1 Tel Aviv	T	12 Motor Freight	NR	R
1936–93‡*	Ichud (Ichud–Igud 1976)	C	1 Petach Tikvah	S	21 Butchers	M	M&R
1936–	Kamah	C	1 Petach Tikvah	P	41 Bakery	M	M
1936–49	Kfar Giladi	N	4 Kfar Giladi	T	11 Passenger Transportation	NR	R
1936–39	Kvutsat Dayagim	N	3 Haifa	P	48 Food	NR	R
1936–38	Machtsevot Ivriot	C	1 Tel Aviv	P	45 Building	NR	R
1936–52	Mechalkei Kerach	C	1 Petach Tikvah	S	21 Produce Ice	NR	R
1936–38	Misaada Coop	C	1 Petach Tikvah	S	22 Restaurant	NR	R
1936–37	Misaada Shell Olei Polin	C	1 Tel Aviv	S	22 Restaurant	NR	R
1936–39	Mivlat	C	1 Tel Aviv	P	43 Printing	NR	R
1936–68	Naalei Arzeino	C	2 Jerusalem	P	49 Shoes	M	M&R
1936–93*	Ot Haifa	N	3 Haifa	P	43 Printing	M	M&R
1936–60‡	Pat Petach Tikvah (Kama)	C	1 Petach Tikvah	P	41 Bakery	M	M&R
1936–71	Tachana Jerusalem	C	2 Jerusalem	T	12 Motor Freight	M	M&R
1936–37	Taxi Rechovot	C	1 Tel Aviv	T	10 Mixed Transportation	NR	R
1936–49	Totseret Bassar	C	5 Rehovot	P	48 Food	NR	R
1936–41	Yalin	C	1 Tel Aviv	P	48 Mineral Water	NR	R
1936–40	Zohar	N	3 Haifa	U	99 Unknown	NR	R
1937–93*	Achvah Jerusalem	C	2 Jerusalem	P	43 Printing	M	M&R

(continued)

Years[1]	Cooperative[2]	Location[3]	Activity[4]/ Product	Org.[5]	Ref[6]
1937–45	Ainbari	C 1 Tel Aviv	U 99 Unknown	NR	R
1937–39	Autobus	C 1 Tel Aviv	S 27 Garage	NR	R
1937–52	Chamah	C 1 Tel Aviv	P 41 Bakery	NR	R
1937–47	Chazak	C 1 Tel Aviv	U 99 Unknown	NR	R
1937–70	Cherut	C 1 Tel Aviv	P 41 Bakery	M	M&R
1937–43	Chever	C 1 Tel Aviv	U 99 Unknown	NR	R
1937–	Dfus Hapoel Hamizrachi	C 1 Tel Aviv	P 43 Printing	HPHM	R
1937–38	Ezran	C 1 Tel Aviv	S 22 Restaurant	NR	R
1937–41	Habochen	C 2 Jerusalem	P 49 Shoes	NR	R
1937–38	Hadelek	U 9 Unknown	U 99 Unknown	NR	R
1937–	Hagamal (Ovdei Zitzif Mechora 1946)	C 1 Tel Aviv	P 45 Building	NR	R
1937–38	Hagilboa	C 1 Tel Aviv	U 99 Unknown	NR	R
1937–39	Hakarton	N 3 Haifa	P 43 Cardboard	NR	R
1937–40	Hamanel	U 9 Unknown	P 49 Shoes	NR	R
1937–40	Haneft	C 1 Petach Tikvah	S 21 Deliver Kerosene	NR	R
1937–41	Hasadeh	C 1 Tel Aviv	P 46 Drilling	NR	R
1937–39	Hasela	C 1 Tel Aviv	P 40 Stoves	NR	R
1937–38	Hasulam	C 1 Tel Aviv	P 40 Ladders	NR	R
1937–46	Kablaney Rechovet	C 5 Rehovot	P 45 Building	NR	R
1937–44	Karchon	N 3 Haifa	S 21 Deliver Ice	NR	R
1937–41	Kayor	C 1 Tel Aviv	P 45 Building	NR	R
1937–49	Lechem	C 2 Jerusalem	P 41 Bakery	NR	R
1937–	Maafiyah Chashmalit	C 5 Kfar Saba	P 41 Bakery	NR	R
1937–39	Maayanot	C 1 Tel Aviv	P 48 Food	NR	R
1937–68	Masperah	C 1 Tel Aviv	S 20 Hairdresser	M	M&R

1937–81	Mechorah	C	1 Tel Aviv	P	45 Building	M	M
1937–39	Merkaz Hachimaim	U	9 Unknown	S	21 Butchers	NR	R
1937–40	Mifratson	C	1 Tel Aviv	S	21 Butchers	NR	R
1937–39	Misrad Kablani	C	1 Tel Aviv	P	45 Building	Gen Z	R
1937–40	Olei Polahiah	N	3 Haifa	S	22 Restaurant	NR	R
1937–39	Rakoa	C	1 Tel Aviv	P	44 Metals	NR	R
1937–38	Sherut Emek Cheffer	C	5 Emek Cheffer	T	10 Misc. Transportation	NR	R
1937–42	Shikuy	C	1 Tel Aviv	P	48 Mineral Water	NR	R
1937–40	Taxi Hadar Hacarmel	N	3 Haifa	T	11 Passenger Transportation	NR	R
1938–55	Al Afinar	N	3 Haifa	T	10 Misc. Transportation	NR	R
1938–41	Aryam	C	1 Tel Aviv	S	20 Grocery	NR	R
1938–52	Charash	C	1 Tel Aviv	P	44 Metals	M	M&R
1938–46	Dfus Cooperativi	C	1 Tel Aviv	P	43 Printing	NR	R
1938–93*	Emek Hayarden	N	4 Afiqim	T	12 Motor Freight	M	M&R
1938–43	Emun	C	1 Tel Aviv	U	99 Unknown	NR	R
1938–45‡	Hachof	C	1 Tel Aviv	T	12 Motor Freight	M	M&R
1938–40	Hakatsavim	N	3 Haifa	S	21 Butchers	NR	R
1938–45	Hamegaper	N	3 Haifa	P	40 Tires	NR	R
1938–	Hasharon	N	3 Haifa	S	20 Misc. Service	M	M
1938–	Hatmua	C	1 Tel Aviv	S	12 Motor Freight	M	M&R
1938–39	Hatsafon	C	1 Tel Aviv	S	23 Cinema	NR	R
1938–43	Kvutsat Banaim	N	4 Bet Alfa	P	45 Building	NR	R
1938–74	Man (Man Dagan 1957)	C	5 Netanya	P	41 Bakery	M	M&R
1938–43	Misaada Hapoel Hamizrachi	C	2 Jerusalem	S	22 Restaurant	HPHM	R
1938–39	Nagarei Rahitim	C	1 Tel Aviv	P	42 Wood	NR	R
1938–40	Nechamah	C	1 Tel Aviv	P	41 Bakery	HPHT	R
1938–54	Shituf	C	1 Tel Aviv	S	20 Misc. Service	M	M
1938–	Tichon Chadash	C	1 Tel Aviv	S	23 Education	NR	R

(continued)

Years¹	Cooperative²	Location³	Activity⁴/ Product	Org.⁵	Ref⁶
1939–46	Alef	N 4 Hadera	P 43 Printing	NR	R
1939–44	Barzel (Avodot Matechet 1939)	C 1 Tel Aviv	P 44 Metals	NR	R
1939–42	Degel	C 1 Tel Aviv	P 48 Food	NR	R
1939–41	Egtonim	C 5 Netanya	T 10 Misc. Transportation	NR	R
1939–56	El Partugal	C 1 Jaffa	S 26 Port Service	NR	R
1939–41	Gimnasiah Ramat Gan	C 1 Tel Aviv	S 23 Education	NR	R
1939–48	Hadar Hasharon	C 1 Tel Aviv	P 50 Soap	NR	R
1939–58	Hakav Haifa	N 3 Haifa	T 12 Motor Freight	M	M&R
1939–41	Hamezin	N 3 Haifa	P 40 Bone Grinding	NR	R
1939–45‡	Hanehag	U 9 Unknown	T 10 Mixed Transportation	M	M
1939–46	Haposhet	C 1 Tel Aviv	S 21 Butchers	M	M&R
1939–40	Hitachdut Hamaafiyot	C 1 Tel Aviv	P 41 Bakery	NR	R
1939–76‡	Igud	C 1 Holon	S 21 Deliver Meat	M	M&R
1939–	Modeolim	C 1 Tel Aviv	U 99 Unknown	NR	R
1939–46	Neeman	N 3 Haifa	S 26 Port Service	NR	R
1939–40	Shimurim	C 1 Tel Aviv	P 48 Food	NR	R
1939–93*	Zifzif (Zifzif Ovdei Tnufah 1954)	N 4 Neveh Chaim	P 46 Sand	M	M&R
1940–42	Avodot Yam	C 1 Tel Aviv	S 26 Port Workers	NR	R
1940–42	Chemical Workers	C 2 Jerusalem	P 50 Chemicals	Heb U	R
1940–41	Cheshev	C 2 Jerusalem	P 45 Building	NR	R
1940–42	Dfus Erets Israel	C 1 Tel Aviv	P 43 Printing	NR	R
1940–42	Gimnasiah Kadimah	C 1 Tel Aviv	S 23 Education	NR	R
1940–43	Gome	C 1 Tel Aviv	P 43 Paper	NR	R
1940–47	Hapoel Hamizrachi	C 2 Jerusalem	P 43 Printing	HPHM	R
1940–40	Kikar Dizengoff	C 1 Tel Aviv	S 22 Restaurant	NR	R
1940–42	Kvutsat Dayagim	N 3 Haifa	P 48 Food	NR	R

1940–41	Lasova	C	1 Tel Aviv	S	22 Restaurant	NR	R
1940–69	Lechem Chamudot	C	1 Petach Tikvah	P	41 Bakery	NR	R
1940–41	Mazor	C	1 Tel Aviv	P	47 Clothing	NR	R
1940–42	Movilim	C	1 Tel Aviv	T	10 Misc. Transportation	NR	R
1940–41	Noam	C	1 Tel Aviv	P	41 Bakery	NR	R
1940–41	Sherut Haemek	N	4 Afula	T	10 Misc. Transportation	NR	R
1940–49	Toveh–Arig	C	1 Tel Aviv	P	47 Weavers	M	M&R
1940–41	Yam Suf	C	2 Jerusalem	P	47 Clothing	NR	R
1941–	Agudat Hashochatim	C	1 Jaffa	S	21 Butchers	NR	R
1941–43	Barad	C	2 Jerusalem	S	21 Deliver Ice	NR	R
1941–49	Chinuch Vetarbut (Gimnasiah Tarbut 1944)	C	1 Tel Aviv	S	23 Education	NR	R
1941–46	Daryan	C	1 Tel Aviv	P	47 Clothing	NR	R
1941–49	Haoperah	C	1 Tel Aviv	S	23 Opera	NR	R
1941–43	Hashomer	C	2 Jerusalem	S	20 Guard Service	NR	R
1941–93*	Mitbachei Hapoalim	C	1 Tel Aviv	S	22 Restaurant	M	M&R
1941–75	Naal	C	1 Tel Aviv	P	49 Shoes	M	M&R
1941–50	Nehagei Haifa (Masa Porek 1942)	N	3 Haifa	T	12 Motor Freight	NR	R
1941–93*	Nesher (Nesher Tours 1960)	C	2 Jerusalem	T	11 Passenger Transportation	M	M&R
1941–42	Pan	N	3 Haifa	T	11 Passenger Transportation	NR	R
1941–42	Perit	C	1 Tel Aviv	P	48 Food	NR	R
1941–42	Teatron	U	9 Unknown	S	23 Theater	NR	R
1941–43	Totseret Beit Lechem	C	1 Tel Aviv	P	41 Bakery	NR	R
1942–46	Amilut	N	3 Haifa	S	26 Port Service	NR	R
1942–44	Arig	C	1 Tel Aviv	P	47 Clothing	NR	R
1942–	Beit Shean Charod	N	4 Bet Hashita	T	12 Motor Freight	M	M&R
1942–56	El Arab	C	1 Jaffa	U	99 Unknown	NR	R
1942–56	El Haklamin	N	3 Haifa	S	21 Butchers	NR	R

(continued)

Years[1]	Cooperative[2]	Location[3]	Activity[4]/ Product	Org.[5]	Ref[6]
1942–56	El Havraya	N 3 Haifa	U 99 Unknown	NR	R
1942–56	El Kanal	N 3 Haifa	U 99 Unknown	NR	R
1942–49	Habasar Hertsliah	C 5 Herzlia	S 21 Deliver Meat	NR	R
1942–44	Hakochav	C 1 Tel Aviv	P 49 Boots	NR	R
1942–50	Haoreg	C 5 Nes Tsiyonah	M 47 Clothing	M	M&R
1942–47	Ovdei Beit Hamitbachayim	N 3 Haifa	S 21 Butchers	NR	R
1942–66	Polan (Yesha 1949)	C 1 Tel Aviv	S 20 Physicians	NR	R
1942–49	Rubin	C 1 Tel Aviv	P 49 Leather	NR	R
1942–	Tachburaa	C 1 Tel Aviv	T 12 Motor Freight	M	M
1942–	Tachburah	N 3 Haifa	T 12 Motor Freight	M	M&R
1942–44	Tev Hadar	C 1 Tel Aviv	P 48 Food	NR	R
1942–58	Tnuvah	C 1 Tel Aviv	S 21 Deliver Milk	NR	R
1943–57	Aguda Lehashbachan	C 1 Tel Aviv	S 21 Deliver Food	NR	R
1943–45	Aguda Lehashbachan	C 1 Tel Aviv	S 21 Deliver Food	NR	R
1943–56	Al Anitzia	C 2 Jerusalem	P 49 Shoes	NR	R
1943–45	Al Asmak	C 1 Jaffa	S 26 Fishing	NR	R
1943–46	Al Fadida	N 3 Haifa	T 10 Misc. Transportation	NR	R
1943–	Al Jadida	C 1 Jaffa	T 10 Misc. Transportation	NR	R
1943–47	As Salokariyya	W 9 Nablus	P 44 Metals	NR	R
1943–	Hagalil Haelyon	N 4 Galil Elyon	T 12 Motor Freight	M	M&R
1943–50	Hamadrim	C 1 Tel Aviv	T 10 Misc. Transportation	M	M&R
1943–47	Hamassia	C 2 Jerusalem	T 11 Passenger Transportation	M	M&R
1943–45	Hayam	C 1 Tel Aviv	S 26 Fishing	NR	R
1943–56	Lie Tasgif	N 3 Haifa	S 20 Clerical	NR	R
1943–	Maabarot Emek Chefer	C 5 Maabarot	T 12 Motor Freight	M	M&R
1943–46	Masaot	C 1 Tel Aviv	T 10 Misc. Transportation	NR	R

1943–49	Poalei Yahalomim	C	2 Jerusalem	P	51 Diamonds	NR	R
1943–46	Shalvat Yam	C	1 Tel Aviv	S	22 Hotel	NR	R
1943–47	Tachbura	C	2 Jerusalem	T	10 Misc. Transportation	NR	R
1943–53	Taxi Carmel	C	1 Tel Aviv	T	11 Passenger Transportation	NR	R
1943–	Textile (Textile Achiezer 1956)	C	1 Tel Aviv	P	47 Textiles	NR	R
1943–45	Totseret Chalav	C	1 Tel Aviv	S	21 Deliver Food	NR	R
1943–50	Yamia	C	2 Jerusalem	T	10 Misc. Transportation	NR	R
1943–54	Yizrael	N	4 Ramat David	T	12 Motor Freight	M	M&R
1944–56	Al Rakha	N	3 Haifa	P	47 Clothing	NR	R
1944–47	As Samkariya	C	1 Jaffa	P	45 Building	NR	R
1944–68	Emun	C	1 Tel Aviv	S	26 Port Service	M	M&R
1944–47	Hakartis	N	3 Haifa	S	23 Theater Agent	NR	R
1944–49	Hakrichiah	C	1 Tel Aviv	P	43 Printing	NR	R
1944–46	Haplitah	C	1 Tel Aviv	P	47 Clothing	NR	R
1944–47	Hasneh	N	3 Haifa	T	10 Misc. Transportation	NR	R
1944–56	Merkaz Hadarom	C	5 Rehovot	T	10 Misc. Transportation	NR	R
1944–80	Ovdei Mitbach	C	1 Tel Aviv	S	22 Restaurant	M	M&R
1944–63	Sadeh Kovesh	C	5 Raanana	S	24 Laundry	M	M&R
1944–46	Shaar Hatsafon	N	3 Haifa	T	10 Misc. Transportation	NR	R
1944–50	Tel Taxi	C	1 Tel Aviv	T	11 Passenger Transportation	NR	R
1944–47	Yediot Hadashot	C	1 Tel Aviv	P	43 Printing	NR	R
1945–47	A.S.H. (Frei 1945)	C	1 Tel Aviv	P	47 Clothing	NR	R
1945–	Al Majdal	N	4 Migdal	P	47 Weavers	NR	R
1945–84	Alumot	C	1 Holon	P	41 Bakery	M	M&R
1945–46	An Maser	N	3 Haifa	T	10 Misc. Transportation	NR	R
1945–55	Atzei Oren Jerusalem	C	2 Jerusalem	P	42 Wood	M	M&R
1945–50	Bagrut	C	2 Jerusalem	S	23 Education	NR	R
1945–47	Bareket	C	1 Tel Aviv	P	51 Diamonds	NR	R

(continued)

Years[1]	Cooperative[2]	Location[3]	Activity[4]/ Product	Org.[5]	Ref[6]
1945–47	Beit Charoshet Leorot	C 1 Petach Tikvah	P 49 Leather	NR	R
1945–55	Brosh Jerusalem	C 2 Jerusalem	P 42 Wood	M	M&R
1945–	Carmeliah	N 3 Haifa	S 22 Restaurant, Hotel	M	M
1945–51	Chaparim	U 9 Unknown	P 40 Misc. Production	M	M
1945–70	Charashei Barzel	C 2 Jerusalem	P 44 Metal, Electrical	M	M
1945–49	Chomrei Binyan	C 2 Jerusalem	P 46 Sand, Quarry	M	M&R
1945–84	Dagan	N 4 Hadera	P 41 Bakery	M	M
1945–93*	Dan	C 1 Tel Aviv	T 11 Passenger Transportation	M	M&R
1945–48	Electron	C 1 Tel Aviv	P 44 Metals	M	M&R
1945–61	Erez	C 1 Tel Aviv	P 42 Wood	M	M&R
1945–57	Eyal	C 1 Tel Aviv	P 47 Textiles	M	M&R
1945–63	Hachofer	C 1 Tel Aviv	U 99 Unknown	NR	R
1945–46	Hadagan	C 2 Jerusalem	P 41 Bakery	NR	R
1945–46	Hakatsavim Haivrim	N 3 Haifa	S 21 Butchers	NR	R
1945–47	Hakorchim Jerusalem	C 2 Jerusalem	P 43 Book Binding	M	M&R
1945–46	Hamahir	C 1 Tel Aviv	S 20 Clerical	NR	R
1945–50	Hamechaber	C 2 Jerusalem	T 11 Passenger Transportation	M	M&R
1945–46	Hamekim	C 1 Tel Aviv	P 45 Building	NR	R
1945–46	Hamgame	C 1 Tel Aviv	T 10 Misc. Transportation	NR	R
1945–	Hamol	C 1 Tel Aviv	P 43 Printing	NR	R
1945–47	Hativ	C 1 Tel Aviv	U 99 Unknown	NR	R
1945–68	Hshichrur	N 3 Haifa	S 23 Cinema	M	M&R
1945–46	Kehat	N 3 Haifa	S 20 Engineering	NR	R
1945–48	Kerach	C 2 Jerusalem	S 21 Deliver Ice	NR	R
1945–50	Keves	C 1 Tel Aviv	S 24 Laundry	M	M&R
1945–47	Kodesh	C 2 Jerusalem	P 40 Religious Objects	NR	R

1945–55	Kooperativ Dfus Vekarton	U	9 Unknown	P	43 Paper	M	M
1945–56	Li La Lo	C	1 Tel Aviv	S	23 Theater	NR	R
1945–58	Mamash Tel Aviv	C	1 Tel Aviv	P	45 Building	M	M&R
1945–50	Misaada Betveriah	N	4 Tiberias	S	22 Restaurant	M	M&R
1945–47	Mutsak	C	1 Tel Aviv	S	23 Plastic Arts	NR	R
1945–46	Netivot	N	4 Hadera	T	10 Misc. Transportation	NR	R
1945–56	Nidbach	C	1 Tel Aviv	P	43 Printing	M	M&R
1945–71	Ovdei Gavish	C	5 Rishon Lezion	P	45 Glass	M	M&R
1945–82	Ovdei Hamaspenah	N	3 Haifa	S	26 Port Service	NR	R
1945–93*	Peled	C	1 Tel Aviv	P	44 Metals	M	M&R
1945–61	Seger	C	5 Rishon Lezion	S	20 Locksmith	M	M&R
1945–77	Shaal	C	1 Tel Aviv	P	49 Shoes	M	M&R
1945–58	Shachaf	C	1 Tel Aviv	S	20 Misc. Service	M	M
1945–50	Shaliach	C	2 Jerusalem	T	10 Misc. Transportation	NR	R
1945–58	Shatef	C	1 Tel Aviv	P	48 Soda Water	M	M&R
1945–47	Shefer	C	1 Tel Aviv	T	10 Misc. Transportation	NR	R
1945–51	Sheleg	N	4 Tiberias	S	24 Laundry	M	M&R
1945–93*	Shelev	C	1 Tel Aviv	T	12 Motor Freight	M	M&R
1945–53	Sherut Hataasiyah	N	3 Haifa	T	11 Passenger Transportation	M	M&R
1945–47‡	Sherut Rakevet	C	1 Tel Aviv	T	12 Motor Freight	NR	R
1945–50	Tsiud Mechani (Haparim 1947)	N	4 Afula	P	44 Metals	NR	R
1945–93*	Yael Tel Aviv	C	1 Tel Aviv	T	12 Motor Freight	M	M&R
1946–55	Agan	C	2 Jerusalem	P	50 Chemicals	M	M&R
1946–47	Al Bayad	C	1 Jaffa	S	24 Laundry	NR	R
1946–	Al Ihhlas	C	1 Jaffa	T	10 Misc. Transportation	NR	R
1946–48	Al Magdal	N	4 Migdal	P	47 Weavers	NR	R
1946–56	Al Toaivhig	N	4 Safed	P	47 Weavers	NR	R
1946–53	Amilan	C	1 Tel Aviv	P	48 Food	NR	R

(continued)

Years[1]	Cooperative[2]	Location[3]	Activity[4]/ Product	Org.[5]	Ref[6]
1946–	Barbur	C 2 Jerusalem	S 24 Laundry	NR	R
1946–47	Charat Netaniah	C 5 Netanya	P 44 Metals	M	M&R
1946–47	Chimiah	N 3 Haifa	P 50 Chemicals	M	M&R
1946–53	Chotzvei Migdal Tsedek	N 4 Migdal Haemek	P 46 Drilling	M	M&R
1946–	El Hadaf	W 9 Bet Sachur	T 10 Misc. Transportation	NR	R
1946–	Even	C 2 Jerusalem	P 45 Building	NR	R
1946–47	Eyn Hatikvah	C 1 Tel Aviv	P 40 Brushes	M	M&R
1946–50	Gal Yam	N 3 Haifa	S 26 Port Service	NR	R
1946–49	Globus	N 3 Haifa	T 10 Misc. Transportation	NR	R
1946–49	Hacherut	C 5 Ramat Hasharon	T 10 Misc. Transportation	NR	R
1946–56	Hadassah	N 3 Haifa	P 44 Metals	NR	R
1946–91	Haets	C 5 Herzlia	P 42 Wood	M	M&R
1946–47	Hakovesh	N 3 Haifa	T 10 Misc. Transportation	NR	R
1946–	Hamasbia	C 2 Jerusalem	P 41 Bakery	NR	R
1946–49	Hamayim	N 3 Haifa	S 23 Cinema	NR	R
1946–	Hameri	C 1 Tel Aviv	T 10 Misc. Transportation	NR	R
1946–56	Hameshuchrar	C 1 Tel Aviv	T 10 Misc. Transportation	NR	R
1946–56	Handasah Tel Aviv	C 1 Tel Aviv	P 40 Misc. Production	M	M
1946–53	Hasholim	C 1 Tel Aviv	S 26 Fishing	NR	R
1946–52	Hayotser	C 5 Ramat Hasharon	P 45 Building	NR	R
1946–61	Hayozem	C 1 Tel Aviv	S 23 Sports	M	M&R
1946–47	Hom Bein	C 5 Rehovot	P 45 Building	NR	R
1946–50	Igud	C 1 Tel Aviv	S 20 Locksmith	M	M&R
1946–55	Kaftor	C 1 Tel Aviv	P 47 Clothing	NR	R
1946–54	Kvutsat Chol	N 3 Haifa	P 46 Sand	M	M&R
1946–47	Lary	C 1 Tel Aviv	U 99 Unknown	NR	R

1946–47	Liket	C	1 Tel Aviv	S	28 Refuse Collection	NR	R
1946–46	May	C	2 Jerusalem	P	48 Meat Products	NR	R
1946–61	Melet Afulah	N	4 Afula	P	46 Cement, Building	M	M&R
1946–47	Mesilah Jerusalem	C	2 Jerusalem	T	12 Motor Freight	M	M&R
1946–49	Mifalenu	N	3 Haifa	T	10 Misc. Transportation	NR	R
1946–49	Mivneh	N	4 Hadera	P	45 Building	M	M&R
1946–47	Mofet	C	1 Tel Aviv	S	20 Advertising	NR	R
1946–47	Nachtom	C	2 Jerusalem	P	41 Bakery	NR	R
1946–53	Naftali	N	4 Binyamina	T	10 Misc. Transportation	NR	R
1946–57	Nahar Vayam	C	1 Tel Aviv	S	26 Sea Transport	NR	R
1946–50	Nitsots	C	2 Jerusalem	P	43 Printing	M	M&R
1946–51	Ovdei Hashiloach	C	2 Jerusalem	P	43 Printing	M	M&R
1946–48	Rechev	C	1 Tel Aviv	T	10 Misc. Transportation	NR	R
1946–53	Refidim	C	5 Raanana	P	40 Upholsterers	M	M&R
1946–47	Reses	N	3 Haifa	S	20 Exterminators	M	M&R
1946–55	Rihut Binyan	C	2 Jerusalem	P	42 Wood	M	M&R
1946–51	Rishon	C	5 Rishon Lezion	P	48 Food	M	M
1946–50	Rishon	C	5 Rishon Lezion	T	10 Misc. Transportation	NR	R
1946–47	Shaavianiah	N	3 Haifa	P	47 Oilcloth	M	M&R
1946–60‡	Shibolet	C	1 Petach Tikvah	P	41 Bakery	NR	R
1946–50	Stam	C	2 Jerusalem	S	20 Religious Objects	NR	R
1946–93*	Tav Tel Aviv	C	1 Tel Aviv	S	20 Engineering	M	M&R
1946–50	Tayar	C	1 Tel Aviv	S	20 Tourism	NR	R
1946–46	Thabihi	C	1 Jaffa	S	45 Building	NR	R
1946–54	Toren	N	3 Haifa	S	20 Engineering	M	M&R
1946–80	Tsedef	C	1 Bnei Brak	P	47 Buttons	M	M&R
1946–49	Tsochek Veochel	C	1 Tel Aviv	P	47 Textiles	NR	R
1946–82	Tsur Jerusalem	C	2 Jerusalem	P	46 Stone	M	M

(continued)

Years[1]	Cooperative[2]	Location[3]	Activity[4]/Product	Org.[5]	Ref[6]
1946–50	Uria	N 3 Haifa	P 44 Metals	NR	R
1946–47	Utz	N 3 Haifa	T 10 Misc. Transportation	NR	R
1946–51	Yahalomei Yahel	C 1 Tel Aviv	P 51 Diamonds	M	M&R
1946–49	Yahalomei Zion	C 2 Jerusalem	P 51 Diamonds	NR	R
1946–53	Zitan	N 4 Hadera	T 10 Misc. Transportation	NR	R
1947–	Al Argul	W 9 Bethlehem	T 10 Misc. Transportation	NR	R
1947–52	Almog	C 1 Tel Aviv	P 51 Diamonds	M	M&R
1947–51	Alon	N 3 Haifa	S 23 Cinema	NR	R
1947–47	Artsi Kafe	N 3 Haifa	S 22 Restaurant	NR	R
1947–70	Bareket	C 1 Tel Aviv	P 51 Diamonds	M	M&R
1947–56	Charziv	C 1 Tel Aviv	P 42 Wood	M	M
1947–54	Chavrei Bursah	U 9 Unknown	P 51 Diamonds	M	M
1947–61	Chavrei Yahalomei Bucharah	C 5 Netanya	P 51 Diamonds	NR	R
1947–51	Dagah	N 4 Acre	P 48 Food	M	M&R
1947–50	Dfus Hadiyuk	C 1 Tel Aviv	P 43 Printing	NR	R
1947–	Dfus Hashomer	N 4 Nahariya	P 43 Printing	NR	R
1947–50	Even Gazit	N 4 Migdal Haemek	P 45 Building	M	M&R
1947–49	Glilit	N 4 Tiberias	T 10 Misc. Transportation	NR	R
1947–93*	Hakoach	C 5 Rishon Lezion	T 12 Motor Freight	M	M&R
1947–56	Hamali	C 1 Jaffa	S 20 Porters	NR	R
1947–	Hanegev	S 6 Beersheba	T 12 Motor Freight	M	M&R
1947–50	Hanikayon	C 1 Tel Aviv	S 20 Cleaning	NR	R
1947–	Hatavor Mizrah	N 4 Kibbutz Mizra	T 12 Motor Freight	M	M&R
1947–62	Higyenah	N 3 Haifa	S 21 Deliver Meat	M	M&R
1947–50	Kemach Dagim	C 1 Tel Aviv	P 48 Food	NR	R
1947–49	Kfor Hamifrats	N 3 Haifa	S 21 Deliver Ice	M	R

Years	Name							
1947–61	M.A.I.	C	1 Tel Aviv	P	43 Printing	NR	R
1947–73	Masa Afulah (Haemek 1948)	N	4 Afula	T	12 Motor Freight	M	M&R
1947–58	Maskit	C	5 Netanya	P	51 Diamonds	M	M&R
1947–93*	Migdal	C	1 Holon	S	23 Art	M	M&R
1947–56	Nagariat Rishon	C	5 Rishon Lezion	P	42 Wood	NR	R
1947–50	Oron	N	3 Haifa	S	23 Theater Agent	NR	R
1947–49	Otsem	N	4 Afula	P	44 Metal, Electrical	M	M&R
1947–65	Ovdei Keren Or	C	1 Tel Aviv	P	44 Metal, Electrical	M	M&R
1947–51	Ovdei Yahalomei Bursah	C	1 Tel Aviv	P	51 Diamonds	M	M&R
1947–49	Poalei Hohovalah	N	3 Haifa	T	12 Motor Freight	NR	R
1947–50	Sheder	C	2 Jerusalem	T	10 Misc. Transportation	NR	R
1947–50	Sheder Tel Aviv	C	1 Tel Aviv	U	99 Unknown	M	M
1947–52	Shoham	C	1 Tel Aviv	P	51 Diamonds	M	M&R
1947–50	Tarshish	C	5 Netanya	P	51 Diamonds	M	M&R
1947–48	Tochen	C	1 Tel Aviv	S	20 Engineering	M	M&R
1947–	Yachad	N	3 Haifa	S	21 Deliver Meat	M	M
1947–71‡	Yotsrim	N	3 Haifa	P	42 Wood	M	M&R
1947–49	Zohar	C	5 Raanana	S	24 Laundry	NR	R
1948–93*	Galei Aviv	C	1 Tel Aviv	S	24 Laundry	M	M&R
1948–62	Hakorech Jaffa	C	1 Jaffa	P	49 Leather	M	M&R
1948–68	Hamaalchim	C	1 Tel Aviv	P	44 Metals	NR	M&R
1948–69	Hamovil	C	1 Tel Aviv	T	10 Misc. Transportation	M	M&R
1948–55	Misaada Shell Hapoel Hamizrachi	C	2 Jerusalem	S	22 Restaurant	HPHM	R
1948–56	Ovdei Hakishon	N	3 Haifa	P	41 Bakery	M	M&R
1948–72	Ovdei Palkeramik	N	3 Haifa	P	40 Ceramics	M	M&R
1948–54‡	Shachar	N	3 Haifa	T	11 Passenger Transportation	M	M

(continued)

Years[1]	Cooperative[2]	Location[3]		Activity[4]/Product		Org.[5]	Ref[6]
1948–50	Shamor	C	1 Tel Aviv	P	51 Diamonds	M	M&R
1948–50	Tsel Noa	C	1 Tel Aviv	P	45 Shades	NR	R
1948–59	Zach	C	1 Holon	S	24 Laundry	M	M&R
1949–77	Achdut Haemek	N	4 Afula	P	41 Bakery	M	M&R
1949–54	Agudat Hatofrot	N	4 Nazareth	P	47 Textiles	None	R
1949–	Akum	C	1 Tel Aviv	S	23 School, Theater	None	R
1949–55	Alchut	N	3 Haifa	S	26 Fishing	None	R
1949–56	Algavish	C	1 Tel Aviv	P	51 Diamonds	HPHM	R
1949–93*	Alon	C	5 Netanya	P	42 Wood	M	M&R
1949–53	Alon	N	4 Ramla	S	20 Misc. Service	M	M
1949–53	Amelim	N	3 Haifa	P	45 Building	M	M&R
1949–60	Arazim	N	4 Hadera	P	42 Wood	None	R
1949–52	Ariach	N	4 Bet Shean	P	45 Building	M	R
1949–56	Arig	S	6 Migdal	P	47 Textiles	None	R
1949–	Atsmaut	N	3 Haifa	P	41 Bakery	None	R
1949–54	Atsmaut	C	1 Jaffa	P	43 Printing	None	R
1949–	Bahat (Ovdei Bahat 1969)	C	5 Netanya	P	46 Cement	HPHM	R
1949–54	Bdolach	N	3 Haifa	S	20 Misc. Service	M	M&R
1949–93*	Beged	N	3 Haifa	P	47 Textiles	M	M&R
1949–54	Brik	C	5 Netanya	P	51 Diamonds	M	M&R
1949–53	Chets	C	1 Jaffa	T	12 Motor Freight	None	R
1949–56	Chitah	C	5 Center	P	41 Bakery	M	M&R
1949–93*	Chof Yam	C	5 Herzlia	P	45 Building	M	M&R
1949–57	Chosen	C	5 Ramatayim	P	45 Bricks	M	M&R
1949–50	Chotsvei Karkur	C	5 Karkur	P	46 Quarry	M	M&R
1949–62	Dachpor	C	1 Tel Aviv	P	46 Digging	M	M&R

1949–58	Dov	C	5 Rehovot	T	12 Motor Freight	None	R
1949–52	Drom Jerusalem	C	2 Jerusalem	P	41 Bakery	M	M&R
1949–84	Dror	S	6 Beersheba	P	41 Bakery	M	M&R
1949–59	Dvorah	C	1 Jaffa	P	48 Sweets	M	M&R
1949–51	Emek Zvulun	N	3 Haifa	T	11 Taxi	None	R
1949–51	Eshel	C	1 Tel Aviv	S	23 Film Making	M	M&R
1949–51	Eshel	C	1 Tel Aviv	P	42 Wood	HPHM	R
1949–56	Even Shtiyah	C	2 Jerusalem	P	48 Soft Drinks	M	M&R
1949–52	Eyn Kerem	C	2 Jerusalem	P	41 Bakery	M	M&R
1949–52	Geulah	C	5 Lod	P	47 Textiles	M	M&R
1949–50	Gilat	C	1 Jaffa	S	27 Garage	M	R
1949–52	Glilim	C	5 Herzlia	P	45 Building	M	M&R
1949–55	Habanaim	C	1 Jaffa	P	45 Building	None	R
1949–56‡	Haboneh	N	3 Haifa	P	42 Wood	M	M&R
1949–50	Hachayat	C	5 Rishon Lezion	P	47 Textiles	M	M&R
1949–53	Hachotsvim	C	5 Migdal Tsedek	P	46 Gravel, Stone	M	M&R
1949–	Hadar Haifa	N	3 Haifa	S	20 Misc. Service	M	M&R
1949–93*	Hagal	N	3 Haifa	S	20 Misc. Service	M	M&R
1949–77	Hagalil	N	4 Safed	P	41 Bakery	M	M
1949–87‡	Hagalil Hamaaravi	N	4 Western Galilee	P	41 Bakery	M	M&R
1949–51	Hakochav	N	4 Acre	P	47 Textiles	M	M&R
1949–51	Halavi	C	2 Jerusalem	P	47 Textiles	HPHM	R
1949–51	Halevenah	C	5 Mishmar Hashivah	P	46 Cement	None	R
1949–69	Halevush	C	1 Tel Aviv	P	47 Textiles	M	M&R
1949–77	Hamaapil	N	3 Haifa	P	41 Bakery	M	M&R
1949–72	Hamachat	C	5 Ramla	P	47 Textiles	M	M&R
1949–51	Hamanof	N	3 Haifa	T	12 Motor Freight	M	M&R
1949–51	Hamasger	C	2 Jerusalem	S	20 Locksmith	M	M&R

(continued)

Years[1]	Cooperative[2]	Location[3]	Activity[4]/Product	Org.[5]	Ref[6]
1949–56	Hamasor	C 1 Tel Aviv	P 42 Wood	M	M&R
1949–51	Hamechashlim	N 4 Safed	S 20 Locksmith	M	M&R
1949–53	Hamechonen	C 1 Tel Aviv	S 20 Fix Machines	M	M&R
1949–55	Hamedayek	C 1 Tel Aviv	S 20 Misc. Service	None	R
1949–53	Hamelaben	C 1 Tel Aviv	P 45 Building	M	M&R
1949–50	Hamelaked	C 1 Tel Aviv	P 45 Building	M	M&R
1949–79	Hamezin	C 1 Tel Aviv	P 48 Sweets	M	M&R
1949–53	Hamonit	N 3 Haifa	T 11 Passenger Transportation	M	M&R
1949–61	Hanagar	C 5 Ramla	P 42 Wood	M	M&R
1949–55	Hanagarim	N 4 Nazareth	P 24 Wood	None	R
1949–60	Haofeh	C 5 Lod	P 41 Bakery	M	M&R
1949–54	Haoleh	C 5 Ramla	P 49 Leather	M	M&R
1949–74	Hapach	S 6 Gedera	S 20 Plumbing, Smithing	M	M&R
1949–55	Hapetach	C 2 Jerusalem	S 20 Tinsmith, Plumbing	M	M
1949–54	Hapoalim	N 4 Acre	P 41 Bakery	None	R
1949–53	Hasabon	N 4 Nazareth	P 50 Soap	None R	
1949–51	Hasela	C 5 Bet Naballa	P 46 Quarry	M	M&R
1949–72	Hasherut	C 1 Jaffa	S 27 Garage	M	M&R
1949–58	Hashmirah	N 3 Haifa	S 20 Guard Service	None	R
1949–51‡	Hasholeh	C 5 Netanya	S 26 Port Service	None	R
1949–	Hashomrom	N 4 Pardes Hanna Karkur	P 45 Building	None	R
1949–60	Hatanur	S 6 South	P 41 Bakery	M	M&R
1949–93*	Hatik Haifa	N 3 Haifa	P 43 Paper	M	M&R
1949–52	Hatsinor	C 1 Tel Aviv	S 20 Plumbing	M	M&R
1949–77	Hayarden	N 3 Haifa	S 20 Plumbing, Tinsmith	M	M&R
1949–57	Kama	C 1 Jaffa	P 41 Bakery	M	R

1949–57	Karnat	C	5 Netanya	P	51 Diamonds	M	M&R
1949–52	Karton Jaffa	C	1 Jaffa	P	43 Paper Boxes	M	M&R
1949–55	Keshet	C	1 Tel Aviv	S	21 Butchers	None	R
1949–69	Ketsef	C	1 Jaffa	P	50 Soap	M	M&R
1949–58	Kfor	N	4 Acre	S	21 Food Service	M	M&R
1949–54	Kfor Hamifrats	N	3 Haifa	S	21 Food Service	M	M&R
1949–53	Kidmah	N	3 Haifa	P	47 Textiles	M	M&R
1949–50	Kim	C	2 Jerusalem	S	21 Food Service	M	M&R
1949–70	Koach	N	3 Haifa	P	44 Metal, Electrical	M	M&R
1949–56	Kol Jerusalem	C	2 Jerusalem	S	23 Cinema	M	M&R
1949–53	Korei Zifzif Netanyah	C	5 Netanya	P	46 Sand	M	M&R
1949–52	Ksut	C	2 Jerusalem	P	47 Textiles	M	M&R
1949–53	Letesh	N	3 Haifa	P	40 Mirrors	M	M&R
1949–60	Maafeh	N	4 Hadera	P	41 Bakery	M	R
1949–67	Mafri	C	1 Tel Aviv	P	48 Food	M	M&R
1949–68	Mamtakim	C	1 Petach Tikvah	P	48 Sweets	M	M&R
1949–60	Manoa	C	1 Jaffa	S	27 Garage	M	M&R
1949–55	Marvadim	U	9 Unknown	P	42 Wood	HPHM	R
1949–51	Masgeriah	C	1 Bet Dagon	P	44 Metal, Electrical	M	M&R
1949–59	Matechit	N	3 Haifa	S	27 Garage	M	M&R
1949–79	Mechalkei Neft	C	1 Tel Aviv	S	20 Misc. Service	M	M&R
1949–	Migdal Haifa	N	3 Haifa	P	41 Bakery	M	M&R
1949–81	Migdan	C	1 Tel Aviv	P	41 Bakery	M	M&R
1949–	Migdaniah (1950)	C	1 Tel Aviv	P	41 Bakery	M	M&R
1949–51	Misaada Netanyah	C	5 Netanya	S	22 Restaurant	M	M&R
1949–51	Mishor	N	3 Haifa	P	45 Building	None	R
1949–51	Musach Machal	C	2 Jerusalem	S	27 Garage	M	M&R
1949–54	Naal Tifert (Naal noy)	C	1 Jaffa	P	49 Shoes	None	R

(continued)

Years[1]	Cooperative[2]	Location[3]	Activity[4]/ Product	Org.[5]	Ref[6]
1949–53	Naalei Netanyah	C 5 Netanya	P 47 Textiles	M	M&R
1949–56	Naalei Hagalil	N 4 Acre	P 49 Shoes	None	R
1949–54	Nachshon	C 1 Tel Aviv	P 47 Textiles	M	M&R
1949–64	Nachtom	C 5 Lod	P 41 Bakery	M	M&R
1949–66	Nagarim	C 5 Lod	P 42 Wood	M	M&R
1949–54	Nagarim Meuchadim	C 1 Jaffa	P 42 Wood	None	R
1949–61	Naknikei Akko	N 4 Acre	P 48 Sausage	M	M&R
1949–51	Naknikei Netanyah	C 5 Netanya	P 48 Sausage	M	M&R
1949–60	Neeman	C 1 Tel Aviv	S 26 Port Service	Ag	R
1949–54	Netech	N 3 Haifa	P 44 Casting House	M	M&R
1949–54	Neter	C 5 Netanya	S 24 Laundry	M	M&R
1949–55	Nirim	C 5 Rishon Lezion	S 20 Locksmith	M	M&R
1949–60	Ofim	C 5 Ramla	P 41 Bakery	M	M&R
1949–70	Ofir	N 3 Haifa	T 12 Motor Freight	M	M&R
1949–53	Olar	U 9 Unknown	P 44 Metal, Electrical	M	M
1949–51	Or Vekoach	C 5 Ramla	P 44 Electricians	M	M&R
1949–56	Orot	S 6 Gedera	P 44 Electricity	M	M&R
1949–62	Orot Jaffa	C 5 Kfar Saba	P 49 Leather	M	M&R
1949–57	Palan Limited	C 1 Tel Aviv	P 44 Brass	M	M&R
1949–52	Pelech	C 5 Netanya	P 47 Textiles	M	M&R
1949–68	Peled	C 5 Rehovot	S 20 Mechanic Locksmith	M	M&R
1949–52	Plovdiv	C 1 Jaffa	P 40 Brooms	None	R
1949–91	Rakat	N 4 Tiberias	S 20 Misc. Service	M	M&R
1949–63	Rakefet	C 1 Tel Aviv	P 47 Textiles	M	M
1949–59	Ramtex	C 1 Ramat Gan	P 47 Textiles	None	R
1949–54	Ripud Haifa	N 3 Haifa	P 42 Wood	M	M&R

1949–51	Ripud Laam	C	1 Tel Aviv	P	42 Wood	M	M&R
1949–57‡	Sabon Hagalil	N	4 Acre	P	50 Soap	M	M&R
1949–56	Sabonat	C	5 Netanya	P	50 Soap	HPHM	R
1949–51	Shachaf	N	3 Haifa	S	20 Misc. Service	M	M&R
1949–51	Shenhav	N	3 Haifa	P	49 Shoes	M	M&R
1949–80	Shibolet	C	5 Nes Tsiyonah	P	41 Bakery	M	M&R
1949–60	Shipon	N	4 North	P	41 Bakery	M	M&R
1949–52	Sholei Hasfog	N	3 Haifa	P	40 Misc. Production	M	M&R
1949–56	Sid	N	4 North	P	46 Cement, Drill	None	R
1949–51	Siv	C	1 Tel Aviv	P	40 Brooms	None	R
1949–55	Slaim	N	4 North	P	45 Building	M	M&R
1949–58	Sova	N	3 Haifa	P	41 Bakery	M	M&R
1949–64	Taim	C	5 Lod	P	41 Bakery	HPHM	R
1949–52	Talal	C	5 Netanya	P	51 Diamonds	None	R
1949–50	Tate	C	5 Karkur	P	40 Brooms, Brushes	M	M&R
1949–57	Telefon	C	1 Tel Aviv	P	44 Telephones	M	M&R
1949–60	Tihur	N	4 Pardes Hanna Karkur	S	24 Laundry	HPHM	R
1949–51	Trico Jaffa	C	1 Tel Aviv	P	47 Textiles	M	M&R
1949–51	Tsdafim	N	3 Haifa	P	45 Building	M	M&R
1949–54	Tsfon Haifa	N	3 Haifa	T	12 Motor Freight	M	M&R
1949–75	Tslil	C	1 Tel Aviv	S	23 Cinema	M	M&R
1949–50	Tsuk	C	1 Bat Yam	P	46 Cement	None	R
1949–54	Umanin	N	4 Acre	P	45 Building	M	M&R
1949–	Vindzor	N	3 Haifa	S	22 Restaurant, Hotel	M	M
1949–51	Yaholomei Hagalil	N	4 Safed	P	51 Diamonds	M	M&R
1949–56	Yatur	C	1 Tel Aviv	T	11 Passenger Transportation	M	M&R
1949–78	Yechiam	N	4 Acre	S	23 Cinema	M	M&R

(continued)

Years[1]	Cooperative[2]	Location[3]		Activity[4]/Product		Org.[5]	Ref[6]
1949–54	Yetsiat Europah	N	3 Haifa	T	12 Motor Freight	M	M&R
1949–54	Yohah	N	3 Haifa	S	20 Misc. Service	M	M&R
1949–68	Zifim	C	1 Tel Aviv	P	40 Misc. Production	M	M&R
1949–62	Zifzif Nahariya	N	4 Nahariya	P	46 Sand	M	M&R
1950–55	Adin	C	1 Petach Tikvah	P	47 Textiles	M	M&R
1950–52	Adin	C	2 Jerusalem	P	48 Food	None	R
1950–93*	Agur	N	3 Haifa	S	20 Misc. Service	M	M&R
1950–64	Aharon	N	3 Haifa	P	41 Bakery	M	M&R
1950–	Alchut	C	5 Netanya	S	20 Repair	M	M&R
1950–59	Alrazon	N	3 Haifa	P	41 Bakery	M	M&R
1950–54	Amir	C	1 Tel Aviv	P	41 Bakery	M	M&R
1950–55	Ariel	C	5 Kfar Saba	P	45 Building	M	M&R
1950–51	Arigei Akko	N	4 Acre	P	47 Textiles	M	M&R
1950–52	Ashkelon	S	6 Migdal Gad	T	12 Motor Freight	M	M&R
1950–55	Atidot	N	4 Acre	P	47 Knitting	M	M&R
1950–57	Atsmon	C	5 Kfar Saba	P	40 Misc. Production	M	M&R
1950–59	Avner	C	1 Petach Tikvah	P	45 Building	None	R
1950–53	Avodot Nagarut	N	4 Bat Shlomo	P	42 Wood	None	R
1950–54	Ayalah	N	3 Haifa	S	21 Butchers	M	M&R
1950–51	Badim	C	5 Raanana	P	47 Textiles	M	M&R
1950–53	Bamah	C	1 Tel Aviv	P	44 Farm Machinery	M	M&R
1950–64	Bar	N	3 Haifa	P	41 Bakery	M	M&R
1950–55	Bashan	N	3 Haifa	P	48 Sausage	M	M&R
1950–53	Bazelet	N	4 Afula	P	45 Building	None	R
1950–53	Binyan Kfar Yasif	N	4 Kfar Yasif	P	45 Building	None	R
1950–54	Binyan Vesid	N	3 Haifa	P	45 Building	None	R

1950–52	Briut	C	5 Rehovot	48 Food	P	M	M&R
1950–51	Chakah	C	1 Tel Aviv	26 Fishing	S	M	M&R
1950–52	Charsit	C	5 Lod	45 Building	P	M	M&R
1950–51	Chatsats	N	4 Nahariyah	45 Building	P	M	M&R
1950–53	Chavatselet	C	5 Rehovot	50 Dyes	P	M	M&R
1950–55	Chemar (Chamra 1951)	C	2 Jerusalem	40 Ceramics	P	M	M&R
1950–64	Chemko	N	3 Haifa	40 Misc. Production	P	M	M&R
1950–54	Chen	C	5 Center	40 Brooms, Brushes	P	M	M&R
1950–51	Cheres	N	4 Acre	40 Ceramics	P	M	M&R
1950–53	Choferet	C	5 Center	46 Sand	P	M	M&R
1950–93*	Chomah Petach Tikvah	C	1 Petach Tikvah	45 Building	P	M	M&R
1950–52	Choshlim	N	4 Givat Ada	44 Metals	P	M	M&R
1950–51	Chotsvei Haemek	N	4 Kfar Baruch	45 Building	P	M	M&R
1950–52‡	Chulon	C	1 Tel Aviv	45 Building	P	M	M&R
1950–51	Chut Vemachat	N	4 Bet Shean	47 Textiles	P	M	M&R
1950–54	Dagan	N	3 Haifa	41 Bakery	P	M	M&R
1950–55	Darooch	C	1 Tel Aviv	99 Unknown	U	M	M
1950–	Dfus Al Itichad	N	3 Haifa	43 Printing	P	None	R
1950–55	Diyuk	C	1 Jaffa	44 Metals	P	M	R
1950–56	Dvorat Zahav	C	2 Jerusalem	48 Food	P	M	M&R
1950–61	Efraty	C	1 Tel Aviv	41 Bakery	P	M	M&R
1950–54	Elef	C	1 Petach Tikvah	24 Laundry	S	M	M&R
1950–50	Even Binyan	N	3 Haifa	45 Building	P	M	M&R
1950–55	Even Vechatsats	N	4 Acre	46 Cement, Drill	P	None	R
1950–51	Eytan	N	4 Bet Shean	49 Shoes	P	M	M&R
1950–50	Gad	S	6 Migdal Gad	26 Fishing	S	M	M&R
1950–55	Galanteriah	C	1 Holon	40 Misc. Production	P	None	R
1950–52	Gershon	C	1 Tel Aviv	40 Plastics	P	None	R

(continued)

Years[1]	Cooperative[2]	Location[3]	Activity[4]/ Product	Org.[5]	Ref[6]
1950–54	Gilboa	N 4 Afula	S 20 Locksmith	M	M&R
1950–53	Habinyan	C 5 Ramla	P 45 Building	NR	R
1950–66	Hachof Hashaket	N 3 Haifa	S 22 Restaurant	M	M&R
1950–78	Hadar	C 5 Center	P 41 Bakery	M	M&R
1950–68	Hadarom	S 6 Gedera	P 41 Bakery	M	M&R
1950–55	Hadaykan	C 1 Tel Aviv	P 47 Textiles	M	M&R
1950–51	Hadfus Hachadash	N 3 Haifa	P 43 Printing	M	M&R
1950–50	Hadizel	C 1 Tel Aviv	S 27 Garage	M	M&R
1950–52	Haganan	C 1 Holon	S 20 Misc. Service	None	R
1950–51	Hagorfim	C 1 Tel Aviv	S 26 Fishing	M	M&R
1950–55	Hakoves	C 1 Tel Aviv	S 24 Laundry	None	R
1950–58‡	Halechem	N 3 Haifa	P 41 Bakery	M	M&R
1950–57	Hamasmer	C 1 Tel Aviv	S 20 Misc. Service	M	M&R
1950–63	Hameasef (Nitsolet 1962)	C 2 Jerusalem	P 40 Recycling	M	M&R
1950–64	Hamechadesh	C 1 Tel Aviv	P 40 Recycling	HPHM	R
1950–52	Hameshubach	C 1 Tel Aviv	P 48 Sausage	M	M&R
1950–51	Hamizron	C 2 Jerusalem	P 40 Mattresses	M	M&R
1950–52	Hanitsots	C 1 Tel Aviv	U 99 Unknown	M	M&R
1950–56	Haof	C 1 Tel Aviv	S 21 Food Service	None	R
1950–52	Haslil	N 3 Haifa	P 47 Knitting	M	M&R
1950–51	Hatikvah	C 2 Jerusalem	S 20 Misc. Service	M	M&R
1950–60	Hatikvah	C 1 Tel Aviv	P 40 Misc. Production	M	M&R
1950–53	Hatsabaim	N 4 Nazareth	S 20 Misc. Service	None	R
1950–93*	Hatsinkografiah	C 1 Tel Aviv	P 43 Printing	M	M&R
1950–54	Hazerem	C 2 Jerusalem	S 20 Misc. Service	M	M&R
1950–55	Homo	N 4 Bat Shlomo	P 49 Shoes	None	R

Year	Name		Location		Industry		
1950–56	Iron	N	4 North	P	41 Bakery	M	M&R
1950–56	Itriot	C	5 Nes Tsiyonah	P	48 Food	M	M&R
1950–59	Kadimah	C	1 Tel Aviv	P	41 Bakery	M	M&R
1950–62	Kali	C	2 Jerusalem	P	41 Bakery	M	M&R
1950–53	Kiduach Hadarom	S	6 Migdal Gad	P	46 Drilling	M	M&R
1950–56	Kivshanei Sid	N	4 Pardes Hanna Karkur	P	46 Limestone	M	M&R
1950–56	Kufsiyon	C	1 Tel Aviv	P	43 Bookbinder	M	M&R
1950–77	Kvasim	C	5 Kfar Saba	S	24 Laundry	M	M&R
1950–56	M.D.A.	N	3 Haifa	P	40 Misc. Production	M	R
1950–55	Maadan Tirah	N	3 Haifa	P	48 Food	M	M&R
1950–57	Maafiyat Karkur	N	4 Pardes Hanna Karkur	P	41 Bakery	M	M&R
1950–51	Maafiyat Tsrifin	C	5 Tsrifin	P	41 Bakery	M	M&R
1950–57	Machat	C	2 Jerusalem	P	47 Textiles	M	M&R
1950–55	Machberet Jaffa	C	1 Tel Aviv	P	43 Paper	M	M&R
1950–62	Makor Hamayim	U	5 Herzlia	P	46 Drilling	M	M&R
1950–53	Makosh	N	9 Nachlat Yehudah	U	99 Unknown	M	M&R
1950–59	Maltrah	U	3 Haifa	P	50 Chemicals	HPHM	R
1950–51	Masad	N	6 Beersheba	P	45 Building	M	M&R
1950–55	Matok	S	4 Acre	P	40 Candles	M	M&R
1950–61	Mazon	N	4 Binyamina	P	41 Bakery	M	M&R
1950–57	Melet	C	5 Netanya	P	45 Building	M	M&R
1950–53	Melet Bat Shl	N	4 Bat Shlomo	P	46 Cement	None	R
1950–54	Melet Natsrat	N	4 Nazareth	P	46 Cement	None	R
1950–53	Menorah	C	1 Jaffa	P	40 Chandlers	None	R
1950–53	Merchavy	C	1 Tel Aviv	P	45 Building	M	M&R
1950–51	Merets	N	4 Acre	S	20 Locksmith	M	M&R
1950–61	Metikah	C	5 Lod	P	48 Food	M	M&R
1950–52	Mifalei Hagalil	N	4 Nahariya	P	47 Textiles	M	M&R

(continued)

Years[1]	Cooperative[2]	Location[3]	Activity[4]/ Product	Org.[5]	Ref[6]
1950–57	Migdal	C 1 Jaffa	P 40 Candles	HPHM	R
1950–58	Migdal Tsedek	C 1 Petach Tikvah	P 46 Gravel	M	M&R
1950–51	Mintsa	N 3 Haifa	U 99 Unknown	M	M
1950–93*	Mirtsefet	C 5 Rehovot	P 45 Building	M	M&R
1950–91	Mishmar Hayam (Shulamit 1954)	N 4 Acre	S 24 Laundry	M	M&R
1950–56	Mitkan	C 5 Raanana	S 20 Locksmith	M	M&R
1950–52	Mitriyot	C 1 Tel Aviv	P 40 Umbrellas	None	R
1950–58	Mizhav (Fridlander 1951)	C 1 Tel Aviv	P 40 Misc. Production	M	M&R
1950–68	Mizrach	C 1 Tel Aviv	P 41 Bakery	M	M&R
1950–59	Moledet	C 1 Tel Aviv	P 41 Bakery	M	M&R
1950–60	Mutsarei Matechet	C 1 Tel Aviv	P 44 Plumbing Parts	M	M&R
1950–54	Nag Hagalil	N 4 Nazareth	P 42 Wood	None	R
1950–50	Nagarei Migdal	S 6 Migdal Gad	P 42 Wood	M	M&R
1950–52	Nagarut	C 1 Jaffa	P 42 Wood	None	R
1950–60	Nahama	C 5 Raanana	P 41 Bakery	HPHM	R
1950–51	Naknik	C 5 Ramla	P 48 Sausage	M	M&R
1950–58	Negba	S 6 Migdal Gad	P 41 Bakery	M	M&R
1950–51	Nehagei Hanegev	S 6 Beersheba	T 12 Motor Freight	M	M&R
1950–55	Nektar	N 3 Haifa	P 48 Food	M	M&R
1950–52	Ofrah	N 3 Haifa	P 46 Cement, Drill	None	R
1950–54	Olah	N 3 Haifa	U 99 Unknown	M	M
1950–61	Omes Jerusalem	C 2 Jerusalem	T 12 Motor Freight	M	M&R
1950–56	Oren Raananah	C 5 Raanana	P 42 Wood	M	M&R
1950–52	Orgim	C 5 Lod	P 47 Textiles	M	M&R
1950–62	Ovdei Masach	C 1 Tel Aviv	S 23 School, Theater	M	M
1950–64	Ovdei Moriyah Jerusalem	C 2 Jerusalem	S 22 Misc. Service	M	M&R

Years	Name		Location	Industry			
1950–64	Ovdei Solex	C	5 Nachlat Ganim	40 Optician	P	M	M&R
1950–54	Ovdei Ziratron	C	1 Ramat Gan	23 School, Theater	S	M	M&R
1950–93*	Oz On	C	1 Tel Aviv	44 Metal, Electrical	P	M	M&R
1950–56	Patbag	N	4 Tiberias	41 Bakery	P	M	M&R
1950–52	Raamses	C	1 Petach Tikvah	46 Cement	P	None	R
1950–70	Rakach	C	1 Tel Aviv	50 Chemicals	P	M	M&R
1950–64	Ramco Chamco	N	3 Haifa	50 Chemicals	P	M	M&R
1950–52	Reafit Tivon	N	4 Tivon	45 Building	P	M	M&R
1950–83	Rechev	C	5 Center	12 Motor Freight	T	M	M&R
1950–51	Retsef	N	4 Pardes Hanna	45 Building	P	M	M&R
1950–62	Revayah	C	5 Netanya	48 Sweets	P	M	M&R
1950–57	Revivim	C	1 Tel Aviv	41 Bakery	P	M	M&R
1950–51	Rishon Lezion	C	1 Rishon Lezion	48 Coffee	P	M	M&R
1950–56	Ronald Jerusalem	C	2 Jerusalem	43 Paper	P	M	M&R
1950–53	Sabon Veshmanim	C	5 Lod	50 Soap	P	None	R
1950–60	Sasgona	C	1 Kiryat Arye	47 Textiles	P	M	M&R
1950–54	Shalvah	C	5 Ramatayim	42 Wood	P	M	M&R
1950–53	Shefa	S	6 Migdal Gad	44 Metal, Electrical	P	M	M&R
1950–57	Shekef	N	3 Haifa	40 Lamps	P	M	M&R
1950–55	Sherut Aliyah Haifa	N	3 Haifa	12 Motor Freight	T	M	M&R
1950–57	Sherutim	C	1 Tel Aviv	27 Garage	S	M	M&R
1950–60	Shichor	N	3 Haifa	27 Garage	S	M	M&R
1950–54	Shikui	N	3 Haifa	48 Food	P	M	M&R
1950–54	Shimorei Akko	N	4 Acre	48 Food	P	M	M&R
1950–54	Shluchot	N	4 Zichron Yaakov	12 Motor Freight	T	M	M&R
1950–77	Shomron	N	4 Zichron Yaakov	41 Bakery	P	M	M&R
1950–51	Shravrav	C	5 Ramla	20 Plumbing, Smithing	S	M	M&R
1950–60	Sichor	N	3 Haifa	27 Garage	S	M	M&R

(continued)

Years[1]	Cooperative[2]	Location[3]	Activity[4]/ Product	Org.[5]	Ref6
1950–55	Sid Bedaburiya	N 4 Daburiya	P 45 Building	NR	R
1950–54	Sid Pkiin	N 4 Pkiin	P 45 Building	NR	R
1950–65	Sigariot Lod	C 5 Lod	P 48 Cigarettes	M	M&R
1950–52	Sova Rechovot	C 5 Rehovot	P 41 Bakery	M	M&R
1950–51	Tachanat Jerusalem	C 2 Jerusalem	P 48 Flour	M	M&R
1950–79	Teidah Tel Aviv (1959)	C 1 Tel Aviv	S 22 Restaurant	M	M
1950–52	Tidhar Chulon	C 1 Holon	P 42 Wood	M	M&R
1950–54	Tsaad	C 1 Tel Aviv	P 49 Shoes	M	M&R
1950–54	Tsach	S 6 Beersheba	S 24 Laundry	M	M&R
1950–81	Tsur	C 1 Tel Aviv	P 45 Building	M	M&R
1950–93*	Tsur Azur	C 2 Jerusalem	P 45 Building	M	M
1950–50	Yarden Tveryah	N 4 Tiberias	S 22 Restaurant	M	M&R
1950–	Yarkon	C 1 Tel Aviv	S 22 Restaurant, Hotel	M	M
1950–52	Yechiel Geul	C 1 Tel Aviv	P 42 Wood	None	R
1950–55	Yitsur Rahitim	C 1 Tel Aviv	P 42 Wood	None	R
1950–54	Yochanan	C 5 Rehovot	S 20 Repair Shoes	M	M&R
1950–52	Zion	U 9 Kfar Aharon	P 40 Recycling	NR	R
1951–54	Aryeh	C 1 Kiryat Arye	P 42 Wood	None	R
1951–56	Atsei Shitim	C 2 Jerusalem	P 42 Wood	M	M&R
1951–56	Atsmon	N 4 Safed	P 48 Food	HPHM	R
1951–	Bahir	C 5 Netanya	S 24 Laundry	HPHM	R
1951–56	Burskaim	C 5 Kfar Saba	P 49 Leather	M	M&R
1951–54	Chisachon	S 6 Beersheba	S 28 Refuse Collection	M	M&R
1951–56	Chitim	C 5 Herzlia	P 41 Bakery	M	M&R
1951–53	Coop Letofrot	N 4 Kfar Kanna	P 47 Textiles	NR	R
1951–53	Coop Tofrot Iblin	N 4 Iblin	P 47 Textiles	NR	R

1951–53	Dayagim	C	5 Netanya	P	48 Food	M	M
1951–54	Dekel	N	4 Safed	P	50 Soap	M	M&R
1951–66	Delek	C	1 Tel Aviv	S	21 Deliver Oil	M	M&R
1951–54	Doron Acre	N	4 Acre	P	40 Misc. Production	M	M&R
1951–54	Etsyon	C	2 Jerusalem	P	41 Bakery	M	M&R
1951–	Galil Maaravi	N	4 Nahariya	T	12 Motor Freight	M	M&R
1951–62	Goren Pardes	N	4 Pardes Hanna	P	41 Bakery	M	M&R
1951–91	Gush Dan	C	1 Tel Aviv	S	20 Misc. Service	M	M
1951–53	Hachalav	C	1 Tel Aviv	S	21 Deliver Milk	None	R
1951–54	Hachorshim	C	5 Raanana	S	20 Misc. Service	M	M&R
1951–52	Haeshel	C	5 Kfar Saba	P	42 Wood	M	M&R
1951–68	Hagalil Hatachton	N	4 Galilee	T	12 Motor Freight	M	M&R
1951–55	Hakodchim	U	9 Zarnuga	P	46 Drilling	HPHM	R
1951–52	Hakodeach Bitsaron	C	1 Bitsaron	P	45 Building	M	M&R
1951–53	Hakoreh	S	6 Migdal Gad	P	45 Building	M	M&R
1951–57	Hamachtsevot	N	4 Kfar Sulam	P	46 Cement, Drill	NR	R
1951–54	Hamakor	C	1 Tel Aviv	P	44 Refrigerators	M	M&R
1951–70	Hamechashel	C	1 Tel Aviv	P	44 Misc. Production	M	M&R
1951–56	Hamehandes	N	3 Haifa	S	20 Misc. Service	M	M&R
1951–56	Hamelaket	N	3 Haifa	S	28 Refuse Collection	M	M&R
1951–52	Hamerahet	C	1 Tel Aviv	P	42 Wood	M	M&R
1951–54	Hanegev	N	3 Haifa	P	40 Misc. Products	M	M&R
1951–52	Haoleh	N	4 Nahariya	P	42 Wood	M	M&R
1951–53	Hasharon	C	5 Netanya	P	41 Bakery	HPHM	R
1951–54	Isah	C	2 Jerusalem	P	48 Food	M	M&R
1951–67	Keter	C	2 Jerusalem	P	50 Soap	M	M&R
1951–52	Kol Movil	C	1 Ramat Gan	S	27 Garage	M	M&R
1951–54	Kol Noa	C	1 Jaffa	P	44 Metal, Electrical	None	R

(continued)

Years[1]	Cooperative[2]	Location[3]		Activity[4]/ Product		Org.[5]	Ref[6]
1951–51	Kolon	C	1 Tel Aviv	S	23 Cinema	None	R
1951–54	Lachtsov	N	4 El Bahaya	P	46 Drilling	NR	R
1951–54	Lakol	N	4 Nazareth	P	49 Shoes	None	R
1951–67	Leket	C	1 Tel Aviv	S	28 Refuse Collection	M	M&R
1951–57	Maalit	C	1 Tel Aviv	P	44 Elevators	M	M&R
1951–52	Maanit	C	1 Tel Aviv	P	40 Misc. Production	M	M&R
1951–54	Machaheh Israel	U	9 Unknown	P	41 Bakery	M	M&R
1951–52	Malbenah	N	4 Kiryat Shmona	P	45 Building	M	M&R
1951–72	Malpach	C	1 Tel Aviv	P	44 Metal, Electrical	M	M&R
1951–53	Masadah	C	1 Tel Aviv	S	20 Architects	None	R
1951–52	Matkon	C	1 Tel Aviv	P	44 Metal, Electrical	M	M&R
1951–56	Meged	S	6 Beersheba	P	50 Chemicals	HPHM	R
1951–54	Meitav	C	1 Tel Aviv	P	47 Textiles	M	M&R
1951–53	Mifaal	C	1 Tel Aviv	P	40 Misc. Production	M	M&R
1951–53	Mivneh	N	4 Nahariya	P	45 Building	M	M&R
1951–53	Mizroniah	N	4 Pardes Hanna Karkur	P	42 Wood	HPHM	R
1951–93*	Movilei Basar Ramat Gan (Gush Dan)	C	1 Ramat Gan	S	21 Deliver Meat	M	R
1951–53	Naalaim Kfar Kana	N	4 Kfar Kanna	P	49 Shoes	NR	R
1951–63	Naalei Kadimah	C	1 Tel Aviv	P	49 Shoes	M	M&R
1951–64	Naalei Lavi (Naalei Hod 1962)	C	1 Tel Aviv	P	49 Leather	M	M&R
1951–55	Naalei Or	C	1 Tel Aviv	P	49 Leather	M	M&R
1951–53	Nagarim	N	4 Pardes Hanna	P	42 Wood	M	M&R
1951–	Netek (Electro–Netek 1964)	C	1 Tel Aviv	P	44 Metals	HPHM	R
1951–55	Niv	N	3 Haifa	P	40 Misc. Production	HPHM	R
1951–52‡	Oromit Chulon	C	1 Holon	P	46 Sand	M	M&R

1951–53	Osef	N	4 Safed	S	28 Refuse Collection	M	M&R
1951–54	Ovdei Arig	C	2 Jerusalem	P	47 Textiles	M	M&R
1951–54	Ovdei Ashim	N	4 Safed	P	40 Misc. Production	M	M&R
1951–53	Ovdei Hadfus	N	3 Haifa	P	45 Building Materials	M	M&R
1951–53	Ovdei Yam Suf	S	6 Gilat	P	41 Bakery	M	M&R
1951–68	Pesach Hovalah	U	9 Unknown	T	12 Motor Freight	M	M
1951–53	Progress	C	1 Tel Aviv	P	40 Misc. Production	M	M&R
1951–54	Ptitim	N	4 Kiryat Bialik	P	48 Food	M	M&R
1951–55	Rama	C	5 Center	P	41 Bakery	M	M&R
1951–60‡	Ramla	C	5 Ramla	P	41 Bakery	M	M&R
1951–53	Rishonei Tsur Shalom	N	4 Rishonei Tsur Shalom	S	20 Misc. Service	None	R
1951–53	Shachak	N	3 Haifa	U	99 Unknown	M	M
1951–54	Shakuf	C	1 Tel Aviv	P	45 Building	M	M&R
1951–52	Shderot Jaffa	C	1 Tel Aviv	S	22 Restaurant	M	M&R
1951–83	Shibolim	C	5 Netanya	P	41 Bakery	M	M&R
1951–57	Shichor	C	5 Netanya	P	43 Paper	HPHM	R
1951–53	Shravravut H.H.	C	1 Tel Aviv	S	20 Misc. Service	HPHM	R
1951–55	Solet Kastinah	S	6 South	P	41 Bakery	M	M&R
1951–57	Tafora	C	1 Petach Tikvah	P	47 Clothing	HPHM	R
1951–64	Talga	C	1 Tel Aviv	S	24 Laundry	HPHM	R
1951–53	Tfirah Tarshicha	N	4 Tarshicha	P	47 Textiles	NR	R
1951–80	Tichnun	C	1 Tel Aviv	S	20 Misc. Service	M	M&R
1951–54	Tslilim	N	3 Haifa	S	23 School, Theater	M	M&R
1951–59	Ugit	C	2 Jerusalem	P	48 Food	M	M&R
1951–52	Universal	N	3 Haifa	S	20 Misc. Service	M	M&R
1951–55	Usha	C	1 Kfar Hamakabi	T	12 Motor Freight	M	M&R
1951–56	Volma	S	6 Tel Arish	P	44 Metal, Electrical	HPHM	R

(continued)

Years[1]	Cooperative[2]	Location[3]	Activity[4]/Product	Org.[5]	Ref[6]
1951–53	Yamaei Elitsur	C 1 Tel Aviv	S 26 Port Service	HPHM	R
1951–52	Yerek Hasharon	C 1 Hadar Yosef	P 48 Food	M	M&R
1951–52	Yuval	C 1 Tel Aviv	P 40 Misc. Production	M	M&R
1951–55	Zikim	C 2 Jerusalem	P 40 Tools	M	M&R
1952–52	Altah	C 1 Tel Aviv	P 47 Textiles	M	M&R
1952–55	Avodot Even	C 5 Rosh Haayin	P 45 Stonework	HPHM	R
1952–63	Deganim	C 5 Rehovot	P 41 Bakery	M	M&R
1952–55	Emun	C 2 Jerusalem	P 41 Bakery	HPHM	R
1952–56	Galei Rinah	C 1 Tel Aviv	P 45 Swimming Pools	None	R
1952–53	Hachut	C 1 Jaffa	P 47 Textiles	M	M&R
1952–93*	Hadofek	C 5 Nes Tsiyonah	P 42 Wood	M	M&R
1952–57	Hashishlul	C 2 Jerusalem	P 44 Metal, Electrical	M	M&R
1952–54	Hashitah	C 5 Ramatayim	P 42 Wood	M	M&R
1952–53	Hayotser Melet	N 4 Hadera	P 45 Building	M	M&R
1952–70	Kemach	N 4 Hadera	P 41 Bakery	M	M&R
1952–68	Kiryat Haovalah	C 2 Jerusalem	S 21 Deliver Ice	M	M&R
1952–54	Korah	N 4 Karkur	P 45 Building	M	R
1952–55	Lumbik	N 4 Acre	P 45 Glass	HPHM	R
1952–57	Masoret	C 2 Jerusalem	P 40 Misc. Production	HPHM	R
1952–64	Matsat Or	N 3 Haifa	P 44 Metal, Electrical	M	M&R
1952–53	Mumchei Binyn	C 1 Tel Aviv	P 45 Building	None	R
1952–54	Nehagei Shefer	C 1 Tel Aviv	T 11 Passenger Transportation	M	M&R
1952–58‡	Noam	N 4 Acre	P 41 Bakery	M	M&R
1952–72	Or Zion	C 1 Tel Aviv	P 40 Candles	HPHM	R
1952–53	Sharon	U 9 Unknown	P 47 Textiles	M	M
1952–60	Shimshon	C 1 Holon	P 49 Leather	M	M&R

Year	Name		Location		Industry		
1952-52	Shivyon	N	4 Hadera	P	47 Textiles	M	R
1952-55	Stam	C	1 Bat Yam	P	40 Religious Writers	HPHM	R
1952-54	Taasiot Reafim	U	9 Unknown	P	45 Building	M	M
1952-93*	Tkumah	S	6 Migdal Ashkelon	P	41 Bakery	M	M&R
1952-54	Yesodot	C	5 Netanya	P	45 Building	M	M&R
1953-62	Chefer	C	5 Center	P	41 Bakery	M	M&R
1953-66	Chermon	C	1 Petach Tikvah	S	21 Deliver Ice	M	M&R
1953-71	Dalya	N	3 Haifa	P	48 Food	M	M&R
1953-55	Haboneh	C	1 Jaffa	P	42 Wood	M	M&R
1953-5	Hamedayek	N	3 Haifa	P	44 Metal, Electrical	M	M&R
1953-55	Hatsolel	N	3 Haifa	S	20 Misc. Service	M	M&R
1953-60	Kedem	N	3 Haifa	P	41 Bakery	M	M&R
1953-55	Kolnoa Bustan	N	4 Acre	S	23 Theater	M	M&R
1953-54	Lehavah	S	6 Beersheba	S	21 Deliver Oil	M	M&R
1953-60	Maariv	C	1 Tel Aviv	P	43 Newspapers	None	R
1953-57	Mikchol	C	1 Jaffa	P	50 Chemicals	M	M&R
1953-54	Misaada Chulon	C	1 Holon	S	22 Restaurant	M	M&R
1953-55	Misaada Kooperativit Petach Tikvah	C	1 Petach Tikvah	S	22 Restaurant	M	M&R
1953-93*	Movilei Basar Petach Tikvah	C	1 Petach Tikvah	S	21 Deliver Meat	M	M&R
1953-80	Shalhevet	C	2 Jerusalem	S	21 Deliver Oil	M	M&R
1953-56	Tnuva RG	C	1 Givatayim	S	21 Deliver Milk	None	R
1953-91	Toval	C	1 Tel Aviv	P	44 Metal, Electrical	M	M&R
1953-55	Tsrichah	U	9 Unknown	P	48 Food	M	M
1953-93*	Yam Suf	S	6 Eilat	P	41 Bakery	M	M&R
1953-57	Ykon	N	4 Karkur	P	41 Bakery	M	M&R
1953-55	Zionah	C	5 Nes Tsiyonah	P	48 Soda Water	M	R

(continued)

Years[1]	Cooperative[2]	Location[3]	Activity[4]/Product	Org.[5]	Ref[6]
1954–58	Amal	U 9 Unknown	P 42 Wood	M	M
1954–79	Beit Chinuch	N 3 Haifa	S 23 School	M	M&R
1954–55	Gama	C 5 Ramatayim	P 43 Paper	M	R
1954–58	Isuf	C 2 Jerusalem	S 28 Refuse Collection	M	M&R
1955–93*	Etsion	U 9 Unknown	P 42 Wood	M	M
1955–58	Hakoreh	N 4 Afula	P 45 Building	M	M
1955–73	Hanagar	C 5 Nes Tsiyonah	P 42 Wood	M	M
1955–64	Hateivah	C 1 Tel Aviv	P 42 Wood	M	M
1955–65	Lehavah	N 3 Haifa	S 20 Misc. Service	M	M
1956–81	Eked	N 4 Tiberias	P 43 Paper	M	M&R
1956–59	Kneset	C 5 Bet Shemesh	P 48 Meat Products	HPHM	R
1956–60	Maaria Beit Shemesh	N 4 Hadera	P 41 Bakery	HPHM	R
1956–66	Neft	C 5 Ramla	S 20 Misc. Service	M	M&R
1956–57	Peer	C 1 Azur	P 47 Textiles	HPHM	R
1957–58	Rihut Azur	C 5 Nes Tsiyonah	P 40 Misc. Production	NR	R
1957–63	Arizah	S 6 Kiryat Gat	P 42 Wood	M	M&R
1957–61	Arizat Lachish	C 1 Tel Aviv	P 40 Misc. Production	None	R
1957–65	Blum	C 1 Holon	P 45 Building	M	M
1957–58	Covaan	C 1 Tel Aviv	P 47 Hats	M	R
1957–59	El Manar	S 6 Eilat	S 23 School, Theater	NR	R
1957–60	Eshel	S 6 Ashdod	P 42 Wood	M	M&R
1957–58	Eshet	C 1 Tel Aviv	P 44 Metal, Electrical	M	M&R
1957–64	Ginun	C 2 Jerusalem	S 20 Misc. Service	M	M&R
1957–65	Hakufsah	N 3 Haifa	P 43 Paper Boxes	M	M&R
1957–60	Hameshaper	N 3 Haifa	S 28 Refuse Collection	M	M&R
1957–60	Hamoded		S 20 Misc. Service	None	R

1957–57	Haparvan	N	4 Nahariya	P	49 Furs	M	M&R
1957–60	Hasak	S	6 Beersheba	P	47 Jute Sacks	M	M&R
1957–70	Ichud	N	4 Karkur	P	41 Bakery	M	M&R
1957–59	Merets Haifa	N	3 Haifa	T	12 Motor Freight	M	M&R
1957–61	Mishmar Hashivah	C	5 Center	P	41 Bakery	M	M&R
1957–58	Ofnat Hanegev	S	6 Beersheba	P	47 Textiles	M	M&R
1957–59	Orot Israel	N	4 Kfar Chasidim	P	49 Leather	M	M&R
1957–60	Ovdei Ashrim	N	4 Safed	P	40 Misc. Production	M	M&R
1957–58	Pinkasan	C	1 Tel Aviv	S	20 Misc. Service	None	R
1957–59	Reses	S	6 Ofakim	S	20 Misc. Service	M	M&R
1957–59	Rihut Veginun	C	1 Ramat Gan	P	42 Wood	M	M&R
1957–58	Rozen	C	1 Tel Aviv	P	47 Textiles	M	M
1957–	Shafir	C	5 Shafir	T	10 Misc. Transportation	HPHM	R
1957–65	Shinei Charsinah	C	1 Tel Aviv	P	40 Misc. Production	M	R
1957–60	Tsur	C	5 Bet Shemesh	P	46 Cement	HPHM	R
1958–65	Achvah Ochana	N	4 Hadera	P	49 Shoes	M	M&R
1958–59	Arnakei Israel	C	1 Tel Aviv	P	49 Leather	M	M&R
1958–93*	Chets	C	5 Ramla	T	12 Motor Freight	M	M&R
1958–93*	Dfus Klali	C	1 Tel Aviv	P	43 Printing	M	M&R
1958–60	Dimonah	S	6 Dimona	T	12 Motor Freight	M	M&R
1958–62	Hacheshbonai	C	5 Raanana	S	20 Accounting	None	R
1958–62	Hamasa	C	5 Center	T	12 Motor Freight	M	M&R
1958–	Harei Jerusalem	C	2 Jerusalem	T	12 Motor Freight	M	M&R
1958–60	Koopergum	N	4 Nahariya	P	40 Misc. Production	M	M&R
1958–76	Nachal Alexander Said	C	5 Netanya	S	20 Misc. Service	M	M&R
1958–60	Papirus	C	2 Jerusalem	P	43 Paper	M	M&R
1958–59	Pragmon Karton	N	3 Haifa	P	43 Cartons	M	M&R
1958–60	Safra	C	1 Tel Aviv	P	43 Paper	M	M&R

(continued)

Years[1]	Cooperative[2]	Location[3]	Activity[4]/Product	Org.[5]	Ref[6]
1958–69	Shefer	C 1 Tel Aviv	P 44 Metal, Electrical	M	M&R
1958–62	Teatron Masechot	C 2 Jerusalem	S 23 Theater	None	R
1959–62	Al Atzlach	N 4 Nazareth	P 45 Building	NR	R
1959–74	Chitah	C 5 Tira	P 41 Bakery	M	M&R
1959–63	Eitan	C 1 Tel Aviv	P 49 Shoes	M	M&R
1959–60	Gazit	S 6 Kiryat Gat	P 45 Building	M	M&R
1959–	Ichud Raananah	C 5 Raanana	P 41 Bakery	HPHM	R
1959–64	Isralt	C 1 Tel Aviv	P 47 Textiles	M	M&R
1959–91	Krichiah	C 1 Tel Aviv	P 43 Paper	M	M&R
1959–83	Maafiah Bet Shean	N 4 Bet Shean	P 41 Bakery	M	M&R
1959–61	Mechonei Iran	C 1 Tel Aviv	S 20 Mechanics	None	R
1959–59	Shaar Hadarom	S 6 Eilat	T 12 Motor Freight	M	M&R
1960–63	Ashdod Yam	S 6 South	S 26 Port Service	NR	M&R
1960–62	El Ragif	N 4 Kfar Kanna	P 40 Misc. Production	M	R
1960–68	Embit	N 4 Pardes Hanna	P 40 Misc. Production	M	M&R
1960–93*	Hamhapech	C 2 Jerusalem	T 12 Motor Freight	M	M&R
1960–81	Hedek	N 4 Kiryat Shmona	P 42 Wood	M	M&R
1960–63	Michun	C 1 Tel Aviv	S 20 Misc. Service	M	M&R
1960–63	Ovdei Hayotsek	C 1 Tel Aviv	P 45 Building	M	M&R
1960–62	Taybet El Mutla	C 5 Tayiba	S 20 Misc. Service	None	R
1961–67	Chen Krichiah	C 1 Tel Aviv	P 43 Paper	M	M&R
1961–67	Chinuch Veomanut	C 1 Tel Aviv	S 23 School, Theater	M	M&R
1961–64	Emet Adrichalim	C 1 Tel Aviv	S 20 Misc. Service	M	M&R
1961–93*	Eshet	N 3 Haifa	P 44 Metal, Electrical	M	M&R
1961–62	Ezrah	S 6 Netivot	S 20 Misc. Service	HPHM	R
1961–66	Gad	S 6 Ashkelon	P 48 Soda Water	HPHM	R

1961–66	Hamegalven	C	5 Nes Tsiyonah	P	45 Building	M	M&R
1961–63	Israel Express	C	1 Tel Aviv	T	11 Passenger Transportation	M	M&R
1961–64	Kachol Lavan	C	1 Tel Aviv	P	50 Chemicals	HPHM	R
1961–62	Kadar Keramicah	N	3 Haifa	P	40 Ceramics	M	M&R
1961–87	Lechem Hasharon	C	5 Center	P	41 Bakery	M	M&R
1961–91	Mifalei Ets	S	6 Beersheba	P	42 Wood	M	M&R
1961–63	Ofot	U	9 Unknown	S	21 Deliver Meat	NR	R
1961–93*	Retsef	C	1 Petach Tikvah	P	45 Building	M	M&R
1961–64	Revivim	C	1 Ramat Gan	S	23 School	M	M&R
1961–62	Tsevet	C	1 Tel Aviv	S	20 Misc. Service	M	M&R
1961–63	Tsiber Chimikali	C	1 Bat Yam	P	40 Misc. Production	M	M&R
1962–65	Achvah	N	4 Osfia	T	11 Passenger Transportation	NR	R
1962–63	Argadim	S	6 Kiryat Gat	U	99 Unknown	M	M
1962–84	Bochen	C	1 Tel Aviv	S	23 School	M	M&R
1962–69	Chosen	C	1 Givatayim	P	45 Flooring	NR	R
1962–63	El Atkan	N	4 Nazareth	P	45 Building	NR	R
1962–	El Barcha	U	9 Bir El Saka	P	48 Produce Oil	NR	R
1962–75	Eshkolot	C	1 Jaffa	S	23 School	M	M&R
1962–63	Katsavei Chulon	C	1 Holon	S	21 Butchers	NR	R
1962–83	Lod Maafiah	C	5 Lod	P	41 Bakery	M	M&R
1962–65	Moniyot Natsrat	N	4 Nazareth	T	11 Passenger Transportation	None	R
1962–66	Mosalat El Nasra	N	4 Nazareth	T	12 Motor Freight	NR	R
1962–67	Movilei Basar	C	2 Jerusalem	S	21 Deliver Meat	NR	R
1962–63	Noi Omanut	N	3 Haifa	S	23 School, Theater	M	M&R
1962–93*	Raanan	C	5 Raanana	S	21 Deliver Meat	M	M&R
1962–63	Ramon	S	6 Mitzpe Ramon	P	40 Misc. Production	M	M&R
1962–63	Tavita	N	4 Nazareth	P	47 Textiles	M	M&R
1962–64	Tavor	N	4 Nazareth	P	48 Food	M	M&R

(continued)

Years[1]	Cooperative[2]	Location[3]	Activity[4]/Product	Org.[5]	Ref[6]
1962-66	Zachal On	C 2 Jerusalem	P 45 Building	M	M&R
1963-66	Aliyah	C 1 Petach Tikvah	P 44 Metals	M	M&R
1963-68	Bedek Bait	S 6 Ashkelon	P 45 Building	M	M&R
1963-66	Beton	N 4 Dalyat El Karmel	P 46 Cement	NR	R
1963-	El Almein	C 5 Tayiba	T 12 Motor Freight	NR	R
1963-	El Jermak	N 4 Beg Jan	T 12 Motor Freight	NR	R
1963-64	Gatron	S 6 Kiryat Gat	P 40 Misc. Production	M	R
1963-65	Givoon	S 6 Kiryat Gat	U 99 Unknown	M	M
1963-66	Haboneh	S 6 Eilat	P 44 Metals	M	R
1963-65	Haganan	N 3 Haifa	S 20 Gardening	M	M&R
1963-67	Hagizrah	N 4 Acre	P 47 Textiles	M	M&R
1963-64	Hanaknik	C 2 Jerusalem	P 48 Food	M	M&R
1963-64	Harakefet	C 1 Azur	P 47 Textiles	M	M&R
1963-66	Kadimah	S 6 Ashdod	P 46 Cement	M	R
1963-63	Kerech	C 2 Jerusalem	P 43 Paper	M	M&R
1963-67	Matachot Arad	S 6 Arad	P 44 Metals	M	M&R
1963-66	Melet	C 5 Center	P 45 Building	M	M&R
1963-66	Merchav	N 4 Tiberias	T 11 Passenger Transportation	M	M&R
1963-66	Nagariat Hasharon	C 5 Tel Mond	P 42 Wood	M	M&R
1963-66	Natsrat Elit	N 4 Nazareth	P 43 Paper	M	M&R
1963-	Platot Chamadiyah	N 4 Chamadiyah	P 42 Wood	M	M&R
1963-65	Salameh	N 4 Shfar Am	P 40 Plastics	NR	R
1963-64	Shafir	C 1 Petach Tikvah	S 24 Laundry	M	M&R
1963-66	Sherutei Carmiel	N 4 Carmiel	S 20 Misc. Service	M	M&R
1963-65	Tafoorah	S 6 Ashkelon	P 44 Electrical	M	M&R
1963-67	Tsomet Achim	S 6 Kiryat Malachi	S 27 Garage	M	M&R

1963–64	Uman	N	3 Haifa	P	44 Metal, Electrical	M	M&R
1963–66	Volta Chashmal	C	2 Jerusalem	P	44 Electrical	M	M&R
1963–65	Yafia	N	4 Yafia	P	42 Wood	NR	R
1963–66	Yeda Vehaskalah	S	6 Beersheba	S	23 School	M	M&R
1963–73	Yeul	C	1 Tel Aviv	S	20 Office Equipment	M	M&R
1964–66	Albani	N	4 Fassutia	P	45 Building	NR	R
1964–93*	Aravah	S	6 Beersheba	P	43 Paper	M	M&R
1964–	Eked	C	2 Jerusalem	P	43 Printing	HPHM	R
1964–	El Burak	N	4 Sachnin	T	11 Passenger Transportation	M	R
1964–65	El Chagara	N	4 Dalyat El Karmel	P	46 Drilling	NR	R
1964–	El Kataf	N	4 Arara	T	11 Passenger Transportation	M	R
1964–	El Muntada	N	4 Shfar Am	T	11 Passenger Transportation	M	R
1964–	El Najar	N	4 Nazareth	P	42 Wood	NR	R
1964–	El Saair	N	4 Maaliya	T	11 Passenger Transportation	M	R
1964–	El Tzadaka	N	4 Um El Fachem	T	11 Passenger Transportation	M	R
1964–68	Erez	C	5 Nes Tsiyonah	P	42 Wood	M	M&R
1964–93*	Ezra	C	1 Tel Aviv	S	20 Cleaning	M	M&R
1964–84	Hakachot	N	3 Haifa	P	41 Bakery	M	M&R
1964–	Hametaken	S	6 Mazkeret Batyah	P	42 Wood	HPHM	R
1964–66	Haofan	N	4 Carmiel	P	44 Metal, Electrical	M	M&R
1964–65	Hatofer	S	6 Ashkelon	P	47 Textiles	M	M&R
1964–66	Hatraktor	C	1 Ramat Gan	P	45 Building	None	R
1964–66	Hayotser	S	6 Beersheba	P	44 Metal, Electrical	M	M&R
1964–68	Isralia	C	1 Tel Aviv	P	40 Misc. Production	M	M&R
1964–66	Jalil	C	4 Jedida	P	45 Building	NR	R
1964–65	K.Sh.T.	N	4 Acre	S	20 Misc. Service	M	M&R
1964–66	Karavan	C	2 Abu Gosh Kiryat Anavim	S	22 Restaurant	M	M&R
1964–93*	Mafteach (Metach)	N	3 Haifa	S	21 Deliver Milk	M	M&R

(continued)

Years[1]	Cooperative[2]	Location[3]	Activity[4]/Product	Org.[5]	Ref[6]
1964–80	Masaot Carmiel	N 4 Carmiel	T 12 Motor Freight	M	M&R
1964–66	Musachim	C 1 Tel Aviv	S 27 Garage	M	M&R
1964–66	Naalei Jerusalem	C 2 Jerusalem	P 49 Shoes	M	R
1964–	Nachal Taasiyah	C 2 Jerusalem	P 40 Misc. Production	HPHM	R
1964–66	Nativ	N 4 Bet Shean	T 12 Motor Freight	M	M&R
1964–65	Nikayon	C 1 Tel Aviv	S 20 Cleaning	M	M&R
1964–68	Rihut Kishut	S 6 Kadima	P 42 Wood	M	M&R
1964–66	Shaish	N 4 Pkiin	P 46 Drilling	M	M&R
1964–93*	Sova	C 2 Jerusalem	S 22 Restaurant	M	M&R
1965–	Atid Tavita	N 4 Nazareth	P 47 Textiles	NR	R
1965–69	Barak	C 1 Tel Aviv	S 20 Misc. Service	M	M&R
1965–	Beit Sefer Le Koop	C 1 Tel Aviv	S 23 Education	None	R
1965–67	Bedek	S 6 Ashdod	S 20 Misc. Service	M	M&R
1965–65	El Majad	C 5 Baka El Garbia	P 46 Cement	M	M&R
1965–	El Rokav	N 4 Nazareth	T 11 Passenger Transportation	NR	R
1965–93*	Gag	C 1 Tel Aviv	P 41 Bakery	M	M&R
1965–67	Gimlaim	C 1 Tel Aviv	S 20 Misc. Service	M	M&R
1965–	Hagalgal	N 4 Kfar Rama	S 27 Garage	HPHM	R
1965–66	Hatikrah	C 1 Tel Aviv	S 20 Misc. Service	M	M&R
1965–66	Kidmah	C 5 Jaljuliya	T 12 Motor Freight	M	M&R
1965–66	Madregot Hadarom	C 5 Nes Tsiyonah	P 45 Building Materials	HPHM	R
1965–66	Manjarat Yarka	U 9 Kfar Yarka	P 42 Wood	NR	R
1965–68	Masaot Majar	U 9 Kfar Majar	T 12 Motor Freight	None	R
1965–68	Movil El Ovaria	S 6 Beersheba	T 12 Motor Freight	M	M&R
1965–93*	Naki	C 1 Tel Aviv	S 20 Cleaning	M	M&R
1965–93*	Or Nikayon	C 1 Tel Aviv	S 20 Cleaning	M	M&R

Years	Name		Location		Industry		
1965–66	Peer	C	1 Tel Aviv	S	20 Misc. Service	M	M&R
1965–69	Peer Hamigdal	N	4 Migdal Haemek	S	20 Misc. Service	M	M&R
1965–66	Peer Plast	s	6 Ashdod	P	45 Building	M	M&R
1965–80	Rahitim	N	4 Ramat Yishai	P	42 Wood	M	M&R
1965–74	Sapir	C	1 Tel Aviv	S	20 Misc. Service	M	M&R
1965–67	Technikot	C	1 Holon	P	50 Chemicals	M	M&R
1965–68	Tikvah Plast	C	1 Petach Tikvah	P	45 Building	M	M&R
1966–67	Al Keren	N	4 Chorfesh	S	20 Misc. Service	M	M&R
1966–77	Beit Hasefer Afikei Daat	s	6 Beersheba	S	23 School	M	M&R
1966–	Daat	s	6 Dimona	S	23 Education	None	R
1966–73	Hamavrik	N	3 Haifa	S	20 Misc. Service	M	M&R
1966–	Lamoshav	C	5 Netanya	S	27 Garage	Ag	R
1966–	Masa	C	1 Tel Aviv	T	12 Motor Freight	Bachan	R
1966–69	Shalom	C	1 Tel Aviv	S	20 Misc. Service	M	M&R
1966–69	Shekef	C	1 Tel Aviv	S	20 Misc. Service	M	M&R
1966–73	Yotzkei Hagalil	N	4 Hatzor	P	44 Metal, Electrical	M	M&R
1967–79	Anak Saba	N	4 Shfar Am	T	10 Mixed Transportation	None	R
1967–78	Bet Tsafafa	C	5 Bet Tsafafa	T	10 Mixed Transportation	None	R
1967–79	Hamarkivim	N	4 Hadera	P	45 Building	M	M&R
1967–69	Korah	C	1 Tel Aviv	P	42 Wood	M	M&R
1967–84	Krichiat Chulon	C	1 Holon	P	43 Printing	M	M&R
1967–	Sherutei Karmiel	N	3 Haifa	S	22 Gas and Food	M	R
1968–70	Achsanyat Noar	C	5 Bar Gyora	S	22 Youth Hostel	Bachan	R
1968–72	Eitan	C	2 Jerusalem	S	23 Arts, Crafts	HPHM	R
1968–70	El Nakel	N	4 Shfar Am	T	10 Mixed Transportation	ACWF	R
1968–82	El Salam	N	4 Kalansua	T	10 Mixed Transportation	ACWF	R
1968–70	El Taazar	C	2 Jerusalem	P	47 Textiles	ACWF	R
1968–	Hashamaim	C	1 Tel Aviv	S	20 Misc. Service	Ag	R

(continued)

Years[1]	Cooperative[2]	Location[3]	Activity[4]/Product	Org.[5]	Ref[6]
1968–91	Keshev Haifa	N 3 Haifa	S 20 Guard Service	M	M&R
1968–80	M.G.T. (Hamevatsea 1968)	N 4 Sharonah	S 20 Farm Machines	M	M&R
1968–69	Matbeat El Salam	C 2 Jerusalem	P 43 Printing	None	R
1968–74	Moniyot Gordon	C 5 Rehovot	T 10 Misc. Transportation	None	R
1968–75	Zvulun	U 9 Ameka	S 20 Farm Machines	M	M&R
1969–93*	Adin	C 5 Hod Hasharon	P 48 Chocolate	M	M&R
1969–	El Maymon	S 6 Gulis	T 12 Motor Freight	ACWF	R
1969–70	El Tasal	S 6 Yarka Gat	T 12 Motor Freight	ACWF	R
1969–70	El Zeytuna	N 4 Kfar Yasif	S 20 Olive Oil	ACWF	R
1969–	Hakotel (Hachomah)	C 2 Jerusalem	S 22 Restaurant	HPHM	R
1969–73	Moriyah Jerusalem	C 2 Jerusalem	P 40 Misc. Production	M	R
1969–77	Talpiyot	N 3 Haifa	P 47 Textiles	M	M&R
1970–72	Achsanyah	U 9 Unknown	S 22 Restaurant	M	M&R
1970–79	Afekah	N 3 Haifa	P 43 Printing	M	M&R
1970–76	Al Na	N 4 Natsrat Ilit	P 44 Metal, Electrical	M	M&R
1970–83	Al Nachlan	C 5 Nachaf	T 12 Motor Freight	ACWF	R
1970–71	Hamidrashah Chulon	C 1 Holon	S 23 Education	M	M&R
1970–72	Hashomrim	C 1 Tel Aviv	S 20 Guard Service	M	M&R
1970–73	Hovalat Hanosea	C 5 Kfar Nachaf	T 10 Misc. Transportation	ACWF	R
1970–73	Kemach Shibolet	N 4 Hadera	P 41 Bakery	M	R
1970–78	Kfar Gant	N 4 Ramat Hagolan	P 40 Misc. Production	HPHM	R
1970–74	Masaot Kvedim	C 5 Rehovot	T 12 Motor Freight	None	R
1970–71	Matachot Arad	S 6 Arad	P 45 Metals	M	R
1970–74	Modiim	C 5 Modiim	P 44 Electrical	M	M&R
1970–76	Movilei Jerusalem	C 2 Jerusalem	T 12 Motor Freight	None	R
1970–71	Mutsarei Fiberglass	S 6 Yerucham	P 45 Polyester	M	M&R

1970–70	Orish	C	1 Or Yehuda	28 Refuse Collection	S	M	M&R
1970–73	Savlan	N	4 Chorfesh	47 Textiles	P	ACWF	R
1970–81	Sh.A.N.	C	2 Jerusalem	20 Cleaning	S	M	M&R
1970–73	Shomrei Arad	S	6 Arad	20 Guard Service	S	M	M&R
1970–72	Shomriyah	C	1 Tel Aviv	20 Guard Service	S	M	M&R
1970–72	Shtichei Hamizrach	N	4 Carmiel	47 Textiles	P	ACWF	R
1970–72	Silgiah Chermon	N	4 Ramat Shalom	22 Restaurant	S	None	M&R
1970–75	Super Kol	N	4 Carmiel	20 Misc. Service	S	HPHM	R
1971–75	Charat	N	4 Bet Shean	44 Metals	P	HPHM	M&R
1971–78	Dadon	N	4 Bet Shean	44 Metals	P	M	M&R
1971–83	Hanechasim	C	1 Tel Aviv	20 Misc. Service	S	HPHM	R
1971–93*	Kalid	C	1 Tel Aviv	20 Repair Office Equipment	S	M	M&R
1971–75	Mamor	N	4 Hatzor	44 Metals	P	HPHM	M&R
1971–71	Mifaal Hadpasah	C	1 Tel Aviv	43 Printing	P	M	R
1971–	Moniyot Atsmon	C	1 Petach Tikvah	11 Taxi	T	NR	R
1971–79	Moniyot Hashalom	C	1 Jaffa	11 Taxi	T	None	R
1971–80	Parag	C	1 Tel Aviv	21 Deliver Meat	S	M	M&R
1971–76	Sarig	C	1 Tel Aviv	47 Textiles	P	HPHM	M&R
1972–75‡	Agur Ashdod	S	6 Ashdod	26 Ship Repair	S	M	M&R
1972–82	Al Shua	N	4 Dir Chana	20 Electrical Power	S	ACWF	R
1972–73	Beit Hasefer Chulon	C	1 Tel Aviv	23 School	S	M	M
1972–73	Chermesh	N	4 Maalot	44 Metals	P	M	M&R
1972–74	Dror Arad	S	6 Arad	27 Garage	S	M	M&R
1972–80	El Anra	N	4 Ilabun	20 Electrical Power	S	ACWF	R
1972–73	Emun Tel Aviv	C	1 Tel Aviv	20 Guard Service	S	M	M&R
1972–77	Filmit	C	2 Jerusalem	45 Fiberglass	P	M	M&R
1972–82	Hagalil Hatachton	N	4 Kfar Chitim	12 Motor Freight	T	M	M&R
1972–75	Hamalbish	N	4 Kiryat Ata	47 Textiles	P	HPHM	R

(continued)

Years[1]	Cooperative[2]	Location[3]	Activity[4]/Product	Org.[5]	Ref[6]
1972–76	Hashalom	S 6 Beersheba	T 12 Motor Freight	HPHM	R
1972–	Moniyot Rechovot	C 5 Rehovot	T 10 Misc. Transportation	None	R
1972–79	Movilei Galil Tachton	N 4 Tiberias	T 12 Motor Freight	M	M&R
1972–75	Optol	N 4 Tiberias	P 45 Building	M	M&R
1972–74	Sh.A.M.	N 4 Hadera	S 28 Refuse Collection	M	M&R
1972–91	Shefa	C 1 Tel Aviv	S 22 Restaurant	M	M
1972–90	Sova	C 1 Tel Aviv	S 22 Restaurant	M	R
1972–74	Srigei Zohar	S 6 Kadima	P 47 Textiles	M	M&R
1973–73	Almagor	C 1 Holon	S 23 Education	M	R
1973–77	Bedek Ashdod	S 6 Ashdod	S 26 Port Service	M	M&R
1973–76	Binyan Vetichnun	C 5 Kfar Saba	P 45 Building	M	M&R
1973–78	El Dayo	C 5 Raanana	S 20 Electric Power	ACWF	R
1973–76	El Manar	U 9 Kabul	S 20 Electric Power	ACWF	R
1973–80	El Shark	C 2 Jerusalem	P 43 Printing	ACWF	R
1973–74	El Turiyah	N 4 Dir El Asad	S 20 Electric Power	ACWF	R
1973–76	Haboneh	C 5 Herzlia	P 45 Building	M	M&R
1973–75	Keshet	N 4 Carmiel	P 43 Printing	M	M&R
1973–86	M.K.M.	N 3 Haifa	P 41 Bakery	M	M&R
1973–80	Midrashiah	C 2 Jerusalem	P 40 Misc. Production	HPHM	R
1973–76	Nidbach Binyan	C 1 Bat Yam	P 45 Building	M	M&R
1973–81	Noor Alfalk	U 9 Kfar Zalpa	S 20 Electric Power	ACWF	R
1973–93*	Sh.N.Ch.	N 3 Haifa	S 20 Cleaning	M	M&R
1973–80	Tochen	C 2 Jerusalem	S 20 Architects	M	M&R
1973–79	Tsemed	C 1 Tel Aviv	S 20 Misc. Service	M	M&R
1973–76	Universal Karton	N 3 Haifa	P 49 Leather, Paper	M	M&R
1974	E.Sh.D.	C 1 Tel Aviv	S 20 Dental	NR	R

1974–85	El Galil	U	9 Ein Elasach	T	10 Mixed Transportation	ACWF	R
1974–84	El Taufic	N	4 Um El Ganum	S	20 Electric Power	ACWF	R
1974–93*	Hazerem	C	5 Kiryat Ono	S	20 Plumbing	M	M&R
1974–77	Kabha	U	9 Bartaa	T	11 Taxi	NR	R
1974–79	Man Dagan	C	5 Netanya	P	41 Bakery	M	M&R
1974–88	Movilei Yerucham	S	6 Yerucham	T	12 Motor Freight	NR	R
1974–74	Shenhav	C	1 Tel Aviv	S	20 Dentist	M	M&R
1974–80	Tfachot	C	5 Netanya	P	45 Building	M	M&R
1975–82	Amaarya	U	9 El Amria Kfar Iblan	S	20 Electric Power	ACWF	R
1975–81	Barik	U	9 Unknown	S	20 Cleaning	M	R
1975–77	El Arishad	N	4 Sachnin	S	23 Teach Driving	ACWF	R
1975–80	El Bark	C	5 Musmus	S	20 Electric Power	ACWF	R
1975–76	El Lahiv	U	9 Parush Romana	S	20 Electric Power	ACWF	R
1975–82	El Marman	U	9 Al Chagnat	S	20 Electric Power	ACWF	R
1975–85	El Tayav	U	9 Baina	S	20 Electric Power	ACWF	R
1975–	Gansh	C	5 Raanana	S	20 Cleaning	M	M&R
1975–	Hakastel	C	1 Tel Aviv	T	11 Taxi	NR	R
1975–86	Hamedayek	N	4 Bet Shean	P	44 Metals	M	M&R
1975–77	Rishonei Yamit	S	6 Yamit	P	40 Misc. Production	NR	R
1975–88	Tachburah Delek	C	1 Tel Aviv	T	12 Motor Freight	Ag	M
1975–93*	Tnufah	N	4 Hadera	P	45 Building	M	M
1975–78	Yesod	C	2 Jerusalem	P	45 Building	M	M&R
1976–85	Al Manir	U	9 Ilut	S	20 Electric Power	ACWF	R
1976–80	Arab Snir	C	5 Lod	S	20 Electric Power	ACWF	R
1976–88	Bartaa	U	9 Bartaa	S	20 Electric Power	ACWF	R
1976–84	El Baha	U	9 Kfar Nin	S	20 Electric Power	ACWF	R
1976–91	El Shahab	U	9 Al Makman	S	20 Electric Power	ACWF	R
1976–82	El Vahag	U	9 Kfar Majar	S	20 Electric Power	ACWF	R

(continued)

Years[1]	Cooperative[2]	Location[3]		Activity[4]/Product		Org.[5]	Ref[6]
1976–79	Hamohalim	C	1 Tel Aviv	S	20 Religious Services	HPHM	R
1976–79	Kdoshey Kahir	N	4 Bet Shean	P	40 Misc. Production	NR	R
1976–79	Kelet	N	4 Natsrat Ilit	T	10 Misc. Transportation	NR	R
1976–93*	Kolnoa Migdal	C	2 Jerusalem	S	23 Theater	M	M
1976–83	M.K.Sh.	N	4 Kiryat Shmona	P	44 Metals	M	M&R
1976–93*	Shor Conservatorion	C	1 Holon	S	23 Music Education	M	M&R
1976–79	Tichnun Vebitsua	S	6 Beersheba	P	44 Electrical	Bachan	R
1976–83	Tova	U	9 Kfar Tova	S	20 Electric Power	ACWF	R
1977–84	Al Aramsha	U	9 Al Aramsha	S	20 Electric Power	ACWF	R
1977–83	Al Biyada	U	9 Al Biyada	S	20 Electric Power	ACWF	R
1977–84	Al Najada	U	9 Al Nadgat	S	20 Electric Power	ACWF	R
1977–88	Al Vahda	U	9 Maavia	S	20 Electric Power	ACWF	R
1977–84	Alfada	U	9 Kakub	S	20 Electric Power	ACWF	R
1977–80	Ayelet Hovalah	C	1 Tel Aviv	T	12 Motor Freight	M	M&R
1977–83	El Afek	U	9 Alzubiya	S	20 Electrical Power	ACWF	R
1977–89	Hamatslichim	N	4 Usfiya	P	45 Building	M	M&R
1977–80	Mazal	U	9 Unknown	P	48 Food	M	M
1977–80	Mazon Lishaat Cherum Babait	C	1 Petach Tikvah	S	21 Deliver Food	M	R
1977–79	Ovdei Hamaafiah	N	4 Kiryat Shmona	P	41 Bakery	M	M&R
1977–83	Ramana	C	5 Ramana	S	20 Electric Power	ACWF	R
1977–87	Salem	C	1 Kfar Salem	S	20 Electric Power	ACWF	R
1978–81	Al Kaharba	N	4 Ein Elsahala	S	20 Electric Power	ACWF	R
1978–87	Al Sana	U	9 El Chaman	S	20 Electric Power	ACWF	R
1978–88	El Shams	U	9 Musharfa	S	20 Electric Power	ACWF	R
1978–79	Kfir	C	2 Jerusalem	P	43 Printing	Bachan	R
1979–86	Al Arian	U	9 Al Arian	S	20 Electric Power	ACWF	R

1979–84	Al Namrud	U	9 Nahaf	T	11 Taxi	ACWF	R
1979–87	Al Tagdil	S	6 El Uzil	S	20 Electric Power	ACWF	R
1979–84	Al Zangaria	U	9 Alzangaria	S	20 Electric Power	ACWF	R
1979–81	El Biar	U	9 Al Biar	S	20 Electric Power	ACWF	R
1979–89	El Charara	U	9 Salama	S	20 Electric Power	ACWF	R
1979–	Irgun Lenehigah	N	3 Haifa	S	23 Teach Driving	NR	R
1979–82	Noach	N	3 Haifa	S	20 Cleaning	M	M&R
1980–84	Al Dachi	U	9 Aldachai	S	20 Electric Power	ACWF	R
1980–92	Al Zrazir	U	9 Al Zrazir	S	20 Electric Power	ACWF	R
1980–84	El Kava	C	5 Mashroa	S	20 Electric Power	ACWF	R
1980–82	El Naora	U	9 Naora	S	20 Electric Power	ACWF	R
1980–82	Mifaley Tkoa	C	2 Jerusalem	P	40 Misc. Production	Bachan	R
1980–82	Tamra Alzabia	N	4 Tamra	S	20 Electric Power	ACWF	R
1981–83	Hala	N	4 Nazareth	S	20 Electric Power	ACWF	R
1981–84	Hamashchetah	C	1 Tel Aviv	S	21 Meat Production Service	NR	R
1981–93*	Omanut Lanoar	C	5 Tel Kabir	S	23 Education	M	M&R
1981–83	Pituach Vekidum	N	4 Galilee	S	20 Tourism	NR	R
1982–83	Gananei Hatikvah	C	1 Tel Aviv	S	20 Gardening	M	M&R
1983–89	Achdut Moniyot	C	1 Petach Tikvah	T	11 Taxi	NR	R
1983–	Merkaz Hasport	C	1 Tel Aviv	S	23 Sports	NR	R
1984–88	Ak Burda	N	4 Nazareth	S	20 Electric Power	ACWF	R
1984–87	Al Iman	U	9 Alsahala	S	20 Electric Power	ACWF	R
1984–87	Al Nagam	N	4 Nazareth	S	20 Electric Power	ACWF	R
1984–93*	Hadofek	C	5 Nes Tsiyonah	P	42 Wood	M	R
1984–	Nativ	N	4 Kiryat Shmona	S	23 Teach Diving	M	R
1985–90	Al Masafar	C	2 Isawiya Jerusalem	T	10 Misc. Transportation	ACWF	R
1985–93*	Beit Hasefer Lemusikah	S	6 Kiryat Gat	S	23 Music Education	M	M&R

(continued)

Years[1]	Cooperative[2]	Location[3]	Activity[4]/ Product	Org.[5]	Ref[6]
1985–91	K.Y.L.	C 1 Tel Aviv	S 20 Misc. Service	M	M&R
1985–88	Maas	C 1 Tel Aviv	S 20 Gardening	M	M&R
1985–	Pituach Netef	U 9 Yehudah	S 20 Misc. Service	Bachan	R
1985–89	Rahitei Tefer	N 4 Tefen	P 42 Wood	M	R
1985–91	Tefen	N 4 North	P 42 Wood	M	M
1986–	Ovdei Haemek	N 4 Afula	S 20 Misc. Service	M	R
1987–	Baalei Miflasot	C 1 Tel Aviv	S 20 Misc. Service	NR	R
1987–	Daf	N 3 Haifa	P 43 Printing	M	R
1987–	Kashrut	C 1 Tel Aviv	S 20 Misc. Service	NR	R
1988–	Habanaim	S 6 Beersheba	P 45 Building	ACWF	R
1988–91	Lamed	C 5 Netanya	T 10 Misc. Transportation	NR	R
1989–	Chasin Esh	S 6 Beersheba	P 40 Misc. Production, Tiles	NR	R
1989–	Harey Yehudah	C 5 Bet Shemesh	T 10 Mixed Transportation	NR	R
1989–	Kvutsat Migvan	U 9 Unknown	S 20 Misc. Service	NR	R
1989–	Moniyot Bakar	N 4 Kfar Makar	T 11 Taxi	NR	R
1990–	Echad	C 1 Ramat Gan	T 10 Misc. Transportation	NR	R
1990–91	El Atid	N 4 Um El Fachem	P 43 Printing	ACWF	M&R
1990–	Galgulya	S 6 Galgulia	T 11 Taxi	NR	R
1990–91	Migvan	S 6 Ashdod	S 20 Misc. Service	M	R
1991–	Arad	S 6 Arad	S 20 Cleaning	NR	R
1991–	Bniyah Veshiputsim	C 2 Jerusalem	P 45 Building	M	R
1991–91	Bonei Hagalil	N 4 Natsrat Ilit	P 45 Building	M	M&R
1991–91	Chashmal Hagalil	N 4 North	P 44 Metal, Electrical	M	M
1991–	Electro Netech	C 1 Bnei Brak	P 44 Electrical	HPHM	R
1991–92	Leshiputsim	S 6 Dimona	P 45 Building	M	R
1991–91	Migvan	N 4 North	P 45 Building	M	M

Year	Name		Location		Category		
1991–	Moniyot Hashalom	C	1 Petach Tikvah	T	11 Taxi	NR	R
1991–	Musach Lakol	N	4 Natsrat Ilit	S	27 Garage	NR	R
1991–91	Musachei Hagalil	N	4 North	S	20 Misc. Service	M	M
1991–91	Omegah	C	1 Bat Yam	P	44 Building Electrical	M	M&R
1991–	Reut	C	5 Rehovot	S	23 Music Education	M	R
1992–	A.A. Shiluv	U	9 Unknown	S	20 Manpower Service	NR	R
1992–	Bonei Haemek	N	4 Migdal Haemek	P	45 Building	M	M&R
1992–	Hamekim	N	3 Haifa	P	45 Production Service	M	R
1992–	Magnet	C	5 Kfar Saba	P	45 Production Service	M	M&R
	Artsi	C	1 Tel Aviv	P	40 Misc. Production	M	M
	Atsmaut	C	1 Tel Aviv	P	47 Textiles	M	M
	Beit Dagon	U	9 Unknown	S	20 Locksmith	M	M
	Chamah	C	5 Tel Mond	P	41 Bakery	M	M
	Chatsats	N	4 Nahariya	P	45 Building	M	M
	Coop Machbesah	U	9 Unknown	S	24 Laundry	M	M
	Eylom	C	5 Ramla	S	23 Cinema	M	M
	Gofer	C	1 Tel Aviv	P	45 Building Tar	M	M
	Hadayag	N	4 Acre	S	26 Fishing	M	M
	Haemek	U	9 Unknown	T	12 Motor Freight	M	M
	Hakrayot	U	9 Unknown	P	41 Bakery	M	M
	Hapachach	C	2 Jerusalem	S	20 Tinsmith, Plumbing	M	M
	Hasatat	N	3 Haifa	P	45 Building	M	M
	Inbar	U	9 Unknown	P	41 Bakery	M	M
	Lachmenu	N	4 Hadera	P	41 Bakery	M	M
	Misaadah	S	6 Beersheba	S	22 Restaurant	M	M
	Nua	U	9 Unknown	T	12 Motor Freight	M	M
	Raanan	N	3 Haifa	P	48 Sweets, Soda	M	M
	Tfirah	C	2 Jerusalem	P	47 Textiles	M	M

(continued)

Years[1]	Cooperative[2]	Location[3]	Activity[4]/ Product	Org.[5]	Ref[6]
	Yachad	N 3 Haifa	S 20 Misc. Service	M	M
	Yahalomey Tsfat	N 4 Safed	P 51 Diamonds	M	M

[1]Years in operation are through 1993, according to the records of either the Registrar of Cooperatives or the Merkaz Hakooperatsia, as noted in the final column. Where both sources were available and offered different dates of formation or dissolution, the earlier date is reported here, except where other sources provided additional information in favor of the later date.

Cases noted with an asterisk (*) were confirmed as still in operation by the Merkaz Hakooperatsia in 1993. All other worker cooperatives known to be affiliated with the Merkaz Hakooperatsia are presumed to be defunct, although in the case of 128 of these organizations no date of dissolution was recorded. Of cases with no known affiliation with the Merkaz Hakooperatsia, a missing date of dissolution may mean that the organization was still in operation in 1993, particularly if the organization had been founded recently. For the year 1988 the Registrar reported a total of 108 worker cooperatives then functioning in Israel, of which only 75 were counted as affiliates of the Merkaz. This means that as many as 33 worker cooperatives outside the Merkaz Hakooperatsia may have been in operation in 1988. An additional 12 worker cooperatives not affiliated with the Merkaz Hakooperatsia were registered by the Registrar in the years 1989–1992.

Cases whose years of operation are noted with the ‡ symbol were involved in mergers with one or more other worker cooperatives, which may still be in operation. Annual reports of the Registrar report statistics on mergers, and the records of both the Registrar of Cooperative Societies and the Merkaz Hakooperatsia contain occasional entries noting that such mergers had occurred. But neither of these sources made systematic efforts to note all cases of dissolutions that took the form of mergers. Some of the information on mergers reported here was supplied by informants in organizations that are still in operation (such as Egged, Ichud-Igud, and Shelev). We are best informed about mergers that gave rise to Egged and Dan, because many of them have been described in documentary sources such as Daniel (1976). Even for these organizations, however, such sources provided only fragmentary information, and the organizations they described could not always be matched unambiguously with worker cooperatives registered with the Registrar or listed by the Merkaz Hakooperatsia. In the case of many mergers, dissolutions were recorded by these sources several years after the date reported by other sources as the year in which the merger had actually occurred.

Mergers for which records could be identified may be summarized as follows. Among bus cooperatives, the most complex set of mergers went into the formation of Egged. Egged was created in 1933 as a merger of Hamahir (1931–1933), Hege (1931–1933), Kadimah (1932–1937), and Hitachdut Hanehagim (1930–1936). At about that same time, a similar set of mergers in the Sharon region created Hasharon Hameuchad (United Sharon, 1930–1942), which in 1942 became part of Egged. Among bus cooperatives in the North, Chever (1934–1954) absorbed Mishmar Mifrats (1934–1937), Hakesher (1935–1941), and other cooperatives, and eventually became part of Shachar (1948–1954). Other cooperatives in the North that are believed to have been included in this series of mergers are Har Hacarmel (1934–1936) and Sherut Haemek (1940–1941). In the South, Hadarom absorbed a cooperative named Yehuda to become Drom Yehuda (1930–1954), which joined Egged at the same time as Shachar. The absorption of Hamekasher (1931–1961) left Dan as the only bus cooperative in Israel remaining outside of Egged.

Dan was created through a parallel but simpler set of mergers. Hamaavir (1928–1945) absorbed Galei-Aviv, which never registered, in 1928. Regev (1930–1932) merged with an unregistered cooperative, Ichud, to create Ichud-Regev (1932–1945). Ichud-Regev merged with Hamaavir in 1945 to form Dan.

The cooperative of drivers in motor freight known as Shelev was created as a merger of a number of other trucking cooperatives, including Hanehag (1939–1945), Sherut Rakevet (1945–1947), Hanamal (1928–1945), Hachof (1938–1945), and Hatikvah (1935–1949).

Among production cooperatives, mergers have been recorded most frequently among cooperative bakeries. In 1958, Noam (1952–1958) merged into Hagalil Hamaaravi (1949–1987), and Halechem (1950–1958) merged into Hamaapil (1949–1977). At about this same time, Pat Petach Tikvah (1936–1960) merged with Kama (1949–1957), and Ramla (1951–1960) merged into Ofim (1949–1960). In the case of the next three mergers of bakeries, the name of the other organization involved in the merger was not recorded. They are Shibolet (1946–1960), Lechem (1935–1964), and Hagalil Hamaaravi (1949–1987). In 1990, the Achdut Bakery (1935–1990) of Haifa was said to have merged into the Achdut Bakery of Tel Aviv, but its assets were sold by the Chevrat Ovdim and turned over to the Merkaz Hakooperatsia.

Other manufacturing activities in which mergers were recorded include woodworking, in which Haboneh (1949–1956) merged into Yotsrim (1947–1971), and construction, where Chulon (1950–1952) of Tel Aviv merged with

(continued)

Oromit (1950–1952) of Holon. In addition, the soap-making cooperative Sabon Hagalil (1949–1957) merged into Ketsef (1949–1969). In the services, two cooperatives that provide port services were dissolved through mergers, Nasholeh Netanya (1949–1951) and Agur Ashdod (1972–1975). In 1976 the butchers' cooperative Igud merged into Ichud, which took the new name of Ichud-Igud (1936–1993).

A total of twenty worker cooperatives are recorded as having dissolved by transforming themselves into companies. Eleven of these are production cooperatives. The incidence of this form of dissolution is particularly high among cooperatives that produce soap (Keter, 1951–1967, and Hadar-Hasharon, 1939–1948) or other chemical products (Kachol Lavan, 1961–1964); cooperatives that produce mineral water (Yalin, 1936–1941) or soda water (Ashkelon, 1961–1966); and diamond cooperatives (Almog and Shoham, both 1947–1952). Forms of production with one recorded instance of transformation into companies are construction (Mizrad Kablani, 1932–1944), textiles (Ramtex, 1949–1959), paper (Hakufsah, 1957–1965), and metals (Dadon, 1971–1978). Among worker cooperatives in transportation, four transformations into companies were recorded, one for a taxi cooperative (Taxi Carmel, 1943–1953) and three for cooperatives listed as providing mixed or unspecified forms of transportation (Aviv, 1936–1937, Hamahim, 1943–1950, and Merkaz Hadarom, 1944–1956). In the services, there were also four, one in a cooperative that provided port services (Gal Yam, 1946–1950) and three from miscellaneous other services, including hairdressing(Masperah, 1937–1968), sports (Hayozem (1946–1961), and accounting (Hacheshbonai, 1958–1962).

2The names of cooperatives are transliterated phonetically, with the additional inclusion of a silent h at the end of words whose spelling concludes with the equivalent letter in Hebrew. Ch should be pronounced as it is in German. In cases in which name changes have been recorded, the alternate name by which the cooperative has been known is given in parentheses.

3Well-known locations (Jerusalem, Nazareth, Acre) are spelled as they most customarily are in English. This led to the choice of Hadera over Chadera, and of Holon over Cholon or Chulon, even though these spellings would seem less preferable if judged by their consequences for pronunciation. Less familiar place names are transliterated more phonetically, as described above.

These locations are categorized in the first place by region, with N signifying the North, C the Center, and S the South. North is defined as beginning at Hadera. Three locations (Bethlehem, Nablus, and Bet Sachur) could clearly be identified as being in the occupied West Bank, signified here with the letter W.

For the analyses reported in chapter 2, the locations of worker cooperatives in Israel were further sorted into six categories: (1) Tel Aviv; (2) Jerusalem: (3) Haifa; (4) other locations in the North; (5) other locations in the Center; and (6) any locations in the South. Tel Aviv is defined here as metropolitan Tel Aviv, or Gush Dan. It includes adjacent cities like Jaffa, Petach Tikvah, and Ramat Gan, but leaves out Rishon Lezion, Rehovot, Herzlia, and Raanana. For the purposes of these analyses, locations that could not be identified, or that were clearly in the occupied West Bank, were assigned the number 9.

4The principal activities identified for each cooperative are as noted in the records of the Registrar of Cooperative Societies or the Merkaz Hakooperatsia. The sectors and industries into which worker cooperatives are sorted are those customarily recognized and differentiated in these sources. There have been some changes over the years in which the meanings and boundaries of these categories have been interpreted. In early publications of the Merkaz Hakooperatsia, cooperatives that did earth moving were viewed as providing a service, but in Daniel (1989) they were listed as production cooperatives that produce sand and cement. The categorizations used here follow the more recent practice. Another convention respected here is the tradition of treating butchers' cooperatives as service cooperatives that deliver meat, rather than as production cooperatives that process food.

Within the transportation sector, the practice of the Merkaz Hakooperatsia is followed in grouping taxi cooperatives with bus cooperatives, but differentiating those two forms of passenger transportation from trucking cooperatives that haul motor freight. While later records tend to observe this distinction, the Registrar in the time of the Mandate often failed to note whether a cooperative provided passenger transportation or hauled freight or did a little of both. For worker cooperatives that are still functioning, or that dissolved through mergers that were recorded, a more precise categorization was possible. Cooperatives that continue to be listed as providing unspecified forms of transportation consist disproportionately of those that perished quickly, as discussed in chapter 2. The Registrar's records are also somewhat inconsistent in their treatment of taxi cooperatives, usually categorizing them in transportation, but on some occasions listing them as services.

For analyses reported in chapters 1 through 3, cooperatives were sorted to the extent that this was possible into the following industrial categories: (10) mixed or unspecified forms of transportation; (11) passenger transportation; (12) motor freight; (20) miscellaneous services; (21) delivery of meat, ice, or oil; (22) restaurants and hotels; (23) schools, theaters, and other cultural activities; (24) laundries; (26) port services, sailing, fishing; (27) garages; (28) refuse collection; (40) miscellaneous production; (41) bakeries; (42) woodworking; (43) printing and paper, including cardboard cartons; (44) metal and electrical products; (45) building materials; (46) sand, cement, and drilling; (47) textiles; *(continued)*

(48) food processing; (49) leather and shoes; (50) chemical products, including soap and pharmaceuticals; and (51) diamonds. The total number of cooperatives within some of these categories may differ slightly from figures shown in tables for chapters 1 through 3, due to a small number of final corrections that were entered shortly before this work went to press.

5Israeli worker cooperatives have never been required to affiliate with a federation or an audit union, but in practice most of them have. In the time of the Mandate, these organizational affiliations were not recorded by the Registrar. Cooperatives are listed here as being affiliates of the Merkaz Hakooperatsia if: (1) the Registrar's records identify them as affiliates of the Merkaz; or (2) the cooperative's name appears on the roster of its members that the Merkaz has maintained since the late 1940s; or (3) the name appears on one of the complete listings of its member cooperatives that the Merkaz published in 1933, 1949, 1960, and 1976. This means that affiliates of the Merkaz Hakooperatsia that ceased operations in the 1920s to 1940s could not be identified unless their names appeared on the initial list of the population that appeared in 1933. For the years 1924–1948, organizational affiliations could be identified for a few additional worker cooperatives because they were apparent from their names (this was true of several cooperatives linked with the religious movement Hapoel Hamizrachi), or because they were rare enough for the Registrar to find them noteworthy (i.e., a single cooperative sponsored by the General Zionists, another by Hapoel Hatzair, a third by Hebrew University in Jerusalem).

Using these procedures, we identified 827 worker cooperatives as affiliates of the Merkaz Hakooperatsia, signified by an "M" in this column. A total of 65 worker cooperatives have been affiliated with or sponsored by the religious Hapoel Hamizrachi movement, as signified by the symbol HPHM in the table. Another 61 worker cooperatives were affiliated with the audit union of Arab Cooperatives of Workers and Farmers (ACWF). Smaller numbers were affiliated with movements that the Registrar describes as promoting "middle class cooperative agriculture" (Registrar of Cooperative Societies, 1989a). These include the Bachan movement, a Likud affiliate (shown in the table as Bachan), which sponsored six worker cooperatives, and Haikhud Hakhaklai (Agricultural Union, abbreviated as "Ag"), which sponsored four. Three organizations sponsored just a single worker cooperative. Two were political parties: the General Zionists (Gen Z in the table), and Hapoel Hatzair (abbreviated as HPHT). The third was Hebrew University (shown as Heb U), which may not actually have been sponsoring a worker cooperative in the years 1940–1942; it may only have been permitting this group of chemical workers to make use of premises that the university owned. In the case of 88 additional worker cooperatives, the Registrar noted that they had no organizational affiliation, signified here by the word "None." For the remaining 427 cooperatives we have no record of their organizational affiliation, noted in the table as "NR."

6Reference is the source of the information provided about each cooperative. "R" is the Registrar of Cooperative Societies, "M" is the Merkaz Hakooperatsia, either its roster of members, or one of its past publications (Cooperative Center, 1933, 1949, 1960, 1976). "M&R" signifies that records about this cooperative could be identified in both of these sets of sources.

GLOSSARY

A list of Hebrew words that are used in the text appears below. Words that have frequently been transliterated into English are spelled here as they are most customarily known in English, except where common spellings encourage serious mispronunciations. Thus *Hevrat Ovdim* is rejected in favor of *Chevrat Ovdim*, and *Kupat Holim* in favor of *Kupat Cholim*, because the relevant letter in Hebrew is pronounced more like the German *ch* than like the American *h*. Otherwise, conventional spellings are favored, as in *kibbutz, kvutzah, Hapoel Hatzair,* and *Poalei Zion*. Less familiar words are transliterated phonetically, with the customary addition of a silent *h* at the end of words that have the equivalent ending in Hebrew, like *aliyah* and *hanhalah*.

Achdut Haavodah (United Labor Party): organized in 1919, by remnants of Poalei Zion and other political movements that had failed to attract many followers in the Yishuv. After having played the leading role in creating the Histadrut and the Chevrat Ovdim, the Achdut Haavodah merged in 1930 with Hapoel Hatzair to form Israel's Labor party (Mapai).

Aliyah (literally, going up or ascending): it has come to mean immigration to the land of Israel. The most influential waves of immigration in Israel's pre-state history are known as the First, Second, Third, and Fourth Aliyot. The First Aliyah of 1882–1903 took the first steps to promote Jewish agriculture, in the process establishing permanent new Jewish settlements at such locations as Rishon Lezion, Petach Tikvah, Rehovot, Hadera, and Rosh Pinah. The Second Aliyah (1904–14) brought the people who would create the kibbutz, the Histadrut, the Chevrat Ovdim, and Labor Party. The Third Aliyah (1919–23) created the Gedud Haavodah, which stimulated the formation of the kibbutz federations and the Chevrat Ovdim. The Fourth Aliyah (1924–31) stimulated the development of Jewish Palestine's cities and of its petite bourgeoisie.

Bank Hapoalim (Worker's Bank): the Bank of the Histadrut, established in 1920 as a conduit for aid from the WZO.

chalutz (pioneer): term applied primarily to the labor Zionist immigrants of the Second and Third Aliyot, or other settlers before and after who became known for their ascetic dedication to agricultural work and for the emphasis they placed on creativity, participation, and improvisation (Eisenstadt, 1967, pp. 17–18).

Chevrat Ovdim (Workers' Society): the holding company established by the Histadrut in 1923 to express its titular control over a large number of subsidiary and affiliated economic enterprises, including the Bank Hapoalim, the Solel Boneh, and the kibbutzim and moshavim.

Diaspora (literally, dispersion): of Greek origin, the term used since ancient times to refer to Jews who live outside the land of Israel.

Gedud Haavodah (Labor Battalion): a national organization of communes with a common treasury created by immigrants of the Third Aliyah in memory of Yosef Trumpeldor in 1920. Although the Gedud itself had ceased to exist by 1927, it had a profound influence on the kibbutz movement and on the creation of the Chevrat Ovdim.

Hamashbir Hamerkazi: initially the purchasing and supply branch of the Chevrat Ovdim, it is now one of Israel's major retailers.

hanhalah (management): the official governing body of an Israeli worker cooperative, empowered to make decisions between meetings of the full membership, or in a large cooperative, of the elected council (vaad).

Hapoel Hatzair (the Young Worker): the Yishuv's nonsocialist workers' party, organized in 1905, which merged with Achdut Haavodah in 1930 to form the Labor Party.

Histadrut: now known in English as Israel's General Federation of Trade Unions, the Histadrut was organized in 1920 as the General Organization of Jewish Workers in the Land of Israel.

Ichud Hakvutzot Vehakibbutzim (Union of Kvutzot and Kibbutzim): Israel's more loosely organized federation of collective agricultural settlements. It originated in 1928 as the Union of Kvutzot, but was expanded in 1951 to include some kibbutzim defecting from Kibbutz Meuchad. The Ichud, or Union, merged in 1980 with Kibbutz Meuchad to form Takam.

Kapai (or more fully, the Kupat Poalei Eretz Israel): known in English as the Palestine Workers' Fund, a conduit for aid from the international Poalei Zion movement to Palestine from 1909. Kapai funded the creation of a number of worker cooperatives until it was taken over by the Histadrut in 1923.

Keren Kayemet (National Fund, established in 1901) and Keren Hayesod (Foundation Fund, established in 1920): funds used by the WZO to buy and own land in Palestine and later Israel.

kibbutz, plural kibbutzim: the more collective of the two major varieties of cooperative agricultural settlement in Israel, in contrast to the more individualistic moshav. When first popularized in the 1920s, this term referred only to larger and more economically diversified collective settlements, which were contrasted with the smaller and more intimate kvutzot. Over time, however, use of the term has broadened to include both of these collective varieties of agricultural cooperative.

Kibbutz Artzi (the National Kibbutz Movement): the more leftist and ideological of the kibbutz federations, established in 1927. Kibbutz Artzi is affiliated in Israel with the political party Mapam, and in the Diaspora with the youth movement Hashomer Hatzair (the Young Watchman).

Kibbutz Meuchad (the United Kibbutz federation): established in 1927. Historically more centralized than the Ichud Hakvutzot Vehakibbutzim, Kibbutz Meuchad merged with the Ichud to form Takam in 1980.

Knesset: the Israeli parliament, established in 1949.

Koor: the manufacturing subsidiary of the Chevrat Ovdim.

Kupat Cholim (literally, Sick Fund): the arm of the Histadrut that provides medical care for all of its members.

Kupat Hakooperatsia (Cooperative Fund): the bank of Israel's worker cooperative movement, which was absorbed into the Bank Hapoalim in the 1960s.

kvutzah, plural kvutzot (group or commune): the smaller, more intimate, and more selective forerunner of the larger and more diversified kibbutz. The remaining kvutzot are currently affiliated with the United Kibbutz Movement, or Takam, and are now viewed more as a variety of kibbutz or as a stage in the development of the kibbutz (e.g., Talmon, 1972; Cohen, 1983), than as a distinct economic form.

Likud (literally, bloc or amalgamation): a unified electoral list of right-wing parties first put together by Ariel Sharon in 1973 that came to power in Israel in 1977. Its most important component was the nationalistic Cherut Party of Menachem Begin and Yitzhak Shamir, who had led the more aggressive wing of the Jewish underground in Palestine in the era of World War II and were the heirs to Zeev Jabotinsky's Revisionist wing of Zionism.

Mandate, Mandatory: refers to the period between 1923 and 1948, when Great Britain governed Palestine under a Mandate from the League of Nations.

mazkirut (secretariat): term used to describe the executive leadership in an Israeli workers' cooperative, which governs the cooperative between meetings of its larger management (hanhalah).

Merkaz Hakooperatsia (Cooperative Center): the organization authorized by the Third Histadrut Congress in 1927 to represent the worker cooperatives affiliated with the Histadrut.

moshav, plural moshavim: the more individualistic of the two major varieties of cooperative agricultural settlement in Israel, in contrast to the more collective kibbutz. In a moshav each household earns its own income from the work of its own members, rather than meeting most needs of the members out of a common purse, as was advocated by the Gedud Haavodah and as practiced by the kibbutz.

moshav ovdim, moshavim ovdim (laborers' moshav): the more common variety of moshav, in which each household lives by the income of its own private fields (or outside employment), while the activity of the cooperative is limited to marketing, distribution, and procurement of equipment, seed, electrification, water, and so on.

moshav shitufi, moshavim shitufim: the more collective variety of moshav. A moshav shitufi organizes its members' work collectively, as on a kibbutz; but unlike the kibbutz, the moshav makes cash payments to its members as compensation for their work, out of which they maintain their own households.

Nir (or Nir Shitufi): officially the legal arm of Israel's Union of Agricultural Workers, it is the legal entity that since 1926 has held title to the collective property on Israel's kibbutzim and moshavim, with the exception of the land, which belongs to the Jewish National Fund.

Palestine: the territory governed by Great Britain under its Mandate from the League of Nations over the years 1923–48. It includes contemporary Israel and the territories currently known as the occupied West Bank and Gaza.

Poalei Zion (Workers of Zion): the most important international political movement among socialist Zionists in the early decades of this century. Its branch in the Yishuv was a forerunner of the Achdut Haavodah in the years before World War I. The growing strength of Poalei Zion in the WZO in the 1920s and 1930s was crucial in enabling the labor leaders in the Yishuv to attain preeminence in the WZO by 1935.

Solel Boneh: the construction company owned by the Histadrut through its economic subsidiary the Chevrat Ovdim. It was created in 1924 as a reorganization of the Histadrut's Bureau of Public Works and Construction Laborers.

Takam: known in English as the United Kibbutz Movement, Takam was created in 1980 through the merger of two kibbutz federations, Kibbutz Meuchad and Ichud Hakvutzot Vehakibbutzim.

vaad (council): the parliamentary or legislative body in Israel's largest worker cooperatives, Egged and Dan. It is from this body that the management (hanhalah) is elected in the second stage of the process by which these cooperatives' leaders are chosen.

World Zionist Organization (WZO): has been the chief organizer of Zionist fundraising efforts in the Diaspora since it was organized by Theodor Herzl in 1897.

Yishuv (literally, settlement): as a proper noun, it refers to the Jewish population in Palestine in the modern pre-state period, especially during the Mandate.

BIBLIOGRAPHY

Aharoni, Yair
1991   *The Israeli Economy: Dreams and Realities.* London and New York: Routledge.

Aharoni, Yair, and Lachman, R.
1982   "Can the Managers' Mind Be Nationalized?" *Organization Studies* 3:33–46.

Alchian, Armen, and Demsetz, Harold
1972   "Production, Information Costs, and Economic Organization," *American Economic Review* 62:777–95.

Aldrich, Howard, Staber, Udo, Zimmer, Catherine, and Beggs, John
1990   "Minimalism and Organizational Mortality: Patterns of Disbanding Among U.S. Trade Associations, 1900–1983," in Jitendra V. Singh, ed., *Organizational Evolution: New Directions.* Newbury Park, CA: Sage, pp. 21–52.

Anderson, John C.
1978   "A Comparative Analysis of Local Union Democracy," *Industrial Relations* 17:278–95.

Applebaum, Levia
1990   "Adjustment to Change Under External Constraints: The Emergence of Diverse Cooperative Frameworks in the Moshav," *Journal of Rural Cooperation* 18:119–31.

Avrahami, Eli
1989   "Yad Tabenkin—Facing a Severe Socio-Ideological Crisis," *Kibbutz Studies,* No. 28 (January), pp. 31–32.

Bar-El, Raphael, ed.
1987   *Rural Industrialization in Israel.* Boulder and London: Westview Press.

Barnett, William P., and Amburgey, Terry L.
1990   "Do Larger Organizations Generate Stronger Competition?" in Jitendra V. Singh, ed., *Organizational Evolution: New Directions.* Newbury Park, CA: Sage, pp. 78–102.

Batstone, Eric
1983   "Organization and Orientation: A Life Cycle Model of French Co-operatives," *Economic and Industrial Democracy* 4:139–61.

Baum, Joel C., and House, Robert J.
1990   "On the Maturation and Aging of Organizational Populations," in Jitendra V. Singh, ed., *Organizational Evolution: New Directions.* Newbury Park, CA: Sage, pp. 129–42.

Ben-Ner, Avner
1984   "On the Stability of the Cooperative Type of Organization," *Journal of Comparative Economics* 8:247–60.

Ben-Ner, Avner
1987   "Preferences in a Communal Economic System," *Economica* 54:207–21.

Ben-Ner, Avner
1988a   "Comparative Empirical Observations on Worker-Owned and Capitalist Firms," *International Journal of Industrial Organization* 6:7–31.

Ben-Ner, Avner
1988b   "The Life Cycle of Worker-Owned Firms in Market Economies: A Theoretical Analysis," *Journal of Economic Behavior and Organization* 10:287–313.

Ben-Ner, Avner, and Estrin, Saul
1991   "What Happens When Unions Run Firms? Unions as Employee Representatives and as Employers," *Journal of Comparative Economics* 15:65–87.

Ben-Ner, Avner, and Neuberger, Egon
1982   "Israel: the Kibbutz," in Frank H. Stephen, ed., *The Performance of Labour-Managed Firms.* London: MacMillan, pp. 186–213.

Ben-Porath, Yoram
1983   "The Conservative Turnabout That Never Was,' *The Jerusalem Quarterly*, No. 29 (Fall), pp. 3–10.

Ben-Rafael, Eliezer
1976   "The Stratification System of the Kibbutz," in Yehuda H. Landau
        et al., *Rural Communities: Inter-Cooperation and Development.*
        New York: Praeger.

Ben-Rafael, Eliezer
1988   *Status, Power and Conflict in the Kibbutz.* Aldershot: Avebury,
        Gower Publishing.

Ben-Rafael, Eliezer
1991   "The Transformation of the Kibbutz: The Test for Socialism,"
        Kibbutz Trends, Nos. 3/4 (Fall/Winter), pp. 73–79.

Berechman, Joseph
1987   "Cost Structure and Production Technology in Transit: An
        Application to the Israeli Bus Transit Sector," *Regional Science
        and Urban Economics* 17:159–34.

Berman, Katrina V., and Berman, Matthew D.
1989   "An Empirical Test of the Theory of the Labor-Managed Firm,"
        Journal of Comparative Economics 13:281–300.

Black, Jeff
1989a   "The CRM Histadrut Platform: Letting Workers Run Hevrat
        Ha'ovdim," *Jerusalem Post,* October 18, p. 9.

Black, Jeff
1989b   "Mapam: Crisis Presents Opportunity for Change," *Jerusalem
        Post,* October 19, p. 9.

Blasi, Joseph
1992   "What Role Should Employee Ownership Play in Russian and
        Eastern European Privatization? Some Lessons From the U.S.
        Experience," *Journal of Employee Ownership Law and Finance* 4,
        No. 4 (Fall), pp. 85–111.

Blasi, Joseph, and Gasaway, James
1993   "Corporate Governance and Employee Ownership: Comparing
        the United States and Russia," paper presented at the Annual
        Meeting of the Society for the Advancement of Socio-Economics,
        New York, New York, March 28.

Blasi, Joseph Raphael, and Kruse, Douglas Lynn
1991   *The New Owners: The Mass Emergence of Employee Ownership
        and What It Means to American Business.* New York: Harper
        Business.

Blumberg, Paul
1968   *Industrial Democracy: The Sociology of Participation.* New York: Schocken Books.

Bonacich, Edna
1972   "A Theory of Ethnic Antagonism: The Split Labor Market," *American Sociological Review* 37:547–59.

Bonacich, Edna
1979   "The Past, Present, and Future of Split Labor Market Theory," *Research in Race and Ethnic Relations* 1:17–64.

Bonin, John P.
1984   "Membership and Employment in an Egalitarian Cooperative," *Economica* 51:295–305.

Brilliant, Joshua
1989   "Kibbutz Group Accepts Debt Rescheduling," *Jerusalem Post,* December 4, p. 1.

Brinkley, Joel
1989   "Debts Make Israelis Rethink an Ideal: The Kibbutz," *New York Times,* March 5, p. 6.

Brod, D.
1990   "The Kibbutzim and Their Debt," *Jewish Spectator* 55(2):32–43.

Brooks, Geraldine
1989   "Saving the Farm: The Israeli Kibbutz Takes a Capitalist Tack to Keep Socialist Ideals," *Wall Street Journal,* September 21.

Bruederl, Josef, and Schuessler, Rudolf
1990   "Organizational Mortality: The Liabilities of Newness and Adolescence," *Administrative Science Quarterly* 35:530–47.

Buber, Martin
1958   *Paths in Utopia.* Translated by R. F. C. Mull. Boston: Beacon Press. First published in English by Routledge & Kegan Paul in 1949.

Buchanan, Robert T.
1978   "The Economic Conditions for Industrial Democracy," *Economic Analysis and Workers' Management* 12:291–301.

Budros, Art
1992   "The Making of an Industry: Organizational Births in New York's Life Insurance Industry, 1842–1904," *Social Forces* 70:1013–33.

Carroll, Glenn R. and Hannan, Michael T.
1989   "Density Dependence in the Evolution of Populations of News-paper Organizations," *American Sociological Review* 54:524–41.

Carroll, Glenn R., and Huo, Yangchung Paul
1986   "Organizational Task and Institutional Environments in Ecological Perspective: Findings from the Local Newspaper Industry," *American Journal of Sociology* 91:838–73.

Central Bureau of Statistics
1977   *Statistical Abstract of Israel 1977*. Jerusalem: Central Bureau of Statistics.

Central Bureau of Statistics
1986   *Statistical Abstract of Israel 1986*. Jerusalem: Central Bureau of Statistics.

Central Bureau of Statistics
1990   *Statistical Abstract of Israel 1990*. Jerusalem: Central Bureau of Statistics.

Central Bureau of Statistics
1992   *Statistical Abstract of Israel 1992*. Jerusalem: Central Bureau of Statistics

Chafets, Ze'ev
1986   *Heroes and Hustlers, Hard Hats and Holy Men: Inside the New Israel*. New York: Morrow.

Cohen, Erik
1983   "The Structural Transformation of the Kibbutz," in Ernest Krause, ed., *The Sociology of the Kibbutz*. New Brunswick, NJ: Transaction Books, pp. 75–114.

Collins, Randall
1975   *Conflict Sociology: Toward an Explanatory Science*. New York: Academic Press.

Conte, Michael A., and Jones, Derek
1985   "In Search of a Theory of Formation of U.S. Producer Cooperatives: Tests of Alternative Hypotheses," in Barbara D. Dennis, ed., *Proceedings of the Thirty-Seventh Annual Meeting*. Madison, Wisconsin: Industrial Relations Research Association, pp. 377–84.

Cooperative Center
1933   *Production and Service Cooperatives Among Workers in Israel in 1933* (Hebrew). Tel Aviv: Cooperative Center.

Cooperative Center
1949   *The Voice of Cooperation* (Hebrew). Tel Aviv: Cooperative Center.

Cooperative Center
1960   *Production and Service Cooperation in Israel in the Years 1948–1958* (Hebrew). Tel Aviv: Cooperative Center.

Cornforth, Chris, Thomas, Alan, Lewis, Jenny, and Spear, Roger
1988   *Developing Successful Worker Co-operatives.* London: Sage Publications.

Craig, Ben, and Pencavel, John
1992   "The Behavior of Worker Cooperatives: The Plywood Companies of the Pacific Northwest," *American Economic Review* 82:1083–105.

Curtis, Michael
1973   "Utopia and the Kibbutz," in Michael Curtis and Mordecai S.Chertoff, eds., *Israel: Social Structure and Change.* New Brunswick, NJ: Transaction Books, pp. 101–13.

Dahl, Robert
1961   *Who Governs?* New Haven: Yale University Press.

Dahl, Robert, and Tufte, Edward R.
1973   *Size and Democracy.* Stanford: Stanford University Press.

Danet, Brenda
1989   *Pulling Strings: Biculturalism in Israeli Bureaucracy.* Albany: State University of New York Press.

Daniel, Abraham
1968   *Producer Cooperation and the Problem of Hired Labor* (Hebrew). Tel Aviv: School of Cooperation Press.

Daniel, Abraham
1972   "Arab Cooperation in Israel," in *Year Book of Agricultural Co-operation.* Oxford: Basil Blackwell, pp. 81–94.

Daniel, Abraham
1975   "The Kibbutz Movement and Hired Labor," *Journal of Rural Cooperation* 3:31–41.

Daniel, Abraham
1976   *Labor Enterprises in Israel.* 2 vols. Jerusalem: Jerusalem Academic Press.

Daniel, Abraham
1986   *A New Model for Producer Co-operatives in Israel.* Saskatoon, Saskatchewan: Centre for the Study of Co-operatives, University of Saskatchewan.

Daniel, Abraham
1989   *Cooperatives in Israel: Success and Failure* (Hebrew). Tel Aviv: Sifriat Poalim.

Darr, Asaf
1993a   "Democratic Ideas in Research on Producer Cooperatives in Palestine (1920–1930)," presented at an International Conference on New Trends in Organizations: Their Impact on Participation, De-Alienation, and Performance, Givat Haviva, Israel, April 14–17.

Darr, Asaf
1993b   "Conflict and Conflict Resolution in Cooperatives: The Case of an Israeli Taxi Station," unpublished working paper. Ithaca, New York: School of Industrial and Labor Relations, Cornell University.

Dean, Macabee
1969   "The Wheels of Tel Aviv Turn *Slowly . . . ,*" *Jerusalem Post,* February 7.

Delacroix, Jacques, and Carroll, Glenn R.
1983   "Organizational Foundings: an Ecological Study of the Newspaper Industries of Argentina and Ireland," *Administrative Science Quarterly* 28:274–91.

Dickenstein, Abraham
1989   "First Steps in the Formation of Cooperatives," in Lieber Losh, ed., *Forty Years of "Shituf:" 1948–1988* (Hebrew). Tel Aviv: Achdut Press, pp. 147–49. First published in 1958.

DiMaggio, Paul J., and Powell, Walter W.
1983   "The Iron Cage Revisited: Institutional Isomorphism and Collective Rationality in Organizational Fields," *American Sociological Review* 48:147–60.

DiMaggio, Paul J., and Powell, Walter W.
1991   "Introduction," in Walter W. Powell and Paul J. DiMaggio, eds., *The New Institutionalism in Organizational Analysis.* Chicago: University of Chicago Press, pp. 1–38.

Domar, Evsai D.
1966   "The Soviet Collective Farm as a Producer Cooperative,"
        American Economic Review 56:734–57.

Don, Yehuda
1968   "Development of Production Cooperatives in Israel: A Statistical
        Analysis," in Yehuda Don and Yair Levi, eds., Public and Co-op-
        erative Economy in Israel. Liege: International Centre of
        Research and Information on Public and Co-operative Economy
        (CIRIEC).

Dow, Greg
1986   "Control Rights, Competitive Markets, and the Labor-
        Management Debate," Journal of Comparative Economics
        10:48–61.

Durkheim, Emile
1933   The Division of Labor in Society. Translated by George Simpson.
        New York: The Free Press. First published in French in 1893.

Edelstein, J. David, and Warner, Malcolm
1976   Comparative Union Democracy: Organization and Opposition
        in British and American Unions. New York: Wiley.

Eisenstadt, S. N.
1967   Israeli Society. New York: Basic Books.

Eistenstadt, S. N.
1985   The Transformation of Israeli Society. London: Weidenfeld and
        Nicolson.

Elon, Amos
1971   The Israelis: Founders and Sons. New York: Holt, Rinehart &
        Winston.

Engels, Frederick
1935   Socialism: Utopian and Scientific. Translated by Edward Aveling.
        New York: International Publishers. First published in German in
        1882.

Engels, Frederick
1939   Anti-Duehring: Herr Eugen Duehring's Revolution in Science.
        Translated by Emile Burns. Edited by C. P. Dutton. New York:
        International Publishers. First published in German in 1878.

Estrin, Saul, and Jones, Derek C.
1992   "The Viability of Employee-Owned Firms: Evidence from
        France," Industrial and Labor Relations Review 45:323–38.

Etzioni, Amitai
1958   "The Functional Differentiation of Elites in the Kibbutz,"
        American Journal of Sociology 64:476–87.

Fichman, M., and Levinthal, D.
1991   "Honeymoons and the Liability of Adolescence: A New
        Perspective on Duration Dependence in Social and Organizational
        Relationships," *Academy of Management Review* 16:442–68.

Fisher, Jeffrey M.
1988   "Cyclical Indicators of the Israeli Economy," *Bank of Israel
        Economic Review* 61:100–31.

Freeman, John, Carroll, Glenn R., and Hannan, Michael T.
1983   "The Liability of Newness: Age Dependence in Organizational
        Death Rates," *American Sociological Review* 48:692–710.

Friedler, Ya'acov
1978   "Egged Takes Internal Quarrel to Court," *Jerusalem Post*,
        December 29.

Getz, Shlomo
1992   *Changes in the Kibbutz* (Hebrew). Haifa: Institute for Research of
        the Kibbutz and the Cooperative Idea, University of Haifa.

Getz, Shlomo, and Rosner, Menachem
1993   "Where Is the Change Leading?" *Kibbutz Trends*, No. 10
        (Summer), pp. 42–45.

Greenberg, Yitzhak
1986   "Chevrat Ovdim: The Process of Decooperativization in the
        Workers' Credit Cooperative" (Hebrew), *Rivon Lekalkalah*
        130:757–71.

Grinberg, Lev Luis
1991   *Split Corporatism in Israel.* Albany: State University of New
        York Press.

Gui, Benedetto
1984   "Basque vs. Illyrian Labor-Managed Firms: The Problem of
        Property Rights," *Journal of Comparative Economics* 8: 168–81.

Gunn, Christopher
1984   *Workers' Self-Management in the United States.* Ithaca: Cornell
        University Press.

Halliday, Terence C., Powell, Michael J., and Granfors, Mark W.
1987   "Minimalist Organizations: Vital Events in State Bar Associations,
        1870–1930," *American Sociological Review* 52:456–71.

Hannan, Michael, and Freeman, John
1987   "The Ecology of Organizational Foundings: American Labor Unions, 1836–1985," *American Journal of Sociology* 92:910–43.

Hansmann, Henry
1990   "When Does Worker Ownership Work?: ESOPs, Law Firms, Codetermination, and Economic Democracy," *Yale Law Journal* 99:1749–816.

Harel, Yehuda
1988   "The New Kibbutz: An Outline," *Kibbutz Currents*, No. 2 (August), pp. 2–5.

Harrison, Michael I.
1981   "Organizational Adaptation in an Industrial Cooperative—Reflections on the Reorganization of the Egged Transport Company in Israel," presented at a Conference on Workplace Democracy and Ownership in Cultural and Historical Perspective, Project for Kibbutz Studies, Harvard University, Cambridge, Massachusetts, June 11.

Hartmann, Heinz
1979   "Works Councils and the Iron Law of Oligarchy," *British Journal of Industrial Relations* 17:70–82.

Helman, Amir
1980   "Income-Consumption Relationship Within the Kibbutz System," in Klaus Bartoelke, Theodor Bergmann, and Ludwig Liegle, eds., *Integrated Cooperatives in the Industrial Society: The Example of the Kibbutz.* Assen, The Netherlands: Van Gorcum, pp. 131–41.

Helman, Amir
1989   "Homo Economicus and the Kibbutz Economic Crisis," unpublished working paper, Ruppin Institute, Israel.

Holyoake, George Jacob
1906   *The History of Co-operation.* 2 vols. Revised ed. New York: Dutton.

Infield, Henrik F.
1946   *Co-Operative Living in Palestine.* London: Kegan Paul, Trench, Truber & Co.

Isacowitz, Roy
1986   "MK Amar Denies Reports of Reserve Duty Bribery," *Jerusalem Post*, January 5.

Janowsky, Oscar I.
1959   *Foundations of Israel: Emergence of a Welfare State.* Princeton:
        Van Nostrand.

Jerusalem Post
1969   "Reshuffle in Dan bus management," *Jerusalem Post*, May 6.

Jerusalem Post
1974a   "Court Rules Expulsion of 2 Egged Members Illegal," *Jerusalem
        Post*, October 23.

Jerusalem Post
1974b   "Egged Rebels Expelled Again," *Jerusalem Post*, October 25.

Jerusalem Post
1984   "Smashing Victory for Ruling Egged List," *Jerusalem Post*, March 8.

Jerusalem Post
1989   "Hapoalim: Why big is beautiful," *Jerusalem Post*, September 8.

Jensen, Michael C., and Meckling, William H.
1979   "Rights and Production Functions: An Application to Labor-man-
        aged Firms and Codetermination," *Journal of Business* 52:469–506.

Jones, Derek C., and Kato, Takao
1993   "The Scope, Nature, and Effects of Employee Stock Ownership
        Plans in Japan," *Industrial and Labor Relations Review*
        46:352–67.

Jones, Derek C., and Schneider, Donald J.
1984   "Self-Help Production Cooperatives: Government-Administered
        Cooperatives During the Depression," in Robert Jackall and
        Henry M. Levin, eds., *Worker Cooperatives in America.* Berkeley:
        University of California Press, pp. 57–84.

Kahana, Nava, and Nitzan, Shmuel
1989   "More on Alternative Objectives of Labor-Managed Firms,"
        Journal of Comparative Economics 13:527–38.

Kardelj, Edvard
1975   "The Integration of Labor and Social Capital Under Workers'
        Control," in Ichak Adizes and Elisabeth Mann Borgese, eds., *Self-
        Mangement: New Dimensions to Democracy.* Santa Barbara: Clio
        Press.

Kardelj, Edvard
1979   "Social Ownership and Socialist Self-Management," *Socialist
        Thought and Practice*, 19 (2): 46–57.

Kardelj, Edvard
1981   *Contradictions of Social Property in a Socialist Society.* Belgrade: Socialist Thought and Practice.

Karmon, Dan
1991   "The Moral and Ideological Basis of the Future Kibbutz," *Kibbutz Trends* 1:49–52.

Karp, Jonathan
1987   "2 Dropped from Egged Board," *Jerusalem Post,* February 14.

Kellerman, Aharon
1993   *Society and Settlement: Jewish Land of Israel in the Twentieth Century.* Albany: State University of New York Press.

Keremetsky, Jacob, and Logue, John
1991   *Perestroika, Privatization, and Worker Ownership in the USSR.* Kent, OH: Kent Popular Press.

Kimmerling, Baruch
1983   *Zionism and Economy.* Cambridge, MA: Schenkman.

Kislev, Y., Lerman, Z., and Zusman, P.
1989   *Credit Cooperatives in Israeli Agriculture.* Washington, D.C.: Agriculture and Rural Development Department, The World Bank, Working Paper WSP156.

Krajewska, Anna
1993   "Profit Sharing and Employee Ownership in Poland," *Journal of Employee Ownership Law and Finance* 5, No. 3 (Summer), pp. 97–116.

Kralewksi, J. E., Pitt, L., and Shatin, D.
1985   "Structural Characteristics of Medical Group Practices," *Administrative Science Quarterly* 30:34–45.

Kramer, Abe
1984   *The Kibbutz Inns of Israel: A Personal Odyssey.* Jerusalem: Carta.

Kressel, Gideon M.
1991   "Managerial Blunders in the Kibbutz Enterprise: The Problem of Accountability," *Journal of Rural Cooperation* 19:91–107.

Labour in Israel
1989   "The 'Perestroika' of Israel Kessar," *Labour in Israel* 33, No. 1 (July), pp. 1–2.

Levi, Yair
1990   "The Recent Crisis in the Moshav Ovdim Sector: Analysis and Some Lessons," *Journal of Rural Cooperation* 18:133–49.

Leviatan, Uri
1980   "Hired Labor in the Kibbutz: Ideology, History and Social Psychological Effects," in Uri Leviatan and Menachem Rosner, eds., *Work and Organization in Kibbutz Industry*. Norwood, PA: Norwood Editions, pp. 64–75.

Lipset, Seymour Martin, Trow, Martin A., and Coleman, James J.
1956   *Union Democracy: The Internal Politics of the InternationalTypographical Union*. New York: The Free Press.

Logue, John, and Bell, Dan
1992   "Worker Ownership in Russia: A Possibility After the Command Economy," *Dissent* 39: 199–204.

Losh, L.
1960   *Guide to Cooperation*. Tel-Aviv: Hapoel Hatzair Cooperative Press.

Losh, L.
1979   "Fifty Years of the Co-operative Centre-Producers' and Services Co-operatives in Israel," *Review of International Cooperation* 72(2): 83–90.

Magid, Joel
1991   "Fading or Flowering: Kibbutz in the 1990s," *Kibbutz Trends* 1:44–46.

Maltz, Judy
1989a   "Koor Buffeted by More Shocks," *Jerusalem Post*, December 8, p. 13.

Maltz, Judy
1989b   "Kibbutzim, Banks, Gov't Sign Debt Agreement," *Jerusalem Post*, December 13, p. 8.

Mansbridge, Jane J.
1980   *Beyond Adversarial Democracy*. New York: Basic Books.

Marcus, Philip M.
1966   "Union Conventions and Executive Boards: A Formal Analysis of Organizational Structure," *American Sociological Review* 31:61–70.

Margolis, Michael
1979   *Viable Democracy.* New York: St. Martin's Press.

Marx, Karl
1972   "Inaugural Address of the Working Men's International Association," reprinted in Robert C. Tucker, ed., *The Marx-Engels Reader.* New York: W. W. Norton, pp. 374–81. Originally published in 1864.

Meister, Albert
1984   "Participation and Democracy in Associations," in his *Participation, Associations, Development, and Change.* Edited and translated by J. C. Ross. New Brunswick and London: Transaction Books, chapter 7.

Meyer, John W., and Rowan, Brian
1977   "Institutionalized Organizations: Formal Structure as Myth and Ceremony," *American Journal of Sociology* 83:340–63.

Michels, Robert
1962   *Political Parties: A Sociological Study of the Oligarchical Tendencies of Modern Democracy.* Translated by Eden Paul and Cedar Paul. New York: The Free Press.

Mill, John Stuart
1909   *Principles of Political Economy.* Edited by W. J. Ashley. London: Longmans, Green, and Co.

Mittelberg, David
1988   *Strangers in Paradise: The Israeli Kibbutz Experience.* New Brunswick, NJ: Transaction Books.

Miyazaki, Hajime
1984   "On Success and Dissolution of the Labor-managed Firm in the Capitalist Economy," *Journal of Political Economy* 92:909–31.

Miyazaki, Hajime, and Neary, Hugh
1983   "The Illyrian Firm Revisited," *Bell Journal of Economics* 14:259–70.

Mondini, Ermanno
1957   "Workers' Productive Societies in Israel," *Review of International Cooperation* 50(1): 14–20.

Nyden, Philip W.
1985   "Democratizing Organizations: A Case Study of a Union Reform Movement," *American Journal of Sociology* 90:1179–203.

Obradovic, Josip
1975   "Workers' Participation: Who Participates?" *Industrial Relations* 14:32–44.

Odenheimer, Alisa
1992/93 "A Paycheck by Any Other Name," *Kibbutz Trends,* No. 8 (Winter), pp. 21–28.

Oked, Yitzhak
1973   "Egged Faction Pressing for Increases in Pay," *Jerusalem Post,* January 24.

Oked, Yitzhak
1985   "Egged Chairman Amar Quits—'Not Linked to Allegations,'" *Jerusalem Post,* September 9.

Olzak, Susan, and West, Elizabeth
1991   "Ethnic Movements and the Rise and Fall of Ethnic Newspapers," *American Sociological Review* 56:458–74.

Oppenheimer, Franz
1896   *Die Siedlungsgenossenschaft, ein Versuch einer positiven Ueberwindung des Kommunismus durch Loesung des Genossenschaftsproblems und der Agrarfrage.* Leipzig: Duncker and Humbolt.

Oppenheimer, Franz
1917   "Collective Ownership and Private Ownership of Land," in Franz Oppenheimer and Jacob Oettinger, *Land Tenure in Palestine.* The Hague: Jewish National Fund, pp. 5–18.

Palgi, Michal
1991   "Worker Participation in Histadrut-Owned Enterprises in Israel," in Raymond Russell and Veljko Rus, eds., *International Handbook of Participation in Organizations,* Volume 2, *Ownership and Participation.* Oxford: Oxford University Press, pp. 285–300.

Perlmutter, Amos
1957   "Ideology and Organization: The Politics of Socialistic Parties in Israel, 1897–1957." Doctoral dissertation, University of California, Berkeley.

Perlmutter, Amos
1970   *Anatomy of Political Institutionalization: The Case of Israel and Some Comparative Analyses.* Cambridge, MA: Center for International Affairs, Harvard University.

Perotin, Virginie
1987   "Conditions of Survival and Closure of French Worker Cooperatives: Some Preliminary Findings," in Derek C. Jones and Jan Svejnar, eds., *Advances in the Economic Analysis of Participatory and Labor-Managed Firms*, Volume 2. Greenwich, CT: JAI Press, pp. 201–24.

Pierson, Frank C.
1948   "The Government of Trade Unions," *Industrial and Labor Relations Review* 1:593–608.

Preuss, Walter
1960   *Co-operation in Israel and the World*. Translated from German into English by Shlomo Barer. Jerusalem: Rubin Mass.

Preuss, Walter
1965   *The Labour Movement in Israel: Past and Present*. Third edition. Jerusalem: Ruben Mass.

Ranger, Moore, James
1991   "If Bigger Is Better, Is Older Wiser?: Age Dependence in Failure Rates of New York Life Insurance Companies," presented at the Annual Meeting of the American Sociological Association, Cincinnati, Ohio, August 25.

Registrar of Cooperative Societies
1938   *Cooperative Societies in Palestine: Report of the Registrar of Cooperative Societies on Developments During the Years 1921–1937*. Jerusalem: Printing and Stationery Office.

Registrar of Cooperative Societies
1968   *The Cooperative Movement in Israel—1968: Report of the Registrar of Cooperative Societies*. Jerusalem: Ministry of Labour.

Registrar of Cooperative Societies
1988   "Cooperation in Israel 1986: Annual Report of the Registrar of Cooperative Societies," *Labour and National Insurance: Monthly Review of the Ministry of Labor & Social Affairs—Israel*, September.

Registrar of Cooperative Societies
1989a   "Cooperation in Israel 1987: Annual Report of the Registrar of Cooperative Societies," *Labour and National Insurance: Monthly Review of the Ministry of Labor & Social Affairs—Israel*, October.

Registrar of Cooperative Societies
1989b   "Cooperation in Israel 1988: Annual Report of the Registrar of Cooperative Societies" (Hebrew), *Labour & Social Affairs and National Insurance: Monthly Review of the Ministry of Labour & Social Affairs—Israel*, No. 8 (December), pp. 333–63.

Reshef, Yonatan, and Bemmels, Brian
1989   "Political and Economic Determinants of Strikes in Israel: A Sectoral Comparison," *Economic and Industrial Democracy* 10:35–57.

Rosner, Menachem
1988   "There Is Nothing New in the New Kibbutz," *Kibbutz Studies*, May, pp. 11–16.

Rosner, Menachem
1991a   "Worker Ownership, Ideology and Social Structure in 'Third-way' Work Organizations," *Economic and Industrial Democracy* 12:369–84.

Rosner, Menachem
1991b   "Ownership, Participation and Work Restructuring in the Kibbutz: A Comparative Perspective," in Raymond Russell and Veljko Rus, eds., *International Handbook of Participation in Organizations*, Volume 2, *Ownership and Participation*. Oxford, Oxford University Press, pp. 170–96.

Rosner, Menachem
1993   "Organizations Between Community and Market: The Case of the Kibbutz," *Economic and Industrial Democracy* 14:369–97.

Rosner, Menachem, Ben David, Itzhak, Avnat, Alexander, Cohen, Neni, and Leviatan, Uri
1990   *The Second Generation: Continuity and Change in the Kibbutz.* New York: Greenwood Press.

Rosner, Menachem, and Blasi, Joseph R.
1985   "Theories of Participatory Democracy and the Kibbutz," in Erik Cohen, Moshe Lissak, and Uri Almagor, eds., *Comparative Social Dynamics: Essays in Honor of S. N. Eisenstadt.* Boulder: Westview Press, pp. 295–314.

Rosner, Menachem, and Cohen, Nissim
1983   "Is Direct Democracy Feasible in Modern Society?: The Lesson of the Kibbutz Experience," in E. Krauss, ed., *The Sociology of the Kibbutz.* New Brunswick, NJ: Transaction Books.

Rosner, Menachem, and Tannenbaum, Arnold S.
1987   "Organizational Efficiency and Egalitarian Democracy in an Intentional Communal Society: The Kibbutz," *British Journal of Sociology* 38:521–45.

Rosolio, Dani
1993   "The Impact of the Economic Crisis on Ideology and Life-Style of Kibbutzim," *Israel Social Science Research* 8(1): 1–10.

Rothschild-Whitt, Joyce
1979   "The Collectivist Organization: An Alternative to Rational-Bureaucratic Models," *American Sociological Review* 44:509–27.

Rus, Veljko
1970   "Influence Structure in Yugoslav Enterprise," *Industrial Relations* 9:148–60.

Russell, Raymond
1984   "The Role of Culture and Ethnicity in the Degeneration of Democratic Workplaces," *Economic and Industrial Democracy* 5:73–96.

Russell, Raymond
1985a   *Sharing Ownership in the Workplace.* Albany: State University of New York Press.

Russell, Raymond
1985b   "Employee Ownership and Internal Governance," *Journal of Economic Behavior and Organization* 6:217–41.

Russell, Raymond
1991   "Sharing Ownership in the Services," in Raymond Russell and Veljko Rus, eds., *International Handbook of Participation in Organizations,* Volume 2, *Ownership and Participation.* Oxford: Oxford University Press, pp. 197–217.

Russell, Raymond
1992   "Employee Shareholding," in Gyoergy Szell, ed., *Concise Encyclopedia of Participation and Co-Management.* Berlin and New York: de Gruyter, pp. 305–17.

Russell, Raymond
1993   "Organizational Theories of the Labor-Managed Firm: Arguments and Evidence," in Samuel B. Bacharach, ed., *Research in the Sociology of Organizations,* vol. 11. Greenwich, CT: JAI Press, pp. 1–32.

Russell, Raymond, and Hanneman, Robert
1992a   "The Employment of Members and Nonmembers in Israel's Production, Transportation, and Service Cooperatives," presented at an International Conference on Theoretical and Applied Aspects of Labor-Managed Firms, Bar-Ilan University, Ramat Gan, Israel, May 25–28.

Russell, Raymond, and Hanneman, Robert
1992b   "Cooperatives and the Business Cycle: The Israeli Case," *Journal of Comparative Economics* 16:701–15.

Russell, Raymond, and Hanneman, Robert
1994   "The Use of Hired Labor in Israeli Worker Cooperatives, 1933–1989," in Derek C. Jones and Jan Svejnar, eds., *Advances in the Economic Analysis of Participatory and Labor-Managed Firms*, Volume 5. Greenwich, CT: JAI Press, pp. 23–51.

Sadan, Ezra
1992   "Primary and Secondary Cooperatives in Disarray: The Latest Experience of Israel's Moshav Cooperatives," presented at an International Conference on Theoretical and Applied Aspects of Labor-Managed Firms, Bar-Ilan University, Ramat Gan, Israel, May 25–28.

Sale, Kirkpatrick
1980   *Human Scale.* New York: Coward, McCann & Geoghegan.

Schachter, Ken
1987   "Dissident Egged Members Cause Uproar at Meeting," *Jerusalem Post,* January 12.

Segel, Mark
1972   "Egged: Power on Wheels," *Jerusalem Post,* November 10: B1, B6, B7.

Shafir, Gershon
1989   *Land, Labor and the Origins of the Israeli-Palestinian Conflict, 1882–1914.* Cambridge: Cambridge University Press.

Shalev, Michael
1984   "Labor, State, and Crisis: An Israeli Case Study," *Industrial Relations* 23:362–86.

Shalev, Michael
1989   "Jewish Organized Labor and the Palestinians: A Study in State/Society Relations in Israel," in Baruch Kimmerling, ed., *The Israeli State and Society: Boundaries and Frontiers.* Albany: State University of New York Press, pp. 96–136.

Shalev, Michael
1990   "The Political Economy of Labor Party Dominance and Decline in Israel," in T. J. Pempel, ed., *Uncommon Democracies: The One Party Dominant Regimes*. Ithaca: Cornell University Press, pp. 83–127.

Shalev, Michael
1992   *Labour and the Political Economy in Israel*. Oxford: University Press.

Shapira, Anita
1984   *"Gedud ha-Avodah:* A Dream that Failed," *Jerusalem Quarterly*, No. 30 (Winter): 62–76.

Shapira, Anita
1989   "Labour Zionism and the October Revolution," *Journal of Contemporary History* 24:623–56.

Shapira, Reuven
1990   "Leadership, Rotation and the Kibbutz Crisis," *Journal of Rural Cooperation* 18:55–66.

Shapiro, Yonathan
1976   *The Formative Years of the Israeli Labour Party: The Organization of Power, 1919–1930*. London: Sage.

Shirom, Arie
1972   "The Industrial Relations Systems of Industrial Cooperatives in the United States, 1880–1935," *Labor History* 13:533–51.

Singh, Jitendra, and Lumsden, Charles J.
1990   "Theory and Research in Organizational Ecology," *Annual Review of Sociology* 16:161–95.

Spiro, Melford E.
1956   *Kibbutz: Venture in Utopia*. Cambridge, MA: Harvard University Press.

Staber, Udo
1989a   "Age-dependence and Historical Effects on the Failure Rates of Worker Cooperatives: An Event-history Analysis," *Economic and Industrial Democracy* 10:59–80.

Staber, Udo
1989b   "Organizational Foundings in the Cooperative Sector of Atlantic Canada: An Ecological Perspective," *Organizational Studies* 10:381–403.

Staber, Udo
1993   "Worker Cooperatives and the Business Cycle: Are Cooperatives the Answer to Unemployment?" *The American Journal of Economics and Sociology* 52:129–43.

Stinchcombe, Arthur
1965   "Social Structure and Organization," in J. G. March, ed., *Handbook of Organizations.* Chicago: Rand McNally, pp. 142–193.

Strauss, George
1977   "Union Government in the U.S.: Research Past and Future," *Industrial Relations* 16:215–42.

Sussman, Zvi
1969   "The Policy of the Histadrut with Regard to Wage Differentials: A Study of the Impact of Egalitarian Ideology and Arab Labour on Jewish Wages in Palestine." Doctoral dissertation, Hebrew University of Jerusalem.

Sussman, Zvi
1973   "The Determination of Wages for Unskilled Labor in the Advanced Sector of the Dual Economy of Mandatory Palestine," *Economic Development and Cultural Change* 22, No. 1 (October): 95–113.

Talmon, Yonina
1972   *Family and Community in the Kibbutz.* Cambridge, MA: Harvard University Press.

Tannenbaum, Arnold S.
1968   *Control in Organizations.* New York: McGraw-Hill.

Teitelbaum, Raoul
1989   "From the Workers' Company to a Democratic Labour Society: The Israeli Experience of the Histadrut Economic Sector," Tel Aviv: Histadrut.

Teveth, Shabtai
1987   *Ben-Gurion: The Burning Ground, 1886–1948.* Boston: Houghton Mifflin.

Tolbert, Pamela S., and Stern, Robert N.
1991a   "Organizations of Professionals: Governance Structures in Large Law Firms," in Pamela S. Tolbert and Stephen R. Barley, eds., *Research in the Sociology of Organizations,* vol. 8. Greenwich, CT: JAI Press, pp. 97–117.

Tolbert, Pamela S., and Stern, Robert N.
1991b   "Inequality in a Company of Equals: Participation and Control in Large Law Firms," in Raymond Russell and Veljko Rus, eds., *International Handbook of Participation in Organizations*, Volume 2, *Ownership and Participation*. Oxford: Oxford University Press, pp. 248–264.

Trattner, Egon
1989   "The Israeli Experience in Rural Industrialization: Achievements, Problems and Forecast," *Journal of Rural Cooperation* 17:57–76.

Uvalic, Milica
1991   "Property Reforms in Yugoslavia," paper presented at the Sixth International Conference of the International Association for the Economics of Self-Management, Cornell University, Ithaca, New York, August 8–11.

Vanek, Jaroslav
1975   "Introduction," in Jaroslav Vanek, ed., *Self-Management: Economic Liberation of Man*. Harmondsworth, Middlesex, England: Penguin, pp. 11–36.

Vanek, Jaroslav
1977   "Some Fundamental Considerations on Financing and the Form of Ownership under Labor Management," in his *The Labor-Managed Economy: Essays by Jaroslav Vanek*. Ithaca: Cornell University Press, pp. 171–85.

Viteles, Harry
1929   "The Jewish Co-operative Movement in Palestine," *Bulletin of the Palestine Economic Society*, 4, No. 1 (June): 1–183.

Viteles, Harry
1932   "The Cooperative Movement," in Harry Viteles and Khalil Totah, eds., *Annals of the American Academy of Political and Social Science*, Volume 164: *Palestine: A Decade of Development*. Philadelphia: American Academy of Political and Social Science, pp. 127–38.

Viteles, Harry
1966   *A History of the Co-operative Movement in Israel*, Book 1: *The Evolution of the Co-operative Movement*. London: Vallentine-Mitchell.

Viteles, Harry
1967   *A History of the Co-operative Movement in Israel*, Book 2: *The Evolution of the Kibbutz Movement*. London: Vallentine-Mitchell.

Viteles, Harry
1968   *A History of the Co-operative Movement in Israel*, Book 5: *Workers Producers Transportation and Service Co-operatives.* London: Vallentine-Mitchell.

Webb, Sidney, and Webb, Beatrice
1920   *A Constitution for the Socialist Commonwealth of Great Britain.* London: Longmans, pp. 154–67. Reprinted in Ken Coates and Tony Topham, eds., *Workers Control.* Revised edition. London: Panther Books, pp. 66–72.

Weber, Max
1968   *Economy and Society.* 2 vols. Edited by Guenther Roth and Claus Wittich. Berkeley: University of California Press.

Weintraub, Dov, and Sadan, Ezra
1981   "Farm Cooperative Organization: A Cooperative Analytical Framework," *Journal of Rural Cooperation* 9:135–61.

Weisskopf, Thomas E.
1992   "Russia in Transition: Perils of the Fast Track to Capitalism," *Challenge* 35, No. 6 (November-December): 28–37.

Whyte, William Foote, and Whyte, Kathleen King
1988   *Making Mondragon: The Growth and Dynamics of the Worker Cooperative Complex.* Ithaca: ILR Press, New York State School of Industrial and Labor Relations, Cornell University.

Williams, Daniel
1989   "Down on the Kibbutz, Israelis Face a Financial Crisis," *Los Angeles Times*, May 19, pp. 12–13.

Williamson, Oliver
1975   *Markets and Hierarchies.* New York: The Free Press.

Williamson, Oliver
1981   "The Economics of Organization: The Transaction Cost Approach," *American Journal of Sociology* 87:548–77.

Williamson, Oliver
1985   *The Economic Institutions of Capitalism.* New York: The Free Press.

Winer, Gershon
1971   *The Founding Fathers of Israel.* New York: Bloch Publishing Company.

Zusman, Pinhas
1988   *Individual Behavior and Social Choice in a Cooperative Settlement: The Theory and Practice of the Israeli Moshav.* Jerusalem: Magnes Press.

Zusman, Pinhas
1990   "The Israeli Smallholder Cooperative Sector and Its Lessons for Rural Cooperatives," *Journal of Rural Cooperation* 18:167–81.

INDEX

A

Achdut Bakery,
of Haifa, 198
of Tel Aviv, 110, 133, 148, 155
Achdut Haavodah ("Labor
Unity"), 24, 25, 26, 27, 32, 36,
54
and the Histadrut, 27, 29
and the labor economy, 27–31,
54
and the WZO, 25
Achdut Press, 34, 98, 132, 148
African countries, immigrants
from, in moshavim, 176
Agassi, Judith, 11
Age, of worker cooperatives,
and hired labor, 114, 119–123,
125, 208
and oligarchy, 131, 132, 134,
208
Age dependence, of mortality, 85,
86
in Atlantic Canada, 88, 89, 95
in France, 88
in Israel, 59, 85–92, 95
in the United Kingdom, 88, 89

Agency theory, 89, 114
Agriculture, in Israel (see also
Kibbutz, Moshav, Rural cooperatives), 177, 180
agricultural cooperatives vs.
capitalist farming, 18–19,
22–23, 32–33, 53, 97, 98, 115,
203
agricultural cooperatives vs.
production cooperatives, 97,
115, 123
value attached to work on the
land, 20, 53, 168, 170
Aharoni, Yair, 17–18, 25, 26,
33–34, 49, 52, 78, 185, 186,
193, 194
Alchian, Armen, 118, 119
Aldrich, Howard, 11, 59, 85, 86
Alienation, in worker cooperatives (see also Oligarchy), 7,
120, 134, 136, 140, 143, 153
Aliyah (see also Immigration), 22
First Aliyah (1882–1903), 18–19
Second Aliyah (1904–1914), 20,
22, 24, 27, 37, 216
Third Aliyah (1919–1923), 21,
27, 28, 37, 216 ,

Fourth Aliyah (1924–1931), 37, 38, 215
Alliance tire factory, 183
"Alternative to Govern," alliance of parties within Egged, 134, 136, 137, 138
Al-Yagon, Orna, 11
Amar, Shlomo, 141, 161
Amburgey, Terry L., 71
Amcor, 179
Anderson, John C., 152
Anti-Semitism, in Poland and Europe, 37
Applebaum, Levia, 177–178
Apter, Moshe, 10
Arab Cooperatives of Workers and Farmers (ACWF), 201
Arabs, Arab laborers, 39, 179
in labor market, 18–19, 22, 32, 33, 37, 38, 98
worker cooperatives of, 38, 78, 201
Asian countries, immigrants from, in moshavim, 176
Assa, David, 142, 143
Atlantic Canada, worker cooperatives in, 71, 79, 88, 95
Atzmon, Mordechai, 143
Audit unions, of cooperatives in Palestine and Israel, 38, 39, 60, 201
Avigur, Shaul, 112
Avis Rent-a-Car, 1
Avrahami, Eli

B

Bakers, cooperatives of (see also Achdut Bakery), 16, 89
in Israel, 39, 40, 50, 89, 91, 92, 203

Balfour Declaration, 24
Bank Hapoalim ("Workers' Bank"), 3, 26, 27, 38, 50, 51, 184, 185, 188, 190
Bank of Israel, 185
Bankers' Trust, 183
Baratz, Joseph, 19
Bar-El, Raphael, 11, 178
Bar-Ilan University, 135
Barnett, William P., 71
Bar-On, Amnon, 10, 197, 198
Basques of Spain. See Mondragon
Batstone, Eric, 120, 121, 132, 133, 150
Baum, Joel C., 59, 85
Beersheba, 188
Begin, Menachem, 52
Belgium, 180
Bell, Dan, 1, 214
Belsberg family, and Koor, 183
Bemmels, Brian, 186
Ben-Gurion, David, 24, 28, 30, 31, 33, 34, 36, 52, 54, 103, 205, 217
Ben-Ner, Avner, 4, 11, 15, 16, 40, 59, 79, 82, 84, 85, 88, 89, 94, 100, 111, 120, 126, 167, 184
Ben-Porath, Yoram, 78, 193
Ben-Rafael, Eliezer, 130, 167, 174, 210
Ben-Tov, Malka, 10
Berechman, Joseph, 160, 204
Berman, Katrina V., 88, 108
Berman, Matthew D., 88, 108
Birth, births, of organizations, cooperatives. See Formation
Black, Jeff, 189, 190
Blasi, Joseph, 1, 210, 214
Blumberg, Paul, 96
Bolivia, 143
Bonacich, Edna, 19, 33

from Eastern Europe, 20, 22
from Europe, 176, 180
from the U.S., 178
Incumbency, advantages of, in
worker cooperatives, 135,
140–144, 146–147, 150
Independence, of Israel, in 1948,
impact on worker cooperatives,
39, 45–46, 49, 55, 66, 77, 78,
203
War of, 39, 76
Industrial cooperatives (see also
Production cooperatives,
Worker cooperatives), 130,
154, 217
Industrialization
of the kibbutz, 123, 168, 170,
171, 178, 195
of the moshav, 177–182, 195
Information costs, 114, 118–119
Infield, Henrik F., 21–23
Institutions, institutional influences
and Israeli worker cooperatives,
5, 34–35, 48, 54–55, 59,
73–78, 82–84, 113, 199,
214–215
and use of hired labor, 7, 100,
104–114, 123–128, 214–216
in environment of Israeli
worker cooperatives, 4–6, 57,
75–76, 93–95, 184–185,
194–195, 218
in labor economy, 4–6, 17–18,
24–26, 31–34, 53, 127, 158,
176, 182, 194–195, 209
Internal control commission
in Dan, 143
in Egged, 140, 141
in Ichud-Igud, 146
Internal courts, in Israeli worker
cooperatives, 137, 146, 157

International Typographical
Union (ITU), 131–132, 151
Isacowitz, Roy, 141, 161
Israel, 2–13, 17, 22, 28, 32, 38, 42,
53, 58, 60, 63, 67, 74, 76, 78,
79, 90, 94–98, 102, 115, 127,
128, 132, 134, 136, 144–147,
149, 153, 163, 166–167, 180,
185, 187–189, 191, 194, 197,
201, 203, 204, 206–209, 218
economy of, 55–56, 80–85,
107–109, 164–165, 175, 177,
183, 184, 193
government of, and worker cooperatives, 41, 44–46, 49–52,
55–56, 59, 68, 73, 77, 92, 93,
105, 113, 124, 138, 141, 161,
162, 202
Land of, 54
law, laws, 114, 143, 188
society of, changes in, 55–59,
75–78, 93, 193–195
Israel Investors Corporation, 183
Italy, worker cooperatives in, 4

J

Jacobson, Dan, 190
Jaffa, 34, 35, 142
Jaffe, Eliezer, 30
JAI Press, 11
Janowsky, Oscar I., 73
Japan, 214
Jensen, Michael C., 154
Jerusalem, 34, 60, 66, 92, 115,
134, 139, 189
Jerusalem Post, 135–137,
141–143, 162, 183, 184
Jewish Agency, 68, 199
Jewish National Fund, 8, 22, 23,
31, 33, 53, 97, 125

S

Sadan, Ezra, 175–177
Sage Publications, 11
Sale, Kirkpatrick, 150, 152, 154, 210
Sand and cement, cooperatives that produce and deliver, 40, 91, 118
San Francisco, worker-owned scavenger firms of, 17, 89, 107, 113–114
Scandals, involving Israeli worker cooperatives, 7, 129, 138, 141–143, 161–163, 204, 205
Scavenger firms, worker-owned, of the San Francisco region, 17, 89, 107, 113–114, 118, 121
Schachter, Ken, 161, 162
Schiff, Zeev, 43, 93
Schneider, Donald J., 79
Schuessler, Rudolf, 59, 85, 86
Seamstresses, cooperatives of, 34
Secondary cooperatives, as cooperatives outside the Merkaz Hakooperatsia, 38
Secretariat (*Mazkirut*), in Israeli worker cooperatives, 135–138, 141, 142, 144
Segel, Mark, 135, 136
Segev. *See* Gush Segev
"Self-help cooperatives," of Depression-era U.S., 79
"Self-labor," 98, 202, 205
Self-management, in Yugoslavia, 130
Sephardic, 193
Services, cooperatives in (*see also* Kalid), 15, 89
in Israel, 35, 43, 61, 100, 106, 109, 122

Settlement Study Centre, 182
Shachar, later merged with Egged, 143
Shafir, Gershon, 5, 11, 18, 19, 21, 23, 26, 33, 97, 205
Shalev, Michael, 5, 11, 32, 33, 52, 78, 107, 193
Shamrock Holdings, and Koor, 183
Shapira, Anita, 27–29, 203
Shapira, Reuven, 173, 210
Shapiro, Yonathan, 21, 23–25, 27–33, 36, 37, 47, 54, 93, 112, 203
Shatin, D., 131
Shinui, party within Egged, 136
Shirom, Arie, 10, 15, 59, 79, 97, 130
Shoes, as product of worker cooperatives in Israel, 49
Shor, conservatory of music, 133, 148
Shoresh Committee, the, 52, 106
Shoresh, S., 52
Singh, Jitendra, 67, 71, 80
Size of organizations,
and democracy, 7, 11, 23, 130–132, 134, 136, 137, 144–145, 147–156, 204, 208, 210, 211
and dissolutions, 85, 86
and hired labor, 119–120, 122–125, 208
Six Day War, June 1967, 107
Smith, Steve, 11
Social ownership, 212–213
Socialism (*see also* Utopian socialism) 2, 3, 5, 129, 207, 208, 212, 213, 218
in Israel 2, 6, 18, 20, 21, 25, 26, 28, 34, 35, 36, 54, 56, 98, 112,